SERVICE INDUSTRY BEHAVIORAL ECONOMIC STRATEGIES

JOHN LOK

Copyright

Contents

Preface

Introduction

How social change influences human behavioral change ? Why human behavior may be influenced by social change? Our individual behavior whether can be influenced to bring negative or positive attitude by social change? I shall attempt to indicate cases to explain whether our individual behavior can be influenced to changed by social environment change. Readers can have more understand how and why social change may influence our behavior in possible. Behavioral economy is one useful and fun social subject. Behavioral economists ususally research how and why human behaviors may influence economy growth or recession, or how and why economy environment changing factor may influence human behavior changes.

In hotel strategy part, I shall explain how any countries aiports ought need to implement in order to achieve excellent service to satisfy travel passengers their changing air planes or waiting air plans to fly to other countries need in whose short time airport staying time. However, one excellent service airport can let travelers to feel the country's airport can provide comfortable staying service , transfer another air plane from gate, shopping or eating entertainment satisfactory feeling. So, one effective airport strategy ought need to plan in order to implement satisfactory airport service performance to raise global travellers choose to go to the country to travel or stay to transfer another air plane. In my this book , I shall attempt to explain some useful airport strategy plan to let readers to understand.

In hotel strategy part, I shall explain how hotel is one kind of booking room living service business. It depends on how many travellers living choice. If it can provide excellent room services to let them to feel comfortable. I believe that the hotel can have good income from travellers. However, any hotels have different design, living room features, entertainment facilities, e.g. restaurants, swimming pools, gym sport etc. different entertainment facilities. Even, on hotel's any facilities can let its travellers to feel similar to another hotel or other hotels facilities. So, in hotel room living service provision market, its competition is very servious.

Due to hotel is one kind of service industy, it is very important to satisfy customer living hotel room and leisure and eating satisfacton. It brings this question: How to implement the hotel's organizational strategy in order to attract travellers to choose to book rooms to live when they are staying in the country? Ought different department supervisor supervise staffs in order to achieve excellent service to satisfy customers needs when they are living in their hotels?

In my this book, I shall explain how different hotel department cooperation and airport department cooperation in order to achieve efficient strategy in order to raise competition. I hope that my readers can have more clear understanding to learn how hotel and airport can implement effective strategy to raise customers number raising aim more easily. The most important, I want readers can feel why service organizational strategies may influence consumer behavioral change.

Prologue

Why human network job behavior may influence economy

Robots take our jobs behavioral and economy influences
Robot job behavior brings economy influences

Intellectual human economic behaviors
What does intellectual human economic behaviors
mean ?
The relationship between social change and human
behavior
How human productive behavior may influence economic development
● New Zealand farmer individual wine productive behavior
● America high technological productive behavior
● China share market investing behavior
Why has any individual country have many people invest share behavior which can influence the country's macro
consumption desire?
Can technology influence human shopping behavioral change?
Why and how human behavior may influence the country's economic growth or recession?
Technology how impacts human behavior changing?
How and why employees behaviors may influence economy development?
Robots invention whether they can help organizations to raise efficiencies or inefficiencies?
Why social behavior may influence organizational strategy needs to be changed ?
How and why human behavior may influence economic growth or recession? p.141-180

CHAPTER I

Implementing airport facility management strategy

Why airport needs to implement FM strategy?
Any organizations ought need to implement FM strategy. Even, any airport which is one providing air planes to fly and stay organization, it also need to provide FM service facility in order to satisfy global traveller passenger individual need when he/she is waiting in the country's airport before he/she catch air plane to fly to another country.
Firstly, we need to know that what organizational FM service means ?
Facility management can help any organizations to reduce
maintenance service expenditure, include airport air plan providing staying and flying organizations?

Facility management provides a variety of non core operations and maintenance services to support any organizations' operation. For logistic organization example, it is possible to provide effective maintenance service to warehouse in order to reduce warehouse facilities to be damaged to bring to spend to buy any new equipment facilities expenditure. So, when the logistic company's warehouse facilities can be maintenance to be the best quality. Then, they can be used these warehouses' machines facilities again. Their performance can assist workers to manufacture any products to keep the most efficiently an raising the best production performance in whole manufacturing process. Then, this logistic company's facility management department can bring to avoid purchase any new machine facilities expenditure spending. One to these warehouses' production machine facilities are kept in the best production performance environment even in long term production need.
The logistic industry's facility management department can create cost savings and efficiency of the warehouse's workplaces. It's machines facilities (production machines) are dealt with the maintenance management of the physical assets maintenance service. FM (facilities management) has been being applied to industrial facilities in logistic and warehouse industry long term as well as maintenance plays a significant role to ensure the full service and the warehousing system, including both building components and equipment in warehouse.
Maintenance service is needed to bring a certain level of availability and reliability of a warehouse facilities system and its components and its ability perform to a standard level of quality. So , it seems that logistic industry's warehouse asset cost reducing. It depends on whether it has one facility management department to provide maintenance service to itself warehouse workplace's production machine facilities and warehouse building itself in order to let workers t feel the manufacturing machines can bring good manufacturing performance to assist them to produce any products in one safe warehouse workplace environment. Hence, the performance measurement of warehouse maintenance issue will be valued to be consider to every warehouse manager and facility manager in logistic industry.
In logistic industry, (FM) works at two level on the one hand, it provides a safe and efficient working environment, which is essential to influence warehouse workers whether how they perform to do their manufacturing tasks or logistic goods delivery tasks in warehouse. When they feel the warehouse is safe environment to work. They will not need to consider anywhere has risk to cause they die by accident in warehouse. Hence, they can concentrate on doing their every tasks . On the other hand, it can involve strategic issues, such as property (warehouse workplace and management, strategy property decision and warehouse facility, e.g. manufacturing machine, facility maintenance and checking planning and maintenance planning development.
However, reducing the operating expense issue will be the main aim when the logistic company feels that it has need to set up one in-house facility management department to carry on any maintenance service for its warehouses' any workplace property and manufacturing machines facilities. So, when the logistic company decides to implement one facility management department, it needs to ensure its facility management department can bring the minimum level of keeping manufacturing performance and efficiency to its warehouses' any manufacturing machines and warehouses' property to avoid to be damaged in short term, such as loss of business due to failure in service,

provision of project to customer satisfaction, provision of safe environment, effective utilisation of workplace space, e.g. warehouse effectiveness and communication between the workers and the logistic managers in the warehouse workplace , due to the warehouse's space is not enough maintenance service reliability to the logistic company's warehouse, responsiveness of the warehouse's worker individual negative emotion problem, due to he/she often feels need to work in one unsafe warehouse working environment. Hence, it seems that poor or unsafe warehouse working environment can influence workers feel negative emotion to work to bring low efficiency (inefficiency) or under productive performance in warehouse. It has relationship to influence they to bring psychological negative emotion feeling to work when the organization lacks one effective warehouse management repairing service to be provided to the warehouse's facilities and properties' maintenance needs in order to avoid ineffective measurement and misleading of performance.

Hence, the logistic company's facilities management department often needs to be reviewed whether its maintenance service level is passed to achieve the lowest repair (maintenance) service standard to its warehouse itself property and manufacturing machine or warehouse delivery tool facilities or warehouse lamps' light whether is enough to let workers to see anything clearly to avoid accident occurrence or see anything to work clearly or the warehouse space areas are enough to let they can have enough space to walk or communicate to their team supervisors or deliver any goods more easily in the short distance between the worker's sending goods location and the delivering goods destination in order to avoid because the lacking enough space to cause the accident occurrence , due to the space is not enough to let they deliver their goods to any locations in warehouse.

Hence, it seems logistic company's (FM) department can contribute to the organization's mission, such as avoiding warehouse accident occurrence, inefficiency, not enough and unavailability of the facility for future needs when the warehouse lacks enough space areas to bring poor performance of facility and dangerous warehouse itself property in warehouse, e.g. safe and reliable operations of material handling equipment and maintenance of warehouse facilities, grounds, security system, utilities, plumbing, heating , enough lighting system, air conditioning, warming heater, fire protection, security system alarm etc. facilities in warehouse.

Hence, it seems that if the logistic company expected to reduce to spend lot of excessive manufacturing machine purchase expenditure, lose of workers' life or bring workplace accidents , due to poor warehouse workplace environment, even bringing lawsuit compensation claim loss , due to the worker individual accident or death is caused from the poor warehouse facilities, or bring negative emotion to let the workers feel they are working in unsafe warehouse workplace environment. Then, it ought choose to set up on facility management department in order to provide enough maintenance service to its warehouse to avoid these non essential expenditure causing , due to these poor warehouse facilities factors.

Hence any logistic company ought choose to set up one itself in -house facility management department, it be better than outsourcing its all facilities service to one facility management (maintenance service provider) to help it to deal any kinds of maintenance service in warehouse. Because it is long term maintenance need to its warehouse's any machines and warehouse itself properties. If it chose to find one outsourcing facilitiy management maintenance service provider to replace its in-house facility management department to deal all related facilities maintenance tasks in warehouse. Then, it is possible that it needs to pay long time facilities maintenance service fee to its outsourcing facility management maintenance service provider more than itself facility management maintenance service provision department.

In conclusion, to decide whether the company ought need or not need facilities maintenance service or either set up in-house facility management department or outsource one facility management maintenance service provider. It depends on whether its organization has how many facilities are used in its workplace, how many staffs are working the workplace, how much size of its workplace, its workplace is office or warehouse or factory, how long time of its facilities' useful time etc. factors , then it can decide whether it needs or does not need one facility maintenance service department or outsourcing facility maintenance service provider to help it to deal any facilities management problem in its organization.

- Facility management role in organization

When one company feels that it has need facility management service. It can choose to set up either in-house facility management department or seek one outsourcing facility management service provider to help it to arrange any facility management service need. However, this facility management role is only one for the organization. It concerns this question: What facility management maintenance function can bring the benefits to the organization? It can define that all services required for the management of building and real estate to maintain and increase their value, the means of providing maintenance support, project management and user management during the building life cycle, the integration of multi-disciplinary activities within the built environment and the management of their impact upon people and the workplace. In traditional, (FM) services may include building fabric maintenance, decoration and refurbishment, plant, plumbing and drainage maintenance, air conditioning maintenance, lift and escalator maintenance , fire safety alarm and fire fighting system maintenance, minor project management. All these are hard services. Otherwise, cleaning , security, handyman services, waste disposal, recycling, pes control, grounds maintenance, internal plants. All these are soft services. Additional services, might also include: pace planning, things moving management, business risk assessment, business continuity planning, benchmarking, space management, facilities contract outsourcing service arrangement, information systems, telephony, travel booking facility utility management, meeting room arrangement services, catering services, vehicle fleet management, printing service, postal services, archiving , concierge services, reception services, health and safety advice, environmental management.

All of these services will be every organization's in-house facility soft or hard services needs. So, it explains why some large organizations feel need one effective facility management department to help them to arrange how to implement facility services efficiently in order to achieve cost reducing, raising efficiency and performance improvement aims because one effective facility management control system can influence employee individual productive effort to be raised or reduced indirectly.

However, (FM) can be selected either setting up one in-house (FM) department or outsourcing its services to one facility management service provider to help the organization to solve any kinds of facilities maintain service problems. One on-house (FM) department is a team, it needs employees to deliver all (FM) services. Some specialist services are needed to be outsourced, when the service is on expertise in the company. The no expertise services will be outsourced to simple service contracts, e.g. lift and escalator (FM) department will have direct labour, but it can outsource some specialist to help it to do some complex facilities management service. So, the team leader can of can manage whose team staffs, such as maintenance technicians run low risk operations . Otherwise, the outsourcing facility management service provider needs to help it to operate high risk operations or maintenance vital plant facility management service. Anyway, it can set up in-house (FM) department to arrange specialist direct labour and outsourced (FM) services to more than one facility management service providers to do different kinds of (FM) services. One of these outsourcing (FM) service provider, who can arrange sub-contractors to assist it to finish any (FM) services of it's outsourcing (FM) services are more complex to compare the other sub-contractors (third parties).

● What is a facility manager's role to provide quality service to satisfy its user needs?

We need to know how quality can be defined in facility management and why it should be defined by the customer? How facility managers can find out customer (user) needs? What are the difficulties in finding out users' needs and in delivering quality services? Whether improving quality always means requiring higher cost?

In general, facility manager's major responsibilities may include these major functional areas: longer range and annual facility planning, facility financial forecasting, real estate acquisition and/or disposal, work specification, installation and space management, architectural and engineering planning and design, new construction and/ or renovation, maintenance and operations management, maintenance and operation management, telecommunications integration, security and general administrative services. When the facility manager had implemented any one of these FM services for those user. How does he/she provide excellent (FM) service quality ot let whose users to feel satisfactory?

In fact, quality issues can not be considered without customer-oriented perspective service quality involves a comparison of expectation with performance. (FM) service quality is a measure of how well to service level delivered matches customer expectation. So, these issues are (FM) service user's general measurement level requirement. The (FM) manager needs to achieve these the minimum performance measurement level to satisfy whose (FM) user's needs.

However, (FM) service quality has three characteristics: Intangibility, heterogeneity, inseparability. But in fact, (FM) service delivered may be through tangible physical aspects, e.g. factory plant workplace building, machine equipment maintenance, intangible (FM) services, e.g. managing space moving in plant to let staffs to work, managing outsourcing cleaners to clean factory equipment. However, all (FM) service performance often varies, due to the behavior of service personnel. Hence, a well developed job specification and training can help to improve the consistence of services of (FM). Any (FM) production and consumption of many services may are inseparable and they are usually interactions between the (FM) client and the contact person from the service provider.

Hence, it seems that service quality is considered as hard to evaluate. In (FM) service quality, it includes physical quality and interactive non-physical service quality. Physical quality is tangibles: The appearance of the physical facilities, equipment, personnel and communication materials. Non-physical services quality means reliability: The ability to perform the promised service dependably and accurately; responsiveness means the willingness to help customers and provide prompot service to let user to feel; assurance mans the competence of the system in its credibility in providing a courteous and secure service and empathy means the approachability, ease of access and effort taken to understand customers' needs.

Hence, a good performance of (FM) manager , he/she ought satisfy the user's tangible and non-tangible both service quality needs. I recommend that he/she can attempt to predict what are the (FM) customer expects in each (FM) service needs. Then, it can make decision what aspect(s) will be the (FM) users major (FM) service need and what aspect(S) won't be the (FM) users major (FM) service need. Then, he/she can make more accurate decision to arrange time, human resource , cost spending amount arrangement whether when it ought concentrate on finishing the (FM) major service tasks as well as whether how he/she ought finish the major (FM) service tasks to be more easily, e.g. how to arrange staffs number to finish, how many the minimum staffs number is needed to be arrange the major (FM) service tasks, time arrangement is important factor, because it can influence whether he/she ought finish the major (FM) service tasks today or tomorrow or later in order to have enough time to finish other non-major (FM) service tasks. Instead of time management, staff number arrangement is also important factor , if he/she arranged the excessive staffs number to do the (FM) major services tasks, then it is possible that it will have shortage of staffs number to finish the non-major (FM) service tasks on the day. So, avoiding either major or non-major (FM) services can not finish on the day. The (FM) manager needs to predict when the major (FM) services and the non-major (FM) services which are necessary to be finished in order to have enough time and staffs to assist him/her to finish every day major and non-major (FM) service effectively. Then, the achievement of his/her (FM) major and non-major tangible and non-tangible services , it will have more chance to be performed efficiently by his/her managed staffs.

In conclusion, in any organizations , (FM) manager needs have good predictable effort to evaluate whether when his/her managed team need to finish the major and/or non-major (FM) tasks as well as whether how he/she ought arrange the accurate time and staff number to finish any major and/or non-major (FM) service tasks on the day. Then, his/her leading of (FM) service team can be managed to work more efficiently in order to satisfy her/his (FM) service user's needs.

How (FM) space moving management
can bring valued add to organizations

There are interesting questions: How (FM) can bring value-add to avoid loss or earn more profit to the organization? Can it influence employees to raise performance and improve efficiency ? Some organizations' (FM) service need which is necessary in order to let employees can raise productivity.

It is based on these assumptions: I assume the organizations have completely either outsourced or in-house their (FM) facility management departments will gain more effect on added value than they have no (FM) function as well as organizations have a strong coordination with the (FM) department will gain more added value than organizations with a weak coordination. Organizations in the profit aim can gain more added value than organizations in the not for profit aim sectors.

In fact, any organization is difficult to confirm it has relationship between improving performance, raising efficiency and owning (FM) function in its organization. (FM) could have to do with the attraction of easy but incomplete indicators of efficiency rather than the necessarily and less direct measures if the effectiveness and the relevance of space moving useful management, e.g. whether building has the enough space to let employees to move to work easy in order to raise efficiency, whether the building has excessive furniture and equipment number and they are putted on wrong places to be caused employees move difficulty in the building in order to influence productive performance.

However, how to arrange space moving management to equipment, e.g. copying machines, faxes, productive machines, they are putted on the locations where have enough space to let employees to move to another locations. For example, the building floor has more than 50 employees, but its space is not enough to let these 50 employees to move to any locations to let them to feel easily often. Then, it is possible to cause they feel nervous pressure and they can feel difficult to work , when they are working in a small office space or factory space or warehouse space. Then, the consequence will be under-predictive efficiency or poor performance to any one of these 50 employees in this office or factory or warehouse.

" Facility management is responsible for coordinating all efforts related to planning, designing, and managing buildings and their systems, equipment, and furniture to enhance. The organizations abilty to compete successfully in a rapidly changing world." (F.Becker)

The author explains equipment, workplace internal space designing, furniture space putting location arrangement will have possible to influence employee individual productive performance or efficiency to be raised or reduced in the workplace. Hence, it seems that, in the value chain (FM) belongs to the activity part of the firm. To make the facilities cooperation with each office or factory or warehouse using space moving facility management. Facility space moving management must be linked strategically, tactically and operationally to other support activity to add value to the organization's office or factory or warehouse space moving management arrangement more effectively.

Thus, how to arrangement space moving management issue it will have possible to influence the organization's employee individual productive performance and efficiency in whose workplace. It seems that (FM) space moving management arrangement have indirect relationship to influence the organization's employee individual performance and efficiency , due to they need often to work in the workplace, if they feel moving difficulty , or excessive equipment , furniture number is putting into the small office, factory or warehouse locations, or they feel the office or factory or warehouse has excessive (a lot of) staffs number to work in the small space of office or factory or warehouse. Then, they can not concentrate nervous on finishing every tasks in possible. In long term, their efficiencies will be poor or inefficiencies or their performance won't be improved or causing poor performance in possible.

Instead of the not enough space moving and excessive staffs number factor, it will bring another question: Can enough information systems equipment cause a more efficient and improved performance to the organization staffs in the workplace?

I assume that the office has 100 employees and it has only ten copying machines. So it means that ten employees use one copying machine. Hence, it brings this question: Is it enough to provide only ten copying machines to average ten employees to use? It depends on other factors, e.g. whether any one of these 100 employees needs to print how many documents per day , whether the five copying machines' locations are far away to separate different locations or they are stored in one printing room in the office, whether the day has how many staffs are absent, whether the day has how many printing machine(s) is/ are broken to need to be repaired. Hence, these unpredictable external environment factors will influence whether the five copying machines number is enough to let these 100 employees to use in the office every day. Hence, facility manager ought need to spend to observe average their copying behaviors every day in order to make data record. Many employees need to use copy machines to print documents, average how many document's page number, they need to print, how much average time spending to print their documents, average how many staff absent number on the day. Even, if the all five copying machines are stored in the printing room, calculating the staffs number whether how many staffs need more than five minutes to walk to the printing room to print their documents many staffs need to spend five minute to walk to the printing room, and they have other urgent tasks to wait to finish. It is possible to influence their efficiency, due to they often need to spend more than five minutes to walk to the printing room to print documents. If there are many staffs need to often to print documents, but their printing task will have many time, e.g. 20 separate printing tasks. Then, they need to spend at least (20x5) 100 minutes to spend time to walk to the printing room to print their documents. It must influence that they should not finish the other urgent tasks on the day. If there are many staffs to spend much time to walk to the printing room in the least 20 separate printing time or more on that day. All the facility manager needs to evaluate whether all the five copy machines are stored in the printing room whether it is the best location decision or they ought need be separated to put on different office locations in their workplaces, even he/she ought need to evaluate whether it is enough copying machines number, when the office has only 5 copying machines. He/she ought need to buy more copying machines number to satisfy any one of these 100 employee individual copying task need.

In conclusion, effective office or factory or warehouse space moving facility management will be one part task of (FM) function. If the office or factory or warehouse can have accurate equipment, machine , furniture number to avoid excessive or shortage number problem to cause employees often feel moving difficult problem in their workplace when they need to move to another location to work in office or warehouse or factory as well as whether the staff needs often spend time to wait the another employee to use the copying machine to print whose document or fax machine to deliver whose document. Then, it is not that fax or printing machines number is not enough to provide the employees to use in the office or warehouse or factory workplace.

Hence, (FM) includes space moving facility management to equipment , machines, furniture number as well as choosing anywhere is(are) the suitable location (s) arrangement to putting or storing these facilities in workplace as well as decision of the staff number and the workplace area size whether it has excessive staffs number to cause these staffs need to work in the small area size of office or warehouse or factory workplace. So, the organization ought need to decide whether it needs to reduce the office's staffs number to let them to work in another more suitable locations in another workplace. Hence, all these facilities space moving management and staffs and workplace size issues will be (FM) manager's consideration issues, because these external environment factors will influence employee individual efficiency and performance to be poor to cause low valued to its organization in long term in possible .

Reference

Becker, F. (1990). " Facility management : a cutting edge field?" property management 8 (2): 25-28.

● Predictive the choosing right

data asset and (FM) analytics

solutions to boost public

transportation service quality , includes airport airplan flying transport service providing organization

Can gather the choosing right data public transportation service station facilities asset and analytics, it can give recommendation to help any organization to boost service quality? (FM) analytics data can be applied to public transportation service industry to be supported how and why the train, train, ferry , ship, air plane, underground train public transportation tools' time arrival and leaving information notice board and automated ticket paying machines facilities are putting on or stored any where locations in order to boost passengers to feel their facilities locations are convenient to let them to buy tickets and see the arrival and leaving time for the next public transportation tool from the information notice electronic board machine. So, it seems that these public transportation tools' station facilities locations can influence passengers to feel the public transportation service company how to consider to its passenger's buying ticket needs and next public transportation tool's arrival and leaving time information needs in order to boost its passengers use service quality and let them to feel better service reliable performance in any train, tram, ferry , ship, underground tram, airplane stations.

As these public transportation service organizations need to learn data analytics represent an opportunity for its ticket paying machine equipment facilities as well as the next transportation tool arrival and leaving time information notice board electronic equipment facilities anywhere the locations are the most suitable to put on or store these equipment to let passengers to walk to the ticket paying machines to buy the ticket to catch the train, tram, underground train, ferry, airplane, taxi, ship more easily. So, they do not need to spend more time to find these facilities locations and spend more time to queue to wait to buy ticket to catch the public transportation tool in stations conveniently. Instead of where is the seeking ticket paying machine location, where is the next public transportation tool arrival and leaving information notice time , these both issues will be any public transportation tool's passenger's main needs.

Hence, how to spend time to seek where the next public transportation tool's arrival and leaving time information electronic notice machine location and where the ticket paying machine location , these both factors will influence any passengers' positive or negative emotion causing. For example, if the passenger feels difficult to find the ticket paying machine in the large area size train station or /and he/she feels difficult to find the train time arrival and leaving information to let him/her to know when the next train will arrive the station. Due to he/she feels difficult to find the train ticket paying machine, he/she needs to spend much time to find any one ticket paying machine in the train station. Then, it will influence him/her to choose another public transportation tool to replace the train public transportation tool, e.g. he/she can choose to catch tram, underground train, taxi, bus, ferry, taxi, ship to replace train. So, it seems ticket paying machine and time arrival and leaving information notice electronic equipment 's location putting or stored choice will be one factor to influence the passenger to choose another kind of public transportation tool to replace train at the moment. When, he/she feels that he/she arrives the destination in the most short time. Then, the public transportation service organization (FM) manager has responsibility to evaluate whether there are enough ticket paying machines number to let passengers do not need to spend more time to queue to buy tickets to catch the public transportation tool in short time as well as there are enough time arrival and leaving for next transportation tool to let passengers to know. It will be their concerning issues when they arrive the public transportation service tool's station.

Hence, predictive passenger individual walking behavior can help the public transportation service organization to choose whether where are the most convenient and attractive locations to let the ticket paying machines and the arrival and leaving time information electronic board machines to be putted on or stored in the suitable station positions in order to let many passengers can find these essential facilities in stations very easily. So, gathering data concerns passenger walking behavior in the public transportation service any stations, which can help the facility manager to make more accurate evaluation to attempt to predict whether where the locations are common places to let passengers to choose to walk daily or where the locations are not common places to let passenger to choose not to walk daily in general. Then, he/she can apply these data of different locations in the stations to evaluate whether anywhere they will have many passengers to choose to walk or whether anywhere they won't have many passengers to choose to walk in order to make more accurate decision whether anywhere are the most suitable locations to let the ticket paying machines and the time arrival and leaving information electronic board equipment to be putter on or stored in order to let them to feel it is so easier to let them to find.

Anyway, calculating each station's passenger number per day issue is important to predict whether where , there are many passengers choose to walk or where, there are not many passengers choose to walk in these different public transportation service stations in order to evaluate whether where the stations' different ought put on paying ticket machines or time arrival and leaving information electronic boards in order to let they feel very easy to buy tickets and seeing the next arrival and leaving time information for the kind of public transportation service tool conveniently in the different stations. Moreover, if the station has no enough ticket paying machines number to be supplied to let passengers need to spend more than ten minute time to wait to buy ticket to catch the kind of public transportation service tool in every queue every day. Then it will cause them to choose another kind of public transportation tool to catch go to working place or entertainment place to replace it to on that day. Then, it will cause these passengers who often do not like to queue in the kind of public transportation service tool's any stations, who will not choose to go to anywhere of this kind of public transportation service tool's any stations again. Hence, in long term this kind of public transportation service tool will lose many passengers. Thus, calculating each station's busy time of passengers number , which can predict when it is the busy time and it can make more accurate decision whether the station has need to increase enough ticket paying machines number in order to bring enough supply number to satisfy passengers' ticket purchase need in the busy time.

In conclusion, gathering above all stations' public transportation service equipment facilities number, storing positions data and every station's passenger walking behavior data, they are necessary to any public transportation tool service industry, because these equipment number and storing locations will influence them to make decisions to choose another kind of public transportation tool to replace it's transportation service if they often feel difficult to find these facilities in its different stations. Thus, it is part of task to facility manager's responsibility if the public transportation service organization expects it won't lose many passengers , due to these external environment factor influence and it also implies cheap ticket price does not guarantee the passengers will choose to catch this kind of public transportation service tool to go to anywhere.

The relationship between facility
management and productive
efficiency, include airport airplan staying and flying service performance improvement

It is one interesting question: Can facility management function bring benefits to raise productive efficiency to organizations? I shall indicate some cases to attempt to explain this possible occurrence chance as below:

● Facility management benefit to office workplace

In private organizations, when the firm has facility management department, whether it can bring efficient administration to influence clerks to work efficiently in office, e.g. reducing administrative time or shorten time to work in administrative processes, in order to achieve minimizing clerk number labor cost. How to design office facilities to let office staffs to feel comfortable to work and reducing their pressure to work. It seems that office working environment will influence office staff individual performance. If the office working environment could improve efficiency and creativity of services to satisfy office workers' comfortable working environment needs. It will reduce every administration manager's working pressure when he/she needs often to find methods to attempt to encourage whose administrative clerks to avoid to waste working time to do some non-major administration tasks. Hence, how to design or allocate or arrange office any facilities' stored locations or whether how many equipment number is the enough to store in the locations, which will influence office employees' working attitude in order to raise or reduce their administration tasks efficiency indirectly, e.g. the office is clean or dirty, whether office reception has enough information telephone switchboard operation facilities, whether every clerk's table has enough computers number to supply to every to use, whether internet speed is fast or slow in order to let any employees can send and receive email to communicate or download any document from internet in short time, whether data processing and computer system maintenance service supply is enough to be repaired to employees' computers immediately when their computers are broken to wait repair, whether website editing facilities operation whether is enough to link to office every staffs in order to let any office staffs can apply internet to do their tasks conveniently in short time.

Hence, all of these general office equipment facilities whether they are enough supplied and their stored positions anywhere are the suitable to assist any clerks to work conveniently, they will influence every office employee's administrative and productive efficiency indirectly as well as all faxes, copying machines, computers, whether internet linking maintenance service time is short or long to prepare to any office employees to use conveniently any time, these different issues will also influence every employee individual efficiency in office. Hence, it concludes that office working environment, facilities supply number, facilities maintenance service and facilities location storing both factors will influence employee individual administrative productive efficiency in office.

● facility management benefits to service working environment

Can effective facility management improve service working environment to raise employee individual work performance? It is a concern about the quality of service to its customer question. The term" standards and goals" are often used to measure staff individual service performance whether he/she can serve to customers to let them to feel this staff's service performance or attitude is good or bad.

Is the service workplace working environment facilities enough, it will influence customer service staff individual performance.

For shopping center service industry case example, for this situtation, e.g. shopping center's facilities are enough or are placed to the suitable locations in order to let the shopping center's customers to feel comfortable to shopping when they enter this shopping center as well as whether the shopping center's facilities can influence the customer service staffs to serve whose shopping customers easily or difficult, due to whether the shopping center's facilities whether are adequate supplied or their locations are the best suitable positions to influence their service performance to let them to feel easier or comfortable to serve their customers in any large size shopping centers. For example, whether the lamps' lighting energy is enough to let the shoppers to feel safe to walk to visit any shops when there are many shoppers were walking to cause crowd and they feel difficult to walk to avoid any body contact to any one in busy time when the shopping center has no enough lights to let them to see anywhere in the shopping center's dark environment. Then it will influence customer service staffs to feel difficult to find any shopping center customers, e.g. when two shopping center customers are fighting in one location where is far away to the shopping customer service staffs and securities in the shopping center, because the shopping center is large and it has no enough light to let the customer service staffs and securities to find their frighting location to deal their fighting behavior and other shopping center's shoppers will feel very dangerous to walk their fighting location to avoid to close them. Then, it will has possible to cause death or hurt to any one of these two fighting shoppers ,even other shoppers' life. Because the shopping center's securities and customer service staffs who need to spend much time to find their fighting location, it will delay they can bring the policemen to their fighting location when they arrive this shopping center's destination in short time in order to solve their fighting behavior to influence all shoppers' life in this shopping center. Hence, the shopping center whether it has enough lamps number and the lamps' light whether is enough, these lighting facilities will influence any shopping center customer service staffs and securities who can spend less time to arrive any locations to deal any urgent matters.

For another situation in shopping center, if the shopping center has no enough paying telephone service facilities to supply shoppers to phone to anyone when they feel need to phone to any in the shopping center. Then, it will lead to some shoppers decide to find where the shopping center's reception's telephone to supply to them to phone call to anyone. If they are ten shoppers are waiting to use the shopping center's reception telephone to phone call to their friend or family within one minute. Thus, it will influence the reception customer service staffs feel difficult to arrange how to distribute the only one telephone to these ten shoppers to use to phone call their friend or family when they are queuing within their one minute waiting time in the shopping center's reception. If these ten shoppers can not use the reception telephone to phone call anyone. hen, they will feel dissatisfactory and complain to the reception service staffs politely. So, lacking enough facilities in the shopping center's any where, it will possible to influence their shopping centers' shoppers to feel all shopping center's service staff individual performance to be poor. It means that if the shopping center expects to improve customer satisfaction to its customer service staff's behavioral performance, it meets have enough facilities to be supplied in the shopping center to let its shoppers to feel it is one comfortable and safe shopping center. In conclusion, shopping center's facilities will have possible to influence shoppers' feeling to evaluate its customer service staffs to evaluate whether their service attitudes are good or poor indirectly.

- Can facility management improve productivity

The productivity means resources (input) is therefore the amount of products or services (output), which is produced by them. Hence, higher (improved) productivity means that more is produced with the same expectation of resource, i.e. at the same cost is terms of land materials, machine, time or labor. Alternatively, it means same amount is produced at less labor cost in term of land, material, machine, time for labor that is utilized. So, it brings this question: How can facility management improve productivity? I shall explain as these several aspects, it is possible to be improved productivity from (FM) successfully.

Improved productivity of farm land: If the farming land has better facility management to bring advantages by using better seed, better facilities of cultivation and most fertilizer. It is in the agricultural sense is increased (improved). So, facility management can bring benefits to any land resource to raise productivity in possible. It implies that the productivity of land used for better facility management of industrial purposes is said to have been increased if the output of products or service within that area of industrial land is increased output aim.

Improved productivity of material: If the factory has improved better equipment by facility management method to assist skillful workers to raise the manufacture cloth number, then the productivity of the cloth number is improved by (FM) method.

Improved productivity of labour: When the factory has good manufacturing equipment facilities to be supplied to improve methods of work to product more producing number per hour, then (FM) improved productivity of worker. Hence, in any workplaces, when organization has good facilities, it will influence employees to raise productivities in possible, because they need often to improved equipment facilities manufacture products to achieve higher production number aim.

● Can facility management raise bank employee
productivity, include airport employee service performance improvement

Bank workplace environment is busy, the bank counter service staffs need to contact many bank clients to help them to serve or withdraw money from bank's counters. Whether does the quality of environment in bank workplace will influence the determination level of employee's motivation, subsequent performance productivity in bank working environment. For example, if the bank's staffs need work under inconvenient conditions , it will bring low performance and face occupational health diseases causing high absenteeism and turnover.

In general, bank size is usually small, it will have many bank clients enter bank to contact counter staffs to need them to help them to save or withdraw money. So, it will bring air pollution the crowd queue in every bank counter challenge when the bank has many people are queue waiting in counters to queue. So, bank working condition problem relates to environmental and physical factors which will influence every bank counter staff individual working performance to serve bank clients satisfactory. However, bank staffs need to deal many documents concern every client personal data every day. So, they need to spend much time to use computer and painting machines. This is particularly true for these employees who spend most of the day operating a computer terminal in bank workplace. As more and more computers are being installed in workplaces, an increasing number of business has been adopting designs for bank offices installment. So, bank needs have effective facilities management design because of demand of bank staffs for more human comfort.

An good equipment facility management for bank staffs to use conveniently, it is assumed that better workplace environment can motives bank employees and produces better productivity. Hence, bank office environment can be described in terms of physical and behavioral components to influence bank staffs to work inefficiently. To achieve high level of bank employee productivity, bank organizations must ensure that the physical environment in conductive to bank different department organizational needs, facilitating interaction and privacy, formality and informality, functional and disciplinarily, e.g. house loan or private loan departments, counter service department, visa card application department.

Thus, in a high safe privacy facility management working environment will let different department bank staffs feel safe to worry about privacy loss in possible. So, the improving bank facility to bring safe and high privacy to avoid bank client individual loss in working environment issue, the facility management can be results to bring these benefits, such as in a reduction in a number of complaints and absenteeism and an increase in productivity.

● Can (FM) create value to organization?
(FM) can reduce managing facilities as a strategic resource to add value to the organization and its overall performance, e.g. saving the energy in building and take care of shuttle buses and parking facilities space management for , on economic efficiency and effectiveness, or good price and value for the organization.

If the organization expects to apply (FM) process to save energy, it depends on possible input factors, i.e. interventions in the accommodation facilities services. So, it seems that the organization expects to save its energy consumption in its building. It needs have good space management facilities between parking its shuttle buses in its property's car park.

Why does space facility management is important to influence efficiency and productivity. For one school's building example, when the school decides none of the two gymnasiums student sport entertainment centers to be built in order to reduce financial cost and higher benefits. Remarkably, the use of space with the school overall strategic goals

, such as creating spaces that better can support the teaching, motivate students and teachers, attract more students and increase the utilisation of existing space to accommodate an increasing number of students.

If it hopes to make high quality teaching facilities on student's choice where to study. The school will need to choose to build either one comfortable and new design facility teaching accommodation or build two gymnasium sport entertainment centers in its limited land space either for students' learning or sport aim. Due to it feels new teaching accommodation can make more attractive to increase students numbers to choose it to study more than building two new gym sport centers to let them do sport in school.

Hence, space choice (FC) management strategy will be one important considerable issue, when the organization has limited land space resources to make choose to build any constructions in order to increase many clients number. Such as the school organization has limited storage land resource to let it to build either two gymnasium sport entertainment centers or one new teaching accommodation in order to attract many students to choose it to learn. Hence, it needs to gather data to make more accurate evaluation to decide how to apply its space facility to choose to build these both kinds of buildings in order to achieve the attractive student learning choice aim, so whether the two sport entertainment activity centers or one new teaching accommodation choice, it needs to gather information to decide whether the school ought to choose to build which kind of building in order to achieve the increase of student number aim, so space facility management will be this school's land shortage problem.

The relationship between facility
management and consumer
behavior, include airport travel passenger service satisfactory feeling

How and why shop facility management can influence consumer individual shopping behavior? If it is possible, what shop facility management factors can influence their consumption decision when they enter the shop to plan to buy anything. I shall indicate some shop case studied to explain whether how and why every shop's facility management can influence consumer individual consumption desire when any one consumer enters any shops.

● Shop's low ceiling height location (FM) influence consumer behavior

Can the shop's ceiling height influence shoppers' shopping behavior? Can the shop's variation in ceiling height can influence how consumers process information to decide to make purchase decision in the shops, e.g. for this situation, when the consumer enters the shop, he/she feels the ceiling height is low and it has a lamp will contact his/her head in possible. So, he/she chooses to move far away from the low ceiling location in the shop. It is possible that shop's ceiling low height and the lamp locates at the ceiling low height position will influence many customers' choices to leave the low ceiling height and lamp location, then the shop's low ceiling height will have possible to influenced many customers to choose to find the another shop to buy the similar kind of products , due to the lamp locates in the low ceiling height, so this lamp and low ceiling height will be possible factor to influence any shoppers who won't choose to walk to this dangerous location in the shop. If the shop's all spaces are ceiling height and it has many lamps are located at the low ceiling height spaces. Then, it will be serious to cause many shoppers do not want to spend too much time to choose any products in the shop because they feel dangerous to walk to the any low ceiling height lamps' locations in the shop.

Hence, hoe to design the different concept may be activated by the showroom ceiling if it were relatively high, as it tends to be in mall stores, versus low, as it is in most strip mall shops and outlet centers. Relatively high ceilings may bring safe shopping emotion to let any consumers to feel thoughts related to freedom, whereas lower ceilings may let consumers to feel dangerous to walk the locations in any shops. Hence it seems any shops ought not neglect whether their ceiling height is tall and the lamps ought avoid to locate in any low ceiling height locations in order to influence consumers number to be decreased.

● Can house facility management influence consumer individual purchase intention?

When one new property is built, whether the property consumers will consider how the new property is facility to influence their purchase intention to the property will the new property's (FM) influence buyers in real estate markets' preferences choice and living interest. Any new property's internal characteristics of the house unit itself , such as rooms available, when example, of external are location, accessibility to utilities services and facilities will have possible to influence the property buyer's final property purchase decision, so it seems that even the property price is cheap, it is not represent the property buyer will choose to buy the property, if he/she feels the property's facility management is poorer to compare other similar kinds of properties.

So, it can help real estate analysts better explain and predict the behavior of decision makers in real estate markets. Property consumers will search for property information, concerns the property's quality, price distinctiveness, ability, facility management, service of the property's external environment to decide whether the property is high value to choose to buy to compare other kinds of properties.

However, the external environmental forces, such as limited resources, e.g. time or financial will influence whose property consumption choice and living the property's satisfaction feeling (represent) a feedback from post-property purchase reflection used to inform subsequent decisions. The process of the property buyer's leaving experience will serve to influence the extent to which the property consumer how to consider future next time property purchases decision and new information methods. Hence, when one property consumer chooses to buy a house, it refers house features are house internal attributes , such as quality of building, the design as well as internal and external design, which are important factors for a property consumer when he/she needs to select and purchases one house.

The other (FM) factors which can influence the property consumers' needs, include living space as features, such as the size of kitchen, bathroom, bedroom, living bath and other rooms available in the house. The environment of housing area is also important factor, e.g. the condition of the hood, attractiveness of the area, quality of houses, type of houses, type of houses, density of housing, wooded area or free coverage, slope of the attractive views, open space, non-residential uses in the areas vacant sites, traffic noise, level of owner-occupation in , level of education in level of income in, security from crime, quality of schools, religious of , transportation , shopping center, sport entertainment can be supplied to close to the house area. All these human related issue of the property's location will also influence the property buyer's living location selection. Hence, above (FM) influence property consumer purchase behavior, it is based on the relationship behavior. The consumer's house purchase intention and house features, living space, environment and distance to recreation center, supermarket, library etc. public facilities variable (FM) factors.

In conclusion, the house internal space facility management and external environment facility management factors will influence property consumer individual house purchase intention.

● The effects of in-store shelf design facility management factor influences consumer behavior

Can every store retailer's shelf design influence supermarket and large retail stores shoppers' behaviors when they visit the stores? However, currently many stores tend to build on traditional and repetitive design for their store shelf layout, it brings results in outdated store layouts.

Another important store shelf layout design aspect, retailer should consider carefully is the allocation of products on shelves. So, it seems that efficient shelf space allocation management does not only minimize the economic threats of empty product shelves, it can also lead to higher consumer satisfaction, a better customer relationship.

Why does supermarket shelves design is important? Any retail tore will sell product category within a shelf. They can use the same nominal category , e.g. crisps next to light crisps, same food product shelf. Anyway, a goal-based shelf display can contain several product, that determine a common consumer goal, e.g. fair trade. Hence, these two categorical product structuring methods are also described in terms of how to put product, or food on shelf benefit and attribute -based product categories.

These shelf design food or product storing method will have more influence consumers to choose to buy the supermarket or retail store food or products more easily , due to products, or food put on their shelf very convenient and systematic to attract consumers' shopping consideration to the supermarket or retail store.

● Music (FM) environment influence consumer consumption desire

Is it possible that shop music (FM) environment can raise consumer purchase desire? In one shop or supermarket, it can provide soft music (FM) equipment to let consumers can listen soft music or songs in the supermarket or retail shop when the are staying to spend more time shopping and whether soft music facility can be expected to raise customer individual value-added options to the music facility shop in the supermarket or retail shop.

Can the music facilities prolong consumers to stay in the store? It is possible that tempo soft music can influence consumers to stay longer time in restaurants and supermarkets and retail shops. It is possible that the different types of music (FM) in any supermarket, restaurant, retail shop owning music listening facility shopping environment. It will have possible to influence consumers to prolong staying in their shops. For example, one wine selling retail shop has classical music (FM) listening equipment to let consumers to listen when they enter the wine shop, it is possible to cause consumers to choose to buy more expensive wine products. Some researchers indicate when the wine shop owns classical music facility to let all consumers can list classical music when they walk in the wine ship, it can evoke the wine consumers to choose to buy purchasing higher prices wine products in the long term classical music listening environment. Otherwise, in a fitness sport center, musical fir and excite or popular music (FM) environment can attract fitness sport players' emotion to play and kind of fitness sport facility longer time. Also, in one supermarket, the soft music facilities listening environment can persuade or attract food consumers to spend more time in the mall consuming food or beverage also purchase other products more easily, due to they will listen soft music to be influenced to choose to prolong staying time in the supermarket. It seems that it has relationship between retail shop's music facility environment and consumer's emotion will be influenced by these different kinds of soft music or songs to raise consumption desire in the supermarket, if some consumers like to prolong to stay longer consuming time in the owning music facility environment's retail shop.

In fact, some researchers indicate the owning background music facility selling environment's ship , it can affect consumer decision making, memory, concentration consumption desire. So, classical , jazz soft music facility ought be installed in restaurants, retail shops, restaurants' environment. Otherwise, popular , exciting, noise, pop music facility ought be installed in fitness sport centers, theme park entertainment parks business places in order to influence fitness sport players or theme park entertainers to prolong playing or entertaining time to feel real sport or entertainment theme park playing machine facility's entertainment enjoyable feeling as well as attracting restaurant or supermarket or retail shop's consumers to prolong their staying time to make consumption decisions. Hence, it seems that music facility environment can raise consumers' consumption desire in possible.

● University bookstore atmospheric factors how to influence student's purchase book behavior?

Any university bookstore how to do international control and structuring of book internal environment to raise students' purchase book desires in university itself school's bookstore, it will be one popular question to any universities. Hence, whether the university bookstore internal (FM) factors include: lighting, music, colors, scents, temperature, layout and general cleanliness as well as university external factors include: the university bookstore shape/size, windows, university parking facility for students availability and location, which can play an influential role of the university bookstore image in order to influence the university itself students to choose to buy books from themselves bookstore or university outside bookstores.

Whether the university student needs to spend how long individual learning time and how much learning nervous to spend time to choose any kinds of book in the universiity bookstore or outside bookstores, this issue , he/she will consider. Because he/she does want to expect spend much time and nervous to choose to buy books in any bookstore. If the university's bookstore physical location and internal (FM) image can let its target student customers to feel it's all book products are stored in any attractive internal book shelves places, e.g. the cheapest and the most expensive different subjects of text books are stored in one system method to bring the positive image of value and quality in order to let university target student customers can find their books' choice location to spend less time to search any books to read in the unviersiity bookstore easily.

However, due to learning time is shortage to every university student of the university's book shelves can display all text books in the attractive right locations in the university bookstore as well as the university's bookstore ought has an adequate space to let university students to walk to anywhere and find any subjects of text books and compare their book sale prices in the bookstore's any shelves' locations easily when they walk to the subject of book shelf location, then they can make accurate decision either to buy the right kind of subject book or not buy it to read in the short time. They will feel their book choice purchase decision making process won't influence their learning time in themselves universiity. Then, the university students will be influenced by themselves university's bookstore's attractive external university facilities in the university's any teaching places and the university's bookstore internal attractive environment facility image which can influence the students to make final choices to buy their liking books to read from their university's itself bookstore. Hence, the university's bookstore internal and external building environment (FM) design factors will influence its students whether choose to buy from themselves bookstore or another outside general bookstore.

● How and why does retail atmospheric environment influence consumers behavior in retail shop?

Any shop's internal facility management design can influence atmospheric environment to influence consumer individual shopping desire, e.g. colour, lighting, music, crowding, design and layout factors, which internal shop (FM) environment can influence the first time shopping visiting client ' cognitive process how to feel the shop store image. Such as if the store's (FM) environment can bring enjoyable and fun and happy image to let them to feel shopping's enjoyment.

In conclusion, when consumers will like to stay longer time in the store. Due to the store's internal (FM) atmospheric environment can attract them to stay longer time in the store. Then, the customer's shopping value will raise and it can bring purchasing intention and shopping satisfaction. How can (FM) influence retail atmospheric physical (FM) environment ? Can (FM) bring indirect relationship to influence how the consumer individual causes positive or negative purchase intention when he/she has influence to prolong staying desire in the store, when the shop has good (FM) , it will bring long time to make consumption chance in the shop.

● Facility management influences

consumer satisfactory service

level, include airport travel passenger satisfactory service performance level

Can facility management (FM) quality influence consumer satisfactory service feeling? Any organization's facility management can improve the effectiveness of the maintenance organization. It can provide improved operational and maintenance functions to maintain the physical environment to support the overall mission. However, any organization will consider whether it improves its facilities, it will raise consumer satisfactory feeling when it provides the service to them, e.g. education service industry, when students need to often to attend any school's classrooms or lecture halls, computer rooms, libraries, all these facilities will be student's learning environment. If these school facilities can be maintenance to let students to feel comfortable to enjoy to study in their schools' any learning locations. Then, it has possible that to bring their enjoyable learning feeling in theirs schools.

● How school's facility management influences student's learning satisfactory feeling.

However, in education industry case, the school's facility management has those criteria can be used to measure effectiveness. Student individual response time between the student's request for computer use service in school computer rooms, library reading service in school library , classroom computer facilities and tables, chairs etc. furniture supplies service and the facility management supply number and available to useful time. If the student believes that the response time is too long when he/she feels need to use any school facilities, the actual number of seconds or minutes, he/she needs to wait how long time to queue to use his/her school's any facilities in library, classroom, computer room. So, the student's queue waiting time to use any his/her school's facilities, it can measure the school's facility management effectiveness.

● Scheduling of preventive maintenance activities.

It schedules of any maintenance activities are not arranged effectively to the school. Then, it will influence students' poor learning facility service to their school. For their situation, when the school's first floor has two men toilets are damaged. They are needed to be required. However, it is one week period, the first floor 100 students can not use the first floor men toilets. Hence, in this week, all 100 students need to go to other floors toilets to often use. They will feel busy and time is not enough when they need to attend to any classrooms to listen the first floor classrooms teachers' lesson. If he/she arrives the first floor classroom too late, due to he/she needs to go to another floor male toilets to queue to use. Then, he/she will feel angry and worries about whose absent or late attending classroom behavior when the lesson's teacher has attended early in the first floor classroom , and he teacher will need him/ her to explain why he/she will go to this classroom lately, if his/her explanation won't be accepted to attend to the first floor classroom too late in the week. So, arrangement maintenance schedule to any school's facilities issue is importnt to influence student's satisfactory feeling to the school. Also, lacking of preventive maintenance activities will bring results in unscheduled shutdown of critical equipment can have an unrecoverable impact on the school's good learning environment providing to student's mission.

In fact, however in any organizations, such as school, ship, office etc. organizations, achieving balance of effectiveness and efficient difficulties and takes time and effort on the part of management and staff. It is not enough to establish an optimal relationship between these two parts. It has another factor that organizations need to consider costs. In today's budget tightening environment, decreasing expenses requires accepting a lower level of efficiency and effectiveness. The goal is to determine the point at which decreasing efficiency and effectiveness is no longer acceptable before that point is reached.

It brings this question : How to apply facility management knowledge to rise efficiency and effectiveness in order to improve quality standard of service to satisfy consumers' needs in short time? Such as school's facilities service case. What factors can influence student's level of satisfaction with regards to higher educational facilities services? It seems that any school's facilities will influence its students how to satisfy its education service indirectly. Because they need often to go to school to learn. So, any school's facilities, e.g. classrooms, computer rooms, libraries, toilets, lecture halls, canteens, sport and entertainment centers, research laboratories, school car parks, student enquiry counters, all these places to the school's any students will attend. So, how raise schools' facilities improvement to satisfy students' learning needs in the school's any locations which will have help to influence it student individual satisfaction level to the school's service, instead of every teacher individual teaching performance service to the school's students.

For any service organizations , such as hotels, restaurant, financial institutions, retail stores and hospitals etc. The physical environment can influence how customers' evaluation of their service. Due to service has intangible nature, so customers will rely on evaluate service quality.

Any higher education institutions are education service providing organizations. They need have comfortable and enjoyable educational environment to be provided to the students to attend the school's any places in order to meet whose learning expectations and studying experience needs. So, the school's facility management will be one factor to influence student's learning satisfaction when they expect to attend the school's any locations or places to let them to feel the school's learning environment have good facility management feeling.

In fact, if the school has comfortable classrooms or lecture halls educational environment to let its students to feel, it will bring assistance to raise their learning satisfactory feeling. So, comfortable learning facility management environment is one kind of school's facility service characteristics, it includes intangibility, perishability, inseparability and variability. So, they are every student individual learning feeling when they are attending to the school's any learning locations. So, school's facility management service feeling will influence whether they expect to choose this school to study. If the school's facility management learning environment is more comfortable and teaching facilities are better to compare other schools' facilities. Then, it will have possible to attract many students to choose this school to study. Such as any educational organizations, instead of the teachers (lecturers and professors) whose educational level is influence students number. The university's building environment will influence students' learning feeling, when they attend in the university. The facilities include laboratories, lecture theatres an offices, but also residential accommodations, catering facilities, sports and recreations centers because university students need have university life feeling to let them to fell the university can give welfare services , e.g. medical services, career guidance, sport entertainment, residential accommodation etc. service, instead of educational learning service in classrooms and lecture theatres. Hence, university's diversification facilities services are needed to satisfy university students to choose it to study, instead of university teacher's educational performance.

When one student can enroll the university to study from secondary education institution. The admitted student will usually consider two aspects to decide to choose the university to study. One aspect is the academic programs, of sequence of courses choices and the another aspect is the university's facilities whether they can satisfy their university life need, e.g. library, dorms, bookstore, food canteen , gym's sport entertainment, education technological facilities in the classrooms and lecture theatres to let the students to feel the university's teaching facilities are achieved his/her learning demand.

So, these two factors (teaching and learning and facilities) are linked to each other to influence student's total school learning experience and attitude towards a particular institution and this is termed as value chain in the student's learning process in the university. Hence, student individual evaluation variables will include teaching staff, teaching method, enrolment and facility enough supply actual service need.

However, the university's facilities, such as any residential accommodation, canteen, library , classroom, lecture theatre, sport gym, entertainment center will be their useful facilities need to satisfy their learning, entertainment and eating ,even living need in residential accommodation in the school's learning life experience every day. If one student chooses to live in the university residential accommodation . All of his/her learning and eating and living time and spending will be calculated to the university's any facilities to let him/her to feel it can provide enough facilities to let him/her to enjoy.

Hence, the facility management factor, such as overall campus environment, library, laboratory, classroom, lecturer theatre size and facility supply of on campus accommodation, welfare right service, parking areas, cafeteria , sport center etc. They will be every students facilities service needs from the university supplies choice. So, any university ought not neglect how to improve itself university's space area facilities to achieve satisfy their needs after they choose this university to study. Hence, any university's facility management will influence how the student's satisfactory learning service feeling when he/she chooses the university to study.

In conclusion, better facility management will attract more students to choose the university to study. Otherwise, worse facility management will not attract more students to choose to study the school. Hence, it seems that the school's facility management factor has relationship to influence student's satisfactory feeling, instead of teacher individual teaching performance factor to the school.

● Property facility management influences householder buying behavior

One new property's low price is attractive factor to influence property buyer individual preference choice. Does the new individual's facility management factor influence the property buyer's preference choice decision, if the property buyer feels its facility management is better than other similar properties, even it's price is higher than other properties. I shall indicate some cases to analyze this possibility as below:

Some properties' facility management service quality has possible to create true value for any property buyers when they consider the calculation ingredients to make decision whether to new property has higher value to choose to buy. The factors may include: price, natural environment, transportation tools convenient available, shopping centers supplies, the neighour quality, and the property's internal facility management etc. factors.

In fact, car or house purchase buyers, they have similar behaviors. It is that car's buyers will consider the car's machines whether they are safe to drive on roads, instead price, manufacture loyalty factors. It is possible that the car's machines quality factor will be preference to any car buyers when they make preference decisions to choose which brand its cars are the suitable. However, if the car's brand is famous and its appearance beautiful and price is cheap. But the car consumer feels its machine qualities are unsafe to let the driver to drive on road. Then, the car's poor machine quality factor will influence the car buyer's decisions to choose to buy this car. It can influence the car buyer individual car purchase decision.

The car buyer's behavior is similar to property buyer's behavior. Although, the new property price is cheap, good neigh ours are living near to the new property's location, shopping centers and transportation tools are available to near to this new property's area. But if the property buyers' feels its facility management is poor quality to compare other similar properties. Then, the poor quality of facility management factor will have possible to influence the property buyers whose final buying decision to choose to buy this new property. It brings this question: How and why can the facility management poor quality factor influence property consumers' preference choice?

In general, all property consumers won't know whether the new property's facility management is good or bad quality , they need to spend time to visit to the new property in order to observe whether its internal facility is satisfactory to his/her acceptable level. In simple, their purchase decision will regard to how to allocate household budget, how the household's economic resources are influenced, e.g. for travelling, visits to restaurants, comparing the different similar types of property product groups, e.g. apartments or houses or houses of a givn size data. For example, if one property's room(s) size is (re) small to compare other kind similar product type of room(s) size. Although the prior property's price is cheaper to compare to the later properties. But, if some property buyers hoped the property has large room(s) size, then the later larger room(s) size which will be possible to some property buyer's preference choice. Even, their property price is more expensive to compare the smaller room(s) size of properties. Thus, the property's room size which will be one major factor to influence property buyers' purchase decision. room's size had relationship to facility management issue. Moreover, if the room's quality and design is attractive, then it will bring more attractive to persuade some property buyers to choose to buy them to live in preference.

Hence, whether the new property is good durable product feeling which will influence householder's choice. If the householder feels the new property has long term durable life to avoid to spend much maintenance expense when they have been living in the new property for a long term period. They will believe it has better facility management, quality to let them to live longer time and the most importance is that they do not need to spend any maintenance expense , due to the property 's any internal facilities are damaged easily.

The external factors may include: culture, reference groups, family, social class and demography of lifestyle as well as internal factors may include: feelings, past property buying and living experience , property knowledge, motivation of the property buyer individual psychology. These both factors can influence any property buyer individual decision making process to do final house purchase behavior. However, internal factors, such as: property knowledge of facility management and property living experience, e.g. how to evaluate to choose to buy the property , due to the property buyer's past living experience for the past property's facilities whether its facilities can satisfy its property buyers' comfortable living needs. This internal factor will be more important to influence any property buyer's property purchase final decision. If he/she feels whose prior old property's facilities are satisfactory. Then, he/she will compare this new property and old property's facilities to decide whether this new property is value to buy. So, the old property's facility will be the measurement standard to compare his/her next new property purchase choice. So, the property purchaser will compare these new and old property's property facilities product knowledge to similarities among property alternative which will influence his/her final decision to choose to buy the new property to live.

It seems that property low price factor must not guarantee to attractive many property buyers' choice. Otherwise, it is assumed that many property buyers like rent or buy to live the property for themselves for long term intention. There are less property buyers expect to sell the first property to earn profit intention. So, they will usually consider whether the property is long term durable product to avoid to pay maintenance expense when they had been living in the property in long term.

Some factors that taking consideration are proximity to the specific location, housing prices, developer's brand, the payment scheme, reference group, which are not the main factors to influence any property buyer individual choice. Because property buyer's need is that the property has good facilities to supply to them to live, e.g. good heater equipment can provide hot water to them to bath in winter or good air conditioners can provide cold temperature to let them to feel cool comfortable feeling in summer in their homes. Good electric tools facilities , when they have need to use electricity in safe environment at home, e.g. car park accessibility facility , level of security facility , surface area facility and housing types, bedroom, bathroom facilities, quality of housing manufacturing raw material, house design , house durable guarantee, speed of complaint responsiveness, specification accuracy, confirmation of building plan service, showing legal file property purchase process service, finance instalments process assistance, speed of responsiveness, officers' skills of presentation. All of above these concern property facility management issues will influence any property buyers' final choice to decide whether the property is value to buy. So, facility management will influence property purchaser individual final decision in possible.

● Hotel facilities influence hotel consumer choice

Travellers choose hotel to live. They will consider price, room comfortable feeling, hotel location , gum sport or entertainment service facility supplies , hotel room booking service etc. factors to decide whether the hotel can achieve every traveller individual minimum living need. However, whether hotel facilities factor will be the main factor to influence travellers' living needs. How and why do travellers consider hotel facilities whether are enough supply or facilities of quality to satisfy their demand to cause their living choice to the hotel final decision.

Usually, hotel's customers won't plan to live too long time, e.g. more than three months in the hotel. Because they are travelling aim. It will bring this question: Does hotel facilities quality consider to influence their hotel living choice if the traveller is short-term traveller to the country? However , some travellers who have effort to spend money to live high class hotels, even their journey is short trip. Hence it seems that short trip , hotel living reason can not influence the high class hotel travellers' living comfortable demand to the high class hotel room. Hence , the high class hotel room's facility management quality is also needed high performance. Even, when they need to eat breakfast, lunch , dinner in the high class hotel canteens or playing any sport equipment, or gum equipment or wathching movie in the hotel's small cinema room . They must need high class hotel can supply more entertainment, restaurant , sport facilities to satisfy their comfortable needs in the high class hotel. Moreover, they must consider safety issue when they are living in the high class hotel. So, thy must demand the hotel have enough five fright equipment in their rooms, or corridors and the stairs to let them can leave the dangerous locations to arrive the most safe locations immediately when the hotel has fire accident occurrence in any where . So, it ensures that the high class hotel's customers must ensure the high class hotel's facilities can satisfy their any one of above these needs before they decide to live this high class hotel.

In fact, high class hotel's room price must be more expensive to compare the low class hotel. So, it explains why high class hotel's consumers will need the hotel has safe and good quality of facilities to let them to feel it is one reasonable price, safe , good service and good facilities' high class hotel to live. Usually, when the traveller arrives the country to travel, the travelers chooses the hotel to live, it is whose first time visit in common. So, he/she ought consider that the hotel environment seems it is good or bad to let the traveller to select to live. If the hotel's facility environment is new and beauty and design colorful to let the first time travellers to feel. Then, it is possible that good facilities environment can influence the first time travellers to select to live, even the hotel's room price is more expensive to compare other similar hotels in the travelling living places. Hence, it explains why hotel facilities can influence traveller individual room booking choice. When he/she is the first time to visit the hotel to select whether to live or not.

● How and why facility management can influence workplace productivity to bring customer satisfaction

Facility management is one part of manufacturers or retailers as their productivity in workplace as their input and functionalistics within physical environment. In fact, facility management in workplace may include: site selection, property disposal, site acquisition, workplace space allocation, space inventory, space forecasting facility management, interior furniture change planning, interior furniture installation, moving maintenance, inventory, design evaluation, employment satisfaction evaluation plan, external maintenance and breakdown maintenance, preventive maintenance, landscape maintenance, energy space facility management, hazardous waste disposal, capital , operating furniture budgeting. So, it seems that one workplace considered whether the workplace's facility is enough to let employees to work in order to raise efficiency and improve productive performance more easily. Then, it will bring this question:

● How and why workplace facility management can influence consumer individual satisfaction?

Strategic FM delivery is essential for business survival. I shall explain why for delivery is important to influence customer satisfaction. In business process view point, an effective and meaningful service to their customer , i.e. the user. For logistic industry, the product's delivery time will influence when the product can be sent to the user's arrival destination. If the product is delayed to sent to the user's home or office or any location destination. The reason is because the logistic product sender has no efficient facility management (FM) arrangement in its warehouse . Then, its warehouse lacks efficient (FM), which will cause users to feel its delivery service is poor and they will complain its delivery service staffs. Then, they will find another delivery service company to replace its service. So, it explains that logistic industry's warehouse (FM) service arrangement can raise efficient time to send any products to their customers in order to let they feel satisfactory service. For example, Amazon online logistic company's warehouse has applied artificial intelligence robotic tools to assist warehouse workers to arrange the different kinds of products to deliver to the right shelves . Then, the warehouse robotics will follow their right product shelves locations to follow the right products to deliver to US domestic or overseas product buyers in the short time and it can avoid the wrong products to deliver to the wrong buyers' risk. Also, the (AI) delivery tools can raise time efficiency to assist Amazon warehouse workers to reduce their work load, and tried to work in large warehouse environment. Although, its warehouse's area is large, the (AI) tools facility can help them to deliver the different products to different shelves in the right locations , e.g. exact product number and the kinds of product to be delivered to the right country' client's shelf location in the warehouse. Also, it implies FM is very important to influence Amazon warehouse delivery efficiency and avoiding delivery wrong occurrence chance. For example, the shelf location belongs to US domestic customers, or the shelf location belongs to Japan customers, or the shelf location belongs to Hong Kong customers, or any other Asia or Western countries' different customers' locations. The warehouse's facility needs have different countries' shelves enough space to put and it also need enough space to let the (AI) tools, robotic delivery workers and human workers both to walk to different shelves locations easily and the different countries' shelves number needs to be calculated accurate. For example, it has how many client number will buy Amazon's the kind product per day. If it has above 5,000 to 10,000 China clients to buy the kind of product. Then, it will need to make judgement how many shelves are placed in the warehouse. So, it can avoid to lack enough shelves to put any different kinds of products to prepare to delivery to China clients in efficient time and it won't avoid to delay to deliver to their homes or offices or any locations in China.

Hence, such as Amazon logistic case, it explains why warehouse's space shelves number and area or locations facility management can influence workers or (AI) delivery tools how to move convenient and avoiding the delivery to the customer's wrong destination chance occurrence and shortening time to deliver products to its clients efficiently. Then, due to the delivering time is shorten and the wrong delivery destination's occurrence chance is also reduced , even it can avoid to deliver the product to wrong client's destination occurrence. Then, the logistic firm's clients will feel more satisfactory to its product sale delivery service and their complaints will be avoided. Hence, it explains effective warehouse (FM) space management service arrangement is essential to any logistic businesses nowadays.

● Facility management brings departmental benefits

Why do organizations need have facility management (FM) service? As above examples indicate that (FM) can improve workplace environment facilities, e.g. warehouse environment to let workers to raise efficiencies or improve performances, even it can influence consumers to raise satisfactory to it's services indirectly, also it can help organizations' equipment to be used long term to cause old and are needed to spend expenditure to maintenance or change new equipment in order to improve better quality . So , it can assist organizations to avoid to spend more expenditure for new equipment purchase or maintenance. All these issues will be facility management service's benefits to an organizations, which can concern raising customers' service satisfaction, raising efficiency or improving productive performance, raising productivity, reducing equipment or property maintenance or new alternation much of expenditure spending, office or warehouse or any workplace space planning arrangement .

However, every organization will need a facility manager or manage whose team effectively . When a facility manager begins to apply FM techniques to solve business problems. The case for FM is made. It is a simple matter of demonstrating a qualified return on the investment required. Every organization's success, FM operation of three key activities: they include: needing a proper understanding of the organization's needs, wants, drivers and goals and knowing when needs to review its changing circumstances, developing an effective facilities solution o support the organization's needs, wants , property drives and contribute to achieve its goals both short term and long term, achievement of reliable delivery of that solution in a managed, measured manner.

So, it bring one question: What are the influential factors to be followed the right direction to FM manager's strategic FM operational decision? The influencing factors may include: ownership, governance sector, complexity and perhaps of most significant, the size of the organization's property portfolio.

In fact, major occupiers feel FM service need, they are large corporate organizations and public service organizations. Their aims usually are to raise. The most marginal improvement in efficiency or effectiveness, these aims are the great significance. Major property occupiers will already have a facilities department or individuals performing the FM function with another department like property, finance or human resource, sale and marketing's facilities.

Usually these FM need occupiers who will encounter this problem: How can apply FM service systems and processes to be developed to improve reliable service delivery making use of the economies of scale, not suffering because of the size of the problem. This question will be facility manager individual concerning question: How to apply (FM) technique to solve the improvement reliable service delivery making use of the economics of scale problem for whose organization?

In reality much of external facilities management benefits to organizations, instead of raising efficiency, improving performance, raising productivity, reducing maintenance expenditure, e.g. energy saving, reducing natural resource waste, increasing local employment, improving supply chain management are all elements of the FM contribution to every organization's need. Hence are the work life balance argument and provision of an effective and safe working environment that supports why some organizations feel need (FM) service to support their organizational development.

Moreover, on cost benefit of space saving efficient view point, space service cost reduction is a key driver for all organizations and the medium, or large sized players will benefit directly from a well coordinated facilities strategy. For example, application FM technique to help warehouse or office space area to save 50% space vacancy to let employees can move easily or putting enough furniture or equipment or many stocks can be putted in warehouses . So, paying more rent expenditure to rent or purchasing another new warehouse or office to satisfy workers or employees' working environment to be better need. If the organization has effective (FM) technique, then it has enough space vacancy to supply to the increase stocks number to be putted inside in warehouse and it can let workers to move safety in available to let staffs to move easily and equipment have enough space to be stored in the limited warehouse space problem.

For greater space savings benefits will bring either long term renting or buying of increasing offices or warehouse number expenditure problem to any organizations, when the organizations' cost or renting or buying accommodation probably accounting for 60 to 70% of total occupancy cost . So a strategic program to release space or the prevent the acquisition of moves can be the most significant consideration to any facility manager, with between 40% and 60% of the workplaces are unoccupied in most offices or warehouses at any given moment in time.

Hence, how to apply (FM) technique to save space occupied areas for employment moving or stocks or equipment saving need in offices or warehouses. This issue will be any facility managers' seeking methods to solve problem. However, the important major advantage of facility management to organizations is that the application of management principle to keep the organization's property assets with the aim of maximizing their potentials. Thus, any organizations' facilities have become important, due to the property facilities' worth will increase if the organization's facility management technique can protect the organization's facilities have good performance. Then, the organization's maintenance expenditure will reduce and it won't need to spend expenditure to buy any new facilities to replace old facilities , due to they often damage factor when they are used old.

In conclusion, it explains why effective FM combines resources and activities can raise work environment improvement, which is essential to the raising employee performance aim. For hotel living service case example, this industry must need have good facility management service because hotels must need to fully equipped in term and facilities for effectiveness to satisfy hotel living clients' demand , hotels ought need good facilities asset management style lead to effectiveness in service delivery, there are benefit derivable from the adoption of facilities management from which other hotels can learn from for their effective operations. Hence, it explains why effective FM can bring benefits to hotels' properties to be more comfortable, beautiful appearances to attract many hotel customers to choose to live the hotel. Because hotel's building industrial kitchens, rooms facilities, equipment , halls of categories, restaurant facilities, gum sport entertainment centers' facilities, fans, elevators, lifts, electrical installation, escalators, baking equipment, recreational facilities, including golf courses which will be important factors to influence hotel clients' comfortable living feeling, if the hotel can keep its all facilities in the best living environment often. Then, it can raise chance to attract many hotel customers to choose it to live. So , hotel industry has absolute need to implement effective FM strategy to keep its properties more attractive to satisfy its clients' living needs.

Instead of hotel industry, logistic transportation industry also needs effective facilities management in warehouse, because of the logistic company's warehouse 's facilities are good, then it will assist to raise employee individual efficiency in the safe and system shelve stored facilities in workplace environment and improving performance.

Consequently, it will bring the shorten time to deliver any products to clients to avoide the delaying time delivery in order to let customers to feel more satisfactory to their services. In simple, it seems that some industries need have effective facilities management techniques to help them to bring long term customer satisfactory feeling, worker individual efficiency raising and performance improvement benefits. Hence, it seems facility management techniques' demand will be increased to some industries in popular in the future because it has help to raise employee individual efficiency , productive performance and client individual satisfactory level consequently.

What benefit will bring to the airport if it implement FM strategy?

How important is airport facility management? Without a doubt, facility management is crucial to ensure operational functions around the airport works efficiently. Airports wish to maintain a positive brand image and keep their customers happy with:

consistent services standard to the customer

a smooth airport operation flow

safe and secure environment

a smooth security screening flow

As the airports dealing with the growing capacity on a daily basis, outsourcing facility management services is a great option because it eases the headaches of managing the physical airport. Moreover, airports save costs, enhance the passenger experience, and spend their time to focus on business growth.

Passengers Expectation

Passenger's satisfaction depends on their experience from the minute they reach the airport, expecting to feel relaxed throughout the check-in, waiting and boarding process. The basic requirements for better customer experience at the airport weigh from the speed of baggage delivery, smooth check-in at the airport terminals, little time taken for security checks and the cleanliness of the facilities.

Even though these days most passengers have obtained a boarding pass before they arrive at the airport, however, not knowing how long it will really take to move through the terminal, passengers tend to arrive very early for flights thus spend more time waiting at the airport. The ground experience before passenger boards an aircraft can be divided into these segments:

getting to the airport

waiting in the terminal before security

passing through security checkpoints

finding the gate

Practical check-in facilities improve arrival and departure flow at the airport. Delays for passengers, airport staff and airline crew resulting in disruptions to airport and airline operations. Therefore, airports and airlines will be backed by the airport assistance roles such as:

ground and luggage handling

luggage claim, recovery, sorting and transfer

delivery and placement in plane

cargo and luggage loading and unloading

luggage transfer

runway support

passenger check-in

reception, embarking and disembarking passengers

management of passenger transfers

flight preparation and management

ticketing, excess luggage management

luggage claim, management of irregularities

Beside improvement the flow of departure and arrival at the airport, passengers consider cleanliness to be a valid circumstance (Batra, 2014). As cleanliness can impact customers' first impression of the service (Harris & Sachau, 2005) and experience (Pijls & Groen, 2012), the sanitary condition of a place such as an airport is a fundamental factor. Hence, airports require regular cleaning and maintenance to maintain their image.

An experienced and knowledgeable facility manager for airport assistant and cleaning tasks often result in better quality output which technical and maintenance tasks can be completed faster and more proficiently. Thus, outsourcing airport assistance and cleaning service are the best solutions to meet the passengers' expectation of the airport facilities at any time.

Improvement airport operational efficiency

Any major airport has lots of customers which most of them are passengers and airlines crew. The passengers demanded useful facilities to use when check-in, waiting and boarding. Airlines required space for aeroplanes, facilities for routine maintenance, places for passengers and flight crews while on the ground. Air-freight companies needed space for cargo aeroplanes. Pilots and the cabin crew needed runways, facilities for aircraft storage and maintenance, and places to relax while on the ground.

The growing capacity of the airport required good planning and operational efficiency. On-time performance is a major parameter for evaluating operational efficiency of airlines; is directly associated with customer satisfaction, and is positively correlated with profitability (Dresner and Xu, 1995; Steven et al., 2012; Mellat-Parast et al., 2015) Top operational efficiency occurs when the right combination of people, processes, and technology come together to optimize business performance.

So, if the airport can provide a clean and safe workplace , it will increase airport staff productivity. Automating daily operations and administrative tasks are crucial to support the airport staff in providing good services consistently. According to a report commissioned by Amadeus Airport, airports can improve operational efficiency through the digital transformation of processes, well-executed data analytics and insight sharing. While delivering excellent passenger experience and improve its operational efficiency, airports also need to increase non-aeronautical (retail) revenue.

For airports, ensuring passengers enjoy a smooth transit through the airport is vital: Spend increases by 2.5% for every minute a customer is in a retail area and not stuck in a queue (Boston Consulting Group, 2018). According to research done by J.D. Power and Associates (2010), it shows that the happier the passengers were at the airport, the more money they spent in the terminal.

Oursourcing FM to airport organizational benefit

Outsourcing facility management will help you attract and retain happy customer and staff. Through highly visible airport improvements and smooth-running terminal operations, outsourced facility management can deliver long-term cost savings by addressing deferred maintenance energy consumption and sustainability. Airports also get strategic direction and help to oversee day-to-day management works in operations, maintenance, technical and systems integration, infrastructure, retail business and space management from the outsourced facility management experts.

Safety and Security

Unfortunately, airports are targets for terrorist activity. For that reason, it's vitally crucial that airports take extremely strict security measures. The facility manager guarantees the airport stays safe and secure by monitoring, checking and improving the security systems, video surveillance system and other airport equipment constantly. Failure to do so may lead to undesirable conditions leading to poor operation, loss, injury, prosecution, and insurance claims to the airports.

However, airports are also introducing effective procedures to optimize the workflow during the security screening in the light of the snail-pace queues. By outsourcing technical maintenance and security service, you are granted access to innovative ideas and leading practices from them that will enhance the quality of your facilities and the airport experience overall. They offer new innovation and effective solution that improves the passenger experience, saves costs, creates efficiencies and adds value.

Why does FM is provided to airport , it can provide facility innovation benefit to let travel passengers feel more comfortable to wait in the country 's airport?

To ensure the efficiency and effectiveness of facility management in coordinating demand and supply of airport facilities and services, continuous innovation and new technology development is useful and necessary to achieve high-quality service offering. According to Skytrax's research, being a global travel leader means constantly striving to improve, innovate and impress. A poll conducted by SITA finds airline passengers are happier when technology ease their way through the airports (SITA Passenger IT Insights, 2019).

According to ACI World Director General, Angela Gittens in the Connected Aviation Today that investing in new and improved infrastructure, as well as making the most of existing infrastructure, is the bedrock on which smooth airport operations and improved passenger experiences are built (Seawright, S, 2019). New technology in surveillance monitoring system enabling digital surveillance streams to travel over the internet so that operators in various airport departments such as police, customs, fire and medic, baggage, and airport operations, can all monitor the video feeds from separate PC workstations.

Airports and airlines can take note that technology solutions can boost passenger satisfaction, every step of the way including the cleanliness of their washrooms. The technology-driven initiative, known as ATALIAN Restroom Management System (AMS), is capable of sending an immediate alert to the cleaning staff for swift action if required. We understand how tough it can be for a major airport to run and maintain a smooth operation while working on multi-tasks at the same time.

What is airport Facility Management?

The facility manager guarantees the airport stays safe and secure by monitoring, checking and improving the security systems, video surveillance system and other airport equipment constantly.

What is the role of facility management?

Facilities managers are responsible for the security, maintenance and services of work facilities to ensure that they meet the needs of the organisation and its employees. Facilities managers essentially look after all of the services that helps a business or other organisation do its work.

What are the 3 main tasks of facilities management?

Four Main Functions of FM

Supporting people.

Establishing processes.

Facilities upkeep and improvement.

Technology integration.

Putting it all together for facilities management.

What is the importance of facility in airport?

Practical check-in facilities improve arrival and departure flow at the airport. Delays for passengers, airport staff and airline crew resulting in disruptions to airport and airline operations. Therefore, airports and airlines will be backed by the airport assistance roles such as: ground and luggage handling.

What are the facilities functions of an airport for it to be considered as international?

International airports include customs and international terminal. Passengers can fly abroad through direct or connecting flights. The international airport can also be used for domestic flights apart from the international.

What are the six main functions of a facility?

Understanding the functions of facilities management

Maintaining & optimising facilities.

Streamlining processes.

Supporting people.

Managing projects.

Integrating technology.

Top Five Benefits of Facilities Management

Asset tracking and management. Tracking assets and budgets through spreadsheets is about as convoluted as it gets. ...

Space optimization. ...

System of record. ...

Cost analysis. ...

Integration. ...

Culminating in a better workplace.

What are examples of facility services?

Some examples include:

Heating, cooling, and ventilation (HVAC)

Plumbing and plumbing fixtures.

Lighting and electrical systems.

Mechanical systems outside of HVAC.

Emergency control systems, such as sprinklers.

What are the types of airport facilities?

Facilities

Check-in facilities, including a baggage drop-off.

Security clearance gates.

Passport control (for some international flights)

Gates.

Waiting areas.

Which kind of facilities is required at airport?

OTHER FACILITIES

Pre-paid Taxi Car Service.

Medical Room.

Baby care room.

Money Exchange Services.

Free Passenger baggage trolleys.

Baggage wrapping services.

Parking space for approx.

What are the facilities provided in airport building?

Main Function of Terminal Airport — Change of Movement Type-From car, train or bus to plane. — Processing (passenger processing space)-Ticket, check-in, security check. — Provide Passenger Facilities - Shopping, toilets, eating, meeting & greeting, business & conference.

What are the airport operations?

Passenger operations include baggage handling and tagging. Terminal operations comprise resource allocation and staff management. Airside operations include aircraft landing and navigation, airport traffic management, runway management, and ground handling safety

How are airports organized?

Airports typically own all of their facilities and make money by leasing them to airlines, air-freight companies, and retail shops and services, as well as by charging for services like fuel and parking and through fees and taxes on airline tickets. The revenues pay off the municipal debt and cover the operating costs.

What is airport Layout?

An Airport Layout Plan (ALP) is a scaled, graphical presentation of the existing and future airport facilities, their location on the airport campus, and pertinent clearance and dimensional information.

What are the challenges of facilities management?

6 facilities management challenges companies face this year

Managing a safe return to the office. ...

Optimizing space utilization in the hybrid workplace. ...

Planning office moves and consolidations. ...

Managing workplace technology. ...

Managing facility maintenance. ...

Rethinking the employee experience.

What is poor facility management?

Buildings are subject to wear and tear or structural depreciation in response to their maintenance neglect which are often manifested in poor facility management. Depreciation in its severe state will reduce the economic lives of buildings and render such buildings in to dilapidation or state of derelict.

What is the critical part of an airport?

In aviation, a critical area refers to a designated area of an airport that all aircraft, vehicles, persons or physical obstructions must remain clear of when one or more Instrument Landing Systems (ILS) are in use, to protect against signal interference or attenuation that may lead to navigation errors, or accident.

What is the need of airport infrastructure?

Role of Airport Infrastructure in National Economy

The quality of airport infrastructure, which is a vital component of the overall transportation network, contributes directly to a country's international competitiveness and the flow of foreign investment.

Why is an airport called an airport?

An airfield would only imply landing strips. An aerodrome added a suffix that implied modernity and more complete facilities, even paved runways, and an airport offered complete facilities for aggregating, moving or receiving, and disaggregating large volumes of people and cargo.'

What are the four airport components?

Components of Airport may include:

Runway.

Taxiway.

Apron.

Terminal building.

Control tower.

Hanger.

Parking.

What is terminal facility?

As used in these regulations the term terminal facilities means all facilities, including waiting room, rest room, eating, drinking, and ticket sales facilities which a motor carrier makes available to passengers of a motor vehicle operated in interstate or foreign commerce as a regular part of their transportation.

What are the 3 key functions undertaken by airports?

Direct effects. Include the activities undertaken at the airport itself: services to passengers (check-in, security, boarding), cargo (loading and unloading), and aircraft (refueling, cleaning).

What are the three parts of an airport?

It includes runways, taxiways, and ramps.

Runway – An area where aircraft takes off and lands. It is made of soft grass, asphalt, or concrete. ...

Ramp – Also called Apron, this area is used for parking the aircrafts. ...

Taxiway – It is a path on the airport that connects the ramp to the runway.

What are the functional areas of an airport?

Departments of Airport

Airport Services English text.

Medical Center.

Postal freight services.

Air Security Service (Security group, control and inspection group)

Department of Accounting and Reporting.

Service for Electrical and technical illumination for the fights.

What is airport Master Plan?

An Airport Master Plan is a critical planning tool for determining the future requirements of an airport and provides a vision for realizing its ultimate potential.

What are the three sections of an airport?

It is customary to classify the several components of an airport in three major catego- ries: airside facilities; landside facilities; and the terminal building, which serves as the interchange between the management alliances: Problems of competition and complexity

Airport facilities management alliances: Problems of competition and complexity

Airport facilities management (AFM) is being delivered through collaboration with airports, through forming networks and strategic alliances. Facilities management (FM) is a function that is adapting because of a changing external environment; strategic alliances is one method used by FM to deliver this change in strategy. This article explores and examines the structure and characteristics of AFM alliances including the problems faced by competition and managerial complexity. This article explores the AFM function, its importance to airports and its strategic and competitive direction. The article concludes that although there are inherent problems in AFM arrangements, these can be effectively managed through well-written contractual documentation.

FM can be defined broadly as a function that consists of numerous managerial activities. More recently, FM is considered to be an integrated approach to operating, maintaining, improving and adapting the buildings and infrastructure of an organisation, to ensure that the built environment supports the primary objectives of the host organisation (Nutt, 2004). In airports, the management activities could be grouped into five main areas: information management, building and property management, civil services, procurement and logistics management, and legal services. FM functions focus on planning and act as a coordinating unit within the firm, aiming to ensure that the function acts as the driving force behind successful operations (van Wagenberg, 1997). The ability of the FM function to translate organisational and individual needs into a balanced and flexible supply of supporting service within an environment that supports these needs is considered one of the successful functions of FM (Klee, 1997).

Increasingly, the primary objectives of organisations are required, or strongly urged, to include environmental commitments. In order for FM to continue to set an environment where the client organisation can deliver its core and supporting business functions, it is likely that FM will need to adapt its processes to include energy management and sustainably orientated processes. This will involve change at the strategic level and would involve the combination of many resources and personnel to design, and redesign the facilities to suit the end user and the system in which the building is used (Edum-Fotwe, 2001; Nutt, 2004). Alternatively, it can be viewed that because there is significant evidence to suggest that the risk of climate change is significant, it should be addressed by all FM managers (Warren, 2010); climate change could legitimately be viewed as a business continuity issue, with natural disasters posing as a risk to the continuation of service provision to a building. Facilities managers have a key role to play in the development of an organisation's Building Continuity Management plan (Warren, 2010). Longer term security of energy supply is an increasingly important issue (Warren, 2010). This is another issue that will require the involvement, if not the total management by, from FM with their knowledge and management of the building systems. The European focus on CO_2 emission reductions and resultant government reduction targets for the built environment are aiming at reducing energy use by encouraging the more efficient use and adaptation of building systems and technology (Williams, 2008). Again FM can have a significant impact on the introduction of sustainable building operations. Strategic alliances have been found to be effective where technological change is the aim (Rothaermel, 2000), adding strength to the notion of using strategic alliances to develop sustainable FM.

The methods to deliver the developing FM function can be described under separate business models: integrated business unit, empowered business unit ('selling' its services to the company), an internal profit-centre or an independent FM service provider (third-party provider). These business models, respectively, can be seen as a life cycle process. The higher the strategic importance of the FM function to the company, the more likely the FM function will be performed by either an internal profit-centre or by an independent provider (Gaya Walters, 1997; Ytsma, 1997). When the FM function is performed by a profit-centre, the FM organisation will try to sell its services outside the company. The most important aspects of the profit-centre are the commercialisation and the performance responsibility of the FM function. When the acquisition of FM services takes place from an independent provider, a higher degree of control is required; this results in a shift from functional FM towards relationship management and the management of cooperative agreements (Gaya Walters, 1997).

Many airports split up their AFM functions into technical, infrastructure, commercial and space management (Frankfurt AFM, 2003; Munich AFM, 2003). Technical management consists of maintaining and developing all technical systems needed to operate an airport. This wide service ranges from vehicle maintenance, security and fire protection down to small technical services. The infrastructure management involves logistics management, including parking, public transport and also the arrangement of cleaning staff, medical services and workplace development. The commercial management function mainly controls relations with third parties (for example, retailers) and contractors, but also performs functions such as business administration and marketing. Airport space management includes building, property and surface management. It provides a framework to support all the other AFM activities.

On conclusion, any airport organizations ought need to implement FM strategy in order to provide comfortable and service performance improvement feeling to encourage any countries travel passengers choose to go to the country to travel or change airplanes in order to raise airport income during any airline air planes renting staying number increases and travel passsnger shopping number increases in the country's airport .

reference

Aaltola, M. (2005) The international airport: The hub-and-spoke pedagogy of the American empire. Global Networks 5 (3): 261–278.

Adler, N. and Berechman, J. (2001) Evaluating multi-hub networks in a deregulated aviation market with an application to Western Europe. Transportation Research, Part A 35: 373–390.

Advani, A. (1999) Passenger-friendly airports: Another reason for airport privatization. Policy Study, Report No. 254. The Reason Public Policy Institute: Los Angeles, pp. 1–26.

Bhadra, D. and Hechtman, D. (2004) Determinants of airport hubbing in the United States: An empirical framework. Public Works Management and Policy 9: 26–50.

Brown, A.W. and Pitt, M.R. (2001) Measuring the facilities management influence in delivering sustainable airport development and expansion. Facilities 19 (5/6): 222–232.

Cranfield University. (2002) Study on the Competition between Airports and the Application of State aid Rules. Final report. Vol. 1, European Commission, DG Energy and Transport, Directorate F-Air Transport.

Edum-Fotwe, F.T. (2001) Review: Facility management: Risks & opportunities. In: B. Nutt and P. McLennan (eds.) Oxford, UK: Blackwell Science, 2000. ARCOM Newsletter, 2, 6–7.

Freathy, P. and O'Connel, F. (1999) Planning for profit: Commercialization of European airports. Long Range Planning 32 (6): 587–597.

Gaya Walters, B. (1997) Organisatiemodellen. In: W. Ytsma (ed.) De vele gezichten van facilities management. Deventer, the Netherlands: Kluwer Bedrijfsinformatie.

Kesharwani, T. (2000) Rapidly growing private presence in airports takes several different forms. ICAO Journal 55 (3): 8–9.

Killing, J.P. (1988) Understanding alliances: The role of task and organizational complexity. In: F.J. Contractor and P. Lorange (eds.) Cooperative Strategies in International Business: Joint Ventures and Technology Partnerships between Firms. Massachusetts/Toronto: Lexington Books.

Klee, H. (1997) Facilities management: een terreinafbakening. In: W. Ytsma (ed.) De vele gezichten van facilities management. Deventer, the Netherlands: Kluwer Bedrijfsinformatie.

Lorange, P. and Roos, J. (1992) Strategic Alliances: Formation, Implementation and Evolution. Cambridge, UK: Wiley-Blackwell.

Nutt, B. (2004) Infrastructure and facilities: Forging alignments between supply and demand. Conference Proceeding of Future in Property and Facility Management II, A Two-day International Conference, University College London, London.

Park, S.H. and Ungson, G.R. (2001) Interfirm rivalry and managerial complexity: A conceptual framework of alliance failure. Organization Science 12 (1): 37–53.

Pels, E., Nijkamp, P. and Rietveld, P. (2003) Inefficiencies and scale economics of European airport operations. Transportation Research Part E: Logistics and Transportation Review 39 (5): 341–361.

Percoco, M. (2010) Airport activity and local development: Evidence from Italy. Urban Studies 47 (11): 2427–2443.

Pitt, M.R. (2001) Strategic direction in the airport business: Enabling or disabling? Facilities 19 (3/4): 150–156.

Pitt, M.R. and Brown, A.W. (2001) Developing a strategic direction for airports to enable the provision of both network and low-fare carriers. Facilities 19 (1/2): 52–60.

Pitt, M.R., Wai, F.K. and Teck, P.C. (2001) Strategic optimization of airport passenger buildings. Facilities 19 (11/12): 413–418.

Rothaermel, F.T. (2000) Technological discontinuities and the nature of competition. Technology Analysis & Strategic Management 12 (2): 149–160.

Schiphol Airport Annual Report (2002) Schiphol Group. http://www.schiphol.nl/SchipholGroup/InvestorRelations/FinancialInformation/AnnualReports.htm.

Tay, L. (2006) Strategic facilities management of Suntec Singapore International Convention and Exhibition Centre. Facilities 24 (3/4): 120–131.

CHAPTER II

AIRLINE AND AIRPORT TRANSPORT STRATEGY

In airline transport industry strategy, I shall attempt to indicate some useful strategies to help airlines to keep travellers number in order to avoid to reduce. I shall indiate as below:

● Airline Oil Price Variable Factor strategy

1.1 Positive social change influence to vehicle fuel consumers

What suitation is positive social change to vehicle fuel consumers. We are entering globalizational competitive society, such as airline fuel case, if the country, e.g. US is increasing vehicle consumers in this year, then US vehicle fuel demand will increase. So, the US vehicle fuel price will be caused to increase. Due to much vehicle fuel demand increases in US this year, so foreign fuel import and US fuel manufacturers will increase to supply to US for vehicle market in this year, due to many US vehicle consumers need to buy fuel to drive their vehicles in US. However, due to fuel natural resource will have limited number to be supplied to manufacture airline fuel, due to much fuel is used to manufacture vehicle fuel in US this year. So, it will cause airline fuel manufacturing and supply shortage challenge. Due to this year, US decreases airline fuel supply, but the US airlines demands fuel number is still increasing. Consequently, vehicle fuel increasing demand factor will cause airline fuel price to be rised in US this year.

For example, air tickets can be bought from internet, so travellers won't need to go to travel agent to buy conventienty. It is due to the global travel industry is increasingly competition. Thus, global travel industry competition will bring negative social change to influences fuel price rising because it will increase traveller numbers and airline flight times to fly. When, traveller's travelling desire demand numbers will be grown up fastly, then their online electronic-ticket buying or consumption behaviors will be rise. Thus, it will also cause online e-ticket price is decreased to attract many travellers to choose to buy e-ticket from online channel more than paper-ticket visiting travel agent channel. Thus, it is negative social change influences to cause fuel price rising due to plane flight flying times will increase and airline company will increase demand to buy many fuel to prepare to fly often. When fuel demand will rise, then the fuel sellers will rise fuel price in possible. Thus, airline industry global competition will being negative social change to influence fuel price raising up and air ticket price falling down to attract many traveller numbers to choose to buy among different travel agents.

Negative social change influence

What suitation is positive social change. I shall indicate economic growth example. When one country has better economic development in the year. Then, employers will have more effort to do businesses. Then, they will create many jobs to provide to the country citizen to do. When, these unemployed people have jobs to do, they will have extra income to save. They can spend extra to prepare to spend to enjoy their entertainment every year, such as travelling. Thus, the positive social change will influence traveller number increasing, then the plane fliging flying times will also increase, it will cause planes need to use much fuel to fly. The result, it will also increase fuel demand, but the fuel natural resource number will decrease , so fuel supply will also decrease. Finally, it will also cause fuel price to be risen.

Also, I shall indicate the financial risk of airline industry evidence from Cathay Pacific airways and China airlines against key determinants of which include interest rate, exchange rate and fuel price risk for the period of January 1996 year to December 2011 year. During this period, these key external factors which were the most serious influence to cause these two airlines choose to change their strategic behaviors.

Due to any these financial risks is difficult to predict and it was also changing often, these factors will also affect any airlines stock returns which arise from changing economic conditions, e.g. fuel price movements and fluctuations in exchange rates. These external unpredicted changing factors will attribute to the air tickets cyclical demand, capital investment, fixed costs of labor and landing rights to this global airline industry.

However, the relationship between fuel price and stock prices varies across economies. The effects of oil price changes in sub-sector indices, such as wood, paper and printing, insurance and electricity. In the past, on global stock exchange market was positively significant in 2011 year. Otherwise, with respect to the U.S.A. aviation industry, some economists suggested that global airlines stock returns were negatively to percentage change in fuel prices related to any airline firm value, e.g. Qantas and Air New Zealand were negatively share price growth to fuel price risk in the short term in the 2011 year.

Thus, it brings this question. Whether positive or negative social change will be one important factor to impact fuel price rising. I feel positive social or negative social change will be one important factor to impact fuel price rising. The reason is such as below:

Nowadays, airline transportation demands are increasing, due to many travelers need to catch planes to travel as well as many cargoes need to be carried to planes to transport to different countries to sell. It seems aviation transportation industry is important to influence the health of the global economy growth nowadays. However, ignorance of internal or external market dynamics, catching travelers business can be detrimental to airline profitability more than carrying cargoes business. Because the demands of travelling different countries' travelers' consumption are still more than the demands of businessmen carrying cargoes in any countries every year. Thus, the travel industry will increase demand to human travelling business more than cargo transportation business. However, the cargo flying transporation demand will rise, due to many global fast speed post businesses are growing. Base on both global cargo flying transportation demand and travellers' flying travelling demand are increasing. Thus, the fuel demand will increase, but the fuel supply will be shortage. So, it will cause fuel price rising consequently.

How can positive or negative social change influence any airlines' air ticket prices to be risen or fallen? In fact, the increase in petroleum price can have chance to affect airlines in a negative manner because increased oil prices have resulted in the reduction of services operations, the number of airline schedules flights, even airline bankruptcies.

Thus, it seems that plan travellers and air flying cargo transportation both demand have been increasing. This social increasing demand change factor, it will be the most influential cause the bad effects to cause airline industry share price reducing or reducing air ticket price or decreasing traveler numbers more than the other factors influence, such as inflation, terrorism, oil shortage, bank interest rate etc. unpredictable external suitation factors.

To support this hypotheses, this are my research questions, such as : Does a combination of terrorism and price of petroleum significantly influence airline profit changing mostly? The alternative hypothesis was base on a significant relationship exists between terrorism, price of petroleum and airline profitability more than other factors, such as inflation, bank interest rate or air ticket price changing of these factors influence. I shall indicate that the first assumption was that terrorism has a negative effect on airline profitability and another assumption was that only external factors as oil prices or terrorism affect airline profitability.

    Terrorisms attack influence

Whether terrorisms attack will influence fuel price rises up or falls down. I feel terrorisms attack to any country, which will cause plan fuel price falls down. Because travellers will feel dangerous and worry about their life safety when they catch the plan to enter the country if the country has serious terrorisms attack risk to cause plan crash accidently.

However the effects of oil price and terrorism on airline profitability was limited to a regional perspective, e.g. the terrorism attack of plane crash event to USA on 11 Sept. After the terrorism attack happened on USA 11 Sept. incident of terrorism attack was restricted to events of skyjacking, attacks on oil production, refinery and distribution. Thus, USA on 11 Sept. terrorism attack will cause oil price falls down , due to it will influence travellers fear death , so who will reduce times to travel to USA after 11 Sept. date terrorism attack occurrence at the year. The oil sellers will reduce oil sale price to attract many airline companies to buy more supply, due to airlines will decrease demand to buy fuel to provide planes to fly when the traveller numbers has decreasing and flying times will be decrease also. Thus, the fuel price will be decreased consequently after the terrorism attacks to any country.

Other types of terrorist activities, such as attacks on financial targets or senior government officials could have an adverse effect on the petroleum and airline industry. I think the disruption of the production or distribution of petroleum because of incidents of terrorism was costly in terms of loss of business and the inflationary effect on fuel dependent products or services.

In fact, some airlines have adopted more fuel saving technology, so whose fuel consumption would not use more than other non fuel saving technology airlines. So, the owned fuel saving technology airlines which will buy less fuel to use. It means that they won't need fear fuel rising to increase their expenditure because they only need to buy less fuel to use and their fuel demand won't fall , even fuel price has risen.

However, it seems fuel price increasing will not be the only factor to influence the airline industry's traveler numbers decreasing, due it is possible that the airlines need to rise air ticket price to riase their profit, sue to their fuel cost has risen. However, due to some airlines which have fuel saving technology, so which can avoid to use more fuel to provide planes to use and which fuel costs will be reduced, then which can provide cheaper air ticket fare prices to compare the non fuel saving technology airlines. The result will cause some non owned fuel save technological airlines will lose travelling customers in this global airline travelling market, also the non fuel saving technology airlines need to renew their fuel technology if which want to keep their competitive abilities to avoid to close down their businesses.

Can airline fuel self-organization avoid
fuel price rising cost

I feel one airline fuel self-organization can avoid fuel price rising to influence cost rising because it doesn't often buy any fuel from fuel suppliers. However, there are some airlines which are the characteristic of airline fuel self organization and they are present in that both of oil fuel production and providing flights service in airline industry. So, these airline fuel self organizations can control the oil fuel price by themselves. However, one airline fuel self organization is also evident in efforts by businesses acts of terrorism against economic targets by adopting proactive steps, such as airline and airport security. So, it seems airline fuel self organization can reduce the risk to avoid oil price raising and terrorism attacks to raise cost in airline industry risk management sector.

Beside, these airline fuel self organizations which have high technology of fuel efficient aircrafts, the use of one aircraft model, the adoption of direct routes versus customer loyalty programs and other operational cost reductions are strategies for increased profitability. It seems these airline fuel self organizations can solve oil price, terrorism etc. external factor influences to raise cost.

Instead of high technology of fuel efficient aircrafts and airline fuel self organization methods can solve terrorism attacks and oil price rising risks. However, I believe that there are other risks are caused to these airline fuel self organizations to raise their airline cost possibly. The risks include such as user factor, such as culture, tradition, education ; economic factor, such as costs, human resources and macro economic factor, such as political stability, economic development, educational policy, health policy, environmental policy. However, these risks occurrences are resulting in the relationship of cause and effect events. These events are not directly observable. Such as, the complexity of relationship between terrorism and airline profitability. Hence, if global airline industry can predict when those risks occur to do protective strategic behavior. It is possible that which can understand when these risk events will occur and to adopt their protective strategic behaviors to influence their outcomes to be positive to avoid any external risk threats on the long term. However, I think hierarchy, airlines fuel self organization efficiency methods which are as possible predictors of user preferences to avoid risk threat events to cause whose airline businesses cost rising to cause failure occurrences in airline industry.

Can tourism industry influence airline
profitability

In my study, I suppose terrorism and the price of petroleum both factors which had properties of distinct and interrelated close relationship to raise airline cost. Moreover, these variables (terrorism and the price of petroleum) displayed differentiation, self replication, efficiency and hierarchy which can cause risk events to airline industry. However, I also think the other internal and external threat factors of airline industry, such as inflation, bank interest rate, business model, service quality, airline fuel or plane engine technology, air ticket pricing, brand loyalty, airline strategic management, government policy and fuel hedging of these factors which can also raise the risks to threaten any airlines existence in airline industry.

There are two basic business models in tourism industry. They are network (full service) and low cost (discount) carriers. The network carrier model employs diversification strategy by increased domestic destinations, serving international routes, providing diverse seating arrangements (business, economy and first class), maintaining a complex system of offering high quality service. Otherwise, low cost (discount) airlines focus on lower air fares. To keep operating costs down, discount airlines offer shorter routes and provide point-to-point destinations rather than through sophisticated flights are primarily in domestic destinations. So, discount airlines operate a common model aircraft fleet, offer a single seating arrangement and cheaper flight services offered to compare network airlines. However, these two basic business models have their unique competitive abilities to provide any airlines existence in tourism industry nowadays.

In fact, natural resource of oil is decreasing in our earth. But as the same time, human demand is increasing and oil supply is decreasing, so it also causes the oil fuel price is increasing to supply to airline industry. It influences not only to airline industry, it also impacts of higher oil fuel price to tourism, such as expansion of airports are made based on expected demand increase.

Tourism has been proven to many adverse events, including terrorism, flight disruptions. Beside, the bad natural climate change influences, such as the volcanic ash cloud event occurred in April 2010 year. So, airline industry need to concern climate change because it will cause high fuel prices indirectly. For example, the event occurred the extreme increase in operating costs for airlines in 2008 year, due to unprecedented prices for aviation fuel also meant, that despite the introduction of fuel charges, so this event causes the global tourism industry recorded losses seriously. Even if alternative fuels become commercially available for airlines which are still likely to be more expensive than present aviation fuel.

Higher airfares in the future are likely to lead to reduction in travel and cause tourists to shift from more distant to closer destination. When some of the economic responses to higher oil prices are obvious assessing the overall economic impacts on tourism is difficult. However, long term changes in global oil price rises will be similar to global changes in other commodity prices, exchange rates and income. It is therefore important to consider the impact of high oil prices on tourism from a general equilibrium perspective rather than relying only on bottom partial equilibrium approaches.

However, I believe tourism and airline industries have close relationship, such as tourism and airline industries are likely to suffer in an environment of high oil prices. Given that tourism destinations receive tourists from a range of origins, it would be useful to understand of some countries are increasing oil prices than others. Such as the net oil importing countries are selling higher oil prices than oil exporting countries generally. For example, New Zealand is an oil import country to provide planes for international visitor arrivals, so its oil fuel price is usually higher to charge to NZ airlines because any NZ airlines need to pay to foreign countries to buy any oil more expensive price. So, NZ airlines usually charge higher airfares to its visitors to compare the other exporting oil countries' airlines. It will impact NZ has negative influence to domestic tourism industry as well as planes need will also be decreased , due to NZ charge high fuel price to cause air ticket price to be raised.

In economic theory, on income effects indicate negative impacts on tourism demand, the exact effects of higher oil fuel prices for specific destinations are far from clear. However, airline industry's different market segments show different sensitivities to air ticket fares changes.

On the first hand, if the visitors are long destinations generally wealthier than average and therefore potentially less affected, as energy costs would be a smaller proportion of their income compared will be those from less wealthy groups. Thus, the more wealthier travelers who won't decrease travelling desire, even the fuel price raises to case the air ticket price to be increased.

On the second hand, oil prices don't translate into higher transport costs especially not on air routes that are highly competitive and that are maintained for strategic reasons. So, non air transportation industry won't influence customer number to be decreased easily.

On the third hand, many other factors shape tourists' decision making, including emotion drivers or those related to images, fashions and perceptions. Increasing environmental protection awareness of tourists could also be an important factor to influence tourism consumption, instead of oil fuel price raising causes air ticket fares raising factor to reduce traveler numbers. However, oil price raising reason causes also due to high use of cars, vans and domestic air transport in some countries, e.g. Hong Kong, China countries, there are many people like to buy cars to drive. So, the private driver numbers are increasing demand to cause these countries' oil fuel prices raise in the short time suddenly. It implies airlines need to consider their country car number whether is increasing or decreasing. If their country car number is increasing, it is possible to cause fuel price to be risen up because car demand is increasing to need to use more fuel and it has less supply of fuel in the year. Otherwise, if their country car number is decreasing, it is possible to cause fuel price to be fallen down because car demand is decreasing to need to use less fuel and it has more supply of fuel in the year.

Is fuel price rising only factor to cause airline risk
in short term

In long run, fuel raising price will not cause risk to airline, due to implications of changes to supply and demand side conditions of oil fuel energy may differ qualitatively. For example, due to investment responses of producers, consumers and governments in alternative energy sources and more energy efficient plants, vehicles are supplied in order to achieve oil fuel price can't be risen seriously.

However, I believe oil fuel rising charge will be an important factor to influence global airline ticket fares to be increased in the short term to cause risk because oil fuel rising charge will be influenced to raise any airlines pressure from other unpredicted factor risk influences.

Firstly, on the bank interest changing factor, e.g. bank interest rate rising which only attract more bank saving. But it can not influence the bank savers who choose to reduce relax time to go to other countries travelling. Otherwise, when the bank savers can save more money to earn higher interest in banks, who will prefer to choose to use their saving to consume travelling. Due to who can earn higher interest rate after a period of saving time. So, I believe who behavioral travelling consumption will be raised when the banks will raise interest rate, then the bank savers won't choose to save more money in banks. So it is possible that who will withdraw more money to consume to go to travelling from banks. It seems bank interest rate changing won't influence bank savers' behavioral travelling consumption to be reduced.

Secondly, on the exchange rate changing factor, although any country's exchange changing will cause other countries' money value to be fallen down or risen up. However, it won't influence any travelers' behavioral consumption to be reduced seriously. Although, it is possible that the traveler won't spend too much to go to shopping when who travel to the another country and arrive the country. But, it is not possible to influence the traveler decides to reduce consumption to buy any air ticket to go to travelling in short time.

Thirdly, any country inflation also can not reduce travelers' travelling consumption easily because inflation can influence consumers who choose to buy cheaper foods and clothing and reduce entertainments in their every day life. But, one country's inflation can not influence it's citizen do not spend much travelling expenditure because travelers only spend one time or two times of travelling every year usually. So, the travelling expenditure rate of any households is not too much to compare daily essential expenditure.

So, it seems that bank interest rate and exchange rate changing and inflation won't influence any travelers' travelling consumption of decisions to be reduced easily in short time. Otherwise, if the oil fuel price raises too much, then global airlines' cost will be raised in long term. So, the airlines only choose to increase their air fare prices to aim to avoid loss possibly in long term. It seems that oil fuel raising price and bank interest rate and exchange rate changing and inflation factors will have direct influence airline income in long term.

● Methods to solve rising air fare prices to decrease travellers'demand
Biofuels energy increases supply
I suggest these methods how to avoid the oil raising price factor to cause airline air fare prices to be risen to lead the risk of traveler numbers to be reduced as below:
The first method: Whether aviation fuel markets will have what benefits from biofuels supply to planes. I shall refer the scope includes trends in jet fuel price, airline response to fuel price, increases and volatility and environmental goals for aviation. The aviation fuel supply industry includes production, distribution and consumption of aviation fuel and it outlines players in the aviation fuel supply chain. For example, at each airport, fuel supply chain organization and fuel sourcing could differ with regard to the role of oil companies, airlines, airport owners and operators and airport service companies. However, major jet fuel purchasers are airlines, general aviation operators,

corporate aviation and the military, with most of the jet fuel in global different countries demanders being used for domestic commercial and civilian flights carrying passengers, cargos or both.

Commercial aviation fuel efficiency has improved dramatically over time, largely due to aircraft and engine upgrades and operational and air traffic control improvements. So, it seems that fuel supply factor can influence airline fare prices majorly. However, jet fuel prices generally correlate with prices of crude oil and other refined petroleum products, such as diesel. So, increasing prices and the persistent price volatility of jet fuel markets import airline industry finances in any countries.

However, airlines use various strategies to manage aviation fuel price certainty, including financial hedges, increased vertical integration and adjustments in aircraft utilization and size to avoid the jet fuel raising price risk.

Investments in alternative aviation fuel could be a mechanism to diversity expose to the price of petroleum. It seems the use of alternative aviation fuel would serve to diversify the fuel mix to reduce the risk of jet fuel monopoly raising price threat. If a diversified fuel mix were to avoid either fuel raising price in short term or to avoid fuel raising price in long term. Potential benefits include reduced actual fuel costs from only choice of jet fuel supply increased price certainty and lessened fuel costs. This diversify could allow airlines to become more consistently profitable and to make other investments in their businesses.

So, biofuels have potential to meet aviation industry needs, possibly including managing risks of upward fuel price trends and fuel price volatility and avoid risks with greenhouse gas emissions. So, the aviation fuels market could use biofuels to reduce greenhouse gas emission and mitigate long-term upward price trends, fuel price volatility or both. What are the challenges of high priced oil for aviation? In fact, nowadays not the resources of oil as such, but much more the insecurity of supply, due to geopolitical instability in combination with a tight oil market makes a scenario with much higher oil prices than the world is currently experiencing not unlikely.

Aviation is completely dependent upon oil as its fuel source. Since no practical energy substitute is readily available for commercial aviation, a scarcity of petroleum relative to demand will present a major aviation policy. In addition, efficiency gains, due to operational measures and new aircraft medium term. In particular, it has been demonstrated that the annual reduction rate in fuel consumption traffic unit is not a constant, but is itself also falling, in contrast to past estimates.

So, a high-priced oil scenario will have severe consequences for demand, airline revenues, the competitive position of airports and eventually airline networks, strategies and fleet development. In particular, transfer demand, short-haul and leisure traffic can be expected to be heavily affected by high oil prices, due to their relative high price sensitivity. Also, different countries' governments or/and airlines are valuable to research another new and potential biofuel energy to substitute oil energy to supply our planes to reduce the threat of oil monopoly supply to influence the cause of air fare raising prices. Because the elasticity is very high to travelers, when the travelers feel air fares are rising high or even low level to influence travelers who will choose not to buy the air tickets to go to travel easily.

Whether will the fuel (oil based inputs) risk be high to compare other costs, e.g. engineering maintenance, employees salaries, general cleaning, security office expenses etc. expenditures to airlines? If the probability-weighted upside effect on firm value when a risk is resolved favorably is greater the risk than the probability-weighted downside effect if the risk is resolved badly, then expected value work not be enhanced by hedging. So, the risk will be resolved badly to any commercial airlines.

Airlines are an interesting case because the direct effect of source of risk resides squarely within the no offset in revenue functions (unlike for oil producers, for example), so value effects from costs feed directly into equity value. Most directly, the risk source is fuel costs to commercial airlines. Jet fuel is of course, a mix product of crude oil, so airlines indirectly face oil price risk. There are reasons to expect that airlines' fuel costs might to convex in oil price (i.e. absent any hedging). For example, oil prices, being generally pro-cyclical in recent times, tend to be highest when airline demand is strong.

In conclusion, airlines are therefore apt to use more high priced fuel than low-priced fuel over time. Airlines can raise air fare benefit is limited by the elasticity of demand. Also, cost functions could be influenced from fuel cost corresponds to upturns in economic activity overall (due to demand pressures on oil related prices), so it causes that airline's capacity delivers their services given their level of fixed capital. The essence of airlines basis risk in the case of jet fuel is essentially the time profile of the refining margin between crude and jet fuel, or the time profile of the price differential between other refined distillates and jet fuel. Thus, it is far from clear that risk management with oil is sure to add value to any airlines. It seems the impact of airline energy and any countries' domestic or foreign airline passenger travel numbers which have direct close relationship.

Reducing terrorism occurrence

Can reduce terrorism occurence to reduce airline failure risk? It needs to judge to determine if a combination of terrorism and the price of petroleum significantly predicted airline profitability and which variable whether the further period was the most significant between the terrorism occurrence and the price of petroleum influence.

I suggest that different countries' governments or airlines need to collect samples of financial records from which country's any airline commercial passengers and cargo airlines on costs of fuel and any airline profitability. Also, gathering the terrorism data were comparison of terrorist attacks on petroleum in oil-producing nations, and incidents of high jacking aboard any country's aircraft.

When any countries' airlines or governments can judge whether the impact of airline energy and terrorism risk level is high or middle or low level. Then, which can use this sample data to measure how to do positive social change to decide either ought rise or reduce employment in commercial aviation industry, or ought need to invest other higher commercial activity in tourist and other travel related service businesses and when is the most right time to adopt of green technologies by the civil aviation manufacturing industry after the terrorism attacks occurrence to any country. It seems that any countries' governments or airlines which ought concern that the event of when the terrorism attacks will occur and gather past sample data to predict when the next time terrorism attacks event will be occurred and the risk will be high or middle or low level to influence global airline industry development.

Will airline industry's ticket price elasticity be influenced by demand and supply factor

In fact, the airline industry is largely dependent on the supply of the oil industry. Otherwise, the oil industry is inelastic. However, the increase or decrease of the price of airfare is directly related to the increase or decrease of the oil's price to fuel the aircrafts because there has no any new energy which can be substituted to oil fuel to airline industry.

So, it seems oil fuel producers are monopolies to control its sale price to be raised easily. Another factor that can affect airline industry to be directly targeted by a tragedy brought about by terrorism. The past four years, from 2001 year to 2005 year, there had been at least $40 billion worth of losses in the airline industry because of the September 11 date terrorism attacks in 2000 year. There had been an expected and significant decrease in the demand for the airline industry services because of the attacks that involved planes hijacking and crashing into key locations like the World Trade Center and the Pentagon in USA. Although, terrorism attacks can bring risk to influence fuel price rising in airline industry. However, this risk occurrence to airline industry is only that after the terrorism attacks occurred. It is possible that terrorism attacks won't occur again in the future.

Otherwise, our concerning ought be the greenhouse emissions and how it affects global warming. The air quality would be better once this new regulations are adopted. However, it would affect large airlines. So, it would increase the price of airfares because of economic fees that airline companies have to cover. Air pollution can give a negative impact on the domestic or oversea owned airline companies for long term. If airlines' planes can use clean fuel to fly, e.g. biofuel, then it will bring benefits to global airlines for long term.

On the positive side, the environment would be healthier as the earth's temperature would rise, and greenhouse effect would be dramatically reduced. This positive effect can come at a cost that is greater than most people perceive. On the psychology view point on travelers, who will be more preferable to catch planes to go to different countries to travel, due to the chance of air pollution and global environmental warm issues will be reduced to low risk to influence our health if planes can use biofuel to be energy to fly in the future one day.

It seems that spending expenditure to research other non polluted biofuel new energy is one solvable method to global airline industry in the future. To solve, any airlines or countries' governments or oil producers ought choose to spend more time to research new biofuel. Otherwise, the predicting when terrorism attacks event will be occurred, it is more difficult to predict the time more than researching to produce new biofuel energy method in the future.

So, I recommend that researching the new biofuel energy or other kinds of energy to substitute the oil energy is the urgent behavioral economy which the airlines or oil producers or different countries' governments which need to concern nowadays.

● Boeing 747 manufacturing fuel cost strategy

For Boeing 747 air plane manufacture example, how it can help airline to avoid travellers number reduces. Boeing 747 air plane manufacture company how achieve air plane manufacturing strategy to reponse airline traveller number market changing. What is fuel conservation strategy to Boeing 747 air plane manufacturing firm? The cost index, (CI) feature of the flight manufacturing computer (FMC) can help airlines significantly reduce operating cost. However, many operators do not take full advantages of this powerful tool. What does CI ratio mean? The CI is the ratio of the time-related cost of an air plane opertation and the cost of fuel. The value of the CI reflects the relative effects of the fuel cost on overall trip cost as compares to time-related direct operating costs.

The equation form, CI= time cost-$/hour / fuel cosst -cents/lb

The numerator of the Ci is often called time refrated direct operating cost (minue the cost of fuel). Items, such as flight crew wages can have an hourly cost associated with them, or they may be a fixed cost and have n variation with flying time engines, anxiliary power units, and air planes can be leased by the hour or owned, and maintenance costs can be accounted for an air planes by the hour, by the calendar or by cycles . As a result, each of these items may have a direct hourly cost or a fixed cost over a calendar period with limited or no correlation to flying time.

What does this air plane fuel, cost strategy advantages to airline companies? In the case of high direct time costs, the airline may direct to time costs, the airline may choose to use a larger CI to minimize time and thus cost . In this case, where most costs are fixed, the CI is potentially very low because the airline is primarily trying to minimize fuel cost. Pilots can easily understand minimizing fuel consumption, but it is more difficult to understand minimizing cost when something other than fuel dominates. So, the cost of the CI ratio. Although, this seems straight toward, issues such among the operating locations, fuel tankering, and fuel hedging can make this calculation complicated. So , this fuel consumption cost, air plan manufacturing strategy can help any airlines to reduce air fuel useful cost and waste fuel.

However, CI can be an extremely useful way to manage operating costs. Because CI is a function of both fuel and non-fuel costs. It is important to use it appropriately to gain the greatest benefit. Appropriate use varies with each airline, and perhaps for each flight.

How low fuel situations can bring less fuel consumed benefit in the more environmentally friendly flight? Fuel conservation strategy can help airlines significantly reduce operating costs. However, many operators do not take full advantage of this powerful tool. Cruise flight is the phase of flight that falls the largest percentages of trip time and trip fuel are consumed typically in this phase of flight, which also impact trip time and fuel significantly can often be avoided through appropriate cruise planning. This fuel conservation strategy includes these characteristics. These objectives which depend on the perspective of the pilot , dispatcher, performance engineer, or operations planner can be groups into five categories , such as:

1. Maximize the distance traveled for a given amount of fuel (i.e. maximum range).

2. Minimize the fuel used for given distance covered (i.e. minimum trip fuel).

3. Minimize total trip time (i.e. minimum time).

4. minimize total operating cost for the trip (i.e. minimum cost, or economy speed).

5. Maintain the flight schedule . The first two objectives are essentially the same because in both cases the airplane will be flown to achieve optimum feel mileage.

In addition to one of the overall strategic objectives for cruise flight, pilots are often forced to deal with shortage term constraints that may require them to temporarily abandon their cruise strategy one or more times during a flight. These situations may include:

Flying a fixed speed that is compatible with other traffic on a specified route segment. Flying aseed calculated to achieve a required time of arrival at a fix. Flying a speed calculated to achieve minimum fuel flow when holding (i.e. maximum endurance). And when directed to maintain a specified speed by a air traffic control. Hence, when the air plane faced with a low fuel situation at destination, many pilits will opt to fly LRC speed, thinking that it will give them , the most miles from their remaining fuel. Also, if fuel prices increase relative to other costs, a corresponding reduction in CI will maintain the most economics operation of the air plane. If however an airline experience rising hourly costs, an increase in CI will retain the most economical operation . For this reason, flight crews typically reserve a recommend CI value from their flight operations department, and it is generally not advisable to deviate from this value unless specific short term constraints demand it.

How it can help air planes to execute for maximum fuel savings efficiently? For example, but times have clearly changed. Jet fuel prices have increased over times from 1990 to 2008 year. At this time, fuel is about 40% oa a tycpical airline's total operating cost. As a results airlines are reviewing all phases of flight to determine how fuel burn savings can be gained in each phase and in totel.

Boeing 777-200 extended range and 747-400 and (long-range, e.g. short range e.g. 717, medium range, e.g. 737-800 with winglate commercail air planes can impact fuel usage. However, flap setting must be appropriate for the situation to ensure air plane safely. Higher flap setting configurations use more fuel than low flags configurations.

The difference is small, but at today's prices the savings can be substantial especially for air planes that fly a light number of cycles each day. Hence, top fuel conservsation strategies for flight crews include: Take only the fuel you need, minimize the use of the nuxiliary power unit, taxi use efficiencly as possible, take off and climb efficiently , fly the air plane with minimum drag, choose routing carefully, strive to mantain optimum attitude, fly the proper cruise speed, descend at the appropriate point, configure in a timely manner.

Fuel conservation is a significant concern of every airline . An airline can choose an approach procedure and flap setting policy that was the least amount of fuel, but it should also consider the trade off involves with using this type of procedure.

Hence, Boeing flight crew can earn benefit, when they fly or air planes, such as to conserve fuel and reduce noise and emissions or to accommodate speed requests by air traffic control. All of these are fuel consumption reducing strategy to airlines.

● How airlines and airports implement successful netwpork strategies

What is airline network strategy ? Network management includes route planning, scheduling optimization, airline business planning and data analysis . How implement airline network strategy, airlines need to evaluate strengths and weaknesses of the current network strategy, identification of additional potential, recommendations for adjustments, network integration, due to merger or cooperation. Fleet and capacity evaluation , analysis of estimated passenger volume over time combined with option aircraft size and frequencies for current and potential future rotes / markets; competition response, modeling of results as an impact of competitor's action and reaction; establishing best practice network managment for new carriers include: route selection, network planning, scheduling, airline business planning includes forecasting of revenues and costs. Finally, any airlines need to establish network planning, such as network optimization and development, traffic and revenue forecasting, market -and -competitor analysis, scenarios for profit-optimized networks include: hub-strategies, evaluation of aliances, cooperation includes: route joint ventures in industry environment.

● Performance measurement system strategy

Any airlines may apply performance measurement methods to design the indicates of performance. Different models and frameworks are excellence models. Any airlines hope to achieve useful performance meaurement strategy. They need to answer these kep questions: Who are the key stakeholders and what they want and need? What strategy airlines have to put into place to satisfy the key stakeholders' want and need? What critical process do airlines need if they want to implement this strategy? What capability do they need to operate and improve this process? What does cost leadership strategy mean? Competitive price is decided for customer . Indoneasia, Malaysia , India and China countries are implementing, it can provide cheaper workforces and the cost of production will be covered.

In aviation service industry, cost strategy , it much relevant to be applied cost carrier, such as Vigin Blus, Ryanair Airways are implementing . However, some airlines combined the low cost carrier and full service ,which is known as low fare limited services.

Innovative marketing strategy is not only how to carry many more passengers, but also how to enable significant reduction in the costs of distribution and marketing. Such a strategy is used as a competitive strategy of low cost tariffs . For example, low cost focus strategy serve tourists or groups with certain destinations, e.g. the flights are carried out by certain airlines.

There are also tourist groups who travel to certain tourist destinations. Passengers only are transported be the tourist destinations, thus departure schedule won't be a basic need, lower price of ticket and flexible departure schedule as well as comfortable cabin are still the standard.

Another improvement of performance method, it is market orientation, it is believed to give psychological and social benefits to the employees , in the forms of greater pride and sense of belonging, as well as greater commitment to the organization.

Another strategy improves to service performance, it is distribution management strategy . Everyone can be brought benefits. It may achieve these benefits: Raising passenger numbers, as some airlines and airports are running at near full capacity. The effects of disruption are only becoming compounded. Social media can help airlines and airports to tackle dissuption management and avoid damaging their reputation with consumers.

So, when discuption is solved. It can help airports reduce discuption cost and damaging their reputation with consumers . Innovation may include: airlines attempt to develop standard procedure for common disruption situations, responding to regulations, such as the delay rule and compensation for cancellations with faster, more proactive decisions, collaborating with air traffic control facilities, airports, themselves views of resources, identify available options.

● What factors influence cost-related management quality ?

Thus, the reduction of costs lies at the core of the low cost airline model, which aims to offer lower fares, elimating some comfort and services that were traditionally quaranteed, e.g. employed to refer to low-cost flight. The use of an airline booking system, the suppression of free-in-flight catering, the use of secondary airports connected through a point-to-point network, and the use of homogeneous fleets are only a part of the innovative choices made by low-cost airlines. However, these are main important factors to influence route structure, type and characteristics of the aircraft cost of labor and management quality . For example, if the airline's pilot, airline passenger service people, cleaners , all salaries can be reduced to employ. Then, the airport or airline's labor cost will be reduced and it can influence it's air ticket price to be also decreased.

When the airline's air tickets price reduces, it will bring competitive low air ticket sale price to win other airline competitors more easily. How air ticket sale attractive prices ? The airline's air plane type and characteristics,, whether they ae comfortable to let passengers catch in their whole trip time. Whether their air planes are new or old model ? Whether their air planes' facilities can satisfy passengers entertainment need, e.g. chair can be bed to let passengers to sleep, television or movie is attractive to watch, music is soft sound etc. psychological entertainment facilities can let the airline passengers feel satisfactory or not.

Final view is management quality, such as whether the airline or airport CEO's management ability performance is either excellent or good or general or poor . They can influence whole airline or airport front -line service staffs' service performance to let passengers or airport visitors feel their services can satisfy their needs when they choose to catch the airline air planes to fly to the country to travel or work, but the country's airport staffs' service performances and airport facilities will influence their revisiting to the country's airport or rebuying the airline's air tickets again.

The final strategy is flying route strategy. I believe that whether the flying route is attractive or not, it can influence passengers to choose the airline preference. Which factors determine choice of flights on the Dhaka-London route? How could the airline be able to cope with the competitive advantages of its major rivals in this flying route? How is the competitive environment for airlines operating in this route? How could the airline sustain its competitive advantage and what can it do to gain more market share in this route?

A successful and attractive flying route design needs to amend and adjust its flying route design strategies and capabilities as the airline firm goes through its flying route design life cycle, when changes in passenger's flying route choice preferences. Hence, any airline needs to know whether what its SWOT (strengths, weaknesses, opportunities, threats) before it decides to implement which flying route(s). Because manay flying routes choicew will be influenced by its current SWOT environment situation. For organization of new flying route to the UK airport from UK , e.g. London ciry airport, the HK airline needs to know whether what its strengths , e.g. customer loyalty, its strengths can provide the most rapid . The most cheapest, the more comfortable flying feeling from HK airport flys to UK London airport or from UK , London city airport flys to HK airport, its UK , London city flying route can provide competitive fare al promotion, extra baggage allowance, airline brand image , whether is famous to UK travellers, providing online seats reservation for any UK , London flights services, airline organization size and airline brand , whether it can get travelling passegners, loyalty or confidence either to fly to UK , London city from UK city airport, or flying to HK city from UK, London city airport, providing regular UK , London flying route schedule, network presence how much UK flying route cost cutting, Uk air planes' aircrafts facilities whether are enough to satisfy HK or UK to catching the airline's air planes flying entertainment needs. Does it one new route development opportunity of direct flughts from HK airport to UK , London city airport. HK air port has enough terminals number to let facilities to provide passengers stay in HK airport when UK , London city travellers arrive HK airport? Does HK airport lacks technologica facilities to satisfy new UK , London city airport flying route development , e.g. providing enough spaces to let air fleets stay in HK airport, aircraft manintenance whether is enough? Does HK airport encounter shortages of experienced front line counter service staffs to serve UK , London city travellers in airport? When the seasonal time is holiday travelling time for UK visitors, is UK new flying route rising fuel cost? Does new entrants to develop another UK , London city flying route from HK? Has new UK , London city from HK flying route , these weaknesses , such as lacking enough resource to develop another another new flying route or no direct flight or long hour flight after the HK airline developed the new UK , London city flying route to the HK airline from HK airport. Has new Uk, London city flying route development enountered these threats: strong competiton, high interest and UK foreign currency exchange rates, raising fuel cost, economic recession decline in the UK airline industry, environmental pollution etc. issues influence UK travellers choose to travel to HK desires. So, SWOT analysis must be needed to consider in order to develop any new flying route in order to avoid servious high cost expenditure loss to any airlines.

So, above these tangible , e.g. fuel cost control , route choice, network cooperation choice and intangible, e.g. service performance factors can influence whether the airline's network cooperation strategy, route choice strategy or low cost strategy can succeed or fail. So, airlines or airports can not neglect these factors to be revised in order to achieve any strategies in success more easily.

CHAPTER III

Airport service performance satisfactory strategy

Airline employee positive emotion method

Emotional labor factor

Airline service industry, front line travelling passengers service workers' emotional challenge concerns cabin crew and airline ground service employee whose service quality or performance how to serve travelling passengers in order to reach service level or satisfy their service performance needs to be accepted. So, how to influence airline service labour individual emotional matter which will be one major factor to let travelling passengers how they feel satisfactory to the airline service.

The question concerns how to let airline service cabin crews and air ground service employees build long term good emotion to serve their airline travelling passengers. Because bad emotional airline service labors will damage the whole airline employers' loyalty as well as reducing travelling passengers number in possible.

Will a lot stresses at work cause bad emotion to airline ground service employees? The hospitality industry comprises of travel and tourism and the major segments include lodgings and cuisines (hotels, restaurants), transport(airlines, rentals, cruise and railway companies), travel and tour operators. All of these related travelling industries' employees , they are emotional labor, whose service performance or service attitude will influence future potential travelling passengers' airline choices to the airline operating servicer again. Any airline service employees in these service sector industries, have to interact with their travelling clients, be its customers on a regular emotion reflecting basis. So, they must be patient to listen any travelling passengers' enquires in order to help them to solve any problems considerably.

Emotional labor is managing one's feelings to generate a publicly accepted facial and bodily display of emotion. Emotional labor is an expression of emotion for a wage. Jobs involve face to face or voice to voice interactions with clients (travelling passengers), jobs demanding the employee to produce and alter an emotional state in other person, and jobs allowing the employer to implement certain amount of control over the emotional activities of the employees, produce or create emotional labor among the employees.

Thus, long time bad emotional airline front labors number increasing, it will influence the airline whole service member performance to be its airline passengers. However, many airline organizations have their owning set of norms or policies that determine these feeling rules. These are specially seen in customer service industries. IN long term, these strict policies will let airline front service staffs feel stress or pressure, because they won't feel to be punished in possible, e.g. without salary continue increasing, dismissal (lose jobs), changing to another position to do more simple or boring job duties, if they are discovered that their working service performances are not satisfied to their airline employers in any time.

So, strict airline organizational policies will be one strict or pressure emotional regulation to any airline front service staffs. This emotional regulation refers to a person's capability to accept and understand his or her experience of emotions to get involved in healthy strategies in managing emotions which are uncomfortable whenever required, when they need to contact their airline passengers every day. In fact, it has possible that they will accept unreasonable complaint from their airline passengers, even they perform very good or they have help their airline passengers to solve any enquiries when they feel any needs, they stay in airports any time. So, it has close relationship among airline front service staffs' emotions and the airline's policy as well as their service attitude. Thus, good airline policy will build good airline service staffs' emotions and good service attitude or service behaviour to serve their airline passengers every day in possible.

Any airline organizations can not neglect to consider how to build (keep) good airline front labor emotion issue. Because they are any airlines' representatives, if they can build good images to let the airline the airline passengers to feel. Then, it will influence many airline passengers to choose to buy the airline tickets to replace other airlines because they like its front airline front staffs' services. SO, any airline organizations need to consider front service staffs' health status and definite psychological or mental diseases more than physical diseases, because many airline front service staffs only need to serve their airline passengers and they do not need to move any heavy things in airports in general. They need to spend more time to contract their passengers more than any things. When their passengers give their passports or/and any related travelling documents, e.g. air tickets to them to check in to find whether they can allow to enter airport restrict areas, and if they give their luggage to them, they also need to help them to measure its size and weight heavy to decide whether they need to pay extra fee and their luggage are permitted either to keep to them together to enter the air planes to fly or separate air planes to fly to destination. So, they need to make accurate judgement need to avoid any error occurrence. They do not allow to do any wrong judgement or error in order to be complain by their airline passengers often. Hence, any airline organizations need have good method to help their airline front service staffs to avoid to do any wrong judgements in order to influence any flights delay or customers' complaints , due to their personal wrong judgement to their passengers cause in possible.

Thus, any airline organizations require to enquire themselves these questions: Is there any influence of emotional labor (surface acting and deep acting) on the general mental health or psychological disease of airline employees? Is these any difference in the experience of emotional labor across demographics (age/gender/mental status/work experience of airline employees influence their service performance? Because above any one factors , such as every airline front service staff individual age, airline service experience, marital status of these factors will influence their emotions to be good or bad to serve their airline passengers every day. Hence , any airline organizations need to investigate every airline front service employee individual background in order to arrange the most suitable policy to train their front line or ground airline service staffs' skill in order to let them to feel less stress or pressure or they can feel happy to enjoy to serve their airline passengers.

On conclusion, reducing airline front or ground service staffs' psychological stress or mental pressure issue which will be the most effective or the best solution to assist them to raise confidence to serve their airline passengers in airports in long time. I believe that it is the most rapid psychological solution method to assist any one airline front or ground service staff to raise service level in short time.

Airports service environment factor

The environment of airports service environment for the airline services, which will also influence travelling passengers' travelling destinations and travelling frequent times choices. The airport price factor includes income growth, aviation technology and local economic / geographical features of the country's domestic or overseas airports both. IN fact, airports, airports are indeed two sides businesses, it has commercial relationship between both airlines and passengers. So, airports' pricing will influence passengers' travelling demands to the airlines in the country. Any countries' airport(s) need(s) to respond how to help themselves country airlines how to increase passengers number and airlines choices in order to achieve attracting traffic on frequent air planes flying aim. Because the country's travelling passengers number increases , it will influence the country's airport(s) ' income increases indirectly, instead of the countries' any airlines themselves incomes.

Hence, any country's airport(s) will be one good platform to let travelling passengers to stay in the country's airport(s). It means that id the country's airport(s) can build good service image and reasonable products sale price and comfortable shopping environment to attract any countries' passengers feel comfortable and worth to stay in themselves countries' airport(s), when they need to transfer air planes to stay in the country's airport, e.g. one hour to five hours short time, even overnight long time staying. However, if they feel the country's airport(s) are(is) more comfortable and clean to stay, less noise, as well as they have enough chairs to let them to sit or sleep and large area to let them to work in the airport ground floor.

Moreover, the country's airport(s) can have enough restaurants , bookshops, any electronic or other kinds product shop[s, even cinema etc. shopping or entertainment services to satisfy the passengers whose eating needs, entertainment needs, shopping needs in the airport. Then, I believe that the country's airport(s) can help itself airlines to attract many passengers to choose to increase travelling times to the country frequently. For example, when the country's airport passengers feel that the airport restaurant food concessionaires will probably provide enjoy positive external gains from having more flights at the airports, additional or better eating facilities are unlikely to provide external benefits to the airlines by stimulating many more passengers with local origins or destinations to use the airport. I believe these airport restaurants can influence the choices of transit passengers whether which country will be their transfer air plane's short journey staying airport destination to fly to their final destinations. Although, transit passengers usually stay to the transfer air plane airport in short time, but they hope that these any one transit staying airport can have any restaurants to provide good taste food to them to eat when they feel hungry, if the transfer air plane country's airport can provide enough restaurants and they can have different food taste choice and reasonable price. Then, the airport's restaurants may attract many short time transit passengers to choose to eat their food, even many passengers will like to choose the country's airline to buy tickets to stay short time to wait to

transfer another air plane to fly to their final destination to replace another country's airport to stay short time.

Hence, it seems that any countries' airports' entertainment, eating and shopping service environment will influence any countries transit passengers whether they ought either choose to stay short time this country's airport in prefer or another country's airport to stay short time in prefer in order to decide to buy the country's airline air ticket for transfer airplane to another destination. Hence, any airports service environment will influence any countries passengers how to make transit airport destination short time staying choice.

However, I also suggest that an airport will place a lower revenue -over cost burden on that side of the travelling market that benefits the other the most. Assuming one passenger

can earn benefit enjoyed by airlines from an extra- passenger using the airport, the airlines will be willing to pay up to this amount to increase passenger enjoyed benefit feeling.

The airport can extract rent from the airlines up to above their allocated costs for providing the airport short time staying platform (transfer air plane short time staying airport) for eating, entertainment, shopping need service of increasing their destination arriving passengers or transfer another air plane passengers number base. This involves transferring the external benefits derived by airlines from additional passengers using the transfer airport to the another destination airport.

On the another view, from a airport location choice perspective, locating or expanding an airport near a city center can reduce or at least contain passenger access costs . But, because land is

like to be more expensive, the airside costs to airlines are serious higher and if the various other external costs of aviation are included. Hence, countryside or the airport is built far away from city center in the country. This location is one reasonable location choice, because it can reduce noise to influence people who are living when air planes are often flying or landing on the airport and the rent cost to the airport's any business renters will be influenced to reduce. Then, their food , product or entertainment service prices charge to the airport consumers will also be reduced. Thus, any airports ought nor neglect their building location choices in any countries because they will influence airport business renters sale prices.

Lean maintenance repair and manual

error factor

Any airlines must need air plans to catch passengers to fly to travel. So, any air plans will need often to fly. Every flight will need long time to fly, e.g. short trip needs to fly less than five hours, even long trip needs to fly more than five hours, even ten hours. If many passengers choose the country to travel, the air plan needs to fly

frequently to catch every flight passengers to go to the travelling destination frequently. So, any airlines air plans often need to check whether they have any engine machines has broken, need to be repaired in possible in order to let passengers feel the airline air plans are safe. If the airline's any air plans have occurred any accidents when they are flying, even the accidents cause any one passengers hurt, even death. Then, these flying accidents will let passengers feel life risk to choose this airline's any air plans to catch to fly. IN special, long time trip(s) flight(s). So, lean maintenance and engine check is needed to consider for any one airplane to any airline in order to improve efficiencies and minimize costs, maintenance, repair, and overhaul services in the aviation industry sector, even avoiding any flying accident occurrence or reducing serious flying accidents occurrence chance to bring any one passenger

hurt, even death when they are catching any one of the airline air plans to travel. Thus, any one of airline safety is one important successful factor to any airlines.

Instead of passenger safety aspect, the flying logistics safety factor is also important. The central tenet of the lean to a flying process can mainfest in a variety of ways , as over stalled

and underused inventory and misallocated labour, time transportation and logistics. From a customer's perspective, value-added activities are necessary and customers are willing to pay for activities(Bamber, 2000, Glass, 2016). For example, improvements caused by lean introduction in aviation industry in order to avoid misallocated labour time, increasing number of old broken tools, and obsolute jigs and fixtures. Aviation MRO services have been reported by the MIT Lean Aerospace Initiative (2005) to result in:

(1) Set up time: 17 to 85 percent improvement.

(2) Lead time: 16 to 50 percent improvement.

(3) Labour hours: 10 to 71 percent improvement.

(4) Cost: 11 to 50 percent improvement.

(5) Productivity: 27 to 100 percent improvement.

(6) Cycle time: 20 to 97 percent improvement.

(7) Airline airplane manufacturing factory floor space: 25 to 81 percent improvement.

(8) Travel distance (people and products): 42 to 95 percent improvement.

(9) Airplanes engine inventory or work in progress: 31 to 98 percent improvement.

(10) Scape, rework , deflects or inspection: 20 to 80 percent improvement.

Hence, any airlines' airplanes need to be achieve any one of above improvement at least percent level in order to keep airplane's accident occurrence chance to the least level.

Moreover, airplanes' pilot employees their flying experiences or flight numbers factor is also important to influence airplane safe flying issue. Because if the pilot has less flying

expereince or he is not proficient pilot, or his flight number is less. This pilot's individual flying factor will also influence the airplan's safety when he is driving the airplane.

So, any airlines need to consider how to train any one of pilot to be one proficient pilot, because id less experienced pilot , he/she is not proficient to drive any one airplane to fly. Then, the flying accident occurrence chance will also raise. It is one critical successful factor to influence passengers' confidence to choose the airline's airplanes to catch, instead of maintenance repair and checking engines factor.

On conclusion, raising travelling passengers' safe confidences factor will be one critical successful factor to influence any airlines' services level, because flying safety issue

must be one important matter to be considered to any passengers when they decide to choose the airline's airplane to catch to fly to any destinations. If one airline can not guarantee any flying accidents won't occur, to cause any passengers hurt or death. Then, any passengers won't have confidence to feel its others services level can satisfy their basic flying enjoyment

needs. Due to passengers' life cost must be no worth calculation more than other service cost. When they choose to catch the airlines' any one airplane to fly to the another destination form the

country's airport. Hence, the influence of human factor in airport maintenance factor will influence any airlines' services feeling level to their passengers because human factor is one of the safety barrier which is used in order to prevent accidents or incidents of aircraft.

Therefore, the question is to which extent the error caused by human factor is included into the share of errors that are made during aircraft maintenance, such as flying

accidents, incidents, injuries, death, damages related to aircraft operation and maintenance. More airlines' detailed analyses have led to the knowledge that it is necessary to study the

interrelation of repair people, machines, airline factory maintenance and manufacturing working environment, and the air planes production processes. Human is the key factor production process and in the process of operation of technical means since gives new value to the object of any one airplane manufacturing process.

As a factor, the human is not perfect and introduces unintentional error in the system. It is important to develop a system of ever identification and to work constantly on error

prevention. The works and activities on aircraft maintenance can produce hidden and active errors on the aircraft. Hidden errors are a type of errors that are seemingly invisible during aircraft

flying. Active errors are errors that occur immediately and result in immediate aircraft damage or injury , even death to any travelling passengers.

Hence, non human or without human factors will be less number to compare human factors to cause any flying incidents or accidents occurrence easily, e.g. damaging engine, old engine (no renew engine), fire, crash etc. different kinds of causes. However, the main causes of human errors to cause any flying accidents may include: lack of communication between the pilot(s)

and airport airplane landing staffs, complacency (assessment of work according to previous working experience), lacking of flying knowledge to the pilot, distraction, lack of

team work, fatigue, lack of materials and technological support), pressure on the work performer, lack of assertiveness (lack of self-confidence or technical approach to work),stress (working under pressure), lack of awareness etc. different human factors. Any one of above human factors will influence any flying accidents cause.

Moreover, instead of human factor, the flying working environment which refers to the space and place for work as well as the conditions of work factor will also influence human

error occurrence increasing chance, e.g. time pressure, equipment and tools enough number supplies, night shift, all of any one work environment factor will also influence human error

occurrence increasing chance in any flight flying. However, the factors that lead to cause of maintenance error may be caused from wrong information system supplies of equipment , aircraft

manufacturer, wrong working equipment and tools, wrong design of aircraft equipment and parts, incorrect working task arrangement, lacking technical education to the aircraft maintenance

workers, employee's bad personality, poor aircraft factory manufacturing working environment, poor airline company organization structure, working management and control and poor

communication etc. different manual or non manual factors.

Hence, all of above any one non manual factors will also raise manual error factor to cause any flying accidents occurrence chances. However, if any airlines hope to satisfy their passengers' flying service level. They must consider non manual and manual both factors for aircraft lean maintenance repair service aspect.

Influence of airside and off airport to airport geographical choice factor

What does airport airside means ? It includes a system of three components: runways, taxiways and agron-gate areas, on which aircraft and aircraft support vehicles operate. It brings this questions: Why can airport airside operation influence passengers feeling to the country's airport and airline services? How does it influence airport ground service staffs' service performance?

In fact, this airside airport physical area choice has direct relationship between aircraft and apron gate areas of the terminal processing of passenger and cargo. They are major factors to influence operations on runway component. It means that airport ground service staffs' service efficiency, used for the passengers and air fright catching any airplanes processing.

Hence, in a geographical sense, landside and airside capacity on how designing and building og geographical area can bring indirect influence to passengers. They need to enter or indirect influence the airport , in special, many flights are staying on the airport runway as well as many passengers need to leave from the airplanes or enter to the airplanes in the same time on the airport boundary. Hence, if the airport has good airside design , then many passengers will feel convenient to leave or enter the airport from the airside areas.

Airports are perhaps truly intermodel terminals in the transportatoin system. They provide an intersafe among air highway, rail and even water way travel. They are an important part of the medium and long distance intercity transportation system in our future transportation tools. Hence, it has enough reasons to support airside geographical airside and off airport factors can influence an airport and its airline flying service providers on its capacity as well as how it's capacity can influence passengers' satisfactory level when they arrive the country's airport. Hence, airport's congestion growth problem that is needed to consider to any airports because when one airport 's congestion is growing.

It will influence passengers service satisfactory level to be fallen down in possible, e.g. capacity is increased by the addition of a new access road, such as additions provide a major increase.Thus, the stair step growth, it will cause congestion growth because if the airport had used many areas for stair step growth and passengers will have less space to let them to walk on the ground and their airport congestion feeling will also increase when passengers are staying to leave the airport or waiting for check in or check out or waiting to transfer another airplane in the country's airport.The major airside factors to influence travelling passengers whose airport service feeling may include as below:

Availability of enough land for expansion for runways, availability of aids to navigation and air traffic control techniques that could result in reduction of separation between aircraft , noise, aircraft mix, load factor, exclusive use and use of gates , enough airside and outside facilities, availability of airspace, whether aircraft large size is enough capacity and where is location of gates, staffing, equipment freight, environmental protection regulation, and community attitudes toward airside operation.

Thus, whether the airport has enough facilities to satisfy passengers staying in its airport service need, it will have indirect influence further passengers increasing or decreasing number problem. For example, if the airport terminal functions are spread over a large geographic area, access and facilities have to be expanded to accommodate the spread-out configuration of the terminal or if terminal facilities are grouped together, the access facilities can be congregated into a smaller geographical area.

The capacity of the landside is a function of the terminal design , which has a major influence on the relative to between airside and landside capacity. Also, these off airport factors can also influence landside capacity, they may include: off airport parking, off airport terminals, urban development pattern, multiple jurisdiction, financial resources etc. issues. The sub factors of the off-airport access functions , they can influence passengers' services feeling to the airport. They may include: user and vehicle characteristics, e.g. occupants per vehicle, separate and preferential guide way subsystems, roadway traffic management, access link to major transportation , transportation connections. All of these airside and off-airport facilities will
influence passengers' servicing feeling when they arrive any countries' airports. Hence, any countries' airports ought not neglect any one of these minor airside facilities of inside airports to outside airports both.

The another geographical choice airport building issue, it is also one critical factor for how the development of airport cities. It will influence passengers' service feeling to any country airport. The questions may include: Why may any country need to develop an airport city? Can it bring economic benefit and attract many passengers to choose to travel the country? Can the airport city reform to raise airport service performance or service level? Airports have become new dynamic centers of economic activity, incorporating several commercial and
entertainment services inside passenger terminals, when developing a hotels and accommodations , office complexes, conference and exhibition centers or leisure facilities choices for leisure passengers and business passengers both.

Airport-centered development may occur at different spatial scales (from the micro scale of the passenger terminal to the regional or metropolitan scale), thus assuming different
shapes and mainfestations. Different concepts to address these developments can be found in the " airport city", airport corridor, and aerotopolis (Guller, M. & Guller, M, 2003).

I shall explain how airport city concept can help to raise passenger service performance feeling in airports and airlines as below:

In general, airport passengers hope airports ought provide these different kinds service and achievement the lowest satisfactory service quality or performance level to let
them to feel, such as air transport needs have complex airport -neighborhood interactions (in what concerns an

eventual development towards the concept of airport city) requires the
identification of thes takeholders involved and an awareness of the relationships between them. Any airport's main task needs to provide traveling, air transport, shipping, entertainment services to the dual market of airlines and travelers. As such, its primary interaction consists of the supply and demand relationship with the users stakeholder group (passengers and airlines), which results in broad terms in the airports aeronautical revenues. Furthermore, non-aeronautical (commercial) revenues also result from the interactions between airport and users, namely from agents such as cargo and passengers oriented organizations who pay rents or concession feeling to the airport authority, depending on the commercial arrangements binding these agents.

Thus, one successful airport city, it ought provide good neighborhood transport service to travelling passengers, e.g. bus, taxi, ferry etc. public transportation service. It aims to avail any airport passengers can catch any one of these public transportation tools to arrive airport or leave the airport easily. It also needs to provide hotel, conference service for business visitors as well as retail shops, cinemas for shopping visitors or entertainment visitors when they are staying in the country's airport(s). Also, it ought provide facilities to any cargo -oriented organizations to deliver any cargo in short time rapidly. So, one airport's any neighborhood facilities have relationship to influence any passengers and airport organizations' service performance feeling between different user agents including: service provision (e.g. between passengers and businesses), business transactions, supply and demand (e.g. between public transport providers and passengers and passengers or visitors) and employer-employee relationships (businesses and workforce , such as airport airline ground service workers). Because if they feel that they can work in one comfortable airport working environment, they will feel happy and enjoyable to serve their passengers more everyday. It means that any airports' facilities will have indirect relationship to influence airport ground service workers' psychology to feel either enjoyable or hate to work in the airport environment often.

On conclusion, airports ought need to consider themselves airside and off airport facilities whether they have enough supplies and innovate their facilities to be better , even perfect in order to satisfy any airport visitors, travelers, user organizations and airport ground service employees to enjoy to work and use their services if they hope their service level or performance is satisfied to their service needs for long term.

Influencing air connectivity to service quality factor

Can air connectivity growth decreases travel costs for attracting travelling passengers, consumers and businesses and facilities global productive growth? This seems to be particularly an issue when airport capacity is scare or when new airports are added to an existing airport system. What is air connectivity ?
Why does air connectivity raise passengers services? How to measure air connective service?

When direct and indirect connectivity relate to the airport connectivity available to local travelling passengers, any airports ought need to raise extra
airline services to raise service quality , e.g. cheaper air ticket price, in-flight service extra service provision, e.g. comfortable and clean and quiet air port waiting environment
service provision and feeling. However, passengers will generally prefer direct, non-stop connections over indirect air connectivity service.

Air connectivity service can assist airlines to raise competitive effort an offer and they provide access to the many destinations with too little demand for a direct flight, such as minimum connecting time differs in quality , due to in-flight time differences, the inconvenience and risk of missing a connection and transfer time for direct or indirect flights. Hence, any airlines can reduce passengers indirect or direct flight in-flight time to wait airplanes arrive to catch when they arrive any airports. This air in flight waiting time shorten service will attract many passengers to choose the airline to catch airplanes if its inflight waiting time to airport passengers is lesser than other airlines' in-flight waiting time in any airports. It can raise airline service quality, due to the airline has many passengers feel in-flight waiting time is shorten than other airlines often.

In fact, airport connectivity is one good concept method to raise passengers' satisfactory service level. One of the important factors for the connectivity of airports may include: The size and economic strength of the local catchment area how drives outbound demand, size and economic activities as well as tourism attractiveness are an important cariable factor in explaining inbound demand (including the propensity to flying demand), landside accessibility drives the size of the catchment area that airlines can serve from a particular airport within a certain landside travel time, apart from the socio-economic variables factor, also cultural , political and the historical ties play a role in explaining demand the origin-destination level factor. All of the research on the factors that explain air level, demand at the origin-destination or airport level is widespread, including gravity modelling (e.g. a bed at al., 2001) and regressions on aggregate

airport demand (Dobruszkes, 2011). All of any one factors may be airport connectivity service to influence passengers' service feeling level in airports and airlines both service quality.

ON airport visit costs aspect, airlines also need to consider airport visit costs in their route development strategy. Visit costs may also influence passenger choice behavior when

airlines pass on higher/lower charges to the passenger through air fares. Although, airport visit costs generally represent a limited share of an airline's total operational costs, this share can be more significant for short haul flights as well as fair airlines. All of any one these airport charges and passenger fees variable may influence passengers airlines choice. They may include:

Fees variable, landing charge, parking charge for their vehicles or aircraft, passenger luggage charge, security charge, boarding bridge charge, noise charge, emission charge, airport development service increasing charge, check -in charge, terminal charge, cargo charge. So, if any one of these charges influence the airline ticket price rises, it will influence passengers' air ticket purchase choice to the airline in possible.

On airport service levels aspect, for keeping and attracting passengers, airlines and airports need to compete with services that improve the passengers experience. Such service

factors concern for immigration and luggage, but also relate to the terminals, waiting transfer another air plane time, shopping facilities, toilets, atmosphere and space cleaniness, friendliness of staff and availability of delicated lounges. Together they determine the image of an airport and its perceived value by passengers and airlines.

On airline routes development aspect, it can also influence passengers choices to the airline, e.g. Australia airline had developed long route to England destination. Any Australia

passengers can fly to England route directly. They do not need to transfer another air plane to go to England. Although, flying time is above 12 hours long time, but it can bring available to

passengers. They do not need to spend time to wait another air plane to transfer to go England in Australia any airports. THus, airline route development strategy airline planners require detailed, accurate information to make new route decisions, but airlines usually do not have the resources to fully evaluate every new route market. So, they need a sound well articulated business case, can convince airlines to introduce new air services, as well as airport / destinations can influence the airline planning process.

For example, Interviewer indicates that new routes are a huge investment and risk to an airline in airline economic view point, if the airline had not gathered any data to evaluate

whether the new route is worth to develop and predict passengers' new route choice behavior. It assumed 75% lead factor will influence any new route development in success. It indicates these different aircraft type and seats per flight, annual passenger requirements data for these aircrafts: Boeing 747 aircraft needs to satisfy 400 at least seats per flight and annual passenger requirement need 219, 000, aircraft airbus A340 aircraft needs 280 at least seats per flight and annual passenger requirements need 153,300 , Boesing 767 to 300 aircraft needs 220 at least seats per flight and annual passenger requirements need 120, 450 . Boeing 737 to 700 aircraft needs 76,650 and regional Jet aircraft needs 100 at least seats per flight and annual passenger requirements need 54,750.

Hence, any airlines need have route priorities strategy before they decide which new flight route(s) will be developed , in order to achieve airlines add service in order of expected profitability, different airlines have pursued different strategies, destinations can move up the priority board with: solid research and analysis (always) and incentives (sometimes).However, any airline questions for new routes may include as below:

What is the current, actual market for a potential route?

How much can my airline stimulate the flight flying market?

How will the competition react?

How much market share will achieve?

How will be the connectivity contribution?

Will the new route be a financial success?

Hence, any airlines need to reduce uncertainty and risk, before they decide to develop any new route market.

The air service development process may include as below:

Step one: market assessment, required a quantify the time size of the existing air travel market

step two: strategy, deficiency analysis and detailed route analysis

step three: business case analysis, packaging and presenting the information to airlines

step fourth: evaluate and negotiate airline incentives

It is the final steps an appropriate incentive, in certain circumstances, helps airlines commit to new air service to satisfy any new route passengers' more satisfactory flying needs.

Similarly, the strategy steps follow: benchmark air services, identify deficiencies, identify new route opportunities, identify potential air service providers, assess viability of potential air services and prioritize route opportunities and target carriers.

Any airlines may find any information concerns new route business cases to decide their countries flying new routes choice , such as: catchment area profile: demographics, economy, tourist etc. information, airport profile : traffic and facilities information market profile; market sizes , top city pairs, traffic leakage etc. information, suggested service : frequency , schedule, airport routing information, route analysis: market share, load factor, stimulation potential, self-diversion etc. information, any airlines' past flying routes strategic considerations etc. information in order to predict and evaluate whether how many further passenger number is flying that they accept to choose the new flying routes travelling needs.

Hence, how to design to impact either the supply or demand for any new flight routes that is only important because of the country has less number of passengers accept to choose the new flying route to fly. Then, the new flying route does not needed to be design to supply to the country's travelling passengers because their acceptance to this new flying route ends are very less. However, the demand level is low new flying route needs to satisfy these three qualifying services criteria, such as: Are new routes only? Increase on existing routes? Does it work service rent incentives? Will the new flying route be satisfied to air service to the airline passengers and airport waiting passengers, e.g. strategically important? Marginally (unprofitable) self-sustaining in the short term? New flying routes only? Increase an existing routes? Service rent incentives?

How can airports afford aggressive airline incentive / fee discounts and still fund route development marketing in a difficult economy? I recommend that the solution method may include new flying route design and developing and maximizing non-aeronautical revenue streams both, such as retail and duty free, food and beverage, parking , loyalty and premium programs and land development to airport building. Marketing funding strategy may be an ineffective incentive for travelling destinations. However, it may not differentiate a market, as route marketing incentives are used by over 80% of communities in the U.S. marketing incentives can be: Unilateral airport pays 100% or cooperative airlines matches some portion, funding amounts are often tied on the capacity of inbound seats to be available on the new flight (flying) route. By calculating the economic impact of new visitors (spend at the destination), a destination can calculate the return on investment in cooperative new flight (flying) route market.

On conclusion, air connectivity is one important factor to influence any country's travelling passengers to the airline's service quality or service level in order to achieve new flying (flight) route design , reducing inflight transfer another airplane waiting time in airport, or marketing development in success. So, any airlines can not neglect this air connectivity will influence their passengers' service quality. Hence, air connectivity factor is also very important to influence any travelling passengers' service satisfactory level.

How to measure and rise airline
service quality

How are airline performing ? Nowadays, the rise of the low cost airlines' competition is serious, due to airlines hope to rise themselves attractions to influence passengers to choose to use their travelling services. So, different airlines have spend long time to build their unique person-to-person passenger services, which passengers use of different airlines, e.g. digital electronic air tickets purchase method. Any airlines hope to make each journey personalized to the individual will gain market share and improve its service quality to be more unique in order to reach the efforts of airlines to build high levels of customer service appears to have been generally noticed by passengers, when they choose to buy the airline's digital electronic ticket or paper air ticket to use its flying service.

Hence, improvement their digital e-ticket purchase experience and communications factor, for example, if any passengers can enter the airline's air ticket purchase website to buy electronic ticket to pre-book seats in the short time rapidly as well as there are enough seats number to supply to them to pre-book. So, they do not need to worry about without any seats to supply to them to catch the airline's flight to fly to anywhere in any time available conveniently. So, it seems that there is plenty of space for airlines to grow and improve their digital experience and communication method to let any passengers to feel, if the airline hopes to let its passengers to feel that it has unique service to compare others airlines.

The aviation industry plays a major role in the aspect of work and leisure to passengers around the global. So, nowadays passengers' demands to any airlines' service quality had been raised. Hence, any airline service industry messengers are under pressure to prove their services are customers oriented service improvement of performance that guarantees competitive advantages to the global travelling marketplace. So, it also implies that any airlines' services performance will be influenced to cause many passengers feel more poor and let passengers dissatisfy the airline's service performance. The, the airline will possible lose many passengers, due to passengers have many airlines choices, they can find any airlines to replace which any one airline to buy air ticket from internet at home immediately.

However, airlines' comfortable seats arrangement service provision feeling factor is still important in preferable to compare other factors, because passengers must need to sit any seats in any air planes. So, whether the air plane can provide new comfortable seats to let passengers to feel this factor is still the most important factor to influence any passengers to choose to the airline's air plane to catch. For example, service comfortability is how passengers observed the quality of service offered them by the airline's cleanliness, quiet zone, shops, restaurants and business pavilion in functioning like staffs, information desk, and in flight announcement are included as tangible features by the passengers (Geraldine et a.,2013). All of these factors are needed often to measure whether their service performances are satisfactory to themselves passengers service needs.

Moreover, the other factors may include service affordability , it can be regarded as given passenger the opportunity to select from inclusive air ticket prices made available to the different group of passengers by the airlines, as a gesture of goodwill , to establish and reinforce customer loyalty and repeat purchases essential for the airline continuity as well as service reliability. it is the probability that airline will carry out its expected function satisfactory as stated in the flight schedule. Hence, there is a strong link between different airlines' service quality variables, airline image and repeat patronage from the passengers.

Service quality is a measure of how well the service level delivered matches passengers expectations to measure service quality based on input from focus groups. It consists of five factors (tangibles, reliability, responsiveness, assurance and empathy). All of these factors will be identifies that how the airline service quality can be satisfactory to its passengers ' psychological and emotion enjoyable service needs.

Any one of these any five service factors will be important to influence the airline's passengers service feeling level to the airline. It means that the passenger will have more chance to choose the airline's service again (repeating purchase its air ticket). Hence, any airlines can not neglect any one of service feeling to its passengers. It needs often to enquire questionnaires to evaluate whether its these five aspects of service quality , if it discovered any of these five aspects of service level is poor, e.g. 5 scale is the best service performance level, then it can attempt to find its error whether which aspects, it needs to very need to reach the 5 scale , the best service performance level when many passengers feel, e.g. enquiring 100 passengers who give 5 scale to reliability service aspect, before reliability service aspect has less than 50% passengers from 100 passengers who feel the airlines concerns this reliable service level aspect questions to be the best. It is one kind of measurement service quality method to any airlines.

Other service performance evaluation factor is satisfaction in the job to every airline front service or ground service staffs to the airline. Job satisfaction describes how content an employee is with his or her job. It is how the employee responses to a job. It can be considered as a part of life satisfaction to one organization, when the employee is working in the organization. Hence, if one airline front service as ground service staff who can feel more job satisfaction to compare his/her prior airline employer. Then, he/she won't be easy to change his/her present airline employer.

However, some factors can influence job satisfaction are pay and benefit, fair performance appraisal, career and promotional opportunities, proper reward and recognition, work-family life balance, the job itself, proper working conditions, leadership chance, autonomy in work.

Job satisfaction can also involve complex number of variables, circumstances, opinions and behavioral tendencies and a variety of work related outcomes, such as commitment, involvement, motivation, satisfaction, attendance. Hence, any airlines also need to concern how let their employees feel job satisfaction issue in order to avoid their leaving turnover number increases, due to job satisfaction and dissatisfaction depend on the expectations what the job supplies for an employee not the nature of the job.

Finally, instead of concerning employees job satisfaction issue, any airlines also need to concern passengers satisfaction issue because it will have any passengers will choose the airline, if it can bring more service satisfaction to let them to feel , then they will become repeat passengers to the airline.

What kinds of factors passengers were looking for and what were the reasons of choosing a specific airline? When one airline often is complained from its passengers. It will have more mistakes to let them to feel or dissatisfy its service. Hence the airlines needs to find which are its mistakes and improve in order to satisfy its passengers' expectations, e.g. finding what are the mistakes to the airlines' serious concern regarding passenger complaints and complaint satisfaction in order to make the airline more likely to meet its passengers' expectation in case of a problem. Hence, any airlines need to concern how to improve its employees' satisfactory service as well as its passengers' satisfactory service both issues as well as how to measure their service quality whether is enough to achieve general service acceptable performance to its passengers.

Reference

A bed, S. Y. A.O. Ba-Fail and S.M. Jasimuddin (2001), " An economatic analysis of international air travel demand in Saudi Arabia". Journal of air transport managmement, vol. 7, pp.143-148.

Bamber, L., & Dale, B.G. Lean production : a study of application in a traditoinal manufacturing environment. Production planning & control, 11 (3), 291-298, 2000.

Dobruszkes, F.M. Lennert and G. Van Hamme (2011). " An analysis of the determinants of air traffic volume for European metropolitan area". Journal of transport geographyy, vol. 19/4/pp.755-762.

Gealdine, O., & David , U.C. (2013). effects of airline service quality on airline image and passengers' loyalty: Findings from Arill Air Nigeria passengers, Journal of hospitality and management tourism, 4(2), 19-28. doi: http://dx.doi: 10.5897/HMT 2013, 0089.

Glass, R., Seifermann, S., & Metternich, J. The spread of lean production in the assembly, Process and maching industry. Procedia CIRP, 55, 278-283, 2016.

Guller, M. & Guller, M. (2003) From Airport to airport city. Editional Gustavo , Gili, Barcel on a.Intervistas Consulting Inc.

Massachusetts Institute Of Technology (MIT), Lean Aerospace Initiative, Available: www.lean.mit.edu, 2005.

CHAPTER IV

Airport organizational long term strategy plan

What does airport long term strategy plan? The analysis of the Airport services has been based around what Inxure refers to as the 'Value Model'. The model is represented in the following diagram. The purpose of the model is to enable a structured and coherent consideration of the important facets which must align and culminate toallow the airport services to provide value to CHRC and the central highlands region. The strategy to any country airport may include as below:

•Assess the current state of the
business and its service
outcomes
•Set goals & objectives the
Airport
•Base this on Council plans and
input from various Council
stakeholders
Future
•Develop a work program to
bridge the gap between current
state and future aspirations for
the Airport
•Prioritise the program based on
risk

Airport Operational Trends

Unlike major capital city airports that typically experience some level of linear growth in passenger movements over successive years, regional airports such as Emerald are subject to a range of influences that lead to greater fluctuations in usage over time. Passenger numbers at Emerald are
influenced by changes in local population, regional workforce development, tourism development,
local events, resource trends and construction cycles and the availability of government services
such as health and access to professional services. A further factor that will impact on future revenue
passenger numbers includes the ongoing provision of scheduled airlines services with appropriate
levels of service including price and frequency to attract prospective users.

SWOT Analysis

A high level, strategic level assessment of the strengths, weaknesses, opportunities and threats for
the Airport has been developed as follows. This SWOT analysis has been considered in the
development of the Business and Operating Models for the business plan.

The Value Model sees the purpose (or vision and strategy) being made up of:

• A clear overall strategic direction or vision for the Airport;
• An understanding of how it links to Council's overall Strategic Framework and then into
tangible and implementable actions and targets; and
• A clear risk appetite and tolerance (i.e. what strategic risks will the organisation take and not
take in respect of the Airport).Components
• Overall Strategic Direction
• Strategy and tactics
• Brand
• Risk Appetite

• Product offerings
• Market strategies and tactics
• Pricing plans
• Customer value propositions
• Financial management
• Resourcing talent management
• Business Systems (Project/Risk/Quality
Management)
• Systems
• Governance (Board, Committees, Programs)
• Performance (Value) Measurement
Core Operations & Projects
(Delivery)
Vision &
Strategy
(Purpose)
Business Model
(How value is created)
Operating Model
(How value is delivered)
he key Principles upon which this Plan is based are;
· Implement a safe, secure and environmentally suitable airport;
· Construct a well-planned airport;
· Develop sound asset management and business practices;
· Ensure strong financial viability and sustainability factors; and,
· Focus on branding and marketing.
There are a number of key objectives that can be immediately implemented, and which
are detailed along with specified actions that will result in the development of a dynamic,
financially viable asset for the community.
Future development and growth should be investigated as funding opportunities arise,
and a review of this plan is recommended every five years to determine whether market
forces have changed or business opportunities have arisen that could benefit this Airport facility.
The Strategic Plan articulated three objectives for Cessnock Airport:
· Be a safe and complying facility that minimises negative impacts on residential
amenity;
· Promote economic and tourism development across the local government area;
and
· Provide a sustainable revenue stream.

Route development programs have become popular with airports worldwide to enhance air connectivity. Enhanced air connectivity of an airport has been found to have a positive and significant impact on the competitiveness and attractiveness of the airport and the regional economy in which the airport is located. However, the drivers behind route development programs and their performance are not always clear; this has been less explored in the literature. A dynamic performance management approach is taken to build a modeling framework in which key drivers affecting route development performance and strategic resources affecting key drivers are identified. Route-level planning is used in an empirical study to demonstrate the dynamic mechanism of airport route development initiatives and performance measurements. The proposed framework can not only provide performance monitoring, but also suggest suitable indicators to evaluate the performance for policymakers in future airport route development.

Airport network connectivity has been viewed as an important factor driving airports' attractiveness to travelers and competitiveness in the industry Theoretically, an accessible and interconnected network will enhance airports' attractiveness; the more attractive the airport, the better its competitive position relative to other surrounding airports serving the same region. The competitive position helps an airport to earn market share and improves productivity through higher passenger volume and freight volume. The increased traffic can leverage commercial revenue for larger airports, but has a lower contribution to regional airports. However, well-connected airports can enhance the national air network efficiency and the development of communities and businesses. Hence, enhancing air connectivity via RD programs has been considered a common strategy for modern airports.

The accumulation and depletion of strategic resources will be affected by the endogenous impacts of the end results. The value of resources in a given time is determined by the strategic policy developed by decision-makers. Then, the resources can be deployed to enhance performance drivers and the intermediate results. Ultimately, this affects the end results. Consequently, organizations will achieve sustainable development via the positive interaction cycles among resources, performance drivers, and end results

In such an environment, aeronautical customers (airlines) and non-aeronautical consumers (passengers) both contribute to enhance and co-create service and product values for airports. Thus, airports have been considered and validated as a two-sided platform instead of a vertical structure . Apart from obtaining revenue from airlines and passengers, the role of airports is to facilitate airlines to provide passengers with air services, and foster a profitable interaction among them, leading to passengers' satisfaction. Particularly, under RD initiatives, airlines are also the partners who contribute to enrich airport services, which attracts more airlines and reinforces airport competition and network effects. In this value chain, passengers are no longer the "passive" consumers located at the end of the value chain because their experience also adds value to airports' service and products. Therefore, on the basis of the <<resources–drivers–outcomes>> logic corresponding to the <<value creation–value capture–outcomes>> process, the value creation, capture, and transfer mechanism of airport RD

Driving factors influencing airport attractiveness are identified and used to track resources and stakeholders. While airport attractiveness is generally conceptualized as driven by straightforward and unambiguous criteria, from the perspective of passenger choices, it could be influenced by the location of an airport, and other utilities passengers gain from services of a particular airport . Location and related factors such as ground transport services are often beyond the control of airports. Hence, airports tend to focus on strategies that can enhance other airport utilities, such as fare level, connectivity, and on-time performance by resident airlines

Meanwhile, flights served by airlines improve airport attractiveness and airport financial performance by increased passenger volume and the subsequent increase in airport revenues. The more connected an airport's network is, the more attractive it is relative to other competing airports in the same region. In addition, the improved network may enhance service level by the airport and stimulate economic growth of the region with more air traffic flow. Thus, routes could be considered a crucial resource and revenue generator for airports. Hence, the conceptual model in Fig 3 can explain why RD is the focus of interest to airport managers and authorities, and provide insights for building the DPM model focusing on the airport RD program.

However, airport attractiveness is determined mainly by three factors, and they are not independent. Within the airport system, air connectivity has various definitions and calculation methods . In general, air connectivity is determined by the number of connections and number of flights, which are directly provided by airlines at an airport to passengers. Airport-fare level is mostly the decision of airlines, which determine the ticket price with consideration to operating costs and market competition. Airport fees account for a large proportion of airline operating costs and affect airfare levels. In terms of on-time performance, airport operating efficiency has effects on on-time performance. In particular, airport capacity utilization affects flight on-time performance and is determined by how the capacity is used by scheduled and operating fight volumes. Therefore, RD influences these three factors directly, which consequently affect airport attractiveness. So, any airport long term strategy plan may include above all elements in order to achieve the airport whole organization operational success.

Chapter 5 Learning airport consumption strategy

Whether do different countries tourists' different lifestyle which can influence their travel consumption behaviors? Even, which countries that they will choose to go to travel. For example, when one tourist who owns himself/herself often to drive to go to anywhere habitually. The tourist's driving car habital behavior which will influence that he /she will feel need to rent car to travel to anywhere habitually , when he/she selects to go to the country to travel. Hence, if he/she feels the tourism destination has no any rent car service providers to provide him/her to rent any car to travel anywhere in the country's travel destination. Does the country lack rent car service factor which will influence that he/she will still choose to go to the country to travel in preference? For example, when one New Zealander's family who own at least one car at home. So, the New Zealand whole family every member can often drive car to go to anywhere , even, one family member had driven one car to leave his/her home. So, driving own car activity or behavior has been one habitual activity to influence the New Zealand every member to feel the travelling destination needs have rent car service provider supplies cars to let them to rent to travel. The driving car lifestyle has caused the whole New Zealander family driving habit. When the family's sons) and/or daughter(s) need(s) to go to school or go to shopping as well as their parents also need to drive their cars to go to office to work in themselves home town often. In common, there are many New Zealanders who will have at least one car at home because they feel that they can drive their themselves cars to go to anywhere in New Zealand more than waiting bus or tram or train or ferry etc. public transportation tools more conveniently. So, New Zealanders' driving own car habit will influence their lifestyle to feel that they also need to rent cars to travel to go to any where to travel to replace to wait public transportation tools choice in the travelling destination during their journey.

For shopping trips is more influenced by their driving car activities. So, it seems that this New Zealander families will be influenced to their tourism destination need, they need the tourism destination has car renting service provider to be supplied anywhere to let them can drive the renting cars to go to anywhere in tourism destination. It means that when the tourim destination has less rent car providers can provide renting car services to drive anywhere or it has none any renting car service providers are existing in the tourism destination. Then, the renting car service providers number shortage or none any renting car service providers to be provided to the country's tourism destination, which will cause the New Zealander families do not perfer to choose to go to the country to travel generally, e.g. Hong Kong, China, Korea these Asia countries have no many rent car service providers in these countries. So, the New Zealand families won't prefer to choose to go these countries to travel when they discover these Asia countries lack enough rent car service providers to let them to drive to travel in themselves conveniently. Otherwise, America, England, Japan etc. countries have many rent car service providers. So, these countries will be this New Zealander families' preferable tourism countries. Thus, the New Zealand families' driving ownership car lifestyle will influence their travel behaviors to choose to go to the country which can have many rent car providers in the tourism country any where tourism destinations in preference.

Thus, whether the country has renting car service providers , it will be variable factor to influence any country's car ownship families' driving car travel behaviors in their journey in order to let they feel that they can drive themselves ownship cars to go to anywhere to travel conveniently, even when they leave their countries. Hence, these countries' car ownship driving habitual families' behaviors will be influenced their tourism destination or location decision choice when the country has many renting car service providers in preference as well as this renting car service provider supplying factor will be more important to influence the habitual driving own car traveller to be preferable choice to compare other factors, e.g. cheap entertainment consumption providers factor which include cheap hotel living fee, cheap food price consumption etc. expenditure in the travelling country.

Thur, it explains that different countries' car ownship tourists , whose driving own car activities will cause their daily lifestyles, then their daily driving own car lifestyles will influence their tourism destination choices indirectly. So, it seems that lifestyle can be a outcome variable (or dependent variable) factor to influence travel behavior in any travelling built environment. The travelling built environment characteristics can include density measures (population density, job density), job-housing density). These travelling buit environment factor can repreent what the city resident's lifestyle. For example, where the location in relation to local centre or regional centre to the country's residents are living. This country resident's living location will cause this country resident's lifestyles , e.g. holiday or leisure whether it is low budget, active and adventurous or frequent traveller with second place or self-orgnized , family oriented or close to home and unadventurour. Hence, the country's living built environment will influence the country's resident's lifestyles. Due to different countries' residents will have different lifestyles. Hence, built environments and lifestlyes have relationship to influence every country's residents when they need to go to other countries to travel in their holidays. For example, frequent travellers are usually living in big and busy cities, otherwise, non -frequent travellers are ususally living in the countrysides, where there are less offices or factories are built to let people to work. So, big city will bring busy feeling to the country's residents, then they will be influenced to feel need to often to go to travel for leisure intention in their holidays. Otherwise, countryside will bring not busy or quiet environment feeling to the country's residents, then they won't feel working feeling when they are living in counryside. So, they won't feel need to go t o anywhere to travel in their holidays often.

Hence, built environment will bring either busy or not busy (quiet environment feeing) to the both different country residents when they are living in the places. Their living places will cause their lifestyles are different. Then, they will be influences to feel have more frequent travelling needs or less frequent travelling needs to explain why every country people will have more or less frequent travelling needs.

- How any why peer-to-peer accommodation can impact business tourism pattern

I shall explain how any why peer-to-peer accomodation can attract business tourisms to choose business tourism intention? Usually , employees or employers buy business trips, why they choose one particular travelling company over another and why the business tourists choose to travel when the peer (more than one buiness tourists) who will choose to peer-to-per accommodation business tourism pattern more than the more expensive hotel living comfortable feeling business tourism pattern.

Business travel agents need to know or understand what reasons the employer or employee feels peer-to-peer accommodation business tourism motivation is more suitable or better to compare hotel living comfortable feeling business tourism pattern. Why can business tourism accommodation choice factor influence the business tourist's business trip choice.

Business trip means work related travel to an irregular place or work and it represents that one employee or more than on employees business tourists whose expenses are paid by the business ,he or she or they work(s) for. So, in employer's business trip expense view point, he/she expects the employee or employees can choose the most cheap expenses for whose business trip. It also means that the explo/er does not expect that it is a high quality journey for the employee's or employees' business trip. The business tourism is year-round, peaking in spring and autumn , but still with high levels of activity in the summer and winter months. It may be long time ot short time, e.g. less than one month or more than one month, evern more than half year for the business trip. When the employee is employees are working permanent full time employment. It is not for leisure intention, it means that the employer does not hope employee or employees spend(s) extra more expense to spend any leisure or goes (go) to any destinations to visit in their/her/his whole business trip.

Hence, it is based on the cheap expenses for the business trip aim, employer usually demands employees or employees to choose the peer-to-peer be cheaper accommodation to live or the employer will help its employee(s) to choose the peer-to-peer cheaper accommodation to live. So, it seems that expensive hotel living facilities won't be the preferable accommodation choice for employer because the business trip pay or reimburse the employee. Hence, business travel agencies ought not help the business tourists to choose expensive travel package, e.g. expensive hotel accommodation on the trip, expensive transportation tools, e.g. taxi renting service to get to buisness meetings, the cheap peer-to-peer cheap hostel accommodation and cheap transportation tool, e.g. travel buses pre-booking service, or cheap restaurant choice vacation incentives package is more attractive to let them/him/her to choose for their/her/his business trip.

A business person or a peer-to-peer business people also have /her expect to take advantage of frequent flyer schemes which allow him/her/them to take leisure trip with airlines when they/he/she is /are accumulated sufficient miles in the chep or tair ticket(s) to catch air plane for businss trip. Hence, he/she /they expect(s) to earn airlines expenses from whose frequent flyer schemes when they/he/she can claim to original air ticket price from whose employer, but in fact, peer-to-peer business tourists or individual business tourist pay lesser ait ticket charge from whose frequent flying program accumulated sufficient miles, even no any payment. So, airlines can benefit the business traveller, such as improved in competition milages programs, quick check in and online check in, lounges with broadband connection etc. service.

Why does peer-to-oeer accommodation living factor is the most influential to any business tourist(s) to choose the travel agent? In employer's business trip expensive view point, if it has many employees need to go to other countries business trips for long days frequently. Then, the employer will consider whether the every day accommodation living cost is expensive or not. So, comparison hotel and peer-to-peer hostle price, hotel accommodation price is usually higher than hostle accommodation rent price. When peer-to-peer accommodation has been shown to positively impact to business trip employers in popular. Because any business spending will be one important considerable factor to influence employers to choose. However, the accommodation renting price will be more influential to impact business tourism cost. Hence, employers will estimate every whole business trip expenses how it can impact peer-to-peer or hotel accommodation choice. So, the living budget factor will be one important influential factor to influence any employers how to choose where are the suitable destination for every individual business tourist or peer-to-peer group business tourists to live. So, it seems small size peer-to-peer hostles are compared to large size expensive hotels more suitable for business tourists.

Although, it is possible that individual employee or a group peer-to-peer employees will feel peer-to-peer hostle is not more safe than hotel accommodation. But, their/his/her employer usually does not consider safety, comfortable environment issue for their/his/her every business trip. They only consider loe accommodation price issue. So, the accommodation choice will be one critical factor to influence employers how to help their individual employee or a group peer-to-peer employees to choose where he/she/they will live when he/she/they arrive(s) the destination for whose every business trip. Hence, it seems that accommodation will be one critical factor to influence anywhere to be chosen to live for any business trips to their individual employee or group peer-to-peer employees' needs.

- ● Factors influence local tourists'

destination choice

What are the main internal and external factors to influence local tourist's domestic travelling choice behaviors and detination choice decision making? What are the social , cultural , personal psychological factors to influence the decision-making of local tourists to travel to different types of tourism destinations in domestic travelling destinations, e.g. attractions, available amenities, accessinility, image price external factors. They can influence local tourist's destination choice behaviors. Does the individual occupational reason can influence local tourist's local destination travelling choice? So, any travel agents need to develop and promote of domestic destination need to determine the factors influencing tourist's destination choice.

In a local destination tourist individual productive way, how loca tourism agents can bring what factors to influence or charge whose local destination travelling behavioral changes. For example, tourist individual behavior and destination choice factor, the comparision between the current local tourism destinations choice and the past local tourism destinations choice factor. Instead of local different travelling destination prices comparison, journeys comparison . What are the other internal and external factor to influence the local tourist's travelling destinations choices behaviors, e.g. attending local festivals, events, taste local cuisine and be part of unique features of a destination. These will be valuable external or internal factors to influence the local tourist's local destinatons choices. So, different countries' local travelling destinations will need have a number og key elements that attract visitors and meet their needs. The key elements may include , for example, primary activities, physical setting and social / cultural attributes primary external activities elements, and secondary elements may include catering and shopping, and addition elements/accessibility and tourists information providing to local tourists.

Due to local destinaton tourism must be cheaper than overseas or foreigh destination tourism. So, the local torust travel agents need to provide thei travelling services to local tourists, more attractions, accessibility , amenities, excellent available packages activities and ancillary services to compare overseas tourism destinations. Because the local tourists will compare the overseas different destinations travelling places to decide whether they ought choose to travel overseas or local different destinations at the moment. So, any entertainment activities concern local destinations which will be local tourists' perferable comparative travelling services to the local travel agent and the overseas travelling service in order to decide whether he/she ought choose local travelling or overseas travelling at the moment.

Hence, local different travelling destinatons attractive factor will be one important influential factor to influence local tourist's travelling choices. However, a tourist's attitude, decisions, activities, ideas or travelling experiences evaluating and searching of any tourism service behaviors will influence the final travelling destinaton choice decision whether he/she ought choose to go to overseas or local travel. He/she will consider how to spend time and money and effort to carry on any kinds of entertainment activitied in whose local or overseas journeys. So, the different destination local and overseas internal travelling price and spending entertainment time in journey and spending effort to arranging every travelling entertainment which every will be one considerable issue to compare budget to overseas and local different travelling destinations. If the tourist feel whose country , e.g. American's local travelling destination budget is spend less than overseas travelling destination too much. Then, the American will choose to local travelling destinations more than overseas travelling destinations and the moment. So, travelling budget will one factor to influence the tourist to choose whether overseas or local travelling.

So, it seems that time, money and effort will be another factor to influence the tourist will be another factor to influence the tourist chooses to go to overseas or local travelling destinations, instead of different travelling entertainment provider choices factor in the local or overseas travelling destinations . Moreover, the tourist's indvidual income, the local and overseas living condition, formation of cultural and aesthetic tasts, price of local and overseas travelling service and discounts, loca and overseas travelling destinations' temperature or weather viable, e.g. number of sunny days, geographical condition, cultural and natural resource, medical tourism etc. external factors will influence the tourist individual final travelling decision to choose either local tourism or overseas tourism entertainment decision.

Airport actual functionality

Instead of airport is one arrical and leaving terminal station place main function for any travelling passengers after the airplances had landed on the country airport's subway. I feel that airport has also another main functions. It can help the country to attract more travellers to choose to go to the country to travel as well as it can persuade them to raise consumption desire in their whole journeys after they leave the travelling country's airport if they feel the country airport's service performance can satisfy their short time staying need. I shall explain why any countries' airports can influence travellers' travelling destinations and travelling shopping choices to be increased or decreased. The future airport will be the assistance role to assist tourim industry development. The factors include, for example, safety and terrorism control, when the travellers feel the country's airport is safe to stay when they catch air planes to arrive the coutry first time. Then, the country's airport can build safe image to let them to feel the country is safe to travel indirectly, traditional cirport service providers will need to seek new service way to deliver value, such as subscription based service models can let travellers to feel the country's airport can provide one comfortable and enjoyable short term travelling staying environment in the country's airport. Then, they bring pleasant emotion to prepare their journey trip after they leave the airport in the foreign country.

So, if the country's airport can let the travellers feel safe and comfortable , then it can bring new exciting and enjoyable feeling to the country's image. Because airport will be any travellers' first time arrival place after they catch airplanes to arrive another country. So, positive or negative airport's image will influence travellers how they feel whether the country , it is worth to choose to travel indirectly. However, airports need have good facilities to satisfy any related airplane service employees or any airport food or product businesses need, instead of travellers' need. For example, it needs have good allocation of terminals and access to facilities , they will be managed and regularly reviewed and regarded their good facility availability , capacity constraints and the best use of available facilities to satisfy any food or product sale shops' sale need and airport passengers' purchase need both in airports or airplane pilots, airplace service employees, irport security employees' comfortable working environment need.

However, airport inside and outside also needs to be arranged enough parking space facilities to let any aircraft parked or stored at the airport from the place where it is parked or stored in order to let any vehicles to be parked in airports or ouside airports easily and conveniently. When any sudden emergency matters occurred, the aircraft subjects to unforeseen operational delays , it should need to contact airport operations control centre to indicate when the expected time of arrival and departure is, there is no need to request a new slot in cases of unforeseen operational delays where the operation will take place within 24 hours of the agreed slot time. For example, of unforeseen operational delays include aircraft technical issues or weather conditions that could not have been planned for. Hence, operationally delayed aircraft must utilise slots in the same manner as originally agreed. If any change to the original slot agreement is required, e.g. a slot must be requested immediately. Moreover, when aircraft subjects to non-operational delays must request new slots immediately, following the correct process in those conditions of use, an example, of a non-operational delay may include delay caused by late running passengers or poor schedule planning. Hence, airport needs have good facilities and communication system to coordinate to any departments to avoid aircraft unforeseen delays to cause airport passengers feel nervous and brings negative and poor emotion to the airport's service performance.

On airport baggage handling function aspect, airport operators must comply with the baggage policy made available to all operators with the airline business management team. For example, where a flight destination or carrier is identified as being at significant or high risk, the operator will pay a charge as notified by management, equating to the cost of any policing cost additional to the services normally provided at the airport for carriers or destinations at lower levels of risk. In fact, airport baggage management needs be checked and delivered in order to help any airplanes' passengers to transport their baggages to follow their airplanes to be delivered to their same destinations when their airplanes are flying with the passengers and whom baggages to arrive the same country's airport at the same time absolutely. So, barrage management operators need submit or demand and in agreed format the already fleets absolutely, such as fleet detail to report these data to include aircraft type and registration, number of seats maximum take off weight kilogrammes of each aircraft owned or operated by the operator, in order to avoid any passengers' luggages wrong delivery occurrence in possible.

Hence, any airports must need to consider above basic passenger service operation in order to avoid any accident occurrences to bring poor airport service attitude feeling. If airport management expected that they have good service performance to satisfy travellers' short term staying needs in themselve countries' airport.

Airport strategies

Any countries' airports expect to increase passenger movements, they must have effective strategies to carry on reviewing any errors and improve performance effectively. For instance, how to keep cost effective measures to lower operating costs and keep good performance on quality, such as for maintenance and cleaning airport cost reducing measures to introduce variable, performance -based elements to encourage productivity gains, how to manage and implement new technological systems to improve information flow and work processes within the country's airport, e.g. airport e-immigration system can allows to receive real-time alerts on any airport building faults. It can reduce airport reliance on manpower in these areas, thus reaulting in better productivity and cost savings for long term airport expenditure. So, high technological strategy system is needed to implement to any country's airport in order to facilitate the handling of more aircraft movements to optimise aircraft handling on runways. Their benefits include reduction of departure flights separation times, reconfiguration of flight routes, and improvements in runway inspection processes.

These new measures can bring effective in improving any country's airport's runway efficiency, developing new infrastructure including the extension of the taxiway, roadway and power supply networks. It aims to satisfy travellers' convenient transportation needs when they arrive any countries' airports and prepare to find suitable transportaton tools to arrive their destinations more easily (airport transportation roadway, taxiway building network strategy).

Hence, any countries' airports need have good strategy to manage a wide range of activities and risks, which are broadly classified into strategic , financial operational, regulatory and investment. Any countries' airports also need to seek how to reduce the occurrence of risks and to minimum potential adverse impact as much as possible, uch as airport risk management strategy. Because when the country has many people are living and they need often to catch airplanes to leave their countries to travel as well as there are many foreign travellers choose to travel the country.

Then, the country's airport must need to expand size and raise good facilities, e.g. more automated immigration gantries are needed to be installed, taxi waiting areas are also needed to be explanded with additional taxi bays constructed to accommodate the higher number of arriving passengers , even increasing airplane subways number to satisfy many airplanes need to fly away from the country's airport or coming airplances fly to the country's airport's landing on runway needs often.

So, airplane subways number expanding strategy and cutomated immigration gate fast checking system is needed when the country has many travellers choose to go to the country travel and/or many local people need to leave themselves countries to travel. For instance, departure and arrival immigration control as well as pre-boarding security screening will be controlled for more efficient deployment of manpower and equipment. Moreover, in the line will the trend of self-service options of airports arrived the world, provisions will be made to have more kioslls for self check in,self-bag -tagging and self bad-drops. The increasing use of these options will help airlines and ground handling agents reduce processing times and staffing requirement. For example, a fully automated to reduce reliance on scare manpower baggage check in and check out system, the baggage handling system will also be equipped with ergonomic lifting aids to enable heavy and odd-sized bags to be handled with ease, even by older workers.

Then, the country's airport must need to increase subways number and immigration fast checking service facility to avoid handling passengers crowd queueing problem often occurs every day. When any airports often let passengers feel time pressure to queue to spend long time to wait immigration checks and leave the airport. It will bring their negative emotion feeling to the country's airport. Then, it is possible to influence they choose to go to the country to repeat travel again. Hence, the country's different airport strategies are needed when the country has increasing travellers number trend as soon as possible.

Another strategy concerns airport emergency service on safe aspect. Any countries' airports need have a highly trained specialist wait that is positioned to provid fast action rescue and fire protection for passengers' life safety ,e .g. aircraft rescue and fire fighting vehicles are needed airport. An incident command and control simulator which provides realistic and interactive simulations of emergency scenarios for the purpose of any sudden accident occurrences in any countries' airports.

So, any countries' airports need to develop an internal digital system to ease labour-intensive work processes like fire safety inspection, incident reporting, logistic management and recording of its personal fitness results, with the new safe system , data entry is needed mobile enabled with the use tablet computers. For example, the airport safe unit can continue to enhance its emergency preparedness and rescue capabilities with the successful staging of two drills, simulated aircraft crashes on land and at sea, as well as any exercises validated crisis contingency plans are recommended to earn strong capability in coordinating rescue efforts involving both the airport community and mutual aid agencies in order to carry on rescuing passengers and airport pilots and service attendants whom life safe service when air planes are crashed on land and at sea.

Another strategy is now aviation facilities strategy, it can support fly, cruise and fly-coach initatives, important options to a rising number of interm travellers, if it can be implemented successfully. It can bring enhancement measures benefits, includes the reduction of departure flight separation times, reconfiguring of flight routes and implementation of aircraft speed control for increased runway use efficiency.

Hence, one successful airport operation , the airport management needs to know how to implement the traveller check out or check in service functions when they arrive the airport or leave the airport and to satisfy its passengers' short term terminal station staying or transfering another airplane's flying need as well as it also needs to know how to implement its different strategies to improve its service performance and to let passengers have more confidence to the country's airport service operators' behavior and they also feel safe when they are staying the country's airport. Hence, any travellers' short term staying feeling in the country's airport , whether the country's airport can bring either positive or negative emotion , which will influence they choose to go to the country to travel again in possible. Hence, airport management can not neglect how to improve airport service performance to satisfy any first time or more time airport visitors' short term staying need.

Long time airport staying and passenger

consumption relationship

It is an interesting question: Can the country's airport service performance influence passengers consumption desire? Nowadays, travelling is a kind of popular entertainment whn working people have holidays, retired people have more savings and students need to go to holiday to feel rest time after they had hard to study. They will choose go to other countries to travel. So, " freguent travelling times" which will increase to any travelling consumers. If the traveller often chooses to go to the country to travel, he must need to permit to enter the country from its airport immigration. If his every visiting time to the country's airport, he feels the country's airports' staffs services are poor performance and he feels that they are not polite or rude attitude to treat him when he needs to check out or check in from the country's airport immigraton gates, even he feels difficult to enquire any airport service staffs, either he feels difficult to find them or they need to spend long time to let him to queue to wait enquiry, even he also needs to spend long time to queue to wait check in or check out in airport immigration gates when he arrives the country's airport or he leaves the country's airport.

All of these negative airport staffs' service attitudes and poor service behavioral feeling, they will cause the frequent traveller doubts whether the country is a worthy travelling place and it is possible to led his negative consumption desire in the country's airport. Then, all of these negative emotion will influence the frequent traveller reduces consumption in the country's airport , even wothut any consumption in the country's airport, when he visits the country to travel every time. So , it seems that airport's service performance will influence travellers carry on more or less consumption in the country's airport. Then, it will influence all the country's airport related retail and restaurant businesses' sales to be reduced indirectly in the country's airport.

Instead of airport service performance intangible factor aspect, the airport's clean, airport itself appearance attractive design, large size and shops and restaurants' suitable locations and internal environment design etc. these tangible factors will also influence travellers' consumption desires in the country's airport. For example, in one special day, e.g. Olympic Games day, the Olympic Games country's airport may complete in record time and its airport can successfully handle a estimate record 85,000 minimum departing passengers a day during the Olympic Games period, twice the number on normal days. Travellers and media will describe the Olympic Games country's airport retail shops and restaurants consumption experience as seamless, magical and unforgettale airport staying experience, if the Olympic games country's airport can provide an excellent service performance on the Olympic games period. Then, it will influence the increasing sale amount in the Olympic Games country airport retail stores and restaurants during period. So , when the country is experiencing special day, such as "Olympic Games " is chosen to carry on competition in the country. Then, in this Olympic Games period, it will attract many travellers to choose to go to this country to travel, due to they have interest to watch Olympic Games competition in this country. This country's airport will represent this country's image. If it 's airport service staffs can provide excellent service to let any one of travellers to feel when they are staying in this country's airport short time and this country's airport itself appearance and design can also be changed more attractive and beautiful and the airport's retail stores and restaurants also design more attractive and beautiful. Then, the travellers' consumption desires will be possible to raise , when they visit this country's airport in first time in this Olympic Games travelling period.

- Global air transport network requirement

In the future, if the country has a strong and affordable global air transport network, it will bring more advantages. Due to many travellers expect to catch air planes which can fly to another country in short time , it can reduce accidents occurrence chance on sky or on sea. So, short time flying can be more attract to compare long time flying. So, it explains that why many travellers prefer to choose one way flying more than transfering another /other air plane(s) flying. Although, they need to pay more air ticket fee. So, if the country's airport can have more subways number and large subways areas to let many arrival air planes and leaving air planes need to fly from land or fly to land in the country's airport frequently. Then, the travellers can buy any air tickets to book same day or next day or later day flught time to fly to any country to travel more easily, when the country's airport has large area size and many subways to let many airplanes can stay in its aircraft subways in same time. Then, the country's airport flight frequency will increase , it means that there are many travellers can catch airplances to fly to other countries in any time very easily from themseleves country's airport. It is time-sensitive feeling to let the country's travellers, they can feel to fly to other countries to travel in short day. They do not need delay to fly to any countries, when the flight airline is either full seat or the time can not permit any air places land on the country's subways.

So, none delaying time sensitive travelling frequent flught model will be one attractive flight flying method to influence the country's travellers choose to frequent travelling behavior. Because they do not change their travelling day, due to airplanes have no enough seats supply or the country's airport has no enough land subways to let any airplanes to stay to cause delaying their flight travelling booking seat day expectly.

So, airport is similar to airline to need to use different customer relationship management to attract returning travelling customers . It brings this question: What are the most attractive motivation factors in airport travel market? I believe that factors may include airport loyalty, various flight time arrangement distribution channel, passenger check in or check out, laggage safe delivery, airpor security service. Moreover, flight schedules are also a main factor influences the travellers' final travelling country choice decision among different travelling countries. However, if the country's airport can build good loyalty image when passengers are staying in the country's airport in short time, it can show a more attractive motivator to increase travellers' consumption desires when they are staying in the country's airport in short time.

Hence, airport 's loyalty seems have relationship to influence travellers' consumption behavior when they are staying in the country's airport. For example, when the different countries' travellers feel enjoyable and happy to stay in the country's airport longer time. Then, their airport long time staying behavior will raise their consumption desire and chance to find any right restaurant to eat food or drink or find any right retail shop to buy right products in airport. Hence , when the country's airport can buil loyal customers relationship. Then, it will bring the advantages or benefits to the airport's any retail shops or restaurants on sale growth aspect, such as : their retention rates will go up easier, their customer referrals will go up easier, the country airport retail shopd and restaurants travelling customers whom spending rates will go up easier, the country airport retail shops and restaurants customers will be loss price sensitive, the costs of retail and restaurant servicing then will go down easier. Hence, if the country's airport customer service performance can maximize travellers' loyalty. It will influence travellers to feel the country airport's retail shops and restaurants have more loyalty to compare other countries airports' retail shops and restaurants loyalty.

So, it implies that any any country airport's loyalty will have relationship to influence its travellers how they feel the country airport's retail shops and restaurants' loyalty. Due to loyalty is intangible and it is obly feeling. So, when the travellers have positive emotion and wheh they are staying in the country's airport long time. Then, they will have positive emotion to spend more time to walk around in the country's airport as well as when they are passing any airport's retail shops or restaurents. Their pleasant emotion may encourage their consumption behaviors to have interest to find any right restaurant to eat food or drink or find any right retail shop to buy any right product in the country's airport in preference easily. Because they had been accepted to spend long time to stay in the country's airport, when they feel interest and surprise to visit the country airport when they arrive. Moreover , the long airport staying time will increase their purchase chance to any the country's airport's retail stores or restaurants in the country 's airport in first time visiting.

How to satisfy customer expectation
for passenger service at airport

When one country's airport can satisfy passengers expectation to accept its service demand, then profitability and passenger number will be influenced to increase. So, airport management needs to focus on how to satisfy any passenger individual need or expectation when he/she needs to stay in whose country's airport for wait to either transferinf another airplance need to carrying on check in or check out in the country's airport immigration gate need in short time.

However, because if the country's airport service can let its passengers feel happy , then they will be super spenders to spend airport staying longer time to consume or entertain in the country's airport. Moreover, it will bring any the country airport's retail shops or restaurante to earn more sale growth indirectly. So, any country airports need to consider how to bring excellent customer services for any passenger individual need in airport. Because its service behavior or performance will have indirect relationship to impact the county airport's any businesses and itself any parking , entertaining services income in airport.

" The concept of managing airport customer expectation on passenger service quality" will be any country airport's main aim. Basically, airport passengers' perception concern how the airport service staffs' service attitudes or performances influence how they feel either negative emotion, such as anger, dissatisfaction, irritation, neutrality or positive emotion, such as happy, satisfaction, pleasure, delight. So, when the airport passenger individual perception is better , then his expected to the country airport individual service staff level will be at the highest level, but if his service expectation is less than his expectation standard, then the airport passenger will dissatisfy with the lowest satisfaction level to be influenced the country airport's other any one service staff by the one airport service staff whose poor performance. Because any one of the country airport's service staff , every one will influence the country airport's image. Of every one has excellent service performance, then, it will let many different counties' passengers feel sympathetic emotion from their every one's behavior. Otherwise, if every one has or most service staffs have poor or not considerate ot not sympathetic service attitude to be let them to feel, then any one of them will let many itself airport's countries' passengers feel the country airport's image is poor. They won't like to spend long time to stay in the country airport, even their short time airport staying behaviors will influence the country airport's any retail shops or restaurants businesses sale growth to be reduced from their short staying time influence.

In general, airport service staffs need to spend some time to answer any passengers' enquiries. So, how they answer their enquiries will influence how their achievement in order to raise the country airport's passengers satisfactions. It may lead a rise in different countries'passengers' loyalty and retention, therefore the country airport can increase many different countries passengers number when the repeating airport visitors , they prefer to choose to go to the country to travel again , due to its airport is attractive reason in possible.

So, any country airport management ought have a policy from how the airport established desirable standard performance, measure it against actual performance to action taken once and revise any unachieved acceptable service level to the acceptable excellent passenger service performance in the country airport. For example, any country airport needs to manage and identify the target passenger segmenation target groups and to make bettwe understand the key elements that have the greatest impact on meeting every different target passenger segmentation group individual expectations and needs from their services in themselves country airport. So, any country airport will have relationship to any one of airline, as well as any one airline will have direct relationship to every passenger when he/she stays in the country airport in short time.

However, instead of restaurants and retail shops; sale relationship will be influenced by the country airport's service performance, airport management also bring more empahsis on non-aeronautical (non related airlined and retail business) revenues, such as shops rents, concessions, car parking service income, consultancy and property developed diversified service incomes. So, airports need to focus directly to enterainment travelling airlines' passengers, meeters, and greeters, business-travelling passengers , users of general aviation services and transfer air plane short time staying visitors, or lone time staying visitors, e.g. the passengers need to live airport hotel for on night or more than one night sleeping before they catch the airplane on the day. So, all these different target passenger segmentations will have different service needs in any country airports.

However, airport passengers' behaviors and expectations of the airport experience depend highly on the types of traveller, they include: demographic characteristics, (i.e. gender, age group, income, sex, occupation) , purpose of trip (i.e. leisure, business), and their circumstances. In general , the passenger can be divided into different group, such as arriving, departing and transfer with different expectation and need, in the way they will be using the airport services and facilities different need and will also influence the behavior of individuals when in the commercial area. For example, passengers who are departing and arriving will require all airport facilities including: car rental, rail, buses access, pre-booking taxi service, check in or check out service, bad processing and security check and vertical and horizontal moving in passenger terminals. Otherwise, transfer passengers will have a short waiting time in airport and their needs will be likely different from those of origin and destination passengers. Some of the transit passengers will need to spend one hour, even more than four hours or half day in the airport. By providing airport facilities that can accommodate their needs, such as a place to lie down and take a short sleep time, free shower, free email public service will mostly give than an enjoyable airport experience. Evem some handicapped people or old people who feel difficult to walk in the airport corridor. Then , the airport will need to arrange the auto -wheel chairs and auto airport vehicle facilities to let service staffs to provide electronic auto wheel chairs to let them to sit down or drive the auto airport vehicle to sit down with them to go to their destination in the airport's any places immediately. For passengers travelling with families may want children play areas, where kids can have a great time when waiting to board the aircraft. They also want the availability of rooms of families travelling with badies equipped with changing facilities, baby crib, microwaved and hot water need. When passengers are on business trip, may want a lounge, with all the business, facilities that they can feel free to use, such as free internet access and other services , such as fax, scan and photocopy machine. Hence, any airport managements need to develop the strategic customer facilities providing service in order to improve the design and delivery of all the facilities and services need by understanding expectation of each passenger segmentation group in their airport staying time.

Finally , in airport unique design aspect, our global airports will need have different unique design to let any travellers to feel that the country's airport can have its unique design to let themm to feel the country airport has itself own airport culture or entertainment features to attract they observe its appearance in order to achieve the increase more travelling visitors number when they feel enjoy to stay in the country airport longer time before they leave the airport. I shall indicate different countries' airports how they will perform themselves different airport cultures and unique design as below:

For China and Hong Kong Chinese airport design example, their airports need have Chinese cultural feeling to let Western travellers to feel their airports' designs and cultures are different to any Western countries' other cultures. So, China anf Hong Kong airports' designs can increase many old big size building photos number in their airports to let foreign visitors can walk on the long glass walkway corridor , when they enter walkway coddidor to walk through different 100 more airplane leaving and arriving gates number and the ground floor is built from heavy glass material. So , any one foreign traveller need to walk through on the long glass walkway corridor to pass any one gates to arrive his/her airplane leaving and arriving gate location and catch airplance to fly. Also, the glass walkway ground floor can let them to see the airport's vehicles and airplanes and people and trees outside environment clearly when they are walking on the airports' all glass material manual made ground floor. It will let foreign travellers feel China and Hong Kong airports building designs are different to the foreign countries' themselves airports' designs as well as Hong Kong and China airports' old building photos will let all leaving passengers feel difficult to forget their old building historical photos and they will know hoe their architectural skills are developed to imprved to build nowadays unqiue desing method from traditional building design method in Hong Kong and China airports. Otherwise, for US, Uk etc. foreign countries their airports designs can increase underground floor fish pool architectural design outside to their airports in order to let any passengers feel that they can see many different kinds of various fishes are swimming. So, their outside large fish pool can let them to feel surprise when they are staying in their any airports, e.g. one beautiful large size fish pool, it can be built to close to their airports and the fish pool can have various kinds of big and small fishes swim in the pool to let passsngers to see, or their airports can appear suddenly and unexpected of a gaping hole in the airport's outside ground, known as a sinkhole. Sometimes, the airport's outside sinkhole will fill up with fresh water to become deep , shaped manual made sinkhole to let passengers to feel they need to enter to the sinkhole and then they can enter the airport. So, the outside large size sinkhole will attract many passengers to stat to observe how the fresh water is entering to the sinkhole interestingly. Then, they will feel surprise when they need to pass though the sinkhole , then they can enter the airport.

In conclusion, attractive airport architectural design will let any passengers can not forget that they had ever visit the country to travel in their travelling experience as well as they can be influenced to like to stay longer time in the country airport by the airport's attractive design and environment influence. The most important influnece, it can influence airport related business income when they like to stay longer time in the airport.

   Cultural distance on satisfaction and

respect travel intention

   Every country cultural difference is different. How and why cultural difference has a real impact on tourist satisfaction and it can also influence to repeat travel. Is cultural tourism one major factor to influence tourist to repeat travelling intention or choice to the country in international tourism choice market? For example, China and

India have similar culture. Their cultural difference is not much, e.g. eating cultural habit is similar , entertainment cultural habit is similar. These both countries people do not want to spend much money in eating and entertainment both aspects. Hence, these two countries people do not consider how to consume to enjoy entertainment and eat expensive food. Hence, it is based on cultural similar reason. These both countries tourists will prefer to choose to repeat travelling either China or India. When the Indian tourists had chosen to go to China to travel in the first time. Then, the Indian tourists will choose to go to China to travel in second time again. Also, the Indian tourists had chosen to go to China to travel in first time. Then, the Chinese tourists will choose to go to India to travel in second time again.

What factors influence China and India tourists respect to travel between these both countries. The factors will include cheap air ticket price, cheap hotel living price , less economic cost factor. However, I believe the similar cultural factor will be the major factor to influence many Chinese and Indian tourist prefer to choose to repeat travelling between these both countries.

As my indication to these both countries people have similar eating habits, choosing foods, low health foods, common foods choice eating at cheap restaurant habitual consumption. Also, they have similar entertainment habits, their entertainment demand is not high. They like to ride bicycles to go to anywhere to travel. They like to go to swim, play basketball, football etc. sports. These all sports are cheap sport consumption. So, it based on similar individual low enjoyment demand and low health, food quality demand similar cultural factors. Chinese and Indian people have no long distance cultural difference between eating and entertainment habitual factor will include them to choose to repeat travelling between these both countries. Due to China and India have many restaurants can provide cheap food or sport service providers can provide different kinds of cheap sport entertainment consumption to satisfy their cheap food and cheap entertainment needs in their journey in China or India anywhere. So, it explains that why these both countries tourists will repeat to travel these both countries again after they had visited China or India to travel in first time. So, the similar cultural factor can impact these both countries tourists to repeat to go to these both countries to travel again. Hence, if these two countries' cultural distance is far or different, then themselves countries' tourists won't choose to repeat travel between themselves when these two countries for cultural distance tourists had visited to another country in first time. Hence, culture has been continuously considered as a much factor which tourists consider in terms of choice of the destination travelling place. Also, it explains cultural distance which can make tourist individual has less satisfaction to concern to tourists to repeat travels.

Otherwise, for far cultural distance two countries case example, such as Chinese and American , these two countries people's eating habit and entertainment cultural needs are different. For eating habit difference example, American like to eat pork, beefs, chickens, potato to replace rice and other foods. Otherwise, Chinese like to wat rice, vegetables more than potatoes, pork , beefs for lunch , dinner . So , their eating habits are very different. Also, American like to drive boats on the season drive cars to go to anywhere to travel on holidays for sports or holiday entertainment activities . Otherwise, Chinese like to play basketball, football, ride bicycle of cheaper sport entertainment on holidays. So, American entertainment activities are more expensive to compare Chinese. Also, US and China , like families whose power distance is different, such as every per family powerful member is parents, who have more power to give opinions to choose anywhere to travel for whose sons and/or daughters whole family members travelling arrangement.

Therefore, if the Us family powerful members, such as at least one son or/and daughter members who need t choose to go to which country to travel if the family powerful members, such as the child/ children's parent feel China's food taste or entertainment activities are totally different to be similar to their country's food taste and entertainment activities habitually after their whole family members had travelled to China in first time before.

Although, their son(s) and daughter(s) will hope to go to China to repeat travel again. But, due to the US family parents are their son(s) and daughter(S) powerful decider to make any travelling decision to choose which country will be next time travelling destination. If their parents feel China's eating and entertainment culture is totally different to their countries. Then, the US family will not choose to repeat travel to the China country again any more easily, because this US family can not feel satisfactory when they visited China in their first time before, due to they feel China 's food and entertainment cultures are totally different to their US country. So, the cultural distance factor will influence the US family don't choose China to go repeat travel again.

Consequently, different countries' similar or different cultural factor will influence the country's tourists choose to repeat travel to the country again. So, any country needs to know what its culture is in order to attract the similar cultural countries tourists to repeat travel to itself country more easily.

Chapter 6 Hotel service strategy

Hotel organizational departments operation

Hotel has different departments, e.g. security deparment, cleaning department, front counter room check in and out department, kitchen cooking department, entertainment facility department, room service department, administration department etc. However, any departments must be very important to influence whole organizational performance. It does not depend on which department is especial important to influence whole organizational service performance. For example, room service department main function is let room living customers to feel comfortable to live in any big, small , middle size hotel rooms. If any one hotel room can not let the customer feels comfortable to live or it is dirty to live. Then, it will bring poor living service performance to cause the customer does not choose to live the hotel to live again. However, it does not mean that room service department must be the most important department in whole hotel organization because all hotel department individual performance and efficiency will influence whole hotel operational efficiency to let all customers to feel. I shall explain all hotel organizations departmental operations as below:

In order to run the Hotel as a functional unit, there are several departments in a hotel which work and coordinate together and the major departments of the hotel are:

1. Front Office Department
2. Housekeeping Department
3. Food and Beverage Service Department
4. Kitchen or Food Production Department
5. Engineering and Maintenance Department
6. Accounts and Credits Department
7. Security Department
8. Human Resources (HR) Department
9. Sales and Marketing Department
10. Purchase Department
11. Information Technology (IT)
1. Front Office Department:

Every day is different with the arrival of new personalities from different walks of life. The Front Office Department is often referred as the nerve centre of the hotel as it is in constant contact with our guests, and has the most diverse operating exposure. Our team is passionate about guest service and look at every possible opportunity to make our guests comfortable during their stay. Our front office associates have a keen intuition that allows them to anticipate our guest's needs and exceed them. With its excellent communication skills, it is not unusual for our staff to multi task and work diligently in order to resolve any issues that may arise.

This department performs various functions like reservation, reception, registration, room assignment, and settlement of bills of a resident guest and the front office department is considered as the nerve centre of a hotel.The front-office staff welcome the guests, carry their luggage, help them register, give them their room keys and mail, answer questions about the activities in the hotel and surrounding area, and finally check them out. In fact, the only direct contact most guests have with hotel employees, other than in the restaurants, is with members of the front-office staff.

Concierge is extra service department – Always At Your Service, concierge is constantly looking for ways to enhance your guest experience. Travel routes, recommendations of tours, attractions, and short cuts around town are just a few services offered by our remarkable Concierge Team, topped by, of course, a lovely friendly welcome!

2. Housekeeping Department:

Every morning is a busy one in the Housekeeping Department. The team has an eminent eye for attention to detail to provide our guests with a spotless guest experience. Our housekeepers are in charge of almost every detail of your stay from the fluffy pillows and sheets in your guest rooms to the replenishment of your bathroom amenities. The Housekeeping Department is a critical function to the hotel's continued success!

The housekeeping department is responsible for the cleanliness, maintenance, and aesthetic upkeep of rooms, public areas, back areas, and surroundings in a hotel and for the immaculate care and upkeep of all guest rooms and public spaces at all times.The staff members who excel in the Housekeeping Departments have an eye for detail and a commitment to the training, development and motivation of a diverse group of talented employees. It is the service and cleanliness that really make an impact on our guests and determine whether they will return and also recommend the hotel to others.

3. Food and Beverage Service Department:

The hotel lounge restaurant are a vibrant bunch with a combination of proficiency and bubbly personalities. Whether it's for breakfast, lunch, dinner cocktails or appetizers, our team will always serve you with a smile.This department looks after the service of food and drinks to guests. The Food which is made in the Kitchen and Drinks prepared in the Bar to the Customers (Guest) at the Food & Beverage premises. Some examples of the food and beverage outlets are Restaurants, Bars, Hotels, Airlines, Cruise Ships, Trains, Companies, Schools, Colleges, Hospitals, Prisons, Takeaway etc.

4. Kitchen or Food Production Department:

An experienced team of chefs offers a great variety of scrumptious dishes to keep our hungry customers happy. Although our chefs work in a fast paced environment, the kitchen is far from what you see on Reality TV! There is a less drama and more fun as our chefs handle the line with their experience, great personalities and talent.All the food and beverages that are served to the hotel guest is prepared in the kitchen. Culinary preparation, as an art and science in the modern kitchen, required more than just a knowledge of food being prepared and the methods of preparation.It is through a knowledge of basic skills, terminology, and rules of the kitchen that a final goal, preparation and service of quality is achieved in the hotel kitchen.

5. Engineering and Maintenance Department:

Running an effective hotel requires careful planning and hard work. Equipment does break down; meaning repairs and regular preventive maintenance are required around the hotel. Our professional Maintenance Team performs a wide range of essential tasks to help ensure a smooth operation resulting in happy guests.

The engineering department is responsible for repairing and maintaining the plant and machinery, water treatment and distribution, boilers and water heating, sewage treatment, external and common area lighting, fountains and water features etc. Also, It looks after the maintenance of all the equipment, furniture and fixture installed in a hotel.

6. Accounts and Credits Department:

The Accounting Team plays a significant role in the managing of hotel expense control aspect. They provide the hotel with relevant financial data and forecasts which are used for daily decision making to ensure we are thriving and keeping the books up to date. The team offers a great support service to all departments with financial recommendations.

This department maintains all the financial transactions. Accounting departments typically handle a variety of important tasks. Such tasks often include invoicing customers, accounts receivable monitoring and collections, account reconciliations, payables processing, consolidation of multiple entities under common ownership, budgeting, periodic financial reporting as well as financial analysis. Also common are setting up adequate internal controls for all business processes (to prevent theft/misappropriation of assets), handling external audits and dealing with banks in order to obtain financing. Taxes are sometimes handled by accounting departments in house, but this work is often contracted to outside tax accountants.

7. Security Department:

The security department of a hotel is responsible for the overall security of the hotel building, in-house guests, visitors, day users, and employees of the hotel, and also their belongings.

8. H R and Admin department:

The Executive Team plays a decisive role in the hotel operations as the final decision-maker. The team is comprised of the Department Heads and is led by the Director of Operations, and the General Manager. The team ensures the smooth running of hotel operations, each member responsible for the management of its own department. Regular meetings are organized to discuss any issues and find ways to continuously improve business profitability and guest experience.

Human Resource department is responsible for the acquisition, utilisation, training, and development of the human resources of the hotel.The role of the HR department also has to do with the administration of an impartial and internal justice system which will promote transparency and openness in organisational communication. The Human resources department also serves as a progressive voice in a common system and strives to ensure competitiveness in the conditions of service for staff.

9. Sales and Marketing Department:

Sales Team works hard to promote the brand and the amenities of the hotel. The Sales Department is in charge of negotiating and prospecting large business and leisure groups, tours operators and individual travellers. The Marketing Department is the analytical backbone of Sales as well as being responsible for increasing exposure for the hotel through various advertising opportunities both in print and on the Web. Be sure to engage with us on our various social media platforms such as, Facebook, Twitter, Google Plus, or Pinterest! The major role of the sales and marketing department is to bring in business and also to increase the sales of the hotel's products and services is the major task of the department.

In addition, catering Department is responsible for the smooth operation and sales of our beautifully appointed conference centre. From corporate meetings to large celebratory events, the catering team must to take ownership of every detail with excellent teamwork and efficient communication in order to meet and exceed the expectations of our clients.

10. Purchase Department:

The purchase department is responsible for procuring the inventories of all the departments of a hotel.

11. Information Technology (IT) / Systems

The Information Technology department is responsible for the day-to-day support of all IT systems, business systems, office systems, computer networks, and telephony systems throughout the hotel/resort. Additionally responsible for Information Technology issues, products, and services at the property. Provides user training and support of all property/site systems, network enhancements, hardware and software support etc.

Above all of different departments are very important to influence any hotel organization's efficiency and service performance. They are inter-connective to influence any service aspects to let any customer to feel whether the hotel overall performance can satisfy his/her living need. For example, if the hotel's front office service performance is poor, this department service staff can not book any rooms vancancy to let any one customer to live when he/she arrives this hotel to check in immediately. Then, many customers will not live the hotel room when he/she walk in to the hotel to prepare book room immediately , then it cause many customers only choose another hotel to live. So, any hotels must need to plan enough big, middle and small size rooms to prepare any customers can live their rooms immediately.

So, front office's room booking budget plan can influence whole hotel customer number.Even, if the hotel's room clearning service can not satisfy any customers feel comfortable to live when they live in dirty room, or any rooms' bath room and sleeping room are dirty, then it will cause any customers won't choose to live this hotel when they travel to this country again, they can choose any one hotel to replace this poor room living service performance hotel significantly. So, it seems that any one hotel department individual performance must influence all customer individual satisfactory level. When the customer feels the hotel can not provide excellent service and/or room living satisfaction to let he/she feels, they the hotel will lose many customers from this kind intangible customer feeling factor easily. Hence, how to implement effective strategy to let customers to feel satisfactory when they choose to live the hotel, it is one important value question to research.

However, I feel that these seven key aspects, any hotel organizations need to consider in order to achieve service efficient raising and provide excellent room living service to let any one customer to feel, they may include as below: A hotel wouldn't run smoothly without the right people and right resources in the right departments. If you're new to the hotel business, or just doing your fair share of basic research, read below for the outline of a hotel's structure. Your exact needs may not be the same as other hotels, which can be affected by the size of your establishment, whether you offer full service or not, and what amenities you have. But most hotels have the following seven areas in common. These areas reflect the various job roles that will need to be filled to keep the organization running. Being aware of these departments can help you plan for future success.

On Executives Service Aspect

These are the decision makers within the business. They may be department heads, managers, or directors. Depending on how your company runs and the size of it, executives may be responsible for some of the other areas discussed below, including accounting, marketing, and at times even front desk services.

On Front Desk Services Aspect

Although no operational segment within a hotel organization is dispensable, it could be argued that very little would happen without the front office staff. These people are constantly in contact with guests, and may even be responsible for taking and handling bookings. Detail-oriented people are often required for this role, since they must meet the exact needs of the guests. Sometimes concierge may also be lumped in with this division of the business, but could be an entirely different department worth building.

On Housekeeping Services Aspect

Keeping your guest rooms clean and tidy is an essential task. Your housekeeping team is typically responsible for every detail within a room, from the cleanliness of the sheets to keeping toiletries stocked.

On Maintenance Facility Management Aspect

Even the best quality utilities and electronics can break and malfunction. In today's tech-oriented world, there is also more to repair and fix in terms of computers, TV screens, game consoles, DVD players, and other cutting-edge tech items than before. Tech can sometimes also be the responsibility of executives or front desk services, depending on what works best for the organization. Additionally, in some cases, maintenance might be lumped in with housekeeping or another role. Again, it depends on the size of your business and the personnel available to you.

On Accounting Administration Management Aspect

Every business needs proper accounting. Tracking expenses and revenue helps you keep a finger on the pulse of the business, so you can make tweaks and adjustments as necessary. The accounting team is usually directly answerable to the executive team, providing them with relevant data and forecasts. They may also make recommendations and offer support for other departments.

On Marketing & Sales Strategy Aspect

Every business requires promotion. The marketing team is responsible for converting prospects into paying guests and spreading the brand message. They must keep up-to-date with the latest marketing channels and practices, including social media, content marketing, OTAs, and so on. Marketing can sometimes become the responsibility of front desk services. But because executives often want control over the exact message that's being shared with their target audience, they will sometimes take it on – especially if they don't have a pre-existing marketing department. Plus, to entrepreneurs, business development is often the most exciting part.

On Managing Kitchen Staff Task Aspect

If you're a full-service hotel, if you offer room service, or both, then it's impossible to keep up with orders and meet your guest's dining needs without competent kitchen staff. Some hotels also need a separate catering team, especially for conference rooms.

When, having the right structure in place is critical to the success of your organization overall. Finding the right balance can be challenging, because human resource is often the most expensive resource of all. At the same time, they are also your greatest resource, and your hotel must cultivate and utilize them well.

All of above deparments are any hotel essential departments in their organizational structure. Any one department's efficiency and function and operation must may influence another department or other departments operation efficienctly. For example, if the cleaning room bed supplied matieral department cleaning staffs efficiencies are low, then, their efficiencies can influence any hotel rooms bed matieral, toilet towel , toilet teeth paste, toilet paper room cleaning supplies have enough supply. So, this deparment has close relationship to influence any hotel rooms have enough clean toilet and hotel room daily materials supplies. Consequently, any it will cause many customers feel hotel rooms' any bed, toilet daily supplies are not enough to be supplied clean hotel bed, toilet daily tools. So, any hotels need to consider how to adjust any department individual operational efficiency absolutely in order to avoid any hotel customers feel poor service performance to your hotel.

Hotel management strategy
● What is hotel management?
Hotel management is really about overseeing every operation of the property. This requires knowledge of distribution strategy, finance, customer service, staff management, marketing, and more. In no way should any of these be treated as 'set and forget'. Hotel management is about constantly evaluating performance is every facet of the business and making necessary adjustments.

Ultimately effective hotel management will not only ensure your hotel stays in business, but is able to profit and grow over time. Think of the hotel as an ecosystem that will get healthier the better you manage it. As your hotel becomes more successful you can upgrade and charge higher rates, pay staff higher wages, and create an experience that guests want to come back for. It can take time to get everything right however. There are many skills you'll already possess but many others you need to learn along the way, or else hire staff that can provide the knowledge for you.

Hotel management definition

Definition of hotel management is that it's 'a field of business and a study, that tends itself to the operational aspects of a hotel as well as a wide range of affiliated topics. Such as: Accounting, administration, finance, information systems, human resource management, public relations, strategy, marketing, revenue management, sales, change management, leadership, gastronomy and more.'Clearly there's a lot to be aware of and many of these functions do require specialists. However not all properties have the luxury of hiring a full team of staff, so it's certainly not impossible to run a successful small hotel business without a range of degrees.

What does hotel management strategy mean? Hotel management strategy may include: service performance management, facility management, cost or expense control management three aspects. Service performance management main aims to let customers to feel the hotel's security is safe when they are living in the hotel, front office service, room service room, even, restaurant food delivery service, entertainment service, such as swimming, gym sport , tennis sport etc. different kinds of whole service can let customers to feel satisfactory as well as facility management service, e.g. swimming pools can let swimmers to feel safe when they are swimming, swimming pools water is warm and clean when they are swimming, swimming pools facility is new, or sport gym running machine, riding machine facility is safe to use and new sport facility can let them to feel to play when they use any kinds of sport tools facility, the hotel room's kitchen tools are clearn, enough provison, kitchen is clean, room is clean, e.g. beds, toilets, drinking cups, plates are clean and enough number provision, when fire occurrence, the stairs areas are large sizes to let many people run on the hotel staires when many customers are running down in the same time. All of any hotel facilities will let customers feel safe or new use in order to let them to feel comfortable to live in the hotel as well as control cost is the main aspect to assist the hotel how to avoid to expend excess expenditure per month. So, how to implement cost control strategy will influence any one hotel income. All of these three aspects may be any one hotel main considerable issues. How to implement effective strategies will be one important discussion issue as below:

Hotel facility management strategy

For hoteliers, hotel management is not one concept. It's hard to really say you've mastered hotel management when it comes with such a range of roles and responsibilities. Being able to adapt, meet challenges, and place yourself on a scale of personal growth is vital for a hotel manager.

There are always new strategies, traveller preferences, or industry technologies emerging that you have to keep track of. Even new roles within hotels and the hotel industry are being created that will affect the way one manages their property.This blog will take you through the major considerations to keep in mind regarding hotel management and throw some tips and ideas along the way, to help you run a better hotel business.

● How managing a hotel as an independent operator?

Hotel operations management: Inventory and revenue

The day to day operations of a hotel are pretty all encompassing. Is everything that guests need in order? Are staff and cleaning schedules organised? Is the occupancy rate where you'd like it to be? Obviously a core aspect of hotel management is to manage your rooms; or your inventory.

Effective inventory management for hotels involves both creating and managing demand, and maximising returns. The investment backing a hotel is tied up in its rooms and the returns can only be gained from selling those rooms optimally.

Here are some strategy basics:

1. Pricing strategy

By driving prices up during high peak periods and knowing how much to discount prices by to ensure rooms are rented during low peak periods, hotels can maximise their return. Through dynamic pricing, businesses can provide discounts and incentives in a controlled way during different seasons.

2. Distribution strategy

Hotels generally advertise their rooms through multiple channels, such as online travel agencies, to optimise reach and promote sales. Distribution management is essential and this involves calculating the minimum numbers of rooms needing to be sold for any given period by each channel. In doing so, you then have the ability to make informed choices regarding reallocation from cancellations or where to list spare rooms to maximise sales.

3. Market segmentation

Being aware of your hotel room visitor need market and the variable preferences, demands and affordability of different demographics are paramount to understanding how to price and distribute your room sales across the various channels. Not only does this help in managing your existing rooms, but it can also allow you to capture more of the market and increase sales and revenue. Flexibility is an important virtue required of hoteliers and being able to understand your clientele and adapt to their needs is vital to building loyalty and guaranteeing profitability.

Revenue management is another huge part of managing your hotel. How do your hotel get smore money coming in and achieve business goals? Smart revenue management and pricing strategies are needed if you want to optimise your Average Daily Rate . I shall recommend some hotel promotion methods as below:

1. Packages, promotions and extras

Packages are any rate that pairs the accommodation with an add-on; it could be free breakfast, free parking, or a ticket to a local event or attraction.Take a look at these methods to make sure your packages offer a unique experience.

Promotions are special rates that can change depending on:

The season or holiday period;

If the guest is a VIP; or,

You want to capitalise on an event.

You can get even more specific by offering things like mobile-only promotions.

Extras are an added expenditure that guests will only realise they want during the booking process. This might include items like champagne and chocolate stocked in their room, shuttle services from the airport, or activities like exercise classes. Extras are an added expenditure that guests will only realise they want during the booking process. This might include items like champagne and chocolate stocked in their room, shuttle services from the airport, or activities like exercise classes.

2. Events and tours

Selling tickets to local events, tours, or offering car rental is a good point-of-sale opportunity to increase your revenue per customer as well as providing a more satisfying experience for your guest.

3. Sell your hotel products

If you offer your guests the chance to buy your shampoo, bath and beach towels, art pieces, linen and so on, it can provide you with extra revenue and might even save you from the cost of replacing items that guests 'accidentally' pack with their own luggage when they depart.

4. Referrals and return business

If your guests give you positive feedback on completion of their stay, encourage them to share their experience with family and friends, and on social media to drive more bookings and brand awareness. You could also set guests up with a promotion code to get a discount the next time they stay. This encourages return business and helps you keep a consistent occupancy rate.

5. Accommodate flexible travellers

Some travellers don't have a set itinerary or allow themselves flexibility with their schedule, so take the opportunity to raise your occupancy and incremental revenue by offering guests a discount for an additional night's stay. Some mistakes have worse consequences than others and depending on the industry, backlash can range from minor to cataclysmic. The type of mistake you make will also have an impact on this. Did it just affect you, or did it also affect your customers?

● Designing hotel website promotion strategy

However, in the hospitality industry almost everything revolves around the customer, and they're the quickest party to point out any flaws. There's also plenty of times where you might simply self-sabotage and fail to get the most out of your business. Human fallibility prevents us from eliminating all our mistakes, but you can certainly look out for some common errors to avoid. I shall indicate some human avoidance mistakes on hotel website design and advertment skillful aspect to cause poor hotel room customer individual experience from your hotel website advertisement as below:

1. Failing to provide basic contact information

A beautiful looking hotel website with a fancy design and stunning features means nothing to the customer if they can't find your address or phone number on the homepage. The basics are something every hotel must get right before anything else. Travellers have all kinds of queries and many of them want to call to get instant clarification, and often people will be calling to make a booking so your phone number is an absolutely essential piece of information.

2. Website scarecrows – autoplay videos and music

Many people book holidays between the hours of 9AM – 5PM, i.e work hours. The last thing they need is for their computer to start blasting commercials or ditties around the office. The first thing they'll do is close your website and it's unlikely they'll return.

3. Incorrect use of social media

It's great to use social media as a marketing avenue but it's important you use it in the right way. You want traffic to be directed to your website and booking pages, not away from them. A common mistake hoteliers make is sending website visitors away to their social media channels immediately after a visitor has landed on the homepage. How many people are going to be coming back once they've been redirected to YouTube for instance?

4. Poor quality photos

There's really no point in investing in a great website design if the photos you integrate into the theme are lacking quality. Travellers want to see what they're paying for and if what they see is a grainy, blurry, or poorly framed image they won't be racing to open their wallets. Paying for high quality photography is worth every penny and you should update your images every couple of years, or every time you refurbish.

5. Downloads for simple information

Does anyone actually enjoy downloading a PDF to their phone or computer? The answer is probably no so why would you make a prospective guest do this? If a traveller wants to view the menu of your hotel restaurant for example, they should be able to do it on your website. Making them download documents is a conversion killer.

6. Connecting to the wrong distribution channels

When you connect to online travel agents manually or via a channel manager, it's still important to do some research. You have to look beyond the four or five biggest channels and find partners that most suit your target market.

7. Ignoring the potential of the local area

Guests are simply buying a hotel room when they come to stay at your hotel. For them, they're paying for an experience delivered by the destination. It would be silly for you not to take advantage of this. Make sure you partner with local businesses and run promotions and packages around local events and attractions.

8. Closing your ears (and mouth) to feedback

Reviews are one of the most important aspects to get right for your hotel. Customer satisfaction and brand reputation are vital if you want to keep the bookings coming in. The worst thing you can do is stay silent online when people leave reviews and feedback on sites like TripAdvisor or your social media pages. You need to respond diligently to both positive and negative reviews.

9. Not paying close attention to seasonality

The price people are prepared to pay for their hotel room will depend on the supply and demand trends over time. Seasonality matters, and you'll have to change rates a number of times during the year to reflect buying behavior and market conditions. This, together with the date and timing release of packages and promotions forms an integral part of your sales and marketing plan.

10. Lacking attention to detail in housekeeping

One of the most common complaints from guests is about dirty rooms or general uncleanliness of the hotel. There should never be any shortcutting when it comes to housekeeping and cleaning. Not only is it a healthy and safety issue, but you open yourself up to a flood of negative reviews. Of course, there are plenty of other pitfalls that could hit your hotel so you have to be constantly diligent and find ways to optimise your processes, reducing the risk of mistakes that could cost you money.

● Hotel and restaurant management strategy

Life gets even more complicated for hotels that also have a restaurant. Since managing a restaurant is a whole other kettle of fish. A study by Leonardo looked at what images travel shoppers viewed the most. Obviously the number one result was guest rooms but the second most viewed was restaurant photos.

This indicates that travel boils down to two primary needs; people want a nice place to sleep and they want a nice place to eat. Most of the time the hotel restaurant is a solid driver of revenue and an integral part of the hotel's identity, so it's ability to help market and sell your hotel should not be underestimated. Here are some reasons your restaurant will drive more bookings and how you can aid the process:

1. Individualise your restaurant

The first thing you need to do is to maximise the quality of your product by treating your hotel restaurant as a restaurant in its own right, rather than a glorified bar only accessible by guests. Turn your restaurant into a premium dining experience that focuses on the whole package including the food, lighting, music, decor, and wine lists. This way, your restaurant won't only be the bait to bring new customers in, but also an incentive for current guests to return when they revisit the area. At the same time it's important to remember who your customers are and understand what they want and what they can afford. Create a menu that will sell, not one you think is cool and trendy, and make sure the pricing is in alignment with the rest of your hotel. Using local produce will help with this.

2. Give your restaurant its own website

Don't let the physical setting of your restaurant deter you from creating a separate website for it. While it should also be featured on your hotel website, a dedicated restaurant website will help maximise revenue and potentially increase traffic to your hotel via page links.The restaurant website should feature large, high-resolution images and videos to showcase the food and decor. Hopefully, if guests land here and see they can also stay in the hotel, they'll be more convinced to stay and book direct.

By cross-referencing both lines of business you'll improve your search engine optimisation and maximise the traffic and conversions you receive. You should make sure everything is optimised for mobile devices and you could also include a direct link to your hotel's booking engine on your restaurant website.

By dedicating a separate website to your restaurant you'll be catering to consumer's need for relevant and distinctive content while also increasing your web presence. It's definitely worth the time and effort, especially if you use a smart intuitive website builder.

3. Make offers or give discounts

Consider offering different restaurant deals for different parts of the week to further encourage people to book with your hotel. Midweek you might advertise via social media or another medium giving away cheaper drinks or free desserts. On the weekend you might include a discounted three-course meal with a booking. As we know, managing a hotel is an extremely complex, stressful, and time-consuming task. The same can be said of running a successful restaurant. Combining both might seem like a fool's errand. And while there's definitely some risks involved in such an enterprise, there's also the opportunity for rich rewards at your hotel.

Hotel restaurant management: How you need to operate

Not only does a successful hotel restaurant have to serve and please your guests at your property, it has to stand on its own as a dining option for anyone in the local area. This is because many guests will want to explore the city and the many options available to them. So if you can't convince your guests to stay in for a meal, you have to attract other paying patrons. Who knows, some diners might even decide to make it a night and book a room directly through your front desk. For this to work the quality of your product has to be high. Your hotel restaurant has to individualise itself and offer a comprehensive dining experience. This means in addition to great food, you need to focus on lighting, music, decor and well thought out wine lists.

Things you need to consider include:

1. Hotel Space

How big will your restaurant attraction be relative to your hotel?

Different departments Staff number

How many patrons can you serve and how many extra staff will you need to oversee this?

2. Restaurent Food Menu

Will you create a menu that sells and is affordable or one that is cool and trendy? Make sure it's in line with who you expect to enter your restaurant.

3. Hotel Room And Food Packages

Obviously giving guests deals and discounts when they book a room direct with you will help increase restaurant traffic and revenue for your property.

● Hotel Restaurant And Hotel Room Bookings good relationship strategy

You should always reserve some tables for your own customers. If a guest walks down to eat and the restaurant is booked out by people not staying at the hotel, the response may be less than favourable.

The main issue is that if your restaurant is receiving poor reviews, it could be turning people off booking a room, no matter how amazing the rest of your hotel is. If it looks like the effort to produce the best possible experience is missing in the restaurant, travellers will assume the same for your whole business and look elsewhere. The same risk applies on the other side of the coin. If your hotel is derided for a poor experience and your occupancy is low, your restaurant could dwindle and die if it relies solely on business from outside the hotel walls.

Your hotel and restaurant have to work in harmony to keep each other strong.

Here are five tips to make your hotel restaurant a success:

1. Strike a balance between class and convenience

For guests already staying at your hotel your restaurant should be a quick and easy place to get a meal. They won't want to spend too much money, nor spend too much time waiting for food if they have other plans. On the other hand, diners coming for the restaurant alone will be expecting first-class ambience, food, and service.To keep everyone hotel customer feels happy and satisfactory when they are living in your hotel, you need to offer a simple but delicious menu that can be eaten in a comfortable setting that also promotes social interaction.

2. Give your restaurant its own website

While it should certainly be featured on your hotel website, a dedicated restaurant website will help maximise revenue and potentially drive extra traffic through your hotel via links. Cross-referencing both lines of business will improve your SEO and help maximise conversions and direct bookings. On your restaurant website, feature large high-resolution images and videos to showcase your food and decor. It will bring attractive and exciting website photos to persuade your potential hotel customers to choose to live your hotel.

3. Create a social media page for your restaurant

If your hotel restaurant has its own website it stands to reason it should have its own Facebook page too. This is especially true if regular events are hosted. Think live music on Friday nights, monthly wine tasting, or happy hours.

It's also useful for posting pictures of your food and dining experience.

4. Offer deals and discounts

You can use different parts of the week and different mediums to drive customers to your restaurant. Before a guest arrives, email them a drink voucher for the restaurant bar. It's likely they'll also grab a meal. You might use social media midweek to promote cheaper drinks or free desserts with every meal order. On the weekend, you could offer a three-course deal when a guest makes a booking.

5. Hire talented hospitality staff

Given the unique challenge of running a restaurant, you need staff that are specifically trained to meet it. Give them the power to create the best possible restaurant experience for your hotel's guests. Hotels and restaurants both form a large part of the hospitality industry and customer service is vital to both. These businesses live and die by customer satisfaction because of the public exposure they're always open to. Guests are only too eager to share stories of their holiday or dining experience – both good and bad.

● Building good cooperative relationship between travel agents and your hotel in your country

Hotel management: Optimising your online travel agent profile. It's common knowledge hotels are at a disadvantage if they aren't engaging online travel agents to boost their distribution and sell rooms. The prominence of OTAs, such as Expedia and Booking.com, continues to grow and they're a proven resource for travellers who use them to discover a diverse range of accommodation options at the best price. Connecting to OTAs will help hotels increase visibility and maintain their occupancy. Your property may even rank higher on search engines – and yet the commission fee from OTAs can feel like a necessary evil if hotels want to accomplish this. However, to make sure you get the full benefit of OTAs and their reach, there's a number of steps you should follow to optimise your hotel's profile. Given your hotel is a brand, your marketing efforts should be consistent across all channels. Don't save your best images and content just for your website, make sure this is also on the OTA websites.

Similar to search engines such as Google, OTAs have their own algorithms for how your property will rank, meaning you need to pay close attention to the following tips:

Here are 6 easy steps to optimise your hotel's OTA profile:

1. Accurately manage your inventory

Because the availability of your rooms will fluctuate due to peak periods or seasonal changes, you need to maintain an accurate inventory across all OTAs to keep your occupancy rate high. Using a channel manager with pooled inventory is the best way to achieve this because travellers won't be disrupted by double booking issues or incorrect data.

2. Cleverly manage your rates and promotions

Guests don't simply use OTAs for a wide range of choice and inspiration, often they're looking for last minute deals and offers. If you have time-sensitive promotions they'll have more chance of being caught and you can more easily sell the remainder of your rooms. It's not hard to make alterations on OTAs to highlight a particular rate or capitalise on seasonal events to attract more guests to your property profile.

3. Carefully respond to reviews

While only 14% of consumers trust traditional advertising, 92% respect reviews on sites such as TripAdvisor. Reviews on OTAs are traditionally reliable because guests can only post a review after they've stayed at the property. However, only 36% of hoteliers respond to reviews on OTA sites. It's important to do an efficient job of managing online reviews.

4. Consider paid advertising

This doesn't have to be restricted to big and rich hotel corporations. It can also be a viable option for independent hotels on a pay-per-click basis. While paid advertising is no guarantee of more bookings, it will help make your property front-of-mind. If your content and aesthetic is strong enough, you should see a rise in revenue and your OTA ranking.

5. Focus on specific markets

Narrowing down your targets will mean you impact a lower volume of customers but you're also more likely to secure the bookings you want if you use certain time periods, events, geo-targeting or other methods to target specific audiences.

6. Understand your competition

It's vital to know who the similar players in your market are so you aren't significantly underselling or overselling your rooms. If you are, you won't be able to compete. On top of this, being aware of their activity may provide an opportunity to snare extra bookings. For example, changing rates could indicate the occupancy of a competitor or a promotion based on something you could also benefit from. There are specific data systems hotels can use to monitor competitors. With an optimised OTA profile, your hotel will not only gain bookings from third-party channels but direct traffic to your website should also increase, helping you to offset the commission fee you pay.

● Hotel restaurant food management strategy

To improve the way you manage your hotel, you have to think about everything and look for ways to save time and money, or increase efficiency. Even small changes can reap big rewards over the course of a financial year. Sticking with the theme of food, there's a big opportunity here. As humans, food represents our most essential connection to the planet and its resources. Yet environmental researchers often surmise that we place less value on food than we used to. Following US hotel kitchen indicates that hotel GDP information. You only have to look at numbers from Hotel Kitchen around food waste to understand their perspective:

In the US alone, an estimated 40% of all food is scrapped

American hotels serve food worth $35 billion each year

It's estimated that 40% of food in customer-facing businesses, such as hotels and supermarkets, goes to waste

How to control food waste in your hotel's kitchen

Fighting food waste at your hotel goes beyond feeding people and helping the environment – it also improves your property's bottom line. Do you really know how much food you throw away each week? Have you worked out its monetary value? Are staff and guests aware of your efforts to be more sustainable and properly manage food waste disposal? According to Hotel Kitchen, more than 90% of staff say they want to take action on tackling food waste. Guests are also becoming increasingly savvy with 60% of those surveyed saying they expect hotels to be actively reducing waste across their operations.

There may be steps your hotel restaurant can take to reduce waste:

1. Get buy in on food waste from your team

Create a team to take ownership of waste reduction and incentivise them. This should include a cook or chef and a kitchen porter (KP). Your KPs see what gets scraped off plates, while a chef will know how leftover ingredients can be better used in future menus.

2. Research waste management software to support processes

Conduct a waste audit, by dividing waste into categories and ensuring staff dispose of it in an appropriately-labelled container. There is weight-based software for this: basically a talking bin that records the weight of different categories of waste according to descriptions entered by staff on a touchscreen. The most well-known of these is probably the Winnow system, which its manufacturer claims typically saves operators 3-5% on food costs – a ROI of up to 10 times within a year. The challenges with using a system like this is that, it requires all waste to go into the same bin, leading to congestion in the kitchen or pot wash, and it can take time to input the data.

3. Assess raw ingredients vs. diners' plates

If conducting a waste audit manually, you'll need to at least split waste into raw ingredients and prepared waste that is left on diners' plates. Almost 10% of raw ingredients are wasted. This includes things like potato peelings and cauliflower leaves, which can be difficult to find a use for. Raw ingredients also covers kitchen prep mistakes. Some 35% of restaurant waste is left on diners' plates. This is most definitely higher in a hotel restaurant, where diners are less likely to take their leftovers home.

4. Asking staff for their frequent observations

Raw ingredients and diners' plates might be the two main categories, but make sure you have as many containers as you have space for. Record the waste, by weight, but also anecdotally. You'll learn more from staff comments: what did they find surprising? Was there an item plated but not eaten? Is there a garnish that customers commonly leave?

5. Following the 'less is more' approach

Assemble as many staff as possible to discuss the results, after a fortnight or a month. When it comes to prepared waste, you may find that it's a result of portion sizes being too large, in which case introduce strict portion controls, possibly using measure scoops that are colour-coded for different items. If lots of butter and preserve is left after breakfast service, consider buying in individual wrapped portions. Keep in mind that, unavoidable post-consumer waste can often be used by farmers as animal feed: all good content for your Instagram stories.

6. Obsessing over food and beverage expiration dates

If you discover that fresh items are going out of date, introduce a strict fridge rotation system and coloured stickers to identify which items to use first. Store new foods on the right fridge and existing on the left to maximise shelf life. Get this ingrained and replicate it in ambient storage areas for rice, herbs and spices, pulses and grains as well. Out of date ingredients can usually be donated to local food banks. Build a relationship with your local food bank operator and post about it on social media to boost your presence in the local community. This may lead to worthwhile involvement in charity events.

7. Sharpen up your kitchen team's knife skills

Meat carcasses should always be used for stock. If staff report that there is still a lot of meat left on bones, check that knives are being properly sharpened and that staff are trained to bone items efficiently. If staff lack butchery and fishmongers skills you'll save on waste by buying, for example, cubed chicken and filleted fish.

8. Using proper peelers for vegetables

Similarly, are staff prepping vegetables properly? You'll see less waste using peelers than knives for most fruit and root vegetables.

9. Allocating some space for composting

Raw vegetable waste can be composted if you have some outside space. A compost area can be simply constructed out of pallets. The resulting compost can be used to improve the soil on site or donated to local allotment groups. It can often be valuable to look at what businesses in other parts of your industry are doing, and seeing how you compare or what you might be able to employ in your own business strategies.

10. Getting customer service ideas from restaurants

There are similarities between service in restaurants and hotels, but also a few differences. Let's see how great customer service in restaurants translates to achieving guest satisfaction in hotels.

A great first step is turning 'service' into 'hospitality'

Service is basically about performing a task; doing something for someone. It denotes a mechanical action. On the other hand, hospitality is about making an impression on someone and going the extra mile to make their experience a memorable one. The interaction involved in hospitality is a genuine one and should be based on a caring attitude. Hospitality is something the best restaurants do extremely well. Customers will generally be served by one waiter their entire visit and will be made to feel like close friends or family, constantly attended to and conversed with warmly. Any requests will be responded to immediately. By the end of the meal, customers will look forward to coming back and seeing their waiter again.

In hotels, guests might interact with many different staff members throughout their stay, meaning they don't always get this personal connection. They may have to wait longer for services and might get frustrated when the staff member doesn't remember their preferences. The attentiveness of restaurants is certainly something hotels can try to replicate. Some things to try is to greet guests by name, get to know their interests, and don't delay when they want attention.

Giving guests a personalised experience at your hotel

A recent report shows full-service and fast food restaurants are revamping their menus and establishing more mobile ordering options, to the delight of customers. Restaurants are adapting their menus and technology to align with shifting consumer preferences. This looks at millennial tastes for fresh food, mobile ordering, and automated kiosks. The bottom line is that restaurants are working hard to please consumers in a way the customers are dictating, resulting in higher satisfaction.

Hotels need to do the same. New technology, both front and backend, needs to be explored if customer service is to improve. Again this comes back to hospitality and personalisation. Give each specific guest what they need. Even if you look at mobile check-in, it's not something everyone wants. Obviously some guests will be in a rush or tired from travel and simply want to get to their room as fast as possible. Others will be craving some human interaction. It's about what's convenient for the individual hotel guest. Technology should be able to help hotels in every regard. Think about how technology can improve the in-room experience, especially when it comes to speeding up room service or cleaning processes. Conversely, if backend tech that makes it easier to manage reservations and distribution is used, more time can be dedicated to guest experience.

Empower staff to solve their own problems

Nothing will frustrate a customer more than a staff member always needing to clear something with their manager. Not only does this take more time, but it makes the staff member look incompetent. Quality restaurants will take difficult or specific requests in their stride and provide customers with any special needs they require. If something goes wrong, their constant hands-on experience allows them to solve it, without the intervention of a manager. Again, it's done with a smile on their face because nothing is too much trouble for a valued customer.

Hotels need to train and empower their staff this way too. A great example is The Ritz-Carlton Hotel Company, where even hourly employees have permission to spend up to $2,000 per guest to solve any problem or dissatisfaction that may arise, without needing to ask for approval or involve management. And it's not the amount of money that's the point; it's the instant no-need-for-approval empowerment, which enables quick solutions for guests.

Hire the right traits in staff at your hotel

The very best restaurant staff show a passion for their job and authentic desire to make people happy. While the hospitality industry is one where skills can be learned on the job and thus standards may be lax, the approach taken to hiring staff must be taken very seriously.

To name just a few, some necessary traits a hotel should find it its staff include:

Empathy

Warmth

Conscientiousness

Enthusiasm

Charisma

● Hotel regular reports for effective hotel management strategy

Reporting on performance is essential to hotel management. You need to collect and analyse accurate data regularly to see where things are working, and what you need to improve on. There are a lot of different parts of the business you'll need reports on to inform your overall strategy. Most of them can be pulled from the systems that you're using such as your property management system and channel manager etc.

Some of the most important information your hotel different department managers need to track includes:

Channel performance

Website performance

Housekeeping

ADR – Average daily rate

Occupancy

RevPAR – Revenue per available room

TrevPAR – Total revenue per available room

Channel performance is key. You need to understand a number of factors about your booking channels. For instance, which channel is delivering the most reservations? Which channel is contributing the most overall revenue? Which channel has the highest cancellation rate? Which has the largest or smallest lead time?

The point is the more information you have about your channel performance, the more tweaks you can make to optimise your distribution mix. Cutting some channels and connecting others, or temporarily pausing, can enable you to maximise revenue.

Given how important direct bookings are, website performance is equally important. Since your booking engine can be included in channel performance you'll be able to see if direct bookings are down. Investigating your website is a good idea. How much traffic are you driving via organic and paid means? What pages are being visited the most? What's the conversion rate on calls to action? How many people are abandoning a booking part of the way through?

Housekeeping is extremely significant. Do you know how long it's taking to clean a room on average? How many guests are arriving to find their room isn't ready yet? Do you have enough cleaning resources or not enough? How efficient are staff?

This is all information you need to report on each and every month to see if your business is on an upward spiral or if standards are dropping. Through your property management and revenue management systems you can track occupancy, ADR, and many other metrics.

● Hotel management software technological strategy

Technology in the hotel industry continues to advance at a rapid pace and hotel management software (HMS) remains essential for hoteliers looking to improve the running of their business. With software, hotel operators can streamline their administrative processes and improve their overall hotel management system. The key to reaping the benefits of an effective hotel management software system is to select the right one for your property. It's critical that you know exactly what this hotel management technology is, and why it is important for you to implement it at your hotel.

What is hotel management software?

Hotel management software is technology that allows hotel operators and owners to streamline their administrative tasks while also increasing their bookings in both the short- and long-term. Your hotel management system is not only important for your own day-to-day operations, but it's a vital part of the overall guest experience. From the beginning of your guests' online booking journey until the completion of their stay and their feedback once they return home, it is necessary for your hotel management technology to enhance their experience with your brand. Finding a hotel management system that offers the features you both need and want is necessary to effectively managing your hotel in a global economic climate.

The purpose of management systems for hotels

Management systems serve several purposes for both hotel operators who manage large chains as well as independent hoteliers. These include:

1. Managing bookings

Your property management system should help you efficiently and effectively manage your bookings. Neither you, nor your staff, should be tasked with manually inputting bookings and managing those across all your distribution channels. A property management system should automate the booking process for you, allowing you to escape the back office and focus more on interacting with your guests. In addition, it significantly reduces the risk of overbooking your rooms, which directly improves the guest experience at your property.

2. Direct bookings

It should allow you to actively drive direct bookings to your website. Travellers today are more apt to book online than they are to call to finalise bookings or partner with a travel agent. Direct bookings allow you to maximise the revenue that you generate per booking. You should only consider software that integrates with an online booking engine.

3. Channel management

Hotel management technology should allow you to easily implement your distribution strategy. Creating partnerships with different types of agents in the industry, such as OTAs and GDSs, is necessary to survive in a competitive, global climate. Managing hotel with software that offers a channel manager will allow you to create and implement a diverse distribution strategy that continually drives bookings.

4. Hotel website

Your hotel administration department software should help enhance your online presence. Your hotel management system is only effective if your guests can reach your brand. Choosing a program that offers a web editor or website creator will allow you to create a clean, appealing and user-friendly website that will encourage guests to book a stay at your property.

Benefits of hotel management technology

When you are selecting hotel management technology for your property, you should consider the many benefits that this system will offer you, including:

1. Reduce time spent on administrative tasks

You hotel can minimise the amount of time spent on administrative tasks. The right hotel management system will do a lot of the work for you, allowing you to focus your efforts and your energy on the big picture. The technology should also provide you with valuable data on how your employees perform their duties and how this affects employee retention, satisfaction and productivity. In today's fast-paced travel environment, it's critical that you automate as many tasks as possible. A property management system can help you tremendously with that.

2. Increase your online presence

Your hotel can increase your brand presence online. Management software that is integrated with your website builder will allow you to accept direct online bookings and develop a user-friendly website. Naturally, this will increase your relevance in the search engine results and allow more travellers to discover your property during their online booking journey.

3. Build relationships with guests

Your hotel will develop a better rapport with your target market segment, while also identifying new markets to tap into. The types of travellers who have always loved staying at your property will appreciate the improved experience. In addition, your new technology will allow you to reach out to new markets that would not have otherwise discovered your brand.

4. Manage your distribution

Your hotel will improve your reach throughout the industry. With a property management system in place that integrates with a channel manager, you will be able to advertise across many channels whilst maintaining rate parity. From the large OTAs and GDSs to individual retail travel agents, you can provide real-time booking information to your agents that will drive bookings.

5. Manage your hotel revenue and cost expenditure control

Your hotel can implement a beneficial revenue management strategy. Using innovative pricing tools that allow you to create a flexible room pricing strategy, you can maximise the revenue that you generate per room at any given moment. Pricing your rooms right is the key to succeeding in this competitive industry, and having these tools available can help you significantly.

6. Increase room bookings

Your hotel will ultimately increase your large , middle and small size room number bookings. At the end of the day, the point of every feature within your hotel management business solution is to boost the bookings that you get at your hotel. Whether your hotel wants to increase your off-season bookings or you want to expand your offerings to new market segments, you will be successful if you select the right hotel management software for your property.

● Hotel property facility management strategy

The first aspect, is your hotel safe facility system. Managing a hotel isn't all about managing the physical property, it's also about managing intangible things like reputation. Any hotel facility issues may influence hotel customers how feel your hotel service performance, for example, when your hotel customers are living in your hotel rooms, during this living period, they feel your hotel fire system is not safe, it will influnece that they choose to reduce room booking living days because they are afraid fire occurs can cause their death. So, any hotel floor fire safe property management facilities will influence any one customer makes booking room days decision whether they can extend days or shorten days to live in your hotel.

Another aspect, is your hotel online booking facility system. It's very simple. Hospitality businesses such as hotels are at risk if they don't focus attention on their online reviews and take control of their reputation management. As more and more guests turn to one another for advice on where to stay in cities around the world, the effectiveness of traditional hotel advertising is declining – while the impact of online hotel reviews is on the rise.

Failure to monitor, manage and respond to feedback will skew your hotel management strategy to issues that are unimportant to customers, as well as provide unhappy customers with ammunition for negative feedback on travel and social media sites. It can be difficult for an individual to get through their lives without significant episodes being recorded on social media channels, let alone a hotel to exist without the blemish of social media complaints.

As the impact of online bookings and digital feedback continues to rise, the importance of reputation management rises with it. Yet while online reputation management is a trend across the hospitality sector, it is still considered an indulgence by some independent hoteliers. Part of this rationale is driven by the confusion around how to deal with both positive and negative feedback online. So here are some standard ways hoteliers can deal with online reviews – regardless of sentiment:

The most feared of all feedback online is a negative review

However, audiences are particularly savvy in determining the value of feedback, not just because the "voice" of the author is on display, but because audiences often apply a filter to their reading of any review. Consciously or subconsciously, they consider the value of any commentary, as well as the relevance of a comment to their own experiences and preferences. So a comment on the convenience of a hotel location to an equestrian events venue will be of potential importance to horse-lovers, yet entirely irrelevant to many other potential guests. Where a rational negative comment is posted, hotels do have options on how to respond.

Acknowledge and Action

For a genuine, reasoned negative comment on customer experience, it is best for hotels to respond in a timely manner (within 72 hours of posting), acknowledging the issue and describing how it will be addressed. Ideally, a follow up post will occur after actioning the issue, and showing how the experience will not be repeated. This is by far the best possible response to negative feedback, because online audiences are far more willing to value action and positive changes in behaviour, than think poorly of the initial negative experience.

Apologise and Compensate

For a negative comment which illustrates an experience that was difficult or impossible to avoid, an appropriate response is to apologise for the poor experience and to privately offer either monetary compensation, or discounts on future bookings. While this is unlikely to totally satisfy the customer with the stated poor experience, it will indicate to other customers, the prioritisation of customer experiences at the hotel. It's important to take compensation offline where possible to avoid inviting those like to complain for free stuff.

Apologise and Thank

For negative comments that focus on pedantic details, the most appropriate response is an apology for the experience and an acknowledgement that this feedback will help shape your hotel's future guest experience strategy. This is far more useful than a response which states that the comment will be passed to a customer service team, because the customer already believes that service is the problem at the property.

How to thank hotel guests for their positive feedback

While most organisations are thrilled with the prospect of positive reviews, an abundance of rave reviews can be just as suspicious to audiences as a series of negative reviews. Therefore, positive reviews also need a response.

Be Humble

Where a positive review is excessive and perhaps gushing, it is wise for firms to thank the guest for their enthusiasm, but to also acknowledge areas where you are attempting to improve. This reinforces commitment to customer service.

Be Delighted

Where positive feedback is sincere and reasoned, the best response for hotels is to express delight and appreciation for the feedback and the desire to serve again in future. This is the easiest response to deliver, but is often the least fulfilled.

Be Appreciative

Where feedback is predominantly neutral, but some aspects are highlighted as being of particular value, it is advisable for hotel managers to express thanks for the feedback and to request further advice on how the organisation could improve in specific areas. Again, try to take this conversation offline with an email or personal phone call. This enables more considered feedback to follow the initial post.

● Reputation management strategy

Reputation management is often considered difficult or time-consuming. Yet the results of research into the importance of reputation management are unarguable: the value of reputation management is substantial and growing. Understanding how to respond to feedback is not just a competitive advantage, but potentially a means of ensuring your hotel stays in business. Your hotel can easily turn complaints around and win hotel guests back – and these basic reputation management responses are your first line of defence.

Hotel property management software

Selecting the right hotel software is critical, particularly in a world where consumers are relying more heavily on their devices with each passing day. An investment this important to your overall success as a hotel operator requires you to do some research.

These are seven questions that you should ask your hotel tech provider as soon as possible:

1. How does your hotel product maintains its relevance in the hospitality industry?

While the core of a technology system may remain the same over time, the reality is that any product geared specifically towards the hospitality industry will need to adapt to changing trends and preferences from travellers. You need to ask this question so you have an understanding of how your technology will help you grow along with the industry.

2. How often can your hotel expects upgrades for your platform?

No piece of technology is perfect, and the best hotel technology providers will make sure that regular updates and upgrades are available for their clients. It's important to have an understanding of how often these upgrades will be available, and how you will be able to successfully implement the upgrades.

3. What level of customer service will I receive from your company?

Unfortunately, far too many hotel technology providers focus on hard sales tactics without much support after the purchase is complete. You will want to verify with your provider that there will be ways to contact and work with staff after the technology has been installed at your hotel.

4. Is your hotel platform secure?

Security should be a top priority of your hotel technology provider. You will want to ask about the details regarding their security features, as it's imperative that both your data and your guests' data is secure.

5. How easily can your hotel personalise your systems?

Hotel technology providers need to offer you a versatile system that includes not only the generic features that are necessary for any hotel, but also the adaptable features that allow you to personalise the platform for your particular brand. Ultimately, your investment in technology needs to result in a system that works specifically for your hotel.

6. What reporting features are available?

When your hotel begin your search for the right hotel technology, you will likely focus first on the property management system. However, you will want to discuss additional features that also are available, with some of the most important being the reporting features. Verify that you'll be able to run detailed reports using live data, as this is the only way to ensure that you can grow your brand.

7. How can your hotel accesses the hotel technology system once implemented?

Be sure that you are investing in a system that allows you to run your hotel from anywhere. You need hotel technology that is optimised for all devices, including smartphones and tablets.

Benefits of a hotel management system

When you are selecting hotel management systems for your property, you should consider the many benefits they'll offer you, including:

1. Reduce time spent on administrative tasks

Your hotel can minimise the amount of time spent on administrative tasks. The right hotel management system will do a lot of the work for you, allowing you to focus your efforts and your energy on the big picture. The technology should also provide you with valuable data on how your employees perform their duties and how this affects employee retention, satisfaction and productivity. In today's fast-paced travel environment, it's critical that you automate as many tasks as possible. A property management system can help you tremendously with that.

2. Increase your hotel online presence

Your hotel can increase your brand presence online. Management software that is integrated with your website builder will allow you to accept direct online bookings and develop a user-friendly website. Naturally, this will increase your relevance in the search engine results and allow more travellers to discover your property during their online booking journey.

3. Build relationships with guests

Your hotel will develop a better rapport with your target market segment, while also identifying new markets to tap into. The types of travellers who have always loved staying at your property will appreciate the improved experience. In addition, your new technology will allow you to reach out to new markets that would not have otherwise discovered your brand.

4. Manage your hotel distribution

Your hotel will improve your reach throughout the industry. With a property management system in place that integrates with a channel manager, you will be able to advertise across many channels whilst maintaining rate parity. From the large OTAs and GDSs to individual retail travel agents, you can provide real-time booking information to your agents that will drive bookings.

5. Manage your hotel revenue

Your hotel can implement a beneficial revenue management strategy. Using innovative pricing tools that allow you to create a flexible room pricing strategy, you can maximise the revenue that you generate per room at any given moment. Pricing your rooms right is the key to succeeding in this competitive industry, and having these tools available can help you significantly.

6. Increase bookings

Your hotel will ultimately increase your bookings. At the end of the day, the point of every feature within your hotel management business solution is to boost the bookings that you get at your hotel.

Hotel property management system

All hotels need some variation of a property management system (PMS). However they come in many different forms and are not all created equal. There are still properties trying to manage their business in a traditional way with books and ledgers, others are using server-based systems, while many used web-based systems.

One of the most valuable things to a hotel manager is time, and money of course. The first two systems listed are a drain on both time and finances, while the latter has obviously become the optimal way to manage hotel operations. Cloud-based PMSs are a superior way to automate and accelerate all the important processes at your hotel such as taking and confirming bookings, managing reservations, generating bills and reports, check-in/out, room transfers, checking/editing availability, guest communication, the list goes in. Cloud-based technology can handle all these tasks with ease because of its ability to deeply integrate with channel managers, booking engines, and revenue management systems. Despite this, there are still concerns over the validity and cost effectiveness of cloud-based PMSs.

Here are five common property management system myths and why we think they're unfounded?

1. You think cloud-based technology is confusing or hard to use

Because it's intangible and seemingly floating in the air, some hotel managers believe using cloud technology will be hard to learn and too confusing to keep track of. The opposite is true. A PMS allows you to keep everything in one place and it can never be lost. You can access your data from any location so long as you have the Internet. The many tasks that you perform using multiple programs or books can be done from one central location with a fully integrated PMS. This also means you can collaborate better with other staff who need access to the same information.

2. You worry that sensitive data is insecure and vulnerable

While the information in your cloud PMS isn't kept under lock and key it is encrypted and backed-up. Nothing is stored 'onsite' so even if your computer breaks or your laptop is lost, your data will remain accessible to you. With data in the cloud you don't have to worry about viruses or bugs, and hacking is much less likely to succeed thanks to firewalls and authentication gateways.

3. Your current software works just as well as cloud-based technology

It's unlikely this is true and even if it is, it won't be for long. Cloud software is constantly being updated and evolved meaning users automatically get the benefits included in their monthly fee. If your current server isn't updated, it becomes slow and vulnerable, while updating it requires extra time and greater cost that has to be done too regularly.

4. You believe a web PMS is only suitable for large hotels

The reality is that smaller or independent hoteliers are often stretched thinner than anyone. With less staff and more responsibility, the time and hassle saved by using a cloud-based PMS is vital and could be the difference between getting the bookings needed for maximum occupancy or losing revenue on empty rooms.

5. You think hotel technology is too expensive

Cloud-based systems are actually very cost effective. You never require any additional hardware, backup solutions, licensing, updates, fixes. There's also no lengthy setup process and with the time you save using it, more resources can be directed towards increasing guest experience and revenue streams. Overall a cloud-based PMS will give you more control over your hotel business, with:

List of hotel property management systems may include as below:

There are literally hundreds of property management systems on the market. The most important aspect when choosing one is to ensure it's easy to use, has all the functions you need, and that it is able to integrate with your other important systems, such as your channel manager.

Some popular examples you might come across include:

Little Hotelier

Mews

Sirvoy

CloudBeds

Frontdesk Anywhere

eZee Frontdesk

Hotelogix

Maestro

OPERA

Avvio

Online booking engine

Essential if your hotel wants to capture direct bookings and reduce the commission you pay to online travel agents (OTAs). The majority of travellers will visit your hotel website even if they discover your property on an OTA.But if you're looking to capitalise on this traffic, your booking engine needs certain features beyond booking as a minimum including:

Seamless online experience for your guests via a customised, two-step booking process. Multi-language and currency capabilities to convert guests from around the globe. Mobile-friendly and Facebook-compatible to reach travellers on-the-go. Upselling capability so you can offer a more personalised stay for your guests. However your hotel booking engine can be a much more powerful tool that you can customise to suit any marketing strategy, allowing your business to maximise its revenue.

Ensure your hotel gets as much value as possible out of your booking engine by following these steps:

1. Prioritise booking engine and website integration

Seamless integration between booking engine and website will make a guests booking experience so much easier. It will be more responsive to mobile, put less pressure on you to design the look of your booking engine, and will maintain your branding throughout the entire booking process. All of this will enhance the trust your customers have in your hotel.

2. Create a strong foundation for search engine optimisation

While not directly related to your booking engine, SEO is vital. If your website isn't optimised for SEO it won't matter how amazing your booking engine is, you won't be attracting sufficient traffic to drive bookings.

3. Implement urgency messages

Urgency messages do exactly what they imply; invoke urgency in the shopper. By drawing attention to rates through urgency messages you can make your guests think they are in danger of missing out, or else getting something other customers aren't. They're a great way of speeding up the booking process and increasing conversions. Examples include 'Book now, pay later!' or 'Only two rooms left!'.

4. Use promo code banners

If you're running a promotion, you want guests to notice it. Display a prominent promo banner on your website using your booking engine so guests can easily view and select applicable dates and benefit from the promotion.

5. Set up an early-bird rate

By selling discounted early-bird rates you can improve your short-term cash flow by collecting full prepayment from the booker. You can control when to flag an early-bird rate via your booking engine extranet.

6. Introduce last-minute rates

Setting attractive last minute rates are good for increasing your short-term occupancy or filling any remaining rooms. Offset the rate by taking a high deposit to limit the amount of cancelled bookings or no-shows. Clearly display these and use them in conjunction with urgency messages.

7. Entice guests with a stay pay deal

Maintain your occupancy by increasing the length of your guests stay. Offer them a discount for one or more of their dates, clearly indicating the price difference and encourage them to book additional nights. Make sure you have control over what night is to be discounted; first, last, cheapest etc.

8. Interest guests in package deals

Packaging up extras like entry to events, attractions, or restaurants gives guests a one-stop shopping experience that they enjoy. Offer options guests can't find on OTAs and again entice them to stay longer. If used intelligently a booking engine can be a hotel marketing and branding tool that will incentivise guests to become loyal to your hotel, further increasing your direct bookings and revenue in the future.

Hotel room management software: Channel managers

A channel manager is a tool that will allow you to sell all your rooms on all your connected booking sites at the same time. It will automatically update your availability in real-time on all sites when a booking is made, when you close a room to sale, or when you want to make bulk changes to your inventory. There's a lot more to a channel manager than simply making life easier for when updating your rates and availability. You can use it to perform many tasks when managing your hotel and its benefits are two-fold in how it can increase bookings and revenue, and enable long term business planning.

Take a look at this comprehensive list of how a channel manager can be used to benefit a hotel.

1. Increase online bookings

With telephone and walk-in bookings on the decline and online bookings on the rise, a channel manager places you in the best position to take advantage of this new traveller booking habit. Connect to more online channels, where more travellers than ever are locking in their stays.

2. Increase hotel revenue

Given a channel manager displays live rates and availability across all your channels at the same time, and updates automatically you can accept bookings faster and almost eliminate the chance of double bookings. In addition, the data you can analyse from your channel manager can ensure your rates are always optimised and you're using the most lucrative channels.

3. Reduce the risk of overbookings

Without a channel manager, you're forced to split your inventory between channels and risk double-bookings or failing to reach full occupancy. Pooled inventory and automated updates of availability and rates in real time means guests can only ever book a room that is actually available.

4. Improve brand recognition

A powerful channel manager will provide two-way unrestricted access to hundreds of booking channels where travellers who would never hear of you can now make reservations at your property. It also makes OTAs more likely to accept your listing because they can be sure your inventory will always be accurate.

5. Boost direct bookings

It may seem illogical but it's true! Many travellers will discover your property first on an OTA, but they want to learn more about you before they book. Often they will visit your website and then make the decision to book their stay. So you get a direct sale, but it was born on the OTA site – resulting in greater profit for your hotel. This is known as the billboard effect.

6. Remove manual processes

Manual data entry is time-consuming and frustrating, we all know that. If you were to use a channel manager and remove this friction, you'd realise just how much more productive you can be. Anything that has to be put on hold can now be prioritised to improve your business.

7. Create a seamless, integrated tech stack

Instead of being required to update information in multiple extranets, a channel manager can integrate with your property management system, central reservation system, or revenue management system as well as your booking engine to create a central control system for the entirety of your hotel's operations. Some channel managers, like SiteMinder, also have a unique connection to Airbnb. Although boutique hotels have already been using Airbnb for some time, there hasn't been a solution for them to manage this channel in conjunction with other partners such as online travel agents – until SiteMinder's partnership.

8. Transform into a powerful business platform

A good channel allows complete transparency of data across all systems and channels, meaning you can use the received information to see which channels or rooms are performing the best. This means you can constantly update your business strategy. Look at reports such as channel yield and channel analysis and your reservation trends to see where things are going right – or wrong!

9. Reduce reliance on traditional booking channels

There's certainly no suggestion that you should leave behind traditional methods such as taking reservations over the phone or via walk-ins. It can be very profitable to save some of your inventory for these methods. However, using a channel manager will ensure you don't have to worry about filling your rooms in this manner. Connecting to a significant number of online booking sites will ensure your occupancy always remains steady.

10. Keep everyone on the same page

Quality channel managers are very easy to use and hotels will regularly have multiple staff members using the system. If the main user is going away or won't be available to make updates they can easily mark important dates in the system so everyone is aware if they need to change a rate or a close a room etc. For example, they may mark school holiday periods so rates can be increased during these peak times.

Hotel management apps technology

In order to enhance productivity at your hotel, you must first ensure you and your team are as organised as possible. This may be easier said than done when you have emails arriving non-stop, content to post and people to manage . Technology has evolved to solve almost any problem. There are many apps in the market to help with everyday challenges. Organised teams get more done and having everything under control also gives you a better grip on the overall success of the business.

Here are five hotel apps to help stay on top of hotel management:

1. Pocket

Have you ever come across interesting articles, videos or websites and ended up forgetting about them? Whenever you find something you want to view later, you can add it to your Pocket – an application and web service for managing reading lists. You can save content directly from your browser or from apps like Twitter, Flipboard, Pulse and Zite. Once saved to Pocket, the list of content is visible on any device (phone, tablet or computer) with access to your account – online and offline helping you share interesting articles with your hotel's team.

2. Astro

If a large part of your day-to-day duties includes sending and receiving emails, Astro will help you focus on what is most important. Astro brings along email and calendar features, powered by an Artificial Intelligence (AI) assistant, which will prioritise your emails, tell you what to follow up on, and help you clean up your inbox. Astro also adds reminders, snoozed emails, and scheduled emails to your calendar, so you can get a complete view of your day. You can also customise the emails you send with Open Tracking, Send Later, Custom Signatures, and much more.

3. Google Calendar

One of the most important parts of management is time management and having your calendar with you on the go can be crucial. Stay on track with your appointments and tasks with Google Calendar. Your events or any meeting requests received via Gmail can be automatically added to your calendar and you'll spend less time managing your schedule. Add images and maps to your appointments, and access your schedule for the day, week and month from any device at any time. You can also gain visibility of your team's work schedule and share your calendar view with them so you can make the most of your day.

4. Trello

Stay up to speed with your team projects using Trello – an easy, free, flexible, and visual way to manage and organise workflow. Trello is divided in boards, with lists representing the workflow. For example, you can have your Social Media Marketing board and inside the lists: To Do, Doing and Done. Every list has cards, representing tasks containing relevant information. For example, the New Years 7 Nights Promotion card will contain the specification of this promotion, such as due date, hotel team members that need to follow the task, checklists and more. As tasks progress along the way, the card will navigate to the next list. With Trello you have a clear and real-time view of the stage your project is at and you'll never lose track of them.

5. Evernote

If sometimes you feel the need for a second brain, meet Evernote – an app designed for note taking, organising tasks lists, and archiving. You can collect everything that matters in one place and find it when you need it, fast. Capture, organise, and share notes from any device and always keep your best ideas in sync and only a click away.

Evernote is not a simple note taking app, you can enhance your notes with links, checklists, tables, attachments, and audio recordings. Even handwritten notes are searchable. From initial brainstorm to finished project, Evernote will give you productivity bliss.

Apps the key to establishing self-service experiences

It's no secret modern-day travellers are becoming more accustomed to hyper-personalised and streamlined service from their hotels. In fact, if the hotel is going to deliver on its promise of quality, your guests expect a personalised and convenient experience.

Hotels can adapt to this growing need by prioritising data, technology, and connectivity. It's important to know what guests want, and also how to provide the appropriate services through hotel systems and applications. The tradition of limiting service and interaction to just your hotel staff and physical property is being outgrown by the ability of technology to automate and make many processes easier for guests. Where travellers once expected to be greeted by a front desk operator, they might now prefer the self-service experience that mobile check-in offers. Given the average person wastes an hour each week waiting in line, it's no surprise that self-service is catching on.

The self-service approach allows staff to be less transactional and focus on establishing genuine connections with guests. With technology in place, hotel employees will no longer be confined to stationary positions within the lobby or left to guess what guest expectations might be. For a better idea of the trends in this area and the enabling power of technology and connectivity, we spoke to four hotel applications to get their perspective.

Being able to adapt, meet challenges, and place yourself on a scale of personal growth is vital for a hotel manager. Hotel management is about overseeing every operation of the property. This requires knowledge of distribution strategy, finance, customer service, staff management, marketing, and more. Effective inventory management for hotels involves both creating and managing demand, and maximising returns. Revenue management is another huge part of managing your hotel. How do you get more money coming in and achieve business goals?

In the hospitality industry almost everything revolves around the customer, and they're the quickest party to point out any flaws. Good management eliminates as many mistakes as possible. Hotel management sometimes also requires the management of a restaurant.

Turn your hotel restaurant into a premium dining experience that focuses on the whole package including the food, lighting, music, decor, and wine lists. This way, your restaurant won't only be the bait to bring new customers in, but also an incentive for current guests to return when they revisit the area.

Similar to search engines such as Google, OTAs have their own algorithms for how your property will rank, meaning you need to pay close attention to how you build your profile on them. Fighting food waste at your hotel goes beyond feeding people and helping the environment – it also improves your property's bottom line. Reporting on performance is essential to hotel management. You need to collect and analyse accurate data regularly to see where things are working, and what you need to improve on. Hotel management software is technology that allows hotel operators and owners to streamline their administrative tasks while also increasing their bookings in both the short- and long-term.

Managing a hotel isn't all about managing the physical property, it's also about managing intangible things like reputation. There are many apps in the market to help with everyday challenges. Organised teams get more done and having everything under control also gives you a better grip on the overall success of the business.

- Keys to an effective hotel distribution strategy

How to increase your hotel's occupancy rate

Effective revenue management strategies for hotels

Essential strategies to increase your hotel room sales

Facility management, or FM, is a broad discipline that includes a variety of industries, from food to technology, manufacturing to e-commerce and beyond. But, though the core of each business may be completely different from even its closest competition, successful facility management practices are easily interchangeable from enterprise to enterprise. As a matter of fact, it is one of the only job titles that can be found in, basically, any small to large organizations, including public entities, like schools and hospitals, to private businesses, like those that manage their inventory in warehouses.But, reciprocal tendencies aside, facility management procedures and techniques must be highly-specialized for the business in which they are being used. Because the discipline covers complex specifics, including business continuity planning and even fire safety, it's key that your organization offers a holistic outlook on its facility management procedures.

- The Core Competencies of Hotel Facility Management strategy

According to the International Facilities Management Association (IFMA), facility management is an interdisciplinary practice that "considers the coordination of people, place, process, and technology." Broken down, this means that a facility manager is responsible for the success of the all facets of the facility, including organization, safety, security, and maintenance, along with the key, everyday operational practices. Facility Management Core Competencies

It may seem like an overwhelming job to put on one person or one small team – and it is an overwhelming job – but what's important to remember is the fact that facility management is just one aspect of what makes a healthy business. Simply put, all necessary departments must work with facility managers to build a business' overall success.

Safety – It's the facility management team's job to ensure the safety of all of the employees and customers occupying the property. This responsibility spans all possible environmental health and safety issues, particularly ones that concern the building and its equipment, specifically. Failure to do so can mean serious business in the form of fines, lost business, or even prosecution if it was deemed that the manager or business' negligence caused casualties or permanent environmental damage. Fire, for example, is usually right at the top of the radars of facility managers because it's a preventable tragedy that, when prepared for sufficiently, can save lives and valuable inventory. A thorough facility management team can protect its company best by guaranteeing that all parts of the facility are up-to-code, its employees are trained well, and all permits and certificates are completely valid. This function entails everything from safe and efficient lighting to flooring choices.

Security – In regards to importance, second to safety is facility security, yet another important piece of the puzzle in which the facility management team must answer to. Though larger companies or ones with particularly pricey inventory or equipment might make the wise choice to outsource its security needs in the form of a private firm, it's still the role of the facility manager to ensure that the firm performs competently. Technology advancements like biometrics and wearables are making it possible to maintain strict access control for high-security areas, but it's up to facility managers to stay on top of these developments and make smart security technology investments. In addition to general safety, it's also important that the facility management team has the technological know-how to safeguard and maintain its priciest hardware. This role is a key one as it doubly affirms that assets are protected just as closely as the safety of the community.

Maintenance and Inspections – No matter the focus of the organization, one of the most heedless things that a facility management team can do is slack off on its building maintenance duties. Every part of the building, including installed machinery such as HVAC systems, must be maintained by the facility management team. Because some facilities contain countless elements that need regular maintenance, establishing and following strict maintenance schedules helps to ensure that all moving and permanent parts of the facility stay up-to-date and working well into the future. Along with general maintenance, inspections are also something that facility management teams must always be ready for. They can prepare the business by conducting internal inspections, as needed, for the many formal regulatory inspections they might incur annually. Of course, the team must also take into account any time the facility undergoes a major change in hardware, level of inventory, or capacity – and, they must also keep their eyes on all changes in laws that could affect their current procedures.

Business Continuity Planning – Part of leading an effective facility management team means planning for "worst case scenarios." This means that each team must sit down with the powers that be to come up with a plan in case disaster strikes and the business can't afford to shut down operations. For example, let's say that a community college endures a major fire and the authorities have deemed the entire main building a total loss. The community college is currently in the middle of a semester which it can't cut short – this is a situation where prior business continuity planning is key. If this were done in the aforementioned scenario, the facility management team would have already come up with alternate locations to hold classes and operate the organization's administrative duties. In addition to the new venue, the team would have already made a solid plan for the temporary facility's security, maintenance, and hardware needs.

Daily Operational Duties – In addition to serving as the safety and security liaisons for the facility, it's also important that facility management teams are organized to handle the inherent day-to-day challenges that might arise. Depending on how the given organization is structured, this can mean anything from mending a leaky roof in the women's restroom to even fixing a jammed fax machine.

Maintenance Operations

No matter the size of the organization, it's key that the higher-ups bring on a facility manager that can hire or outsource a reliable, competent team. And, because not every company is filled with safety-minded individuals, it is the job of this manager to act as an advocate for the workers and/or customers that occupy their facility. Having this level of tenacity and attention-to-detail in the facility management spectrum is necessary – in fact, it can save a business or even a life.

Operations and Management Strategies

The current presiding global facilities management organization, the International Facility Management Association, calls for these leaders to take a more tactical and shrewd approach when it comes to protecting the future of their business' properties. In the IFMA's Strategic Facility Planning white paper, the organization makes a call for facility managers to carry out SFP (strategic facility planning) as it "helps to avoid mistakes, delays, disappointments, and customer dissatisfaction." In addition to the aforementioned safety and maintenance-heavy responsibilities, the IFMA wants managers to begin looking beyond their normal duties so that they can better aid in the efficiency of their organizations.To do this effectively, managers must compile two things: 1) a strategic facility plan and 2) a master plan for the facility. Let's take a look at how each one can better strengthen the overall productivity of the business:

Strategic Facility Plan (SFP) – In order to compile a comprehensive SFP, the IFMA urges managers to first become acquainted with three very important things: the core values or changing values of the organization and how facilities must reflect the values, the compiling of an in-depth analysis of the facility, including location, capability, and condition, and, finally, a fundamental understanding of how the organization's goals might make for the ramping up or down in regards to facilities. If the manager can confirm each and every one of these benchmarks with the appropriate departments and find a way to support their organization's ambitions while carrying out effective day-to-day practices, then they will be acting as a truly "strategic" support system. This blend of "current" and "future" allows for all parties involved to grapple with changes as they come in the most effective manner possible.

Facility Master Plan – Any facility manager should already be constantly re-working their facility's master plan, a framework that looks at the "physical environments that incorporate the buildings," but that doesn't mean that each is as comprehensive as it could be. Let's take a look at what a holistic master plan that takes both the day-to-day tasks as well as the future space use analyses into consideration.

Here's what a facility master plan in a hotel should include:

Zoning, regulation, covenant assessments

Space standards/benchmarks descriptions

Program of space use

Workflow analyses

Engineering assessment and plan

Block, fit, or stacking plans

Concept site plan or campus plan

Architectural image concepts

Long-term maintenance plan

Construction estimates

Phasing or sequencing plan (the sequence or projects)

Once a hotel facility manager does the proper footwork to make contact with all departments that influence their facility, they will be better equipped to support their organization as it makes profitable moves in the future.

Project Management for Streamlined Facilities

Because the name of the game for facility managers is safety, maintenance, and planning, it surely comes as no surprise to you that the manager must also develop and execute a laundry list of projects to ensure that everything on and in the building is running smoothly. Facility Management Equipment Log.

Here are some examples of how project management tactics can streamline a facility's overall efficiency:

The establishment of project schedules that include both scope and budgetary needs

Advising all workers, including employees and consultants, on development and work progress

Maintaining transparent databases on each and every project to ensure that higher-ups are advised of any changes to schedule, budget, or manpower in real time

The compiling of comprehensive training schedules to ensure that all employees are properly certified for any regulatory changes that may arise

Conducting budget estimates for all proposed construction projects

Coordinating any service or maintenance upgrades for the facility's systems

Conduct meetings and get approval for necessary space alterations which might be necessary for the modernization of the space

Developing internal audit processes to ensure that all applicable regulatory standards are met, including the new ISO 41001, Facility management – Management systems – Requirements with guidance for use

Hotel Facilities Demand Organization

Best Leadership Practices for Facility Managers

Facility management is a big, often complex job that requires a strong, forward-thinking, and most of all, responsible leader who thinks about their facility's needs in as holistic of a manner as possible. In addition to possessing these qualities, the most informed managers either have years of diverse industry experience under the belt or have earned a specialized degree in the discipline. Continuing education is also common in the field, and there are a number of facilities management courses that can help facility managers stay up-to-date on current trends and best practices.

Facility Management Role

So, now that we have an idea of what an adept facility manager might look like on paper, let's delve into the most effective leadership practices they can implement to guarantee the safety and efficiency of their organization:

They are on the same page as the higher-ups in regards to the future – As mentioned throughout this guide, being a powerful facility manager means looking ahead into the future. From compiling business continuity plans in the event of a disaster to keeping an open line of communication with other departments, the manager understands that they will only be a true leader if their facility and staff are ready to roll with the changes.

They know how to plan and budget – Facility managers know the current value of every part of their facility's infrastructure – and how much it will take to upgrade. They also have an acute understanding of how their budgetary needs might ebb and flow moving forward so that they can accurately propose budgetary changes to the powers that be.

They have a feel for developing a great team – Depending on the specific needs of the organization, the facility manager might be responsible for the hiring and training of the facility workers, contractors, or even consultants. This means that the manager needs to have an innate understanding of the duties and restraints of each position and how they can best work together to make the most capable team possible. Remember, these team members are ultimately in control of the safety and security of the facility, very important jobs that can break an organization in regards to liability if something were to go awry.

They are willing to listen – It's only natural for facility managers to become frustrated with higher-ups calling for big shifts who might be physically disconnected with the facility, but that doesn't mean that they are wrong. Dynamic leaders collaborate with all departments by listening to their propositions and ideas. By doing so, they create an open, safe line of communication that, no matter the outcome, will strengthen interdepartmental relations.

Hotel Facility management is a challenging job, and it's one that grows increasingly complex as technology advancements reshape old processes into newer, streamlined approaches. The best facility managers understand exactly how to balance smart technology investments that boost efficiency while minimizing risks (e.g., fiscal and safety risks) for a positive influence on the bottom line. In short, facility management is the backbone of operations across a multitude of industries today.

In business world, the perspectives of entrepreneurial Strategies are crucial for growth. Driven by this urge, the strategic management has modeled concepts and principles towards this managerial cause. In its approach, the strategy evaluates the business operational environment and focus on the inner working of a company. In this case, it develops methodological advances and ideas that follow and target at predicting the transformation of the management practice. This paper aims to examine the strategies of management employed by the Marriott Hotels executives. For example, The Marriott Hotels choose the 'generic' strategy.The differentiation Strategy is the 'generic' approach chosen by The Marriott Hotels to market it products in the highly competitive hotel industry. Marriot International is an enterprise that has successfully employed the business-level generic strategies. The business is a global franchise or and a lodging and hotel facilities entity. These products display the Marriott facility to be the one of the top players in the accommodation sector, and the phenomenon is projected to be stabilised for a number of future years. This projection is anchored on the various competitive advantages at the disposal of the company (Marriott International Brands 34). These advantages include cost, uniqueness, and their competitiveness extent. The Marriott Global Incorporation follows a variety of strategies at the entrepreneurial level. The plans are showcased by the Marriott's vast brand portfolio that enables them to command a strong market presence in the hospitality industry. This approach is part of the strategy for the entity persuinng differentiation. The Marriot Incorporation differentiation plan is factored in developing a service and product that satisfies, in a unique way, the need of its customer. The approach is affected by the provision of several options of lodging that ranges from average to premium priced packages. The secret of value-addition offered by the uniqueness of the firm warrant it to peg a higher premium charge for hotels in the upmarket.

The way through which Marriott Hotels is implementing its strategy of differentiation

For example, Marriott Hotels is implementing its strategy of differentiation by integrating its market segmentation strategies with its every operation step. The Marriott management immediately realized, from the beginning, that one brand of the whole hotel enterprise could not offer adequate catering to every need of the guests (Harmon 2). As a result, the hotel chain utilized an extensive strategy of differentiation by creating various hotel brands. Each of the product names offered services to varied clients in the hospitality market. In this strata, products range from the low-end to high-end services. The upscale offers comprise of such products as Marriott JW Resorts, Ritz Carlton and Spas that are packaged for customers who desire luxurious and high-end accommodations (Marriott International Brands 34). Others are the Marriott Courtyard with a designed in-room space offices for the business traveler. The Fairfield Inn product offers quality service for the budget travelers. This mix of a variety of brands ensures that the Marriott International meets and fulfills any desire of every consumer regardless of her or his purchasing power. In this segmentation, the JW Marriott, Ritz Carlton, Marriott Resorts, and Hotels are promoted towards the clients desiring more experience in upscale lodging. These customers also have a strong will to pay a relatively higher cost of an added luxurious amenity. The Marriott Courtyard segment offers the business travelers an office space set-up in their units where they may be productive after business trip hours. Springhill Suites segments is a hotel offering that is moderate for a family or a single traveler with living area for unwinding before embarking on a good rest at nights (Harmon 2). The Townplace Suites and Residence Inn give accommodations an extended stay for traveler's searching for a place that is more like home. These hostels encompass living areas, full-size kitchens and sleeping quarters. In addition, the hospitality chain has a budget traveler suite with accommodations of Marriott quality. In overall, the firm has as a Marriott for all form of occasions. These products and helps the chain in its noble mission of molding loyalty to its customers. As illustrated, through this segmentation Marriott Hotels has implemented its strategy of differentiation in a unique way.

Evaluation of the Marriott Hotels' current strategy in the light of the analysis

In my opinion, the market segmentation strategy used by the hotels is a proper approach to creating a wide base of consumer. There is success for the company in this strategy, especially by segmentation its market in threefold and allocating specific price to each brand. These three categories of products. For example, the company has substantially served the high-end market in the Marriott JW Resorts, Ritz Carlton, and Spas products that are packaged for customers who desire luxurious and high-end accommodations. In addition, The Marriott Courtyard segment offers the business travelers an office space set-up in their units where they may be productive after business trip hours (Harmon 2). Springhill Suites segments is a hotel offering that is moderate for a family or a single traveler with living area for unwinding before embarking on a good rest at nights. The Townplace Suites and Residence Inn give accommodations an extended stay for traveler is searching for a home-like place. As a result, every consumer need is properly and adequately catered for without compromise in the high-quality service pursued by the Marriott Hotels management.

In my opinion, the hotel has other strategies that it may exploit. These include the Franchising and the approach Cost Leadership in its marketing mix. In addition to the market segmentation, the company should try to strengthen each brand as per its category. In this case, the firm will be able to create a strong brand identity with its consumers at all its levels of the market. As a result, it will be able to capture the mass market for its products. The increased demand will enable the firm to move high volumes of products thereby increasing its turnovers. As a result, it will be able to design a proper pricing system, as high turnovers will have high-profit levels. In addition, the company may employ the franchising strategy. In this case, it will be able to forego its traditional direct control of its hotels especially in the economies overseas. As a result, it might now concentrate its crucial business (Harmon 2). Furthermore, it will win in substantially reduce the financial risk associated with enormous businesses while allowing a more non-participatory global growth. The company may use this opportunity of franchising, as many investors are willing to collaborate with it due to its strong Marriott brand. This strategy will offset the threat of stiff competition the company is facing from its rival as Hilton and other hotels.

- Hotel cost / expense control management strategy

For hotel owners looking to grow their business, a robust revenue management strategy is of the utmost importance, helping to optimise business results. However, under the broader revenue management umbrella, there are many smaller strategies that can help to facilitate growth. In this article, you find nine revenue management strategies that those in the hotel industry can employ to achieve this ultimate objective.

What is Revenue Management?

Revenue management is a popular concept within the hotel industry, and is used to optimise a hotel or resort's financial results by maximising revenue. The accepted definition is: selling the right hotel room, to the right customer, at the right time, for the right price, via the right channel, with the best cost efficiency.Typically, it requires businesses to make effective use of performance data and analytics to predict demand, establish a dynamic pricing model and maximise the amount of revenue that the company brings in. Although revenue management is applicable to other industries, it has significance in the hospitality industry because hotels deal with a perishable inventory, fixed costs and varied levels of demand. Revenue management is considered important because it takes the guesswork out of key pricing decisions. More extended information about revenue management you can read in the article "What is revenue management?".

Revenue Management Strategies

1. Understand Your Market

In order to implement a successful revenue management strategy, it is imperative that you have a clear understanding of your market, where demand comes from and the various different local factors that might affect seasonal demand. You also need to be aware of your audience and their needs, wants and expectations.

Learn From Our Expert Partners

Moreover, you need to understand the competition that exists within the market and make strategic decisions regarding price, discounts and advertising with this competition in mind. Remember, this competition may not always be obvious, and may not always be in the same location as your hotel.

2. Segmentation and Price Optimisation

The concept of selling the right room to the right person at the right price requires you to appropriately segment your customer base. To do this, you need to identify different 'types' of customer and then look at these different segments and evaluate when they book hotel rooms or hotel facilities, how they book them and other habits. When this is carried out, it allows you to optimise prices for those different segments. One of the key advantages of this is that once prices are optimised for a particular segment, price changes can be minimised. This, in turn, can help to generate customer loyalty from those who appreciate the price consistency you offer.

3. Work Closely With Other Departments

Next, it is important to achieve close collaboration between the various different hotel departments, such as sales and marketing, in order to ensure that your revenue management strategies and their individual departmental strategies are in alignment with one another, and so that you can address challenges collectively. Identify key departmental decision-makers and bring them on board. Work with them to make adjustments to your revenue management strategies, rather than imposing your will, which might be met with resistance. Close collaboration will also help to ensure that you are always presenting consistent messages to customers and clients.

4. Forecasting Strategies

One of the most important aspects of revenue management is forecasting, which allows you to anticipate future demand and revenue, enabling necessary adjustments to be made. Within the hospitality industry, high-quality forecasting relies on accurate records being kept, including occupancy, room rates and revenue. Most forecasting strategies rely heavily on using historical data to spot trends. For example, if you notice an upturn in business in the past three Julys, it is sensible to assume the same may occur next time. However, forecasting also requires an awareness of current bookings, competitors' performance, local events and wider industry trends.

5. Embrace Search Engine Optimisation

Search engines offer one of the single biggest opportunities for those operating in the hotel industry to attract customers, which makes search engine optimisation an important part of a robust revenue management strategy. Through SEO, hotel owners can improve the visibility of their website on search engine results pages. As a consequence, you can improve the chances of attracting business from customers who are not specifically searching for your hotel, but who are searching for a hotel in your location. To achieve this, it is best to operate a solid content marketing strategy, and ensure your website's design is optimised for SEO purposes.

6. Choose the Right Pricing Strategy

There are many different pricing strategies out there, and no one strategy will guarantee success. Instead, those in the hospitality sector need to consider the best strategy for their particular hotel, based on what they have to offer, who they are trying to attract and what strategy their competitors are employing. A competitive pricing strategy, where prices are set based on other hotels prices, puts your business in direct competition and is good when your hotel has more to offer than your rivals do. Yet, in slow seasons, a discount strategy might be best, because a low-paying customer is better than an empty room. Another option is the value-added approach, where rates are higher, but additional value is provided through extras and freebies.

7. Incentives For Direct Bookings

While it is certainly important to cater for all distribution channels and meet customers where they are, rather than where you want them to be, it is also sensible to try to maximise the number of direct bookings that are made. The primary reason for this is because direct bookings do not require the commission to be paid to third parties, which means they are ideal for maximising revenue. One option is to offer exclusive incentives, such as loyalty points, or freebies, for customers who book directly through your own website.

Increase Revenue by Outsourcing Revenue Management

Revenue management is a proven concept, based on the idea of using data and analytics to optimise financial results. It also requires specific skills and knowledge, which means that it can be more effective to outsource revenue management to a third party that specialises in this area.

8. Focus on Mobile Optimisation

For those in the hotel industry, mobile has become one of the single most important revenue streams. As a result, any hotel or resort that is operating without having prioritised mobile optimisation is already operating at a distinct disadvantage compared to their competitors. Make sure your website is optimised for mobile viewing, meaning it loads quickly, the pages display properly on mobile devices and all buttons are fully functional. In addition, you need to ensure your booking process is also optimised, so that customers can book rooms from their mobile device, without needing to switch to desktop.

9. Work With a Freelance Revenue Manager

Finally, in many cases it can be beneficial to enlist the help of a freelance revenue manager, who will be able to bring knowledge, expertise and experience into your organisation. Freelancers are used to coming into hotels and getting to work quickly, and can work as and when you need them. Appointing a full-time revenue manager internally means employing them full-time, but a freelancer will only need to be paid for the work they actually do, meaning less of their time will be wasted. Moreover, because of their established expertise, you will be able to save money on costs associated with training them.

The concept of selling the right hotel room, to the right customer, at the right moment, for the right price, via the right channel is important for maximising revenue and facilitating growth. By following the nine revenue management strategies above, owners in the hospitality industry can improve their chances of achieving this.–

● Hotel service management strategy

For hotels, successful marketing depends on addressing a number of key points. These include: what a company or an industry like a hotel is going to produce; how much a hotel is going to charge; how that particular hotel is going to deliver its products or services to the guests; and how it is going to tell its customers about its products and services. Traditionally, these considerations were known as the 4Ps of the hotel industry — Product, Price, Place, and Promotion. As marketing became a more sophisticated discipline in the hospitality industry, a fifth 'P' was added and implemented— People. And recently, two further 'P's were added, mainly for service industries (like the hospitality industry)— Process and Physical evidence. These considerations are now known as the 7 Ps of service marketing in the hotel industry and sometimes referred to as the marketing mix of the hospitality industry!

In the realm of hotels, marketing is a technique of guiding the customers to choose your goods and service rather than electing the products of your rivals. If a hotel is not accounting for this aspect to make their brand more relevant, they are hampering their profit level, sales, and occupancy. The key for all hotels is to search the correct channel of marketing (which may be Display Advertising, Email Marketing, Pay-Per-Click Advertising (PPC) or Online Public Relations) and disclosing the accurate message in order to influence the targeted guests.

How to manage luxury hotel

The hotel industry has welcomed an unprecedented level of luxury. The rising demand for this extravagance is the increasing guest pursuit of meaningful, personalized experiences that are at the same time unique, exclusive and memorable. At luxury hotels, we work with a number of hotels that offer such services. From this first-hand experience, we have seen that luxury hotel guests don't want to be seen as capricious and wasteful. They value their privacy, yet seek out luxury stays for the unique surprises and thrills that hotel management can offer.However, it may have different kinds of service peformance strategies for luxury and not luxury hotel service perfomance, it may differ as below:

Outstanding Luxury Hotel Services hotel positioning strategy

1. Paparazzi Police

Keeping their vacation private is the minimum that your guests can ask of your luxury hotel, right? But, if for instance you have celebrity guests whose daily life involves being followed by paparazzi, maintaining such privacy presents challenges.To solve this paparazzi problem, for example the Las Ventanas hotel in Los Cabos, Mexico came up with an innovative solution to ensure their guests' privacy and an enjoyable stay. This hotel's staff are equipped with reflective screens, which protect their guests from prying photographers. These "Paparazzi Police" use their screens to shine light at the photographers, which ruins their photos.

2. Personalized Firework Display

We focus on Las Ventanas again, as the luxury hotel offers a spectacular personalized, private fireworks show. Costing around $1,700 per minute, guests can easily personalize it to their liking. It is another service that helps create a truly unique, unforgettable experience in a part of the world that is known for its mesmerizing natural beauty.

3. Hot Air Balloon Ride

Breathtaking experiences are a favorite of luxury hotel guests prepared to pay extra for the privilege. One such experience is a ride in a hot air balloon. And one such hotel that offers this service is the Kale Konak Hotel, located atop Cappadocia in Turkey. Leveraging its position amid a location of natural splendor, this hotel helps its guests by organizing a hot air balloon ride, which promises a stunning experience of a lifetime.

How can your hotel take advantage of its surroundings to offer thrilling adventures and experiences?

4. Sunscreen-Spraying Booths

Hotel guests don't want to worry about anything when they enjoy the beach or the resort pool at remote and exclusive locations. And if there's one thing that can ruin a vacation, it's sunburn. Proactive hotels take it upon themselves to help guests prevent burning up by including sunscreen-spraying booths as a standard luxury hotel service. In particular, many Caribbean hotels offer this service, loved by solo travelers, couples and families alike. After all, even if a guest carelessly forgets to apply sunscreen and suffers the consequences, they are much more likely to associate your hotel with the negative experience. By offering sunscreen-spraying booths, you cancel out this possibility and create a value-added service for your guests, so they can enjoy their vacation in full.

5. Sunscreen-Spraying Booth

For hotels that are located with expansive countryside hills nearby, paragliding is a luxury service that ticks all the boxes. It can be relatively inexpensive to run, offers a riveting add-on experience, and will hep move you head and shoulders above your competition. A novel twist is to offer a paragliding route from atop a hill to the hotel entrance at the bottom. With the help of a professional paragliding expert, the most demanding and fearless of guests can enjoy an extreme sport and make a rock-star entrance at your hotel.

6. Secret, Invite-Only Room

It is an increasing trend to offer a secret or hidden service. But the catch is that it can't be bought by money. Certain luxury desires can only be attained with the right contact, recommendation, knowledge or invite. Think of the appeal of speakeasy bars, or exclusive, secret societies. Take advantage of this winning trend by creating a secret, invite-only room in your hotel. Make it exceptionally beautiful or intriguing, or offer services that are unobtainable to "regular" guests. Choose a secluded or forbidden area of your hotel for its location. And of course, this secret room cannot be advertised on your official channels, such as your website.

7. In-Suite Shopping

Luxury is never having to pack a suitcase, no matter where you go or for how long. Take inspiration from London's

Hotel Café Royal, which offers its guests a personalized, curated styling service for all occasions during their stay. Guests check in without luggage and find a selection of clothes handpicked by a personal stylist to choose from in their suite upon arrival. By offering your guests this luxury option, you make them feel like pop stars. And not only is it extremely convenient, everyone loves discovering a new outfit to wear and feeling like a VIP.

8. Complimentary Luxury Car Drives

Some of the very best 5-star luxury hotels offer their guests luxury cars during their stay too, for free. Hotels like The Peninsula Beverly Hills in California provide their guests with Rolls-Royce and Infiniti cars, having developed a strong relationship with the high-end car manufacturers. If you have the budget to ramp up your luxury hotel with this complimentary service, it will help serve as a magnet for guests eager for exclusive experiential stays. And if not, there are other options. For instance, you can approach high-end car leasing companies to enquire about reaching an agreement. And it doesn't have to be luxury cars. You could also tap into the growing importance of sustainability to guests by offering premium eco-friendly cars.

9. No-Internet Digital Detox Zone

C-suite executives and stressed millionaires with companies and scores of people dependent on their decisions and attention find it difficult if not impossible to disconnect. With so much responsibility on their shoulders, they are often available around the clock, seven days a week. Even if they do get an opportunity to get some much needed time off, they are often interrupted by a colleague who needs their input on the latest emergency or major decision at their company. Cue the growing prevalence of no-internet resorts. No WiFi, no mobile internet signal and no onsite computers to access the web. Completely and utterly offline.

This digital detox is increasingly sought after by hyper-connected individuals who want to get away from it all, even if only for a few days, offering them total peace and quiet, without the fear of their phone blowing up with calls, messages and emails. For typically busy company executives and such individuals in an ultra-connected world, this kind of opportunity to unwind and relax "off the grid" is an increasingly exclusive luxury.

On conclusion, more and more hotels are trying to make their guests' stay as special as possible so in the near future, many of these unconventional services will be offered by more luxurious hotels all over the world. This being said, a great hotel manager goes beyond what customers say they want, helping them to realize their wildest dreams by combining fun, joyful experiences with exclusive, unique services that make them feel important.

For hotels, successful marketing depends on addressing a number of key points. These include: what a company or an industry like a hotel is going to produce; how much a hotel is going to charge; how that particular hotel is going to deliver its products or services to the guests; and how it is going to tell its customers about its products and services. Traditionally, these considerations were known as the 4Ps of the hotel industry — Product, Price, Place, and Promotion. As marketing became a more sophisticated discipline in the hospitality industry, a fifth 'P' was added and implemented— People. And recently, two further 'P's were added, mainly for service industries (like the hospitality industry)— Process and Physical evidence. These considerations are now known as the 7 Ps of service marketing in the hotel industry and sometimes referred to as the marketing mix of the hospitality industry!

Hence, in the realm of hotels, marketing is a technique of guiding the customers to choose your goods and service rather than electing the products of your rivals. If a hotel is not accounting for this aspect to make their brand more relevant, they are hampering their profit level, sales, and occupancy. The key for all hotels is to search the correct channel of marketing (which may be Display Advertising, Email Marketing, Pay-Per-Click Advertising (PPC) or Online Public Relations) and disclosing the accurate message in order to influence the targeted guests.

Before providing an excellent service is experienced, it first has to be delivered. It, therefore, means that the process of choosing to use a service might be perceived as risky since one is buying something that is intangible. To reduce this uncertainty, physical evidence such as case studies should be used. This can be done by keeping the facilities clean, well decorated and tidy. The physical evidence that is demonstrated by an organization should be able to confirm the assertions of the customers. Although it might not be possible for the customers to experience the service before they have purchased, the customers can talk to other customers with experience!

GUEST ENGAGEMENT GUEST EXPERIENCE HOTEL INDUSTRY HOTEL MARKETING HOTEL REVENUE MANAGEMENT MARKETING

Hotel-sales-strategies-direct-bookings

Your worst nightmare as a hotelier is walking down the halls of your hotel and realising that rooms are empty. There's a sad stillness that not only marks the sign of a quiet moment, but also the sign of a failing business strategy. In order to avoid this situation at any point during the year – even during the slow travel season – you need to implement sales strategies that will improve business and continually bring in more guests. The first, and most obvious reason, to focus on increasing hotel room sales is because this will drive revenue. With additional revenue on-hand, you are able to provide guests with the service they expect, as well as move the hotel forward into the future. Before you can dabble in additional packages, add-on excursions and luxury upgrades, you must be able to sell rooms. Another reason to prioritise hotel room sales techniques is to provide guests with the atmosphere that they expect. A vacant or nearly empty hotel is not a good look to people who are staying there. You want to be able to sell as many rooms as possible so that you can provide your guests with a lively, charismatic environment.

● Essential hotel room sales strategies

Every hotelier needs to implement sales strategies that work best for their own target market as well as for their local destination. Ultimately, it is up to the hotel operator or manager to create a customised sales strategy that will drive the most room sales at their own individual property, but these are some of the top hotel room sales strategies to consider:

1. Hotel group sales strategy

This strategy may require an overhaul of your normal marketing and sales approach. The idea is to sell rooms and meeting spaces to corporate groups; it's important you can offer a deal for both. Landing these types of sales requires innovation but it can be very beneficial for repeat business if you do. The most cost effective way to secure group bookings is by connecting directly to planners. You can list your property on venue marketplaces where planners can view floorplans, photos, and unique differentiators. It's also important to segment your target audience so you can make compelling offers to the right kind of groups for your property.

2. Hotel direct sales strategy

With this sales strategy, the priority is to earn direct bookings online from as many guests as possible. Direct bookings are the most beneficial booking for hotel operators because these bookings generate the most revenue. There are no agents or other distribution partners that must be paid a commission when a guest books directly online. In order to implement a direct booking strategy, hotel managers should invest in an online booking system that syncs with their existing website and property management system. Hotel operators should also prioritise their social media strategy when focusing on increasing direct bookings.

3. Destination marketing sales strategy

This type of sales strategy requires a hotel operator to work with other tourism business professionals in their destination to promote the region as a whole. Through a destination marketing campaign, local businesses team up to target the most powerful inbound tourism markets and drive more traffic to the general area.

4. Cross-promotional sales strategy

With this sales strategy, hotel managers need to identify and evaluate various large events that will be taking place in the local region throughout the calendar year. Then, the hotel operator needs to come up with a promotion that can coincide with the event, ultimately allowing them to earn an influx of bookings that they may not otherwise have had. Opportunities that are ideal for a cross-promotional sales strategy include an upcoming industry conference, a concert or a major sporting event.

5. Guest rewards sales strategy

Many travellers today, particularly the powerful millennial generation, value the opportunity to earn rewards with the companies that they do business with. Hotels, in particular, have great success with rewards programs. In a guest rewards sales strategy, the manager or operator should develop a system that rewards guests for staying frequently, for purchasing upgrades, and for referring friends and family members. A rewards sales strategy often generates repeat bookings, which are particularly lucrative for hotel operators.

6. Revenue management sales strategy

This type of sales strategy aims to maximise the number of rooms booked at any point in the year, regardless of the typical travel traffic at that particular point in time. Typically, a revenue management plan requires hotel operators to drop room rates during the low season in order to encourage bookings, while raising rates during high traffic times. During these moments, guests are going to be willing to pay higher rates to get a room, so it's worthwhile raising rates to generate more revenue per available room.

Other room selling techniques in hotels

Large, overarching, strategies are vital to drive a consistent level of business at your hotel but there are other smaller tactics you can use to sell your rooms or generate more revenue from each guest:

Upselling – Upselling is the process of selling a more expensive version of the service or product your customer is buying. The methods you use to upsell need to be handled with a degree of delicacy. The timing, tone, and regularity with which you upsell is the key to the success of your efforts. You don't want to seem pushy so treat it as an exercise in awareness rather than a sales pitch. Make sure guests know what options are available to them but let them initiate any further interest.

Re-marketing – Re-marketing allows you to reach out to potential guests who have visited your site without finalising their booking. Many travellers will visit a variety of different websites to explore their options during the research phase of their online booking journey. With re-marketing strategies, you can access these customers again at different points during their online booking experience and remind them to visit your site again to book with you.

Incentives or cross-selling – Cross-selling is the process of selling an additional, supplementary product or service to complement the product or service your customer is buying. Offering incentives in the form of additional products or services may just be the thing that gets your guest to confirm a booking. Think added-value items like a free massage, or a local tour.

Build local partnerships – Unless your hotel is located in a remote or isolated destination, there should be plenty of other businesses and attractions you can form a mutually beneficial partnership with. Co-promoting with restaurants, specialty shops like ski hire, adventure companies, theme parks, or museums can help lead to easy and effective marketing. And these kind of partnerships can work no matter how the guest is planning their trip – be it to book accommodation first, or create their itinerary before looking for a hotel.

Make booking easy on your website – The importance of a good website experience for travellers can't be overstated. Nothing will drain their excitement quicker than a slow, confusing, or convoluted website. Make sure yours is clean, intuitive, mobile-friendly, and has clear action buttons such as 'book now' for potential guests to click. When direct bookings are so valuable, your website has to be a priority.

● Hotel promotion strategy

Promotions are great because you can be very flexible and targeted with what you offer, and often they'll grab the attention of travellers searching online. This is where it can actually be useful to steer into what guests might expect, such as promotions around seasons, themes, events, direct, bookings, or partnerships.

1. Seasonal promotions

Most destinations experience a low season, where tourism is not as active as other parts of the year. However, with the right deals your hotel doesn't have to suffer through empty rooms and hallways. Try to incorporate discounts with eye-catching promotions like 'Summer Getaways' and 'Winter Retreats' and remind travellers how beautiful your destination is and how much they can see when there are less crowds.

2. Themed promotions

These will be attention-grabbing and very relevant for travellers looking into booking a stay in the area. For example you might offer promotions around honeymoons or anniversaries if you're in a romantic locale, adventure deals if you're out of the major cities, or ultimate relaxation experiences if you're a coastal hotel. Appealing to different lifestyles or family setups is always a good idea.

3. Event-based promotions

It makes a lot of sense to capitalise on events and include them in your promotions. People will already be researching these events so if your hotel has a deal on in conjunction with them, awareness of your hotel should increase along with site traffic. These events might include music or art festivals, Easter or Christmas events, circuses, travelling markets, sporting events etc. With a booking you might offer discounted tickets, adapt the hotel experience to match the events, create special rates.

4. Direct booking promotions

Placing exclusive promotions within your booking engine on your website will give travellers an incentive to book direct instead of via an OTA. It will also help establish your hotel website as your most important distribution channel and help increase profit by eliminating OTA commission fees. The incentive might be a discount, or it might also be an added extra such as a bottle of wine, restaurant voucher, or amenity gift cards.

5. Partnership promotions

Combining with other businesses will reduce the cost of promotion and marketing, and give you wider coverage as long as your partner holds up their end of the bargain. It may also give you access to a new market and create ongoing business. Common partnerships include those with theme parks, restaurants, cinemas, museums, sporting arenas, adventure and tour guides. It's one thing to create your promotions, but remember you need people to see them. Always advertise on your social media channels and ensure your search engine optimisation is strong

6. Mobile-only promotions

Year on year, nearly every statistic points to an upsurge of mobile usage on hotel, travel, and booking websites, with projected numbers even more prominent. As quick as online booking overtook more traditional and outdated methods, mobile is starting to usurp desktop. Implementing smart and effective mobile strategies will boost customer experience and keep your hotel competitive within an industry that never stops innovating.

● Hotel packages strategy

Use other businesses to enrich your packages – Combining your services with that of another tourist attraction in the area is a surefire way to add value to your packages. It also gives you a lot of flexibility on what you can offer guests. Tickets to zoos, tours, theme parks, museums are always popular as are restaurant vouchers. Even concerts or one-off events can be leveraged as short-term packages. This way you can cater for many different guests, those interested in adventure and those more excited by shopping or fine dining.

Promote one-stop shopping – Savvy travellers will look at your packages and wonder exactly what kind of deal they're getting. Unless you and your business partner agree to offer discounted prices it's likely the combined price of a room and a tour package will be similar to the components purchased separately. This is why you need to advertise the convenience and quality of what you're offering, rather than spruiking the cost.

Be creative with your choices – Guests might become rather bored if they see yet another 'romance' package. Try incorporating more interesting content into your packages and their names. For instance a 'bucket list' package might include a selection of passes or discounts to the absolute must-sees of the local area. This will be an attractive option for guests because it's likely they already interested in visiting those landmarks. For business travellers, always focus on convenience such as a package delivering breakfast to their room, free dry cleaning, and transport services.

Use your own property to add value – While most packages include a room and some type of external activity, you can make your packages even more enticing by adding your own service to the mix such as spa-treatments or a bar tab. Guests will want to experience your amenities and they'll be more likely to pay to do so if it's included in a package.

Cater for speciality markets – Never ignore families. Often it's the children you're appealing to most because parents will be looking for activities that will occupy the kids. The same principle applies if you're a pet-friendly hotel. You must also consider guests with disabilities and people with specific occupations that you can give personalised packages to. Don't forget to promote any new packages you create, be they long-term or one-off. Use Facebook, Twitter, Instagram, and your email sends to drum up business. Send any information along to your local tourism office so they can do the same. Another thing to consider is what you want to achieve with your packages. Sometimes they can create a lot of brand awareness, even if they don't attract much business directly.

direct-sales-hotel

To the average traveller you and your competitors will often appear very similar. That's why you need to present an offer that tips the balance and convinces an undecided traveller yours is the best hotel for them. Package deals and extras are an easy, but extremely effective way of doing this, providing you take the right approach.

Your hotel distribution strategy and how it impacts sales

Implementing a successful sales strategy requires you to have an effective distribution strategy. Hotel operators must network with industry professionals as well as agents to sell their rooms to the maximum number of people in a variety of target market segments. Common agents that are included in any distribution strategy include retail travel agents, visitor information centres, local businesses, online travel agents, and destination marketing organisations. Hotel operators and managers must recognise that their distribution network is a fluid, living entity, and they should constantly be looking for new and innovative ways to reach out to new agents and distributors.

In addition to expanding and developing a diverse distribution network, hotel operators must be able to effectively distribute their rooms to all of their agents in real-time. The only way to do this is to partner with a channel manager that connects to your property management system. With a channel manager, hotel operators can provide their live availability to every distribution agent that they have, regardless of their location or time zone. This allows them to sell as many rooms as possible — including securing those valuable last-minute bookings. It also significantly reduces the risk of overbooking rooms at the property, particularly during high-volume times. A channel manager is necessary to implement any sales strategy that a manager wishes to employ at their individual property.

Hotel sales tools

Your hotel sales tools include anything that enable you to bring a guest into your hotel. This might mean your social media accounts, your email marketing campaigns, the phone on your front desk, guest feedback, or back-end hotel technology solutions.Though when you think of tools as objects or functional pieces of software you might consider these to help inform your sales strategy:

Social networks

Analytics tools such as Google

Survey tools

Online travel agents

Property management tools

Booking engines

Channel managers

Website builders

Identifying and using the right tools will depend on your property and the guests you want to attract but for the most part all properties need the same tools. The difference comes in how you use them. Data is extremely important so using tools that can give you detailed reporting functions is a great step to take. With enough data at your disposal, you can make informed decisions about how you sell, gaining an edge over any competitors who are following a 'cookie-cutter' approach. Obviously you need to be smart about you use the budget at your hotel and look at tools which will make life easier while helping deliver more revenue to the business.

Hotel sales software

When you think of sales software in a hotel context, it's better to think distribution software. Three key pieces of technology that could help you are a channel manager, online booking engine, and website builder. While they may not be strictly thought of as sales software, they are the key to driving sales and revenue in the hotel industry.

Channel manager

This is one of your greatest allies when distributing your rooms because it's a tool that manages all the different online travel agents (OTAs) you sell your rooms through, such as Booking.com, Expedia or Airbnb. The main operating principle is called "pooled inventory" which means updates to rates and availability are made automatically across all connected channels whenever and wherever a booking is made. Enabling a more effective way to promote your rooms will naturally create an increase in sales. Read our guide on channel managers to learn more.

Booking engine

Also a reservation system, this will secure online bookings from direct channels such as your own website and social media pages like Facebook. An online booking engine has become essential, especially with the rise of social media. Creating a friction-less experience for guests when they book direct will boost your conversion and improve your sales results. Read our guide on booking engines to learn more.

Website builder

This takes away the need for you to hire a web designer. Instead you can use this software to create a beautiful, search engine optimised, guest converting website in minutes. You simply have to provide your content and choose from a number of available templates. Your website is a major selling point for travellers – winning them over with an amazing first impression is imperative. With the right technology in place, you will be able to easily and effectively implement your hotel room sales strategies. To learn more about these hotel sales tools and to find out if they are the right choice for your hotel property, check out how they work in a video demo.

What to expect from these hotel room sales strategies? When you sell hotel rooms, you do more than just get another guest in the door of your property. You are able to improve your hotel business in its entirety. Here are a few of the benefits that you will realise when you employ hotel room sales strategies that are designed to increase hotel room sales:

You will generate more revenue consistently throughout the entire year. An effective hotel sales strategy allows you to earn as much revenue as possible, regardless of the seasonal ebbs and flows of the tourism industry. You will be able to make improvements to your property. As you begin to earn more revenue from your bookings, you can make improvements that will generate buzz about your brand and continue to sell more rooms. Finally, you will be able to move beyond standard sales strategies and begin creating packages that increase the revenue you generate per guest. Once your sales steadily increase, you can begin to expand your offerings. Romance packages, adventure packages and luxury upgrades allow you to sell more rooms while also boosting the revenue you earn per booking.

● Hotel revenue management technology

What is revenue management for the hospitality industry? Revenue management refers to the strategic distribution and pricing tactics you use to sell your property's perishable inventory to the right guests at the right time, to boost revenue growth. Other products such as your amenities and food and beverage offerings will also come into the picture. Revenue management revolves around measurement of what customers from different segments are willing to pay, and this can only be done by measuring and monitoring the supply and demand of your hotel rooms.

Every traveller has a maximum value they can offer your hotel; revenue management is about capturing as much of this value as you possibly can. Preferably you'll do this by convincing the guest to book direct, purchase extensions, up-sells or extras, and become a return visitor. The best strategies are based on the understanding that hotel pricing is fluid, and can change from one day to the next. This is why you should never be afraid to increase your rates. Customers actually expect increases over time – most businesses where consumers spend money are varying their prices based on demand and shifts in costs.

Effective hotel revenue management strategies can also help hoteliers:

Better manage resources

Protect against rostering too many staff during slow periods

Ensure adequate numbers of staff are working during the busiest times

With all this in mind, revenue management can drive the entire business plan when implemented effectively. Your hotel distribution strategy is also a vital part of your revenue management plan. Make sure you are on the internet distribution channels that promote your destination online. They have strong marketing power and can put your hotel in front of many customers you can't contact directly.

How to increase hotel revenue? Many strategies come into play when driving more revenue to your hotel, and many of them don't involve raising prices or playing with your rates much at all. Not least of these is satisfying your customer. If the product you offer is universally recognised as quality, you have the grounding to charge a higher price. If guests feel like they are getting maximum value for their money, it's very likely they'll be willing to spend more. Getting more out each individual guest who stays with you is a great way to increase the overall revenue of your hotel. For instance, guaranteed revenue from a guest you convince to stay an extra night by discounting the additional night might be worth your while, especially in low season.

A list of general tactics you can use to improve your hotel's revenue stream:

Be bookable online

These days travellers enjoy the flexibility, convenience, and value of booking online. By connecting to online travel agents/more online travel agents you'll easily see an uplift.

Build a revenue culture

Who's on your revenue team? Everyone! Anticipatory service + proactive revenue-minded employee = emotionally connected customer with engaged loyalty and higher revenue returns.

Sell other hotel products

Revenue opportunities extend far beyond simply selling your rooms. Think about the amenities you have on site and what your are charging for them, and go even further by offering hotel guests the chance to purchase items like soap, utensils, towels etc – especially if your hotel has a unique sense of style.

Leverage events and attractions

Local events and attractions are a great opportunity to put together packages for guests or offer additional services such as transport. The benefits are two-fold – guests will enjoy their stay more and your hotel will generate more income.

As you move away from tactics and towards fully fledged strategies around your revenue and room sales, you need to start understanding your key performance indicators (KPIs). Once you know what you should be looking at you can start analysing the data and developing ways to manipulate them in your favour.

As an introduction, these are the metrics you can explore:

Occupancy rate

ADR (Average daily rate)

RevPAR (Revenue per available room)

TrevPAR (RevPAR + ancillaries)

GOPPAR (Gross operating profit per available room)

RevPASH (Revenue per available seat hour) – useful if you have a hotel restaurant

The principle that you should always keep in mind is to assess market conditions in real-time and adapt accordingly.

Revenue management strategies

You need a revenue management strategy to remain sustainable – that's the short story. Ideally, you'll even be able to turn a tidy profit each year. The best hotel revenue management strategies recognise that hotel pricing is fluid, and can change from one day to the next. It's critical that any hotelier creates a revenue management strategy that is adaptable to the current conditions. Often it's more important to focus on your own business and be confident than to worry too much about competitors, at least at first.

Every hospitality business strategy has to have the customer at its heart. How do travellers behave in the current landscape? How do they book and travel? How do they experience and explore? What do they require? What are their expectations? It's vital you have an idea of these factors if you want to squeeze the most value out of each guest that enters your door. The better you know the guest the more guest loyalty you can generate, which is extremely important for recurring revenue. If you know you have a certain amount of guests returning each year, that's more rooms you don't have to worry about and you can focus more on upselling and cross-selling.

Hotel pricing strategies

There's no pricing strategy that is perfect for any hotel. Each property must consider the pricing strategy, or strategies, that work best for its particular brand. A revenue manager will spend a lot of time analysing data and other influencing factors to ensure the business is operating with the best possible chance to maximise income.

There are a number of questions that should surround your pricing strategies:

What do your guests want?

Which strategy will complement the business mix?

How will different strategies affect connected channels and distribution partners?

How does your strategy integrate with your channels?

Who are the experts that can help determine the right strategy?

With all that in mind, the first priority of pricing should be forecasting. This way you can predict demand so you can get travellers to book early. Then you can raise rates later as availability drops and demand increases. (This is an ideal pricing structure known as the "ascending model" whereby pricing increases closer to an arrival day.) We'll talk more about forecasting and analysis later.

What is dynamic pricing?

Dynamic pricing involves changing room rates daily or even within the day based on real-time market data. Taking supply and demand into account, prices should fluctuate regularly if you want to maximise revenue. This pricing option is well suited in today's market and is one many hoteliers opt to use.

Dynamic pricing examples

Put simply, there will be days where supply and demand will be very different depending on the time of day. In the morning you may have lower rates because your occupancy is low, as is demand. However by that evening supply may have reduced and demand grown. Many factors can drive this, such as competitors putting up their no vacancy signs or setting rates slightly too high, or travellers arriving late for events the next day and so on. You can raise your rates to take advantage of the shifting market and earn more revenue than if you'd kept your rates static.

What is open pricing?

Open pricing defines the flexibility hotels around the globe have to set their prices at different levels depending on the various target markets and distribution channels they deal with.

This luxury of choice allows hotels to forecast more accurately. For example, a high-end hotel may usually attract guests who no budget constraints but in the off-season bookings will drops and the hotel can drop rates to attract travellers who normally would not be able to afford the stay. While the average daily rate of the hotel will be lower, occupancy will remain steady and revenue will continue to turnover.

Other hotel pricing strategies

There are numerous pricing strategies you can use at your hotel as part of your broader revenue management strategy, many of them in conjunction. Here's a list of the most common pricing strategies your hotel might find useful:

1. Value-added pricing

You can set your room rates higher than the local competition while also offering more extras in the basic package. This gives the illusion that the hotel offers a premium experience that focuses on value rather than just low rates.

2. Discount pricing

Used in slow seasons to boost occupancy by dropping base rates. Revenue can be made up through other services in the hotel.

3. Price per segment

Offering the same product at different prices to different types of customers. E.g 'family rate'

Length of stay

When demand outweighs supply, it can help to implement a rule where guests are 'obligated' to stay a minimum number of days. In such cases, lower rates may not be necessary.

4. Positional pricing

Basing your rates off brand strength and reputation.

5. Penetration pricing

Positioning yourself as the cheapest in the market. Be mindful of how travellers will perceive your hotel – you need to retain the opportunity to sell at higher rates.

6. Skimming

Positioning your hotel among the most expensive. Price leaders often achieve among the highest profitability, however the consumers need to clearly understand the reasons that they would pay more for staying at your hotel.

What does hotel market segmentation mean?

Segmenting is a key aspect of revenue management. It allows you to differentiate between the travellers who are coming to your hotel and devise uniques strategies for all of them. For example, the approach you take with young adventurers will be very different to a business professional. However segmentation is more complex than simply business vs leisure, and you can use it to discover trends within your hotel business.

One of the best ways to identify and filter segments is by their reason for travel. Think family holiday, wedding, tourist event, adventure, relaxation, business, etc. However, more and more hotels are adopting a different strategy and defining market segment by how a reservation was made, e.g. Expedia as a market segment. This is known as "blended segmentation" – combining the reason for stay and method of booking. Hotel chains have adopted different applications of this traditional definition of a market segment and channels. Some hotel chains and groups identify a channel as an OTA, and then identify the likes of Booking.com's reward program and Expedia's Egencia (for corporate travel) as sub-channels.

Further segmentation factors that you should take into account include:

Length of stay

Days of the week of stays

Lead time (how long before arrival do they book)

Cancellations

No show ratio

Once you have a good grip on market segments you can start to decide which groups your business wants to focus on more, and which to close out at different times of the year. By drilling down further you might realise certain segments have higher cancellation rates and you could want to resist marketing to them. Each segment will have a unique opportunity for you to gain extra business or revenue.

Here's a quick snapshot of the possibilities:

Loyalty or rewards members – Offer discounts

Mobile booking – Use mobile exclusive promotions

Direct bookings – Make offers that only exist on your website

Walk-ins – Entice extra spending with your amenities

Corporate – A chance to negotiate rates with large companies

Online travel agents – Advertise special event packages

Groups – Combine with tour operators and attractions

Every piece of analysis you do helps you build the optimal business mix for your hotel, so it's important to look at all your options. If selling is a problem, there's always a new way to sell or new market to target. If spending is the problem, there's always a way to entice customers to open their wallets again.

Hotel price forecasting

Forecasting is not only important for rate setting, but also for budgeting purposes. Accurate and effective forecasting requires a strong foundation in historical data. By budgeting and forecasting in advance you'll have plenty of time and opportunity to make strategy adjustments. If you know one point in the year is particularly valuable to your hotel, write your forecast immediately for that period a year in advance. For example, try writing your December 2021 forecast on January 1st 2020.

Key components of an effective forecast include:

Occupancy

Revenue

Room rates

Turnaways/Regrets/Denials – tracking of reservations that are turned away or not booked, and is a critical measurement of demand. Ideally your turnaways are captured and measured on your online as well as direct/ telephone requests.

Spend per room

Reservations

Market trends

Hotel budgeting and demand forecasting

It's a good idea to create demand calendar prior to setting your budgeting plan so you know exactly what you're dealing with. Most hotels forecast every day for next 30 days and every week for next 90 days. A lot of hoteliers do this in a spreadsheet after extracting data from their PMS, but this is where you need really cool tech – and a really easy system – that can do it all in one place.

Take into account factors from last year and also the upcoming year. Mark the following as things to track:

RevPAR last year

Groups or events last year

Demand level indicator last year (High, Medium, Low, Distressed)

Public/bank holidays

School holidays

Indications of increased demand

This will allow you to make informed pricing strategies based on solid data sets.

Before you reach your ideal budget you have to take into account influences such as sales resources, online marketing and distribution, refurbishment needs, and developments your competitor set is making. Your budget should be developed on the basis of this question: at which rate and how many rooms can you sell for every future day? For example, how do you anticipate the business demand and the leisure demand per country? At which rate can you sell on the upcoming months? How will your main corporate accounts behave?

Two distinct demand measurements are constrained demand and unconstrained demand.

1. Constrained demand

Maximum demand for amount of rooms (the maximum number of bookings you could get based on the number of rooms) limited by the physical inventory.

2. Unconstrained demand

Maximum bookings you could get with unlimited rooms based on demand and not limited by the actual physical inventory.

You should identify when unconstrained demand is above the capacity of the hotel. This is an important part of your hotel revenue management strategy. The unconstrained demand will help you calculate your Last Room Value for certain dates, and possible length of stay restrictions that may apply.

Hotel benchmarking

Hotels will commonly benchmark against their competition to evaluate performance. It's not the definitive way to track performance, nor should it be treated as an authority, but it does enable you to see where you stand and how travellers might react.

You'll be required to benchmark on criteria such as:

Prices

Product (luxury, mid-range, economy?)

Level of service

Location

Distribution channel

Remember a competitor is only a competitor if they're targeting the same markets as you, and even then you might not be competing for the same segments at the same time. However, if you can anticipate their strategies, making your own adjustments will become much easier. In the context of the competitor set, results can often look very different. Perhaps you thought you only had an average year when in fact your competitors were much worse off and you were the stellar hotel in the area. Or vice versa.

On conclusion, hotel price control/income management strategy may bring below these benefits to any hotels as below, they may include as below:

1. Less costly errors

While larger hotels might be able to hide or easily overcome a pricing mistake, smaller hotels have less margin for error. An incorrect price at a small hotel will have a bigger impact on ADR and RevPAR.

2. Get more revenue out of every room

With fewer rooms, maximising the rate for each room becomes more critical. The data your technology provides will help you understand who you should be targeting and when. What will be the most valuable demand for you? For example, do you offer rates for group business? Do you offer discounts for long stays?

3. Know your competitors better

To get your own pricing strategy right, you need to know what your immediate competitors are doing. With a pricing intelligence tool you can get an instant all-in-one overview of your competitors rate activity, meaning you can concentrate on why they are adjusting and how/if you should respond.

4. It makes your hotel 'bigger'

Large, branded hotels will already have an RMS in place – and dedicated revenue managers to manage them – and while independent hotels may not be able to afford a robust solution, pricing intelligence tools are an affordable substitute. These use the data and its own algorithms to carry out a real-time analysis of the state of the market, and of demand, in order to calculate ideal room rates. Increasing your data visibility and analysis capabilities gives you more ammunition to compete with large hotel groups who are able to devote full-time staff to revenue management.

5. Manage your time efficiently

Automated market intelligence will allow you to instantly access and act upon pricing data. Knowing when the market will be an easy sell-out or in a quiet period will not only enable you to optimise rates, but with a dependable forecast, you can organise your staff more effectively and improve the guest experience.

6. You can be proactive

The more data you have access to, the less reactive you'll be. Rather than reacting to your competitors all the time, you'll better understand demand, make your own projections, and set intelligent rates.

7. Understand your guests better

A RMS can tell you more about customer behaviour and allow you to attract more bookings. For example, do guests prefer it when your rate applies to every night of their stay, or will they accept varying rates, or do they prefer a total stay price?

8. Your data will come from a single source

Instead of combing through your own data, and then individually doing the same for competitors, an RMS will collate everything for you in one place. Depending on your system, you can do this for up to 15 competitors. If you are a smaller hotel that is new to revenue management strategies, doing everything manually might have you tearing your hair out.

Hence, any hotels can not neglect to consider how to implement price and income management strategy in order to achieve the highest profit aim.

Hotel room living service consumer psychological factors

What are some noticeable hotel service trends in the industry ?

Travellers of today are diverse and want to stay in a place which lets them live out their individuality. They want a hotel which adapts to them, not the other way around. The quest for individualised experiences sets them apart from older generations and has created a challenge for many hoteliers. Guests expect convenience, simplicity and the same instant gratification they enjoy in other areas of their lives. However, hotel and resort staff face the daunting task of handling an endless array of guest issues with a limited team. No matter how well trained front desk staff might be, there are always occasions where long lines form and waiting guests become frustrated. Even a five-minute wait in a check-in line can result in a 50% reduction in guest satisfaction scores. Moreover, guests have become accustomed to the Airbnbs of the world where everything offered to them is extremely relevant and guest has the option to tweak the experience themselves. A similar trend is seen among major hotel chains, where they are using loyalty solutions to promote offers and services based on the guests' preferences and guests have the ability to check-in using mobile. Independent hotels are slowly but steadily starting to embrace such solutions. Personalisation of guest service is no longer a trend, but an obligation for hotels. For example, traditional check-in times were designed for a guest that no longer exists. With long haul travel now very much mainstream, 40% of guests are either arriving on flights before 7AM or leaving on flights that take off after 6PM. Tailoring check-in/check out times to your guest's travel plans is the next battleground of personalisation."

What's the power of automation for hotels and guests?

By combining powerful segmentation with a high-conversion platform, upselling can really help deliver the five R's of revenue management: Selling the right room on the right channel to the right customer at the right time at the right price. Using segmentation properly allows you to target and market to a variety of potential buyers with varying needs, behaviors and budgets. Doing this well will provide you data needed to understand the success of your current revenue strategies and adjust them to maximise your topline in the future. Software providers can take most of that work off your hands. Setting up your segments is done in a matter of minutes, and the software handles the rest, like making sure the segments you choose are offered attractive deals in automatically sent emails."

Can AI platforms or chatbots raise travellers living hotel room choice need ?

Artificial Intelligence (AI) platforms or chatbots can be used to answer simple guest questions and requests freeing up hotel staff to focus on the most complicated guest issues. With mobile keys, bluetooth technology allows mobile devices to communicate directly with the door lock on a guest room.Automation technology can also be leveraged to enhance communication between the hotel staff and guest. Platforms like ours at OpenKey also gives hotels the ability to offer mobile dining, valet requests, concierge, and other guest services – in addition to a digital key – from a mobile app.

I believe that AI technology can boost your hotel brand perception. Automating guest communication opens up a tremendous potential for the hotel. Typically pre-arrival or confirmation emails have been seen as just a system-generated message verifying that a reservation has been made. But this is the first time guest hears about you. "Wouldn't it be nice, if you could delight the guest with a warm greeting, in their own language, with offers that are specific to their profile or segment? With proper tools, this can be easily achieved. For exmaple, if a guest booked a standard room, the system may automatically offer the deluxe room. Or if the airport is far away, offer them a fully arranged taxi service. If targeted properly, upsell and cross-sell efforts can significantly improve guest satisfaction as offers are more relevant. When should you send the offer and who should you send it to? Hotels often send their upsell offers too early when the pain point the hotel is looking to solve is not front of mind for the guest. How should you change your offer depending on the nature of the guest? We'll change how we target and what we offer guests depending on nationality and travel time.

Moreover, AI technology is helping hotels to be more efficient. From the perspective of some hotels which apply AI technology, these hotels look to elevate their service, mobile technology will help us deliver a simplified and efficient guest experience. Today's traveller wants to save time and enjoy their travel, not wait in check-in lines. These hotels could help their customers can be happier about adding a tech solution that will ultimately benefit to their per booking hotel rooms service before they catch pair planes to arrive their country. So, they do not need to spend much time to find the best suitable hotel to live when the hotel can apply AI technology to help them to make hotel choice decision. For example, hoteliers are slowly beginning to understand that technology is not here to replace the human touch but to complement it. Historically guest-facing technology was seen as a toy they can live without. But more and more guests expect these types of convenience services and hotels are realising, this is the new norm. Most guests are not overly expressive about their wants and needs. This means, without tech, it will become extremely difficult to deliver superior guest experience.

How important is connectivity for hoteliers and the platforms they use? As a minimum we need the reservation data from hotel guests, which can be gleaned from the PMS, channel manager, or OTA. So it's important these systems are able to integrate easily with each other. Connectivity is the most important influential factor: Without it any lacking AI technological communication assistance hotels can't automate their services for their clients, which means adding manual work to the hotel's front desk, which simply doesn't work. The ability for technology to continue to help hotels run their businesses, hinges on the providers ability to connect into the hotel's tech stack. Moreover, hoteliers completely understand the pivotal role of tech, but their hands have been tied by the lack of connectivity offered by their incumbent technology systems.

On conclusion, hotel management is about overseeing every operation of the property. This requires knowledge of distribution strategy, finance, customer service, staff management, marketing, and more. Effective inventory management for hotels involves both creating and managing demand, and maximising returns. Revenue management is another huge part of managing your hotel. How do you get more money coming in and achieve business goals?

In the hospitality industry almost everything revolves around the customer, and they're the quickest party to point out any flaws. Good management eliminates as many mistakes as possible. Hotel management sometimes also requires the management of a restaurant. Turn your hotel restaurant into a premium dining experience that focuses on the whole package including the food, lighting, music, decor, and wine lists. This way, your restaurant won't only be the bait to bring new customers in, but also an incentive for current guests to return when they revisit the area. Similar to search engines such as Google, OTAs have their own algorithms for how your property will rank, meaning you need to pay close attention to how you build your profile on them. Fighting food waste at your hotel goes beyond feeding people and helping the environment – it also improves your property's bottom line. Reporting on performance is essential to hotel management. You need to collect and analyse accurate data regularly to see where things are working, and what you need to improve on. Hotel management software is technology that allows hotel operators and owners to streamline their administrative tasks while also increasing their bookings in both the short- and long-term. Managing a hotel isn't all about managing the physical property, it's also about managing intangible things like reputation. There are many apps in the market to help with everyday challenges. Organised teams get more done and having everything under control also gives you a better grip on the overall success of the business.

● How and why hotel managers need to attempt to predict customer booking hotel room behavior or booking hotel room need psychology?

Any hotel management ought need to learn how to predict hotel entertainment consumer individual need in order to attract consumer living choice or increase consumers number easily. I assume that if the hotel can provide the room living service can let any hotel consumers to feel such ad themselves homes feeling. It will influence them to live longer time to stay in the hotel (prolonging hotel room booking days) in the hotel because they can feel themselves homes living feeling. How can make hotel room booking consumers to feel the hotel rooms are such as their homes living feeling? it is one interesting question to discuss. I shall explain as below;

Building hotel living holiday leisure feeling, this factor is very important to influence hotel living consumers to make final extending proplonging living consumers to make final extending or prolonging living days in the hotel. Holidays, by definition , are non-working times, an extended period of anticipated recreation, especially away from home, they can be days of festivity when no work is done. The prolem and opportunity for hotel living entertainment service providers, is that when hotel living customers are on holiday, or at leisure. Hotels need to give a chance of getting away from living holidays, new changing the batteries and for some a change of holiday living of entertainment lifestyle. Hence, if the hotel can let all customers to feel home comfortable living feeling to enjoy their one part of entertainment activity in the whole journeys. The hotel may persuade any one customer (hotel room living customers to prolong any one customer (hotel room living customers to prolong living days in the hotel).

Will the broad framework of leisure defined as time, there are many variations. In general, defining leisure as the time when someone is not working primarrily for money. So, if the hotel room living customer can feel that he/she spends the booking room living fee is value to choose the hotel room to live. The hotel room is such as unoccupied time or free time in whose journey time. Due to he/she feels that this living hotel room time is whose entertainment time. It is essential, then this unoccupied time may persuade him/her to prolong booking hotel room living time in the hotel. For example, he planned to stay 5 days in the hotel, but because he/she feels that the hotel can provide entertainment activities time to attract him/her to stay longer time in the hotel, e.g. gym sport facilities are very attractive sport playing entertainment or hotel restaurant can provide good taste food eating time in special dinner, breakfast, lunch time or swimming pool is beautiful design and large size and it can let him/her to feel actual natural beach environment feeling. Then, any one these extra entertainment facilities or services factors may influence any one customer to spend extending living time in the hotel. Such as this cause, this hotel living customer may feel need to live more two to three days, even more days in this hotel. Hence, hotel leisure as time psychological factor is also important to influence any one hotel room living customer to influence any one hotel oom living consumer to make extending living time decision easily, when they feel this hotel has themselves homes feeling.

Kraus & Bates (1975) add experiencing to the activity. Recreation consists of activities or experiences with are carried on volutarily in leisure time. They are chosen by participants, either for pleasure or to satisfy certain personal needs when provided as part of organized community programs, creation must be designed to achieve constructive goals.

Hence, if the hotel can consist any recreation actvities or experiences to let any one hotel living customer to enjoy to live when are carried on voluntarily in their leisure time. They can choose any kinds of leisure activities to play and live in the hotel, if the hotel any one kind of leisure activity can satisfy their leisure needs. Then, the hotel's any kind of leisure activity can achieve constructive goals to persuade any one hotel room living consumer likes to spend extra money to enjoy any kinds of hotel leisure facilties, instead of spending extra hotel room living expenditure to proplong hotel time in the hotel. Hence, it seems that whether the hotel can provide attractive leisure facilities to let consumers to relationship to influence they their long living or staying time in the hotel.

When asked what were the three most important factors in the development of hotel. Thus equality applied to most leisure facilities ideally, a public transport location may influence any one hotel room customer to choose which hotel location is the nearest to public transport in order to pay cheap transport fee to catch the public transport. This is one low transport fee cost factor to influence the potential hotel room customer choice.

Hence, any hotel's location will be chosen to build to near many public transport tools, e.g. buses, underground trains, taxis, trains station locations. It aims to attract the hotel room booking potential customers can pay cheap public transport fee to arrive their hotel conveniently. They do not need to spend long walking time to arrive their hotels after they catch any one kind of public transport tool to arrive their hotel destinations. Moreover, they do not need to spend long time to find where the hotel locates when they leave the bus stop. So, geographical location factor will be another main factor to influence hotel consumer choices.

The model is based on comparing demand and supply economc theory:

1. identifying where hotel demand is located, whether and to what extent, hotel rooms number demand exceeds hotel rooms number supply in the geographical area and whether , and where, the city has much land to provide space capacity to permit to build hotels number exists in the geographical area in the city.

2. Moreover, local demand is measured on the basis of the number of hotel visits per week in peack period for any hotel room needs determined by:

The total number of travelling visitors in the month rate , the demand rate, the proportion of residents who want to book room to live in the hotel, instead of overseas travelling visitors, the desired frequency of visits, how often overseas travellers want to visit the country and the proportation of visits which arise in the normal peiods per month, such as christmas, New Year etc. public holidays.

So, all of these hotel visitors public transport fee cheap demand number and hotel geographical locations, hotel entertainment facilities , hotel comfortable living feeling, hotel safety, hotel food taste, public holiday and visitor individual travelling need, air ticket price main factors which will influence any one hotel's room demand and supply number absolutely in behavioral economic theory view, instead of hotel environment and service performance basic element factor.

On conclusion, all of these any one element may influence any one hotel customers numner increases or decreases absolutely. Hence, any one hotel management can not neglect to learn how to implement their hotel management strategies effectively.

   ref.

Kraus , R. & Batees , B. (1975). Creation leadership and supervision, W.B. Saunders, philadelphia, P.A.

How to supervise teams in hospitality industry

Any hotels need effective supervisors to supervise their teams in different department in order to raise service efficiency. How to supervise teams which is one important question to any hotels? I shall attempt to explain as below: In hospitaloty industry, alomst everything depends on the psycical labour of many hours (non-managerial workers), waiters, mix drinks, wash dishes, checkquests, clean room, carry bags, mop floors, even security etc. All of these teams must need a supervisor to manage their make products and/or perform services. The human resources for personnel, and training departments are example of staffs who advise line departments, such as the food and beverage department on matters including hiring, disciplining and training.

In general, supervisor responsibility may include: achieving or exceeding the expected results, on time and on budget, planning or determining priorities. Organizing (scheduling), motivating (creative a positive work environment), controlling (monitoring and taking corrective action if mistakes are outside acceptable limits), communicating effectively.

In the reality, in a hotel you may have 5,000 minimum customers are day. You deal with your supervisors. You deal with your subordinates, and you deal with your guests, all coming at you from different directons. Salepeople , deliveries, inspectors, customer complaints and applicants . You jobs interrupt you. So , you are likely to have only a few seconds available when you make many important decisons.

You will feel bus to deal any of either above, these matters every day. Hence, in effective hotel organization, it needs have effective scientific management, it incudes these elements: Standardization, of work procedures, tool and conditions of work through design of work methods by specialists, careful selection of competent people, after training, and elimination of these (traineers) who could not or would not perform, complete and constant overseeing of the work, with total obedience from the worker' incenive pay for meeting the fair day for meeting the fair day's work standard, the worker's share of the increased productivity.

How to innovate hotel tasks to be work simplification or searching for the best way of performance tasks ? Supervisors can use time-and-motion study techniques, developing ways of simplifying tasks than often doubled or triples what a worker would do. This methods and principles had a great impact in food service kitchen, where work simplification techniques have been explored widely adopted. This methods ewere adopted although the idea that have hotel worker should share in the benefits of increased productivity seldom went along with the rest of the system. For example, in hotel kitcehen department , every cooking steep is systematized, and the cooker, dish cleaner is simply taught to run the kitchen dish cleaning machines, cooking machines follow the rules, and speak given phrases. When the kitchen bell rings, the cooker turns the hamburgers on dispenser one time, where is no room for deviation.

How a supervisor can build a positive work climate in his/her hotel department ? He/She needs to know his/her employee expectation and need. You may wonder whethet their performance will meet your expectation, and you may have some plans for improving productivity. But you may not realize that what there people expect from you and how you meet their expectations may have as much to do with their performance as your expectation of them. However, your staffs also expect you to be qualified to supervise. First, they want you to have worked in the area in which you are supervising: a hotel, room, a hotel kitchen, a hotel restaurant, lowing into a big motel from a job in a budget motel, you may also improve yourself. Your staffs want to feel that you understand the operation well and appreciate the work , they are doing. They want to feel that they and their jobs are in good hands, that you are truly capable of directing their work.

● Behavior modification supervising strategy

Behavior modification explains a newer method for improving performance. It explains all behavior is a function of its consequences; people behave as they do because of positive or negative consequences to them. If the consequences are positive, they will trend to repeat the behaviors, if they are negative, they will trend not to . Hence, if you are hotel kitchen cookers their supervisor, you need to give praise , or appreciation to the cookers , whose cooking skills can be improved when they can cook good taste foods ro satisfy hotel restaurant customer individual eatting feeling. Every time, you need to give praise to the excellent cooker's cooking performance. Then, his/her cooking skills will be improved , due to your praise.

It is possible that he/she feels salary will be increased by your praise. Otherwise, when you feel the cooker's cooking skill is worse and your cookers their cooking foods taste are also worse and they can not satisy your cookers their customers' eatting taste needs often. Then , you ought not punish or blam to let him/her by your oral blaming or pubishment threat (without salary increasing threat). Consequently, his /her cooking skill can not be improved, even worse. You ought attempt to help him/her to find whether which aspects of cooking skills , he/she is felt to need to learn how to improve hir/her cooking skill to be better, and you ought teach him/her how to cool the kinds of food to be better taste. Consequently, his/her cooking skill will be improved by your teaching and patience excuse attitude.

● How to design clear job analysis?

Any one hotel team ought need have clear job analysis to let their departments supervisors and staffs to know whether what aspects of tasks , they need to do in order to achieve actual work performance improvement. For example, sever job units example, it may include: Stock service station, set tables, great quests, explain menu to customers, take food and beverage orders and complete guest check, pick up order and complete plate preparation, serve food, recommand wines and serve them, total and present check, perform side work, operate equipment , meet dress and grooming stantards, observe sanitation procedures and requirements, maintain good customer relations, and desired check arrange.

Hence, any one hotel restaurant server can know whether how they require the setting standards, training and evaluation jst as the actual work sequences do. Such units appears in ither jobs as well , and the same standards will apply in each case in the hotel any departments performance standards from the heart of the job description and they describe the what, how to and how wells of a job.

1. What the employee is to do?

2. How it is to be done?

3. To what extent it is to be done?

It means that any hotel department staffs and supervisors they need to know concern their job requirement such as : How much, how well, how soon. For example, " one waitor or waitress job at acertain restaurant. The server will take food and beverage orders for up to five tables with 100 % accuracy, using standard house procedures." It is the hotel restaurant waitor/waitress general job standard acceptance level.

Hence, waitor/waitress supervisor can folle this guideline to know how to supervise his/her staffs and evaluate whose job performance in the hotel restaurant.

On conclusion, due to hotel is one service industry, any hotel's different department effective supervising management, they need have good job standard, training and fair evaluation performance system, fair compensation and pubishment system, instead of the department supervisor whose supervising effort or ability whether is proficient or worse in order to influence whose team serving performance effectively and efficiently . However, any organization itself management team and supervising team will need have good communicating technique in order to let any department supervisor knows how to supervise his/her team effectively in order to achieve improvement service performance aim.

CHAPTER V

Learning airport consumption strategy

Whether do different countries tourists' different lifestyle which can influence their travel consumption behaviors? Even, which countries that they will choose to go to travel. For example, when one tourist who owns himself/herself often to drive to go to anywhere habitually. The tourist's driving car habital behavior which will influence that he/she will feel need to rent car to travel to anywhere habitually , when he/she selects to go to the country to travel. Hence, if he/she feels the tourism destination has no any rent car service providers to provide him/her to rent any car to travel anywhere in the country's travel destination. Does the country lack rent car service factor which will influence that he/she will still choose to go to the country to travel in preference? For example, when one New Zealander's family who own at least one car at home. So, the New Zealand whole family every member can often drive car to go to anywhere , even, one family member had driven one car to leave his/her home. So, driving own car activity or behavior has been one habitual activity to influence the New Zealand every member to feel the travelling destination needs have rent car service provider supplies cars to let them to rent to travel. The driving car lifestyle has caused the whole New Zealander family driving habit. When the family's sons) and/or daughter(s) need(s) to go to school or go to shopping as well as their parents also need to drive their cars to go to office to work in themselves home town often. In common, there are many New Zealanders who will have at least one car at home because they feel that they can drive their themselves cars to go to anywhere in New Zealand more than waiting bus or tram or train or ferry etc. public transportation tools more conveniently. So, New Zealanders' driving own car habit will influence their lifestyle to feel that they also need to rent cars to travel to go to any where to travel to replace to wait public transportation tools choice in the travelling destination during their journey.

For shopping trips is more influenced by their driving car activities. So, it seems that this New Zealander families will be influenced to their tourism destination need, they need the tourism destination has car renting service provider to be supplied anywhere to let them can drive the renting cars to go to anywhere in tourism destination. It means that when the tourim destination has less rent car providers can provide renting car services to drive anywhere or it has none any renting car service providers are existing in the tourism destination. Then, the renting car service providers number shortage or none any renting car service providers to be provided to the country's tourism destination, which will cause the New Zealander families do not perfer to choose to go to the country to travel generally, e.g. Hong Kong, China, Korea these Asia countries have no many rent car service providers in these countries. So, the New Zealand families won't prefer to choose to go these countries to travel when they discover these Asia countries lack enough rent car service providers to let them to drive to travel in themselves conveniently. Otherwise, America, England, Japan etc. countries have many rent car service providers. So, these countries will be this New Zealander families' preferable tourism countries. Thus, the New Zealand families' driving ownership car lifestyle will influence their travel behaviors to choose to go to the country which can have many rent car providers in the tourism country any where tourism destinations in preference.

Thus, whether the country has renting car service providers , it will be variable factor to influence any country's car ownship families' driving car travel behaviors in their journey in order to let they feel that they can drive themselves ownship cars to go to anywhere to travel conveniently, even when they leave their countries. Hence, these countries' car ownship driving habitual families' behaviors will be influenced their tourism destination or location decision choice when the country has many renting car service providers in preference as well as this renting car service provider supplying factor will be more important to influence the habitual driving own car traveller to be preferable choice to compare other factors, e.g. cheap entertainment consumption providers factor which include cheap hotel living fee, cheap food price consumption etc. expenditure in the travelling country.

Thur, it explains that different countries' car ownship tourists , whose driving own car activities will cause their daily lifestyles, then their daily driving own car lifestyles will influence their tourism destination choices indirectly. So, it seems that lifestyle can be a outcome variable (or dependent variable) factor to influence travel behavior in any travelling built environment. The travelling built environment characteristics can include density measures (population density, job density), job-housing density). These travelling buit environment factor can repreent what the city resident's lifestyle. For example, where the location in relation to local centre or regional centre to the country's residents are living. This country resident's living location will cause this country resident's lifestyles , e.g. holiday or leisure whether it is low budget, active and adventurous or frequent traveller with second place or self-orgnized , family oriented or close to home and unadventurour. Hence, the country's living built environment will influence the country's resident's lifestyles. Due to different countries' residents will have different lifestyles. Hence, built environments and lifestlyes have relationship to influence every country's residents when they need to go to other countries to travel in their holidays. For example, frequent travellers are usually living in big and busy cities, otherwise, non -frequent travellers are ususally living in the countrysides, where there are less offices or factories are built to let people to work. So, big city will bring busy feeling to the country's residents, then they will be influenced to feel need to often to go to travel for leisure intention in their holidays. Otherwise, countryside will bring not busy or quiet environment feeling to the country's residents, then they won't feel working feeling when they are living in counryside. So, they won't feel need to go t o anywhere to travel in their holidays often.

Hence, built environment will bring either busy or not busy (quiet environment feeing) to the both different country residents when they are living in the places. Their living places will cause their lifestyles are different. Then, they will be influences to feel have more frequent travelling needs or less frequent travelling needs to explain why every country people will have more or less frequent travelling needs.

● How any why peer-to-peer
accommodation can impact
business tourism pattern

I shall explain how any why peer-to-peer accomodation can attract business tourisms to choose business tourism intention? Usually , employees or employers buy business trips, why they choose one particular travelling company over another and why the business tourists choose to travel when the peer (more than one buiness tourists) who will choose to peer-to-per accommodation business tourism pattern more than the more expensive hotel living comfortable feeling business tourism pattern.

Business travel agents need to know or understand what reasons the employer or employee feels peer-to-peer accommodation business tourism motivation is more suitable or better to compare hotel living comfortable feeling business tourism pattern. Why can business tourism accommodation choice factor influence the business tourist's business trip choice.

Business trip means work related travel to an irregular place or work and it represents that one employee or more than on employees business tourists whose expenses are paid by the business ,he or she or they work(s) for. So, in employer's business trip expense view point, he/she expects the employee or employees can choose the most cheap expenses for whose business trip. It also means that the explorer does not expect that it is a high quality journey for the employee's or employees' business trip. The business tourism is year-round, peaking in spring and autumn , but still with high levels of activity in the summer and winter months. It may be long time ot short time, e.g. less than one month or more than one month, evern more than half year for the business trip. When the employee is employees are working permanent full time employment. It is not for leisure intention, it means that the employer does not hope employee or employees spend(s) extra more expense to spend any leisure or goes (go) to any destinations to visit in their/her/his whole business trip.

Hence, it is based on the cheap expenses for the business trip aim, employer usually demands employees or employees to choose the peer-to-peer be cheaper accommodation to live or the employer will help its employee(s) to choose the peer-to-peer cheaper accommodation to live. So, it seems that expensive hotel living facilities won't be the preferable accommodation choice for employer because the business trip pay or reimburse the employee. Hence, business travel agencies ought not help the business tourists to choose expensive travel package, e.g. expensive hotel accommodation on the trip, expensive transportation tools, e.g. taxi renting service to get to buisness meetings, the cheapt peer-to-peer cheap hostel accommodation and cheap transportation tool, e.g. travel buses pre-booking service, or cheap restaurant choice vacation incentives package is more attractive to let them/him/her to choose for their/her/his business trip.

A business person or a peer-to-peer business people also have /her expect to take advantage of frequent flyer schemes which allow him/her/them to take leisure trip with airlines when they/he/she is /are accumulated sufficient miles in the chep or tair ticket(s) to catch air plane for businss trip. Hence, he/she /they expect(s) to earn airlines expenses from whose frequent flyer schemes when they/he/she can claim to original air ticket price from whose employer, but in fact, peer-to-peer business tourists or individual business tourist pay lesser ait ticket charge from whose frequent flying program accumulated sufficient miles, even no any payment. So, airlines can benefit the business traveller, such as improved in competition milages programs, quick check in and online check in, lounges with broadband connection etc. service.

Why does peer-to-oeer accommodation living factor is the most influential to any business tourist(s) to choose the travel agent? In employer's business trip expensive view point, if it has many employees need to go to other countries business trips for long days frequently. Then, the employer will consider whether the every day accommodation living cost is expensive or not. So, comparison hotel and peer-to-peer hostle price, hotel accommodation price is usually higher than hostle accommodation rent price. When peer-to-peer accommodation has been shown to positively impact to business trip employers in popular. Because any business spending will be one important considerable factor to influence employers to choose. However, the accommodation renting price will be more influential to impact business tourism cost. Hence, employers will estimate every whole business trip expenses how it can impact peer-to-peer or hotel accommodation choice. So, the living budget factor will be one important influential factor to influence any employers how to choose where are the suitable destination for every individual business tourist or peer-to-peer group business tourists to live. So, it seems small size peer-to-peer hostles are compared to large size expensive hotels more suitable for business tourists.

Although, it is possible that individual employee or a group peer-to-peer employees will feel peer-to-peer hostle is not more safe than hotel accommodation. But, their/his/her employer usually does not consider safety, comfortable environment issue for their/his/her every business trip. They only consider loe accommodation price issue. So, the accommodation choice will be one critical factor to influence employers how to help their individual employee or a group peer-to-peer employees to choose where he/she/they will live when he/she/they arrive(s) the destination for whose every business trip. Hence, it seems that accommodation will be one critical factor to influence anywhere to be chosen to live for any business trips to their individual employee or group peer-to-peer employees' needs.

● Factors influence local tourists'
destination choice

What are the main internal and external factors to influence local tourist's domestic travelling choice behaviors and detination choice decision making? What are the social , cultural , personal psychological factors to influence the decision-making of local tourists to travel to different types of tourism destinations in domestic travelling destinations, e.g. attractions, available amenities, accessinility, image price external factors. They can influence local tourist's destination choice behaviors. Does the individual occupational reason can influence local tourist's local destination travelling choice? So, any travel agents need to develop and promote of domestic destination need to determine the factors influencing tourist's destination choice.

In a local destination tourist individual productive way, how loca tourism agents can bring what factors to influence or charge whose local destination travelling behavioral changes. For example, tourist individual behavior and destination choice factor, the comparision between the current local tourism destinations choice and the past local tourism destinations choice factor. Instead of local different travelling destination prices comparison, journeys comparison . What are the other internal and external factor to influence the local tourist's travelling destinations choices behaviors, e.g. attending local festivals, events, taste local cuisine and be part of unique features of a destination. These will be valuable external or internal factors to influence the local tourist's local destinatons choices. So, different countries' local travelling destinations will need have a number og key elements that attract visitors and meet their needs. The key elements may include , for example, primary activities, physical setting and social / cultural attributes primary external activities elements, and secondary elements may include catering and shopping, and addition elements/accessibility and tourists information providing to local tourists.

Due to local destinaton tourism must be cheaper than overseas or foreigh destination tourism. So, the local torust travel agents need to provide thei travelling services to local tourists, more attractions, accessibility , amenities, excellent available packages activities and ancillary services to compare overseas tourism destinations. Because the local tourists will compare the overseas different destinations travelling places to decide whether they ought choose to travel overseas or local different destinations at the moment. So, any entertainment activities concern local destinations which will be local tourists' perferable comparative travelling services to the local travel agent and the overseas travelling service in order to decide whether he/she ought choose local travelling or overseas travelling at the moment.

Hence, local different travelling destinatons attractive factor will be one important influential factor to influence local tourist's travelling choices. However, a tourist's attitude, decisions, activities, ideas or travelling experiences evaluating and searching of any tourism service behaviors will influence the final travelling destinaton choice decision whether he/she ought choose to go to overseas or local travel. He/she will consider how to spend time and money and effort to carry on any kinds of entertainment activitied in whose local or overseas journeys. So, the different destination local and overseas internal travelling price and spending entertainment time in journey and spending effort to arranging every travelling entertainment which every will be one considerable issue to compare budget to overseas and local different travelling destinations. If the tourist feel whose country , e.g. American's local travelling destination budget is spend less than overseas travelling destination too much. Then, the American will choose to local travelling destinations more than overseas travelling destinations and the moment. So, travelling budget will one factor to influence the tourist to choose whether overseas or local travelling.

So, it seems that time, money and effort will be another factor to influence the tourist will be another factor to influence the tourist chooses to go to overseas or local travelling destinations, instead of different travelling entertainment provider choices factor in the local or overseas travelling destinations . Moreover, the tourist's indvidual income, the local and overseas living condition, formation of cultural and aesthetic tasts, price of local and overseas travelling service and discounts, loca and overseas travelling destinations' temperature or weather viable, e.g. number of sunny days, geographical condition, cultural and natural resource, medical tourism etc. external factors will influence the tourist individual final travelling decision to choose either local tourism or overseas tourism entertainment decision.

Airport actual functionality

Instead of airport is one arrical and leaving terminal station place main function for any travelling passengers after the airplances had landed on the country airport's subway. I feel that airport has also another main functions. It can help the country to attract more travellers to choose to go to the country to travel as well as it can persuade them to raise consumption desire in their whole journeys after they leave the travelling country's airport if they feel the country airport's service performance can satisfy their short time staying need. I shall explain why any countries' airports can influence travellers' travelling destinations and travelling shopping choices to be increased or decreased. The future airport will be the assistance role to assist tourim industry development. The factors include, for example, safety and terrorism control, when the travellers feel the country's airport is safe to stay when they catch air planes to arrive the coutry first time. Then, the country's airport can build safe image to let them to feel the country is safe to travel indirectly, traditional cirport service providers will need to seek new service way to deliver value, such as subscription based service models can let travellers to feel the country's airport can provide one comfortable and enjoyable short term travelling staying environment in the country's airport. Then, they bring pleasant emotion to prepare their journey trip after they leave the airport in the foreign country.

So, if the country's airport can let the travellers feel safe and comfortable , then it can bring new exciting and enjoyable feeling to the country's image. Because airport will be any travellers' first time arrival place after they catch airplanes to arrive another country. So, positive or negative airport's image will influence travellers how they feel whether the country , it is worth to choose to travel indirectly. However, airports need have good facilities to satisfy any related airplane service employees or any airport food or product businesses need, instead of travellers' need. For example, it needs have good allocation of terminals and access to facilities , they will be managed and regularly reviewed and regarded their good facility availability , capacity constraints and the best use of available facilities to satisfy any food or product sale shops' sale need and airport passengers' purchase need both in airports or airplane pilots, airplace service employees, irport security employees' comfortable working environment need.

However, airport inside and outside also needs to be arranged enough parking space facilities to let any aircraft parked or stored at the airport from the place where it is parked or stored in order to let any vehicles to be parked in airports or ouside airports easily and conveniently. When any sudden emergency matters occurred, the aircraft subjects to unforeseen operational delays , it should need to contact airport operations control centre to indicate when the expected time of arrival and departure is, there is no need to request a new slot in cases of unforeseen operational delays where the operation will take place within 24 hours of the agreed slot time. For example, of unforeseen operational delays include aircraft technical issues or weather conditions that could not have been planned for. Hence, operationally delayed aircraft must utilise slots in the same manner as originally agreed. If any change to the original slot agreement is required, e.g. a slot must be requested immediately. Moreover, when aircraft subjects to non-operational delays must request new slots immediately, following the correct process in those conditions of use, an example, of a non-operational delay may include delay caused by late running passengers or poor schedule planning. Hence, airport needs have good facilities and communication system to coordinate to any departments to avoid aircraft unforeseen delays to cause airport passengers feel nervous and brings negative and poor emotion to the airport's service performance.

On airport baggage handling function aspect, airport operators must comply with the baggage policy made available to all operators with the airline business management team. For example, where a flight destination or carrier is identified as being at significant or high risk, the operator will pay a charge as notified by management, equating to the cost of any policing cost additional to the services normally provided at the airport for carriers or destinations at lower levels of risk. In fact, airport baggage management needs be checked and delivered in order to help any airplanes' passengers to transport their baggages to follow their airplanes to be delivered to their same destinations when their airplanes are flying with the passengers and whom baggages to arrive the same country's airport at the same time absolutely. So, barrage management operators need submit or demand and in agreed format the already fleets absolutely, such as fleet detail to report these data to include aircraft type and registration, number of seats maximum take off weight kilogrammes of each aircraft owned or operated by the operator, in order to avoid any passengers' luggages wrong delivery occurrence in possible.

Hence, any airports must need to consider above basic passenger service operation in order to avoid any accident occurrences to bring poor airport service attitude feeling. If airport management expected that they have good service performance to satisfy travellers' short term staying needs in themselve countries' airport.

Airport strategies

Any countries' airports expect to increase passenger movements, they must have effective strategies to carry on reviewing any errors and improve performance effectively. For instance, how to keep cost effective measures to lower operating costs and keep good performance on quality, such as for maintenance and cleaning airport cost reducing measures to introduce variable, performance -based elements to encourage productivity gains, how to manage and implement new technological systems to improve information flow and work processes within the country's airport, e.g. airport e-immigration system can allows to receive real-time alerts on any airport building faults. It can reduce airport reliance on manpower in these areas, thus reaulting in better productivity and cost savings for long term airport expenditure. So, high technological strategy system is needed to implement to any country's airport in order to facilitate the handling of more aircraft movements to optimise aircraft handling on runways. Their benefits include reduction of departure flights separation times, reconfiguration of flight routes, and improvements in runway inspection processes.

These new measures can bring effective in improving any country's airport's runway efficiency, developing new infrastructure including the extension of the taxiway, roadway and power supply networks. It aims to satisfy travellers' convenient transportation needs when they arrive any countries' airports and prepare to find suitable transportaton tools to arrive their destinations more easily (airport transportation roadway, taxiway building network strategy).

Hence, any countries' airports need have good strategy to manage a wide range of activities and risks, which are broadly classified into strategic , financial operational, regulatory and investment. Any countries' airports also need to seek how to reduce the occurrence of risks and to minimum potential adverse impact as much as possible, uch as airport risk management strategy. Because when the country has many people are living and they need often to catch airplanes to leave their countries to travel as well as there are many foreign travellers choose to travel the country. Then, the country's airport must need to expand size and raise good facilities, e.g. more automated immigration gantries are needed to be installed, taxi waiting areas are also needed to be explanded with additional taxi bays constructed to accommodate the higher number of arriving passengers , even increasing airplane subways number to satisfy many airplanes need to fly away from the country's airport or coming airplances fly to the country's airport's landing on runway needs often.

So, airplane subways number expanding strategy and cutomated immigration gate fast checking system is needed when the country has many travellers choose to go to the country travel and/or many local people need to leave themselves countries to travel. For instance, departure and arrival immigration control as well as pre-boarding security screening will be controlled for more efficient deployment of manpower and equipment. Moreover, in the line will the trend of self-service options of airports arrived the world, provisions will be made to have more kioslls for self check in,self-bag -tagging and self bad-drops. The increasing use of these options will help airlines and ground handling agents reduce processing times and staffing requirement. For example, a fully automated to reduce reliance on scare manpower baggage check in and check out system, the baggage handling system will also be equipped with ergonomic lifting aids to enable heavy and odd-sized bags to be handled with ease, even by older workers.

Then, the country's airport must need to increase subways number and immigration fast checking service facility to avoid handling passengers crowd queueing problem often occurs every day. When any airports often let passengers feel time pressure to queue to spend long time to wait immigration checks and leave the airport. It will bring their negative emotion feeling to the country's airport. Then, it is possible to influence they choose to go to the country to repeat travel again. Hence, the country's different airport strategies are needed when the country has increasing travellers number trend as soon as possible.

Another strategy concerns airport emergency service on safe aspect. Any countries' airports need have a highly trained specialist wait that is positioned to provid fast action rescue and fire protection for passengers' life safety ,e .g. aircraft rescue and fire fighting vehicles are needed airport. An incident command and control simulator which provides realistic and interactive simulations of emergency scenarios for the purpose of any sudden accident occurrences in any countries' airports.

So, any countries' airports need to develop an internal digital system to ease labour-intensive work processes like fire safety inspection, incident reporting, logistic management and recording of its personal fitness results, with the new safe system , data entry is needed mobile enabled with the use tablet computers. For example, the airport safe unit can continue to enhance its emergency preparedness and rescue capabilities with the successful staging of two drills, simulated aircraft crashes on land and at sea, as well as any exercises validated crisis contingency plans are recommended to earn strong capability in coordinating rescue efforts involving both the airport community and mutual aid agencies in order to carry on rescuing passengers and airport pilots and service attendants whom life safe service when air planes are crashed on land and at sea.

Another strategy is now aviation facilities strategy, it can support fly, cruise and fly-coach initatives, important options to a rising number of interm travellers, if it can be implemented successfully. It can bring enhancement measures benefits, includes the reduction of departure flight separation times, reconfiguring of flight routes and implementation of aircraft speed control for increased runway use efficiency.

Hence, one successful airport operation , the airport management needs to know how to implement the traveller check out or check in service functions when they arrive the airport or leave the airport and to satisfy its passengers' short term terminal station staying or transfering another airplane's flying need as well as it also needs to know how to implement its different strategies to improve its service performance and to let passengers have more confidence to the country's airport service operators' behavior and they also feel safe when they are staying the country's airport. Hence, any travellers' short term staying feeling in the country's airport , whether the country's airport can bring either positive or negative emotion , which will influence they choose to go to the country to travel again in possible. Hence, airport management can not neglect how to improve airport service performance to satisfy any first time or more time airport visitors' short term staying need.

Long time airport staying and passenger
consumption relationship

It is an interesting question: Can the country's airport service performance influence passengers consumption desire? Nowadays, travelling is a kind of popular entertainment whn working people have holidays, retired people have more savings and students need to go to holiday to feel rest time after they had hard to study. They will choose go to other countries to travel. So, " freguent travelling times" which will increase to any travelling consumers. If the traveller often chooses to go to the country to travel, he must need to permit to enter the country from its airport immigration. If his every visiting time to the country's airport, he feels the country's airports' staffs services are poor performance and he feels that they are not polite or rude attitude to treat him when he needs to check out or check in from the country's airport immigraton gates, even he feels difficult to enquire any airport service staffs, either he feels difficult to find them or they need to spend long time to let him to queue to wait enquiry, even he also needs to spend long time to queue to wait check in or check out in airport immigration gates when he arrives the country's airport or he leaves the country's airport.

All of these negative airport staffs' service attitudes and poor service behavioral feeling, they will cause the frequent traveller doubts whether the country is a worthy travelling place and it is possible to led his negative consumption desire in the country's airport. Then, all of these negative emotion will influence the frequent traveller reduces consumption in the country's airport , even wothut any consumption in the country's airport, when he visits the country to travel every time. So , it seems that airport's service performance will influence travellers carry on more or less consumption in the country's airport. Then, it will influence all the country's airport related retail and restaurant businesses' sales to be reduced indirectly in the country's airport.

Instead of airport service performance intangible factor aspect, the airport's clean, airport itself appearance attractive design, large size and shops and restaurants' suitable locations and internal environment design etc. these tangible factors will also influence travellers' consumption desires in the country's airport. For example, in one special day, e.g. Olympic Games day, the Olympic Games country's airport may complete in record time and its airport can successfully handle a estimate record 85,000 minimum departing passengers a day during the Olympic Games period, twice the number on normal days. Travellers and media will describe the Olympic Games country's airport retail shops and restaurants consumption experience as seamless, magical and unforgettale airport staying experience, if the Olympic games country's airport can provide an excellent service performance on the Olympic games period. Then, it will influence the increasing sale amount in the Olympic Games country airport retail stores and restaurants during period. So , when the country is experiencing special day, such as "Olympic Games " is chosen to carry on competition in the country. Then, in this Olympic Games period, it will attract many travellers to choose to go to this country to travel, due to they have interest to watch Olympic Games competition in this country. This country's airport will represent this country's image. If it 's airport service staffs can provide excellent service to let any one of travellers to feel when they are staying in this country's airport short time and this country's airport itself appearance and design can also be changed more attractive and beautiful and the airport's retail stores and restaurants also design more attractive and beautiful. Then, the travellers' consumption desires will be possible to raise , when they visit this country's airport in first time in this Olympic Games travelling period.

- ● Global air transport network requirement

In the future, if the country has a strong and affordable global air transport network, it will bring more advantages. Due to many travellers expect to catch air planes which can fly to another country in short time , it can reduce accidents occurrence chance on sky or on sea. So, short time flying can be more attract to compare long time flying. So, it explains that why many travellers prefer to choose one way flying more than transfering another /other air plane(s) flying. Although, they need to pay more air ticket fee. So, if the country's airport can have more subways number and large subways areas to let many arrival air planes and leaving air planes need to fly from land or fly to land in the country's airport frequently. Then, the travellers can buy any air tickets to book same day or next day or later day flught time to fly to any country to travel more easily, when the country's airport has large area size and many subways to let many airplanes can stay in its aircraft subways in same time. Then, the country's airport flight frequency will increase , it means that there are many travellers can catch airplances to fly to other countries in any time very easily from themseleves country's airport. It is time-sensitive feeling to let the country's travellers, they can feel to fly to other countries to travel in short day. They do not need delay to fly to any countries, when the flight airline is either full seat or the time can not permit any air places land on the country's subways.

So, none delaying time sensitive travelling frequent flught model will be one attractive flight flying method to influence the country's travellers choose to frequent travelling behavior. Because they do not change their travelling day, due to airplanes have no enough seats supply or the country's airport has no enough land subways to let any airplanes to stay to cause delaying their flight travelling booking seat day expectly.

So, airport is similar to airline to need to use different customer relationship management to attract returning travelling customers . It brings this question: What are the most attractive motivation factors in airport travel market? I believe that factors may include airport loyalty, various flight time arrangement distribution channel, passenger check in or check out, laggage safe delivery, airpor security service. Moreover, flight schedules are also a main factor influences the travellers' final travelling country choice decision among different travelling countries. However, if the country's airport can build good loyalty image when passengers are staying in the country's airport in short time, it can show a more attractive motivator to increase travellers' consumption desires when they are staying in the country's airport in short time.

Hence, airport 's loyalty seems have relationship to influence travellers' consumption behavior when they are staying in the country's airport. For example, when the different countries' travellers feel enjoyable and happy to stay in the country's airport longer time. Then, their airport long time staying behavior will raise their consumption desire and chance to find any right restaurant to eat food or drink or find any right retail shop to buy right products in airport. Hence , when the country's airport can buil loyal customers relationship. Then, it will bring the advantages or benefits to the airport's any retail shops or restaurants on sale growth aspect, such as : their retention rates will go up easier, their customer referrals will go up easier, the country airport retail shopd and restaurants travelling customers whom spending rates will go up easier, the country airport retail shops and restaurants customers will be loss price sensitive, the costs of retail and restaurant servicing then will go down easier. Hence, if the country's airport customer service performance can maximize travellers' loyalty. It will influence travellers to feel the country airport's retail shops and restaurants have more loyalty to compare other countries airports' retail shops and restaurants loyalty.

So, it implies that any any country airport's loyalty will have relationship to influence its travellers how they feel the country airport's retail shops and restaurants' loyalty. Due to loyalty is intangible and it is obly feeling. So, when the travellers have positive emotion and wheh they are staying in the country's airport long time. Then, they will have positive emotion to spend more time to walk around in the country's airport as well as when they are passing any airport's retail shops or restaurents. Their pleasant emotion may encourage their consumption behaviors to have interest to find any right restaurant to eat food or drink or find any right retail shop to buy any right product in the country's airport in preference easily. Because they had been accepted to spend long time to stay in the country's airport, when they feel interest and surprise to visit the country airport when they arrive. Moreover , the long airport staying time will increase their purchase chance to any the country's airport's retail stores or restaurants in the country 's airport in first time visiting.

How to satisfy customer expectation
for passenger service at airport

When one country's airport can satisfy passengers expectation to accept its service demand, then profitability and passenger number will be influenced to increase. So, airport management needs to focus on how to satisfy any passenger individual need or expectation when he/she needs to stay in whose country's airport for wait to either transferinf another airplance need to carrying on check in or check out in the country's airport immigration gate need in short time.

However, because if the country's airport service can let its passengers feel happy , then they will be super spenders to spend airport staying longer time to consume or entertain in the country's airport. Moreover, it will bring any the country airport's retail shops or restaurante to earn more sale growth indirectly. So, any country airports need to consider how to bring excellent customer services for any passenger individual need in airport. Because its service behavior or performance will have indirect relationship to impact the county airport's any businesses and itself any parking , entertaining services income in airport.

" The concept of managing airport customer expectation on passenger service quality" will be any country airport's main aim. Basically, airport passengers' perception concern how the airport service staffs' service attitudes or performances influence how they feel either negative emotion, such as anger, dissatisfaction, irritation, neutrality or positive emotion, such as happy, satisfaction, pleasure, delight. So, when the airport passenger individual perception is better , then his expected to the country airport individual service staff level will be at the highest level, but if his service expectation is less than his expectation standard, then the airport passenger will dissatisfy with the lowest satisfaction level to be influenced the country airport's other any one service staff by the one airport service staff whose poor performance. Because any one of the country airport's service staff , every one will influence the country airport's image. Of every one has excellent service performance, then, it will let many different counties' passengers feel sympathetic emotion from their every one's behavior. Otherwise, if every one has or most service staffs have poor or not considerate ot not sympathetic service attitude to be let them to feel, then any one of them will let many itself airport's countries' passengers feel the country airport's image is poor. They won't like to spend long time to stay in the country airport, even their short time airport staying behaviors will influence the country airport's any retail shops or restaurants businesses sale growth to be reduced from their short staying time influence.

In general, airport service staffs need to spend some time to answer any passengers' enquiries. So, how they answer their enquiries will influence how their achievement in order to raise the country airport's passengers satisfactions. It may lead a rise in different countries'passengers' loyalty and retention, therefore the country airport can increase many different countries passengers number when the repeating airport visitors , they prefer to choose to go to the country to travel again , due to its airport is attractive reason in possible.

So, any country airport management ought have a policy from how the airport established desirable standard performance, measure it against actual performance to action taken once and revise any unachieved acceptable service level to the acceptable excellent passenger service performance in the country airport. For example, any country airport needs to manage and identify the target passenger segmenation target groups and to make bettwe understand the key elements that have the greatest impact on meeting every different target passenger segmentation group individual expectations and needs from their services in themselves country airport. So, any country airport will have relationship to any one of airline, as well as any one airline will have direct relationship to every passenger when he/she stays in the country airport in short time.

However, instead of restaurants and retail shops; sale relationship will be influenced by the country airport's service performance, airport management also bring more empahsis on non-aeronautical (non related airlined and retail business) revenues, such as shops rents, concessions, car parking service income, consultancy and property developed diversified service incomes. So, airports need to focus directly to enterainment travelling airlines' passengers, meeters, and greeters, business-travelling passengers , users of general aviation services and transfer air plane short time staying visitors, or lone time staying visitors, e.g. the passengers need to live airport hotel for on night or more than one night sleeping before they catch the airplane on the day. So, all these different target passenger segmentations will have different service needs in any country airports.

However, airport passengers' behaviors and expectations of the airport experience depend highly on the types of traveller, they include: demographic characteristics, (i.e. gender, age group, income, sex, occupation) , purpose of trip (i.e. leisure, business), and their circumstances. In general , the passenger can be divided into different group, such as arriving, departing and transfer with different expectation and need, in the way they will be using the airport services and facilities different need and will also influence the behavior of individuals when in the commercial area. For example, passengers who are departing and arriving will require all airport facilities including: car rental, rail, buses access, pre-booking taxi service, check in or check out service, bad processing and security check and vertical and horizontal moving in passenger terminals. Otherwise, transfer passengers will have a short waiting time in airport and their needs will be likely different from those of origin and destination passengers. Some of the transit passengers will need to spend one hour, even more than four hours or half day in the airport. By providing airport facilities that can accommodate their needs, such as a place to lie down and take a short sleep time, free shower, free email public service will mostly give than an enjoyable airport experience. Evem some handicapped people or old people who feel difficult to walk in the airport corridor. Then , the airport will need to arrange the auto -wheel chairs and auto airport vehicle facilities to let service staffs to provide electronic auto wheel chairs to let them to sit down or drive the auto airport vehicle to sit down with them to go to their destination in the airport's any places immediately. For passengers travelling with families may want children play areas, where kids can have a great time when waiting to board the aircraft. They also want the availability of rooms of families travelling with badies equipped with changing facilities, baby crib, microwaved and hot water need. When passengers are on business trip, may want a lounge, with all the business, facilities that they can feel free to use, such as free internet access and other services , such as fax, scan and photocopy machine. Hence, any airport managements need to develop the strategic customer facilities providing service in order to improve the design and delivery of all the facilities and services need by understanding expectation of each passenger segmentation group in their airport staying time.

Finally , in airport unique design aspect, our global airports will need have different unique design to let any travellers to feel that the country's airport can have its unique design to let themm to feel the country airport has itself own airport culture or entertainment features to attract they observe its appearance in order to achieve the increase more travelling visitors number when they feel enjoy to stay in the country airport longer time before they leave the airport. I shall indicate different countries' airports how they will perform themselves different airport cultures and unique design as below:

For China and Hong Kong Chinese airport design example, their airports need have Chinese cultural feeling to let Western travellers to feel their airports' designs and cultures are different to any Western countries' other cultures. So, China anf Hong Kong airports' designs can increase many old big size building photos number in their airports to let foreign visitors can walk on the long glass walkway corridor , when they enter walkway coddidor to walk through different 100 more airplane leaving and arriving gates number and the ground floor is built from heavy glass material. So , any one foreign traveller need to walk through on the long glass walkway corridor to pass any one gates to arrive his/her airplane leaving and arriving gate location and catch airplance to fly. Also, the glass walkway ground floor can let them to see the airport's vehicles and airplanes and people and trees outside environment clearly when they are walking on the airports' all glass material manual made ground floor. It will let foreign travellers feel China and Hong Kong airports building designs are different to the foreign countries' themselves airports' designs as well as Hong Kong and China airports' old building photos will let all leaving passengers feel difficult to forget their old building historical photos and they will know hoe their architectural skills are developed to imprved to build nowadays unqiue desing method from traditional building design method in Hong Kong and China airports. Otherwise, for US, Uk etc. foreign countries their airports designs can increase underground floor fish pool architectural design outside to their airports in order to let any passengers feel that they can see many different kinds of various fishes are swimming. So, their outside large fish pool can let them to feel surprise when they are staying in their any airports, e.g. one beautiful large size fish pool, it can be built to close to their airports and the fish pool can have various kinds of big and small fishes swim in the pool to let passsngers to see, or their airports can appear suddenly and unexpected of a gaping hole in the airport's outside ground, known as a sinkhole. Sometimes, the airport's outside sinkhole will fill up with fresh water to become deep , shaped manual made sinkhole to let passengers to feel they need to enter to the sinkhole and then they can enter the airport. So, the outside large size sinkhole will attract many passengers to stat to observe how the fresh water is entering to the sinkhole interestingly. Then, they will feel surprise when they need to pass though the sinkhole , then they can enter the airport.

In conclusion, attractive airport architectural design will let any passengers can not forget that they had ever visit the country to travel in their travelling experience as well as they can be influenced to like to stay longer time in the country airport by the airport's attractive design and environment influence. The most important influnece, it can influence airport related business income when they like to stay longer time in the airport.

Cultural distance on satisfaction and
respect travel intention

Every country cultural difference is different. How and why cultural difference has a real impact on tourist satisfaction and it can also influence to repeat travel. Is cultural tourism one major factor to influence tourist to repeat travelling intention or choice to the country in international tourism choice market? For example, China and India have similar culture. Their cultural difference is not much, e.g. eating cultural habit is similar , entertainment cultural habit is similar. These both countries people do not want to spend much money in eating and entertainment both aspects. Hence, these two countries people do not consider how to consume to enjoy entertainment and eat expensive food. Hence, it is based on cultural similar reason. These both countries tourists will prefer to choose to repeat travelling either China or India. When the Indian tourists had chosen to go to China to travel in the first time. Then, the Indian tourists will choose to go to China to travel in second time again. Also, the Indian tourists had chosen to go to China to travel in first time. Then, the Chinese tourists will choose to go to India to travel in second time again.

What factors influence China and India tourists respect to travel between these both countries. The factors will include cheap air ticket price, cheap hotel living price , less economic cost factor. However, I believe the similar cultural factor will be the major factor to influence many Chinese and Indian tourist prefer to choose to repeat travelling between these both countries.

As my indication to these both countries people have similar eating habits, choosing foods, low health foods, common foods choice eating at cheap restaurant habitual consumption. Also, they have similar entertainment habits, their entertainment demand is not high. They like to ride bicycles to go to anywhere to travel. They like to go to swim, play basketball, football etc. sports. These all sports are cheap sport consumption. So, it based on similar individual low enjoyment demand and low health, food quality demand similar cultural factors. Chinese and Indian people have no long distance cultural difference between eating and entertainment habitual factor will include them to choose to repeat travelling between these both countries. Due to China and India have many restaurants can provide cheap food or sport service providers can provide different kinds of cheap sport entertainment consumption to satisfy their cheap food and cheap entertainment needs in their journey in China or India anywhere. So, it explains that why these both countries tourists will repeat to travel these both countries again after they had visited China or India to travel in first time. So, the similar cultural factor can impact these both countries tourists to repeat to go to these both countries to travel again. Hence, if these two countries' cultural distance is far or different, then themselves countries' tourists won't choose to repeat travel between themselves when these two countries for cultural distance tourists had visited to another country in first time. Hence, culture has been continuously considered as a much factor which tourists consider in terms of choice of the destination travelling place. Also, it explains cultural distance which can make tourist individual has less satisfaction to concern to tourists to repeat travels.

Otherwise, for far cultural distance two countries case example, such as Chinese and American , these two countries people's eating habit and entertainment cultural needs are different. For eating habit difference example, American like to eat pork, beefs, chickens, potato to replace rice and other foods. Otherwise, Chinese like to wat rice, vegetables more than potatoes, pork , beefs for lunch , dinner . So , their eating habits are very different. Also, American like to drive boats on the season drive cars to go to anywhere to travel on holidays for sports or holiday entertainment activities . Otherwise, Chinese like to play basketball, football, ride bicycle of cheaper sport entertainment on holidays. So, American entertainment activities are more expensive to compare Chinese. Also, US and China , like families whose power distance is different, such as every per family powerful member is parents, who have more power to give opinions to choose anywhere to travel for whose sons and/or daughters whole family members travelling arrangement.

Therefore, if the Us family powerful members, such as at least one son or/and daughter members who need t choose to go to which country to travel if the family powerful members, such as the child/ children's parent feel China's food taste or entertainment activities are totally different to be similar to their country's food taste and entertainment activities habitually after their whole family members had travelled to China in first time before.

Although, their son(s) and daughter(s) will hope to go to China to repeat travel again. But, due to the US family parents are their son(s) and daughter(S) powerful decider to make any travelling decision to choose which country will be next time travelling destination. If their parents feel China's eating and entertainment culture is totally different to their countries. Then, the US family will not choose to repeat travel to the China country again any more easily, because this US family can not feel satisfactory when they visited China in their first time before, due to they feel China 's food and entertainment cultures are totally different to their US country. So, the cultural distance factor will influence the US family don't choose China to go repeat travel again.

Consequently, different countries' similar or different cultural factor will influence the country's tourists choose to repeat travel to the country again. So, any country needs to know what its culture is in order to attract the similar cultural countries tourists to repeat travel to itself country more easily.

CHAPTER VI

Hotel service strategy

Hotel organizational departments operation

Hotel has different departments, e.g. security deparment, cleaning department, front counter room check in and out department, kitchen cooking department, entertainment facility department, room service department, administration department etc. However, any departments must be very important to influence whole organizational performance. It does not depend on which department is especial important to influence whole organizational service performance. For example, room service department main function is let room living customers to feel comfortable to live in any big, small , middle size hotel rooms. If any one hotel room can not let the customer feels comfortable to live or it is dirty to live. Then, it will bring poor living service performance to cause the customer does not choose to live the hotel to live again. However, it does not mean that room service department must be the most important department in whole hotel organization because all hotel department individual performance and efficiency will influence whole hotel operational efficiency to let all customers to feel. I shall explain all hotel organizations departmental operations as below:

In order to run the Hotel as a functional unit, there are several departments in a hotel which work and coordinate together and the major departments of the hotel are:

1. Front Office Department
2. Housekeeping Department
3. Food and Beverage Service Department
4. Kitchen or Food Production Department
5. Engineering and Maintenance Department
6. Accounts and Credits Department
7. Security Department
8. Human Resources (HR) Department
9. Sales and Marketing Department
10. Purchase Department
11. Information Technology (IT)

1. Front Office Department:

Every day is different with the arrival of new personalities from different walks of life. The Front Office Department is often referred as the nerve centre of the hotel as it is in constant contact with our guests, and has the most diverse operating exposure. Our team is passionate about guest service and look at every possible opportunity to make our guests comfortable during their stay. Our front office associates have a keen intuition that allows them to anticipate our guest's needs and exceed them. With its excellent communication skills, it is not unusual for our staff to multi task and work diligently in order to resolve any issues that may arise.

This department performs various functions like reservation, reception, registration, room assignment, and settlement of bills of a resident guest and the front office department is considered as the nerve centre of a hotel.The front-office staff welcome the guests, carry their luggage, help them register, give them their room keys and mail, answer questions about the activities in the hotel and surrounding area, and finally check them out. In fact, the only direct contact most guests have with hotel employees, other than in the restaurants, is with members of the front-office staff.

Concierge is extra service department – Always At Your Service, concierge is constantly looking for ways to enhance your guest experience. Travel routes, recommendations of tours, attractions, and short cuts around town are just a few services offered by our remarkable Concierge Team, topped by, of course, a lovely friendly welcome!

2. Housekeeping Department:

Every morning is a busy one in the Housekeeping Department. The team has an eminent eye for attention to detail to provide our guests with a spotless guest experience. Our housekeepers are in charge of almost every detail of your stay from the fluffy pillows and sheets in your guest rooms to the replenishment of your bathroom amenities. The Housekeeping Department is a critical function to the hotel's continued success!

The housekeeping department is responsible for the cleanliness, maintenance, and aesthetic upkeep of rooms, public areas, back areas, and surroundings in a hotel and for the immaculate care and upkeep of all guest rooms and public spaces at all times.The staff members who excel in the Housekeeping Departments have an eye for detail and a commitment to the training, development and motivation of a diverse group of talented employees. It is the service and cleanliness that really make an impact on our guests and determine whether they will return and also recommend the hotel to others.

3. Food and Beverage Service Department:

The hotel lounge restaurant are a vibrant bunch with a combination of proficiency and bubbly personalities. Whether it's for breakfast, lunch, dinner cocktails or appetizers, our team will always serve you with a smile.This department looks after the service of food and drinks to guests. The Food which is made in the Kitchen and Drinks prepared in the Bar to the Customers (Guest) at the Food & Beverage premises. Some examples of the food and beverage outlets are Restaurants, Bars, Hotels, Airlines, Cruise Ships, Trains, Companies, Schools, Colleges, Hospitals, Prisons, Takeaway etc.

4. Kitchen or Food Production Department:

An experienced team of chefs offers a great variety of scrumptious dishes to keep our hungry customers happy. Although our chefs work in a fast paced environment, the kitchen is far from what you see on Reality TV! There is a less drama and more fun as our chefs handle the line with their experience, great personalities and talent.All the food and beverages that are served to the hotel guest is prepared in the kitchen. Culinary preparation, as an art and science in the modern kitchen, required more than just a knowledge of food being prepared and the methods of preparation.It is through a knowledge of basic skills, terminology, and rules of the kitchen that a final goal, preparation and service of quality is achieved in the hotel kitchen.

5. Engineering and Maintenance Department:

Running an effective hotel requires careful planning and hard work. Equipment does break down; meaning repairs and regular preventive maintenance are required around the hotel. Our professional Maintenance Team performs a wide range of essential tasks to help ensure a smooth operation resulting in happy guests.

The engineering department is responsible for repairing and maintaining the plant and machinery, water treatment and distribution, boilers and water heating, sewage treatment, external and common area lighting, fountains and water features etc. Also, It looks after the maintenance of all the equipment, furniture and fixture installed in a hotel.

6. Accounts and Credits Department:

The Accounting Team plays a significant role in the managing of hotel expense control aspect. They provide the hotel with relevant financial data and forecasts which are used for daily decision making to ensure we are thriving and keeping the books up to date. The team offers a great support service to all departments with financial recommendations.

This department maintains all the financial transactions. Accounting departments typically handle a variety of important tasks. Such tasks often include invoicing customers, accounts receivable monitoring and collections, account reconciliations, payables processing, consolidation of multiple entities under common ownership, budgeting, periodic financial reporting as well as financial analysis. Also common are setting up adequate internal controls for all business processes (to prevent theft/misappropriation of assets), handling external audits and dealing with banks in order to obtain financing. Taxes are sometimes handled by accounting departments in house, but this work is often contracted to outside tax accountants.

7. Security Department:

The security department of a hotel is responsible for the overall security of the hotel building, in-house guests, visitors, day users, and employees of the hotel, and also their belongings.

8. H R and Admin department:

The Executive Team plays a decisive role in the hotel operations as the final decision-maker. The team is comprised of the Department Heads and is led by the Director of Operations, and the General Manager. The team ensures the smooth running of hotel operations, each member responsible for the management of its own department. Regular meetings are organized to discuss any issues and find ways to continuously improve business profitability and guest experience.

Human Resource department is responsible for the acquisition, utilisation, training, and development of the human resources of the hotel.The role of the HR department also has to do with the administration of an impartial and internal justice system which will promote transparency and openness in organisational communication. The Human resources department also serves as a progressive voice in a common system and strives to ensure competitiveness in the conditions of service for staff.

9. Sales and Marketing Department:

Sales Team works hard to promote the brand and the amenities of the hotel. The Sales Department is in charge of negotiating and prospecting large business and leisure groups, tours operators and individual travellers. The Marketing Department is the analytical backbone of Sales as well as being responsible for increasing exposure for the hotel through various advertising opportunities both in print and on the Web. Be sure to engage with us on our various social media platforms such as, Facebook, Twitter, Google Plus, or Pinterest! The major role of the sales and marketing department is to bring in business and also to increase the sales of the hotel's products and services is the major task of the department.

In addition, catering Department is responsible for the smooth operation and sales of our beautifully appointed conference centre. From corporate meetings to large celebratory events, the catering team must to take ownership of every detail with excellent teamwork and efficient communication in order to meet and exceed the expectations of our clients.

10. Purchase Department:

The purchase department is responsible for procuring the inventories of all the departments of a hotel.

11. Information Technology (IT) / Systems

The Information Technology department is responsible for the day-to-day support of all IT systems, business systems, office systems, computer networks, and telephony systems throughout the hotel/resort. Additionally responsible for Information Technology issues, products, and services at the property. Provides user training and support of all property/site systems, network enhancements, hardware and software support etc.

Above all of different departments are very important to influence any hotel organization's efficiency and service performance. They are inter-connective to influence any service aspects to let any customer to feel whether the hotel overall performance can satisfy his/her living need. For example, if the hotel's front office service performance is poor, this department service staff can not book any rooms vancancy to let any one customer to live when he/she arrives this hotel to check in immediately. Then, many customers will not live the hotel room when he/she walk in to the hotel to prepare book room immediately , then it cause many customers only choose another hotel to live. So, any hotels must need to plan enough big, middle and small size rooms to prepare any customers can live their rooms immediately.

So, front office's room booking budget plan can influence whole hotel customer number.Even, if the hotel's room clearning service can not satisfy any customers feel comfortable to live when they live in dirty room, or any rooms' bath room and sleeping room are dirty, then it will cause any customers won't choose to live this hotel when they travel to this country again, they can choose any one hotel to replace this poor room living service performance hotel significantly. So, it seems that any one hotel department individual performance must influence all customer individual satisfactory level. When the customer feels the hotel can not provide excellent service and/or room living satisfaction to let he/she feels, they the hotel will lose many customers from this kind intangible customer feeling factor easily. Hence, how to implement effective strategy to let customers to feel satisfactory when they choose to live the hotel, it is one important value question to research.

However, I feel that these seven key aspects, any hotel organizations need to consider in order to achieve service efficient raising and provide excellent room living service to let any one customer to feel, they may include as below:

A hotel wouldn't run smoothly without the right people and right resources in the right departments. If you're new to the hotel business, or just doing your fair share of basic research, read below for the outline of a hotel's structure. Your exact needs may not be the same as other hotels, which can be affected by the size of your establishment, whether you offer full service or not, and what amenities you have. But most hotels have the following seven areas in common. These areas reflect the various job roles that will need to be filled to keep the organization running. Being aware of these departments can help you plan for future success.

On Executives Service Aspect

These are the decision makers within the business. They may be department heads, managers, or directors. Depending on how your company runs and the size of it, executives may be responsible for some of the other areas discussed below, including accounting, marketing, and at times even front desk services.

On Front Desk Services Aspect

Although no operational segment within a hotel organization is dispensable, it could be argued that very little would happen without the front office staff. These people are constantly in contact with guests, and may even be responsible for taking and handling bookings. Detail-oriented people are often required for this role, since they must meet the exact needs of the guests. Sometimes concierge may also be lumped in with this division of the business, but could be an entirely different department worth building.

On Housekeeping Services Aspect

Keeping your guest rooms clean and tidy is an essential task. Your housekeeping team is typically responsible for every detail within a room, from the cleanliness of the sheets to keeping toiletries stocked.

On Maintenance Facility Management Aspect

Even the best quality utilities and electronics can break and malfunction. In today's tech-oriented world, there is also more to repair and fix in terms of computers, TV screens, game consoles, DVD players, and other cutting-edge tech items than before. Tech can sometimes also be the responsibility of executives or front desk services, depending on what works best for the organization. Additionally, in some cases, maintenance might be lumped in with housekeeping or another role. Again, it depends on the size of your business and the personnel available to you.

On Accounting Administration Management Aspect

Every business needs proper accounting. Tracking expenses and revenue helps you keep a finger on the pulse of the business, so you can make tweaks and adjustments as necessary. The accounting team is usually directly answerable to the executive team, providing them with relevant data and forecasts. They may also make recommendations and offer support for other departments.

On Marketing & Sales Strategy Aspect

Every business requires promotion. The marketing team is responsible for converting prospects into paying guests and spreading the brand message. They must keep up-to-date with the latest marketing channels and practices, including social media, content marketing, OTAs, and so on. Marketing can sometimes become the responsibility of front desk services. But because executives often want control over the exact message that's being shared with their target audience, they will sometimes take it on – especially if they don't have a pre-existing marketing department. Plus, to entrepreneurs, business development is often the most exciting part.

On Managing Kitchen Staff Task Aspect

If you're a full-service hotel, if you offer room service, or both, then it's impossible to keep up with orders and meet your guest's dining needs without competent kitchen staff. Some hotels also need a separate catering team, especially for conference rooms.

When, having the right structure in place is critical to the success of your organization overall. Finding the right balance can be challenging, because human resource is often the most expensive resource of all. At the same time, they are also your greatest resource, and your hotel must cultivate and utilize them well.

All of above deparments are any hotel essential departments in their organizational structure. Any one department's efficiency and function and operation must may influence another department or other departments operation efficienctly. For example, if the cleaning room bed supplied matieral department cleaning staffs efficiencies are low, then, their efficiencies can influence any hotel rooms bed matieral, toilet towel , toilet teeth paste, toilet paper room cleaning supplies have enough supply. So, this deparment has close relationship to influence any hotel rooms have enough clean toilet and hotel room daily materials supplies. Consequently, any it will cause many customers feel hotel rooms' any bed, toilet daily supplies are not enough to be supplied clean hotel bed, toilet daily tools. So, any hotels need to consider how to adjust any department individual operational efficiency absolutely in order to avoid any hotel customers feel poor service performance to your hotel.

Hotel management strategy
● What is hotel management?
Hotel management is really about overseeing every operation of the property. This requires knowledge of distribution strategy, finance, customer service, staff management, marketing, and more. In no way should any of these be treated as 'set and forget'. Hotel management is about constantly evaluating performance is every facet of the business and making necessary adjustments.

Ultimately effective hotel management will not only ensure your hotel stays in business, but is able to profit and grow over time. Think of the hotel as an ecosystem that will get healthier the better you manage it. As your hotel becomes more successful you can upgrade and charge higher rates, pay staff higher wages, and create an experience that guests want to come back for. It can take time to get everything right however. There are many skills you'll already possess but many others you need to learn along the way, or else hire staff that can provide the knowledge for you.

Hotel management definition

Definition of hotel management is that it's 'a field of business and a study, that tends itself to the operational aspects of a hotel as well as a wide range of affiliated topics. Such as: Accounting, administration, finance, information systems, human resource management, public relations, strategy, marketing, revenue management, sales, change management, leadership, gastronomy and more.'Clearly there's a lot to be aware of and many of these functions do require specialists. However not all properties have the luxury of hiring a full team of staff, so it's certainly not impossible to run a successful small hotel business without a range of degrees.

What does hotel management strategy mean? Hotel management strategy may include: service performance management, facility management, cost or expense control management three aspects. Service performance management main aims to let customers to feel the hotel's security is safe when they are living in the hotel, front office service, room service room, even, restaurant food delivery service, entertainment service, such as swimming, gym sport , tennis sport etc. different kinds of whole service can let customers to feel satisfactory as well as facility management service, e.g. swimming pools can let swimmers to feel safe when they are swimming, swimming pools water is warm and clean when they are swimming, swimming pools facility is new, or sport gym running machine, riding machine facility is safe to use and new sport facility can let them to feel to play when they use any kinds of sport tools facility, the hotel room's kitchen tools are clearn, enough provison, kitchen is clean, room is clean, e.g. beds, toilets, drinking cups, plates are clean and enough number provision, when fire occurrence, the stairs areas are large sizes to let many people run on the hotel staires when many customers are running down in the same time. All of any hotel facilities will let customers feel safe or new use in order to let them to feel comfortable to live in the hotel as well as control cost is the main aspect to assist the hotel how to avoid to expend excess expenditure per month. So, how to implement cost control strategy will influence any one hotel income. All of these three aspects may be any one hotel main considerable issues. How to implement effective strategies will be one important discussion issue as below:

Hotel facility management strategy

For hoteliers, hotel management is not one concept. It's hard to really say you've mastered hotel management when it comes with such a range of roles and responsibilities. Being able to adapt, meet challenges, and place yourself on a scale of personal growth is vital for a hotel manager.

There are always new strategies, traveller preferences, or industry technologies emerging that you have to keep track of. Even new roles within hotels and the hotel industry are being created that will affect the way one manages their property.This blog will take you through the major considerations to keep in mind regarding hotel management and throw some tips and ideas along the way, to help you run a better hotel business.

● How managing a hotel as an independent operator?

Hotel operations management: Inventory and revenue

The day to day operations of a hotel are pretty all encompassing. Is everything that guests need in order? Are staff and cleaning schedules organised? Is the occupancy rate where you'd like it to be? Obviously a core aspect of hotel management is to manage your rooms; or your inventory.

Effective inventory management for hotels involves both creating and managing demand, and maximising returns. The investment backing a hotel is tied up in its rooms and the returns can only be gained from selling those rooms optimally.

Here are some strategy basics:

1. Pricing strategy

By driving prices up during high peak periods and knowing how much to discount prices by to ensure rooms are rented during low peak periods, hotels can maximise their return. Through dynamic pricing, businesses can provide discounts and incentives in a controlled way during different seasons.

2. Distribution strategy

Hotels generally advertise their rooms through multiple channels, such as online travel agencies, to optimise reach and promote sales. Distribution management is essential and this involves calculating the minimum numbers of rooms needing to be sold for any given period by each channel. In doing so, you then have the ability to make informed choices regarding reallocation from cancellations or where to list spare rooms to maximise sales.

3. Market segmentation

Being aware of your hotel room visitor need market and the variable preferences, demands and affordability of different demographics are paramount to understanding how to price and distribute your room sales across the various channels. Not only does this help in managing your existing rooms, but it can also allow you to capture more of the market and increase sales and revenue. Flexibility is an important virtue required of hoteliers and being able to understand your clientele and adapt to their needs is vital to building loyalty and guaranteeing profitability.

Revenue management is another huge part of managing your hotel. How do your hotel get smore money coming in and achieve business goals? Smart revenue management and pricing strategies are needed if you want to optimise your Average Daily Rate . I shall recommend some hotel promotion methods as below:

1. Packages, promotions and extras

Packages are any rate that pairs the accommodation with an add-on; it could be free breakfast, free parking, or a ticket to a local event or attraction.Take a look at these methods to make sure your packages offer a unique experience.

Promotions are special rates that can change depending on:

The season or holiday period;

If the guest is a VIP; or,

You want to capitalise on an event.

You can get even more specific by offering things like mobile-only promotions.

Extras are an added expenditure that guests will only realise they want during the booking process. This might include items like champagne and chocolate stocked in their room, shuttle services from the airport, or activities like exercise classes. Extras are an added expenditure that guests will only realise they want during the booking process. This might include items like champagne and chocolate stocked in their room, shuttle services from the airport, or activities like exercise classes.

2. Events and tours

Selling tickets to local events, tours, or offering car rental is a good point-of-sale opportunity to increase your revenue per customer as well as providing a more satisfying experience for your guest.

3. Sell your hotel products

If you offer your guests the chance to buy your shampoo, bath and beach towels, art pieces, linen and so on, it can provide you with extra revenue and might even save you from the cost of replacing items that guests 'accidentally' pack with their own luggage when they depart.

4. Referrals and return business

If your guests give you positive feedback on completion of their stay, encourage them to share their experience with family and friends, and on social media to drive more bookings and brand awareness. You could also set guests up with a promotion code to get a discount the next time they stay. This encourages return business and helps you keep a consistent occupancy rate.

5. Accommodate flexible travellers

Some travellers don't have a set itinerary or allow themselves flexibility with their schedule, so take the opportunity to raise your occupancy and incremental revenue by offering guests a discount for an additional night's stay. Some mistakes have worse consequences than others and depending on the industry, backlash can range from minor to cataclysmic. The type of mistake you make will also have an impact on this. Did it just affect you, or did it also affect your customers?

● Designing hotel website promotion strategy

However, in the hospitality industry almost everything revolves around the customer, and they're the quickest party to point out any flaws. There's also plenty of times where you might simply self-sabotage and fail to get the most out of your business. Human fallibility prevents us from eliminating all our mistakes, but you can certainly look out for some common errors to avoid. I shall indicate some human avoidance mistakes on hotel website design and advertment skillful aspect to cause poor hotel room customer individual experience from your hotel website advertisement as below:

1. Failing to provide basic contact information

A beautiful looking hotel website with a fancy design and stunning features means nothing to the customer if they can't find your address or phone number on the homepage. The basics are something every hotel must get right before anything else. Travellers have all kinds of queries and many of them want to call to get instant clarification, and often people will be calling to make a booking so your phone number is an absolutely essential piece of information.

2. Website scarecrows – autoplay videos and music

Many people book holidays between the hours of 9AM – 5PM, i.e work hours. The last thing they need is for their computer to start blasting commercials or ditties around the office. The first thing they'll do is close your website and it's unlikely they'll return.

3. Incorrect use of social media

It's great to use social media as a marketing avenue but it's important you use it in the right way. You want traffic to be directed to your website and booking pages, not away from them. A common mistake hoteliers make is sending website visitors away to their social media channels immediately after a visitor has landed on the homepage. How many people are going to be coming back once they've been redirected to YouTube for instance?

4. Poor quality photos

There's really no point in investing in a great website design if the photos you integrate into the theme are lacking quality. Travellers want to see what they're paying for and if what they see is a grainy, blurry, or poorly framed image they won't be racing to open their wallets. Paying for high quality photography is worth every penny and you should update your images every couple of years, or every time you refurbish.

5. Downloads for simple information

Does anyone actually enjoy downloading a PDF to their phone or computer? The answer is probably no so why would you make a prospective guest do this? If a traveller wants to view the menu of your hotel restaurant for example, they should be able to do it on your website. Making them download documents is a conversion killer.

6. Connecting to the wrong distribution channels

When you connect to online travel agents manually or via a channel manager, it's still important to do some research. You have to look beyond the four or five biggest channels and find partners that most suit your target market.

7. Ignoring the potential of the local area

Guests are simply buying a hotel room when they come to stay at your hotel. For them, they're paying for an experience delivered by the destination. It would be silly for you not to take advantage of this. Make sure you partner with local businesses and run promotions and packages around local events and attractions.

8. Closing your ears (and mouth) to feedback

Reviews are one of the most important aspects to get right for your hotel. Customer satisfaction and brand reputation are vital if you want to keep the bookings coming in. The worst thing you can do is stay silent online when people leave reviews and feedback on sites like TripAdvisor or your social media pages. You need to respond diligently to both positive and negative reviews.

9. Not paying close attention to seasonality

The price people are prepared to pay for their hotel room will depend on the supply and demand trends over time. Seasonality matters, and you'll have to change rates a number of times during the year to reflect buying behavior and market conditions. This, together with the date and timing release of packages and promotions forms an integral part of your sales and marketing plan.

10. Lacking attention to detail in housekeeping

One of the most common complaints from guests is about dirty rooms or general uncleanliness of the hotel. There should never be any shortcutting when it comes to housekeeping and cleaning. Not only is it a healthy and safety issue, but you open yourself up to a flood of negative reviews. Of course, there are plenty of other pitfalls that could hit your hotel so you have to be constantly diligent and find ways to optimise your processes, reducing the risk of mistakes that could cost you money.

● Hotel and restaurant management strategy

Life gets even more complicated for hotels that also have a restaurant. Since managing a restaurant is a whole other kettle of fish. A study by Leonardo looked at what images travel shoppers viewed the most. Obviously the number one result was guest rooms but the second most viewed was restaurant photos.

This indicates that travel boils down to two primary needs; people want a nice place to sleep and they want a nice place to eat. Most of the time the hotel restaurant is a solid driver of revenue and an integral part of the hotel's identity, so it's ability to help market and sell your hotel should not be underestimated. Here are some reasons your restaurant will drive more bookings and how you can aid the process:

1. Individualise your restaurant

The first thing you need to do is to maximise the quality of your product by treating your hotel restaurant as a restaurant in its own right, rather than a glorified bar only accessible by guests. Turn your restaurant into a premium dining experience that focuses on the whole package including the food, lighting, music, decor, and wine lists. This way, your restaurant won't only be the bait to bring new customers in, but also an incentive for current guests to return when they revisit the area. At the same time it's important to remember who your customers are and understand what they want and what they can afford. Create a menu that will sell, not one you think is cool and trendy, and make sure the pricing is in alignment with the rest of your hotel. Using local produce will help with this.

2. Give your restaurant its own website

Don't let the physical setting of your restaurant deter you from creating a separate website for it. While it should also be featured on your hotel website, a dedicated restaurant website will help maximise revenue and potentially increase traffic to your hotel via page links.The restaurant website should feature large, high-resolution images and videos to showcase the food and decor. Hopefully, if guests land here and see they can also stay in the hotel, they'll be more convinced to stay and book direct.

By cross-referencing both lines of business you'll improve your search engine optimisation and maximise the traffic and conversions you receive. You should make sure everything is optimised for mobile devices and you could also include a direct link to your hotel's booking engine on your restaurant website.

By dedicating a separate website to your restaurant you'll be catering to consumer's need for relevant and distinctive content while also increasing your web presence. It's definitely worth the time and effort, especially if you use a smart intuitive website builder.

3. Make offers or give discounts

Consider offering different restaurant deals for different parts of the week to further encourage people to book with your hotel. Midweek you might advertise via social media or another medium giving away cheaper drinks or free desserts. On the weekend you might include a discounted three-course meal with a booking. As we know, managing a hotel is an extremely complex, stressful, and time-consuming task. The same can be said of running a successful restaurant. Combining both might seem like a fool's errand. And while there's definitely some risks involved in such an enterprise, there's also the opportunity for rich rewards at your hotel.

Hotel restaurant management: How you need to operate

Not only does a successful hotel restaurant have to serve and please your guests at your property, it has to stand on its own as a dining option for anyone in the local area. This is because many guests will want to explore the city and the many options available to them. So if you can't convince your guests to stay in for a meal, you have to attract other paying patrons. Who knows, some diners might even decide to make it a night and book a room directly through your front desk. For this to work the quality of your product has to be high. Your hotel restaurant has to individualise itself and offer a comprehensive dining experience. This means in addition to great food, you need to focus on lighting, music, decor and well thought out wine lists.

Things you need to consider include:

1. Hotel Space

How big will your restaurant attraction be relative to your hotel?

Different departments Staff number

How many patrons can you serve and how many extra staff will you need to oversee this?

2. Restaurent Food Menu

Will you create a menu that sells and is affordable or one that is cool and trendy? Make sure it's in line with who you expect to enter your restaurant.

3. Hotel Room And Food Packages

Obviously giving guests deals and discounts when they book a room direct with you will help increase restaurant traffic and revenue for your property.

● Hotel Restaurant And Hotel Room Bookings good relationship strategy

You should always reserve some tables for your own customers. If a guest walks down to eat and the restaurant is booked out by people not staying at the hotel, the response may be less than favourable.

The main issue is that if your restaurant is receiving poor reviews, it could be turning people off booking a room, no matter how amazing the rest of your hotel is. If it looks like the effort to produce the best possible experience is missing in the restaurant, travellers will assume the same for your whole business and look elsewhere. The same risk applies on the other side of the coin. If your hotel is derided for a poor experience and your occupancy is low, your restaurant could dwindle and die if it relies solely on business from outside the hotel walls.

Your hotel and restaurant have to work in harmony to keep each other strong.

Here are five tips to make your hotel restaurant a success:

1. Strike a balance between class and convenience

For guests already staying at your hotel your restaurant should be a quick and easy place to get a meal. They won't want to spend too much money, nor spend too much time waiting for food if they have other plans. On the other hand, diners coming for the restaurant alone will be expecting first-class ambience, food, and service.To keep everyone hotel customer feels happy and satisfactory when they are living in your hotel, you need to offer a simple but delicious menu that can be eaten in a comfortable setting that also promotes social interaction.

2. Give your restaurant its own website

While it should certainly be featured on your hotel website, a dedicated restaurant website will help maximise revenue and potentially drive extra traffic through your hotel via links. Cross-referencing both lines of business will improve your SEO and help maximise conversions and direct bookings. On your restaurant website, feature large high-resolution images and videos to showcase your food and decor. It will bring attractive and exciting website photos to persuade your potential hotel customers to choose to live your hotel.

3. Create a social media page for your restaurant

If your hotel restaurant has its own website it stands to reason it should have its own Facebook page too. This is especially true if regular events are hosted. Think live music on Friday nights, monthly wine tasting, or happy hours.

It's also useful for posting pictures of your food and dining experience.

4. Offer deals and discounts

You can use different parts of the week and different mediums to drive customers to your restaurant. Before a guest arrives, email them a drink voucher for the restaurant bar. It's likely they'll also grab a meal. You might use social media midweek to promote cheaper drinks or free desserts with every meal order. On the weekend, you could offer a three-course deal when a guest makes a booking.

5. Hire talented hospitality staff

Given the unique challenge of running a restaurant, you need staff that are specifically trained to meet it. Give them the power to create the best possible restaurant experience for your hotel's guests. Hotels and restaurants both form a large part of the hospitality industry and customer service is vital to both. These businesses live and die by customer satisfaction because of the public exposure they're always open to. Guests are only too eager to share stories of their holiday or dining experience – both good and bad.

● Building good cooperative relationship between travel agents and your hotel in your country

Hotel management: Optimising your online travel agent profile. It's common knowledge hotels are at a disadvantage if they aren't engaging online travel agents to boost their distribution and sell rooms. The prominence of OTAs, such as Expedia and Booking.com, continues to grow and they're a proven resource for travellers who use them to discover a diverse range of accommodation options at the best price. Connecting to OTAs will help hotels increase visibility and maintain their occupancy. Your property may even rank higher on search engines – and yet the commission fee from OTAs can feel like a necessary evil if hotels want to accomplish this. However, to make sure you get the full benefit of OTAs and their reach, there's a number of steps you should follow to optimise your hotel's profile. Given your hotel is a brand, your marketing efforts should be consistent across all channels. Don't save your best images and content just for your website, make sure this is also on the OTA websites.

Similar to search engines such as Google, OTAs have their own algorithms for how your property will rank, meaning you need to pay close attention to the following tips:

Here are 6 easy steps to optimise your hotel's OTA profile:

1. Accurately manage your inventory

Because the availability of your rooms will fluctuate due to peak periods or seasonal changes, you need to maintain an accurate inventory across all OTAs to keep your occupancy rate high. Using a channel manager with pooled inventory is the best way to achieve this because travellers won't be disrupted by double booking issues or incorrect data.

2. Cleverly manage your rates and promotions

Guests don't simply use OTAs for a wide range of choice and inspiration, often they're looking for last minute deals and offers. If you have time-sensitive promotions they'll have more chance of being caught and you can more easily sell the remainder of your rooms. It's not hard to make alterations on OTAs to highlight a particular rate or capitalise on seasonal events to attract more guests to your property profile.

3. Carefully respond to reviews

While only 14% of consumers trust traditional advertising, 92% respect reviews on sites such as TripAdvisor. Reviews on OTAs are traditionally reliable because guests can only post a review after they've stayed at the property. However, only 36% of hoteliers respond to reviews on OTA sites. It's important to do an efficient job of managing online reviews.

4. Consider paid advertising

This doesn't have to be restricted to big and rich hotel corporations. It can also be a viable option for independent hotels on a pay-per-click basis. While paid advertising is no guarantee of more bookings, it will help make your property front-of-mind. If your content and aesthetic is strong enough, you should see a rise in revenue and your OTA ranking.

5. Focus on specific markets

Narrowing down your targets will mean you impact a lower volume of customers but you're also more likely to secure the bookings you want if you use certain time periods, events, geo-targeting or other methods to target specific audiences.

6. Understand your competition

It's vital to know who the similar players in your market are so you aren't significantly underselling or overselling your rooms. If you are, you won't be able to compete. On top of this, being aware of their activity may provide an opportunity to snare extra bookings. For example, changing rates could indicate the occupancy of a competitor or a promotion based on something you could also benefit from. There are specific data systems hotels can use to monitor competitors. With an optimised OTA profile, your hotel will not only gain bookings from third-party channels but direct traffic to your website should also increase, helping you to offset the commission fee you pay.

● Hotel restaurant food management strategy

To improve the way you manage your hotel, you have to think about everything and look for ways to save time and money, or increase efficiency. Even small changes can reap big rewards over the course of a financial year. Sticking with the theme of food, there's a big opportunity here. As humans, food represents our most essential connection to the planet and its resources. Yet environmental researchers often surmise that we place less value on food than we used to. Following US hotel kitchen indicates that hotel GDP information. You only have to look at numbers from Hotel Kitchen around food waste to understand their perspective:

In the US alone, an estimated 40% of all food is scrapped

American hotels serve food worth $35 billion each year

It's estimated that 40% of food in customer-facing businesses, such as hotels and supermarkets, goes to waste

How to control food waste in your hotel's kitchen

Fighting food waste at your hotel goes beyond feeding people and helping the environment – it also improves your property's bottom line. Do you really know how much food you throw away each week? Have you worked out its monetary value? Are staff and guests aware of your efforts to be more sustainable and properly manage food waste disposal? According to Hotel Kitchen, more than 90% of staff say they want to take action on tackling food waste. Guests are also becoming increasingly savvy with 60% of those surveyed saying they expect hotels to be actively reducing waste across their operations.

There may be steps your hotel restaurant can take to reduce waste:

1. Get buy in on food waste from your team

Create a team to take ownership of waste reduction and incentivise them. This should include a cook or chef and a kitchen porter (KP). Your KPs see what gets scraped off plates, while a chef will know how leftover ingredients can be better used in future menus.

2. Research waste management software to support processes

Conduct a waste audit, by dividing waste into categories and ensuring staff dispose of it in an appropriately-labelled container. There is weight-based software for this: basically a talking bin that records the weight of different categories of waste according to descriptions entered by staff on a touchscreen. The most well-known of these is probably the Winnow system, which its manufacturer claims typically saves operators 3-5% on food costs – a ROI of up to 10 times within a year. The challenges with using a system like this is that, it requires all waste to go into the same bin, leading to congestion in the kitchen or pot wash, and it can take time to input the data.

3. Assess raw ingredients vs. diners' plates

If conducting a waste audit manually, you'll need to at least split waste into raw ingredients and prepared waste that is left on diners' plates. Almost 10% of raw ingredients are wasted. This includes things like potato peelings and cauliflower leaves, which can be difficult to find a use for. Raw ingredients also covers kitchen prep mistakes. Some 35% of restaurant waste is left on diners' plates. This is most definitely higher in a hotel restaurant, where diners are less likely to take their leftovers home.

4. Asking staff for their frequent observations

Raw ingredients and diners' plates might be the two main categories, but make sure you have as many containers as you have space for. Record the waste, by weight, but also anecdotally. You'll learn more from staff comments: what did they find surprising? Was there an item plated but not eaten? Is there a garnish that customers commonly leave?

5. Following the 'less is more' approach

Assemble as many staff as possible to discuss the results, after a fortnight or a month. When it comes to prepared waste, you may find that it's a result of portion sizes being too large, in which case introduce strict portion controls, possibly using measure scoops that are colour-coded for different items. If lots of butter and preserve is left after breakfast service, consider buying in individual wrapped portions. Keep in mind that, unavoidable post-consumer waste can often be used by farmers as animal feed: all good content for your Instagram stories.

6. Obsessing over food and beverage expiration dates

If you discover that fresh items are going out of date, introduce a strict fridge rotation system and coloured stickers to identify which items to use first. Store new foods on the right fridge and existing on the left to maximise shelf life. Get this ingrained and replicate it in ambient storage areas for rice, herbs and spices, pulses and grains as well. Out of date ingredients can usually be donated to local food banks. Build a relationship with your local food bank operator and post about it on social media to boost your presence in the local community. This may lead to worthwhile involvement in charity events.

7. Sharpen up your kitchen team's knife skills

Meat carcasses should always be used for stock. If staff report that there is still a lot of meat left on bones, check that knives are being properly sharpened and that staff are trained to bone items efficiently. If staff lack butchery and fishmongers skills you'll save on waste by buying, for example, cubed chicken and filleted fish.

8. Using proper peelers for vegetables

Similarly, are staff prepping vegetables properly? You'll see less waste using peelers than knives for most fruit and root vegetables.

9. Allocating some space for composting

Raw vegetable waste can be composted if you have some outside space. A compost area can be simply constructed out of pallets. The resulting compost can be used to improve the soil on site or donated to local allotment groups. It can often be valuable to look at what businesses in other parts of your industry are doing, and seeing how you compare or what you might be able to employ in your own business strategies.

10. Getting customer service ideas from restaurants

There are similarities between service in restaurants and hotels, but also a few differences. Let's see how great customer service in restaurants translates to achieving guest satisfaction in hotels.

A great first step is turning 'service' into 'hospitality'

Service is basically about performing a task; doing something for someone. It denotes a mechanical action. On the other hand, hospitality is about making an impression on someone and going the extra mile to make their experience a memorable one. The interaction involved in hospitality is a genuine one and should be based on a caring attitude. Hospitality is something the best restaurants do extremely well. Customers will generally be served by one waiter their entire visit and will be made to feel like close friends or family, constantly attended to and conversed with warmly. Any requests will be responded to immediately. By the end of the meal, customers will look forward to coming back and seeing their waiter again.

In hotels, guests might interact with many different staff members throughout their stay, meaning they don't always get this personal connection. They may have to wait longer for services and might get frustrated when the staff member doesn't remember their preferences. The attentiveness of restaurants is certainly something hotels can try to replicate. Some things to try is to greet guests by name, get to know their interests, and don't delay when they want attention.

Giving guests a personalised experience at your hotel

A recent report shows full-service and fast food restaurants are revamping their menus and establishing more mobile ordering options, to the delight of customers. Restaurants are adapting their menus and technology to align with shifting consumer preferences. This looks at millennial tastes for fresh food, mobile ordering, and automated kiosks. The bottom line is that restaurants are working hard to please consumers in a way the customers are dictating, resulting in higher satisfaction.

Hotels need to do the same. New technology, both front and backend, needs to be explored if customer service is to improve. Again this comes back to hospitality and personalisation. Give each specific guest what they need. Even if you look at mobile check-in, it's not something everyone wants. Obviously some guests will be in a rush or tired from travel and simply want to get to their room as fast as possible. Others will be craving some human interaction. It's about what's convenient for the individual hotel guest. Technology should be able to help hotels in every regard. Think about how technology can improve the in-room experience, especially when it comes to speeding up room service or cleaning processes. Conversely, if backend tech that makes it easier to manage reservations and distribution is used, more time can be dedicated to guest experience.

Empower staff to solve their own problems

Nothing will frustrate a customer more than a staff member always needing to clear something with their manager. Not only does this take more time, but it makes the staff member look incompetent. Quality restaurants will take difficult or specific requests in their stride and provide customers with any special needs they require. If something goes wrong, their constant hands-on experience allows them to solve it, without the intervention of a manager. Again, it's done with a smile on their face because nothing is too much trouble for a valued customer.

Hotels need to train and empower their staff this way too. A great example is The Ritz-Carlton Hotel Company, where even hourly employees have permission to spend up to $2,000 per guest to solve any problem or dissatisfaction that may arise, without needing to ask for approval or involve management. And it's not the amount of money that's the point; it's the instant no-need-for-approval empowerment, which enables quick solutions for guests.

Hire the right traits in staff at your hotel

The very best restaurant staff show a passion for their job and authentic desire to make people happy. While the hospitality industry is one where skills can be learned on the job and thus standards may be lax, the approach taken to hiring staff must be taken very seriously.

To name just a few, some necessary traits a hotel should find it its staff include:

Empathy

Warmth

Conscientiousness

Enthusiasm

Charisma

● Hotel regular reports for effective hotel management strategy

Reporting on performance is essential to hotel management. You need to collect and analyse accurate data regularly to see where things are working, and what you need to improve on. There are a lot of different parts of the business you'll need reports on to inform your overall strategy. Most of them can be pulled from the systems that you're using such as your property management system and channel manager etc.

Some of the most important information your hotel different department managers need to track includes:

Channel performance

Website performance

Housekeeping

ADR – Average daily rate

Occupancy

RevPAR – Revenue per available room

TrevPAR – Total revenue per available room

Channel performance is key. You need to understand a number of factors about your booking channels. For instance, which channel is delivering the most reservations? Which channel is contributing the most overall revenue? Which channel has the highest cancellation rate? Which has the largest or smallest lead time?

The point is the more information you have about your channel performance, the more tweaks you can make to optimise your distribution mix. Cutting some channels and connecting others, or temporarily pausing, can enable you to maximise revenue.

Given how important direct bookings are, website performance is equally important. Since your booking engine can be included in channel performance you'll be able to see if direct bookings are down. Investigating your website is a good idea. How much traffic are you driving via organic and paid means? What pages are being visited the most? What's the conversion rate on calls to action? How many people are abandoning a booking part of the way through?

Housekeeping is extremely significant. Do you know how long it's taking to clean a room on average? How many guests are arriving to find their room isn't ready yet? Do you have enough cleaning resources or not enough? How efficient are staff?

This is all information you need to report on each and every month to see if your business is on an upward spiral or if standards are dropping. Through your property management and revenue management systems you can track occupancy, ADR, and many other metrics.

● Hotel management software technological strategy

Technology in the hotel industry continues to advance at a rapid pace and hotel management software (HMS) remains essential for hoteliers looking to improve the running of their business. With software, hotel operators can streamline their administrative processes and improve their overall hotel management system. The key to reaping the benefits of an effective hotel management software system is to select the right one for your property. It's critical that you know exactly what this hotel management technology is, and why it is important for you to implement it at your hotel.

What is hotel management software?

Hotel management software is technology that allows hotel operators and owners to streamline their administrative tasks while also increasing their bookings in both the short- and long-term. Your hotel management system is not only important for your own day-to-day operations, but it's a vital part of the overall guest experience. From the beginning of your guests' online booking journey until the completion of their stay and their feedback once they return home, it is necessary for your hotel management technology to enhance their experience with your brand. Finding a hotel management system that offers the features you both need and want is necessary to effectively managing your hotel in a global economic climate.

The purpose of management systems for hotels

Management systems serve several purposes for both hotel operators who manage large chains as well as independent hoteliers. These include:

1. Managing bookings

Your property management system should help you efficiently and effectively manage your bookings. Neither you, nor your staff, should be tasked with manually inputting bookings and managing those across all your distribution channels. A property management system should automate the booking process for you, allowing you to escape the back office and focus more on interacting with your guests. In addition, it significantly reduces the risk of overbooking your rooms, which directly improves the guest experience at your property.

2. Direct bookings

It should allow you to actively drive direct bookings to your website. Travellers today are more apt to book online than they are to call to finalise bookings or partner with a travel agent. Direct bookings allow you to maximise the revenue that you generate per booking. You should only consider software that integrates with an online booking engine.

3. Channel management

Hotel management technology should allow you to easily implement your distribution strategy. Creating partnerships with different types of agents in the industry, such as OTAs and GDSs, is necessary to survive in a competitive, global climate. Managing hotel with software that offers a channel manager will allow you to create and implement a diverse distribution strategy that continually drives bookings.

4. Hotel website

Your hotel administration department software should help enhance your online presence. Your hotel management system is only effective if your guests can reach your brand. Choosing a program that offers a web editor or website creator will allow you to create a clean, appealing and user-friendly website that will encourage guests to book a stay at your property.

Benefits of hotel management technology

When you are selecting hotel management technology for your property, you should consider the many benefits that this system will offer you, including:

1. Reduce time spent on administrative tasks

You hotel can minimise the amount of time spent on administrative tasks. The right hotel management system will do a lot of the work for you, allowing you to focus your efforts and your energy on the big picture. The technology should also provide you with valuable data on how your employees perform their duties and how this affects employee retention, satisfaction and productivity. In today's fast-paced travel environment, it's critical that you automate as many tasks as possible. A property management system can help you tremendously with that.

2. Increase your online presence

Your hotel can increase your brand presence online. Management software that is integrated with your website builder will allow you to accept direct online bookings and develop a user-friendly website. Naturally, this will increase your relevance in the search engine results and allow more travellers to discover your property during their online booking journey.

3. Build relationships with guests

Your hotel will develop a better rapport with your target market segment, while also identifying new markets to tap into. The types of travellers who have always loved staying at your property will appreciate the improved experience. In addition, your new technology will allow you to reach out to new markets that would not have otherwise discovered your brand.

4. Manage your distribution

Your hotel will improve your reach throughout the industry. With a property management system in place that integrates with a channel manager, you will be able to advertise across many channels whilst maintaining rate parity. From the large OTAs and GDSs to individual retail travel agents, you can provide real-time booking information to your agents that will drive bookings.

5. Manage your hotel revenue and cost expenditure control

Your hotel can implement a beneficial revenue management strategy. Using innovative pricing tools that allow you to create a flexible room pricing strategy, you can maximise the revenue that you generate per room at any given moment. Pricing your rooms right is the key to succeeding in this competitive industry, and having these tools available can help you significantly.

6. Increase room bookings

Your hotel will ultimately increase your large , middle and small size room number bookings. At the end of the day, the point of every feature within your hotel management business solution is to boost the bookings that you get at your hotel. Whether your hotel wants to increase your off-season bookings or you want to expand your offerings to new market segments, you will be successful if you select the right hotel management software for your property.

● Hotel property facility management strategy

The first aspect, is your hotel safe facility system. Managing a hotel isn't all about managing the physical property, it's also about managing intangible things like reputation. Any hotel facility issues may influence hotel customers how feel your hotel service performance, for example, when your hotel customers are living in your hotel rooms, during this living period, they feel your hotel fire system is not safe, it will influnece that they choose to reduce room booking living days because they are afraid fire occurs can cause their death. So, any hotel floor fire safe property management facilities will influence any one customer makes booking room days decision whether they can extend days or shorten days to live in your hotel.

Another aspect, is your hotel online booking facility system. It's very simple. Hospitality businesses such as hotels are at risk if they don't focus attention on their online reviews and take control of their reputation management. As more and more guests turn to one another for advice on where to stay in cities around the world, the effectiveness of traditional hotel advertising is declining – while the impact of online hotel reviews is on the rise.

Failure to monitor, manage and respond to feedback will skew your hotel management strategy to issues that are unimportant to customers, as well as provide unhappy customers with ammunition for negative feedback on travel and social media sites. It can be difficult for an individual to get through their lives without significant episodes being recorded on social media channels, let alone a hotel to exist without the blemish of social media complaints.

As the impact of online bookings and digital feedback continues to rise, the importance of reputation management rises with it. Yet while online reputation management is a trend across the hospitality sector, it is still considered an indulgence by some independent hoteliers. Part of this rationale is driven by the confusion around how to deal with both positive and negative feedback online. So here are some standard ways hoteliers can deal with online reviews – regardless of sentiment:

The most feared of all feedback online is a negative review

However, audiences are particularly savvy in determining the value of feedback, not just because the "voice" of the author is on display, but because audiences often apply a filter to their reading of any review. Consciously or subconsciously, they consider the value of any commentary, as well as the relevance of a comment to their own experiences and preferences. So a comment on the convenience of a hotel location to an equestrian events venue will be of potential importance to horse-lovers, yet entirely irrelevant to many other potential guests. Where a rational negative comment is posted, hotels do have options on how to respond.

Acknowledge and Action

For a genuine, reasoned negative comment on customer experience, it is best for hotels to respond in a timely manner (within 72 hours of posting), acknowledging the issue and describing how it will be addressed. Ideally, a follow up post will occur after actioning the issue, and showing how the experience will not be repeated. This is by far the best possible response to negative feedback, because online audiences are far more willing to value action and positive changes in behaviour, than think poorly of the initial negative experience.

Apologise and Compensate

For a negative comment which illustrates an experience that was difficult or impossible to avoid, an appropriate response is to apologise for the poor experience and to privately offer either monetary compensation, or discounts on future bookings. While this is unlikely to totally satisfy the customer with the stated poor experience, it will indicate to other customers, the prioritisation of customer experiences at the hotel. It's important to take compensation offline where possible to avoid inviting those like to complain for free stuff.

Apologise and Thank

For negative comments that focus on pedantic details, the most appropriate response is an apology for the experience and an acknowledgement that this feedback will help shape your hotel's future guest experience strategy. This is far more useful than a response which states that the comment will be passed to a customer service team, because the customer already believes that service is the problem at the property.

How to thank hotel guests for their positive feedback

While most organisations are thrilled with the prospect of positive reviews, an abundance of rave reviews can be just as suspicious to audiences as a series of negative reviews. Therefore, positive reviews also need a response.

Be Humble

Where a positive review is excessive and perhaps gushing, it is wise for firms to thank the guest for their enthusiasm, but to also acknowledge areas where you are attempting to improve. This reinforces commitment to customer service.

Be Delighted

Where positive feedback is sincere and reasoned, the best response for hotels is to express delight and appreciation for the feedback and the desire to serve again in future. This is the easiest response to deliver, but is often the least fulfilled.

Be Appreciative

Where feedback is predominantly neutral, but some aspects are highlighted as being of particular value, it is advisable for hotel managers to express thanks for the feedback and to request further advice on how the organisation could improve in specific areas. Again, try to take this conversation offline with an email or personal phone call. This enables more considered feedback to follow the initial post.

● Reputation management strategy

Reputation management is often considered difficult or time-consuming. Yet the results of research into the importance of reputation management are unarguable: the value of reputation management is substantial and growing. Understanding how to respond to feedback is not just a competitive advantage, but potentially a means of ensuring your hotel stays in business. Your hotel can easily turn complaints around and win hotel guests back – and these basic reputation management responses are your first line of defence.

Hotel property management software

Selecting the right hotel software is critical, particularly in a world where consumers are relying more heavily on their devices with each passing day. An investment this important to your overall success as a hotel operator requires you to do some research.

These are seven questions that you should ask your hotel tech provider as soon as possible:

1. How does your hotel product maintains its relevance in the hospitality industry?

While the core of a technology system may remain the same over time, the reality is that any product geared specifically towards the hospitality industry will need to adapt to changing trends and preferences from travellers. You need to ask this question so you have an understanding of how your technology will help you grow along with the industry.

2. How often can your hotel expects upgrades for your platform?

No piece of technology is perfect, and the best hotel technology providers will make sure that regular updates and upgrades are available for their clients. It's important to have an understanding of how often these upgrades will be available, and how you will be able to successfully implement the upgrades.

3. What level of customer service will I receive from your company?

Unfortunately, far too many hotel technology providers focus on hard sales tactics without much support after the purchase is complete. You will want to verify with your provider that there will be ways to contact and work with staff after the technology has been installed at your hotel.

4. Is your hotel platform secure?

Security should be a top priority of your hotel technology provider. You will want to ask about the details regarding their security features, as it's imperative that both your data and your guests' data is secure.

5. How easily can your hotel personalise your systems?

Hotel technology providers need to offer you a versatile system that includes not only the generic features that are necessary for any hotel, but also the adaptable features that allow you to personalise the platform for your particular brand. Ultimately, your investment in technology needs to result in a system that works specifically for your hotel.

6. What reporting features are available?

When your hotel begin your search for the right hotel technology, you will likely focus first on the property management system. However, you will want to discuss additional features that also are available, with some of the most important being the reporting features. Verify that you'll be able to run detailed reports using live data, as this is the only way to ensure that you can grow your brand.

7. How can your hotel accesses the hotel technology system once implemented?

Be sure that you are investing in a system that allows you to run your hotel from anywhere. You need hotel technology that is optimised for all devices, including smartphones and tablets.

Benefits of a hotel management system

When you are selecting hotel management systems for your property, you should consider the many benefits they'll offer you, including:

1. Reduce time spent on administrative tasks

Your hotel can minimise the amount of time spent on administrative tasks. The right hotel management system will do a lot of the work for you, allowing you to focus your efforts and your energy on the big picture. The technology should also provide you with valuable data on how your employees perform their duties and how this affects employee retention, satisfaction and productivity. In today's fast-paced travel environment, it's critical that you automate as many tasks as possible. A property management system can help you tremendously with that.

2. Increase your hotel online presence

Your hotel can increase your brand presence online. Management software that is integrated with your website builder will allow you to accept direct online bookings and develop a user-friendly website. Naturally, this will increase your relevance in the search engine results and allow more travellers to discover your property during their online booking journey.

3. Build relationships with guests

Your hotel will develop a better rapport with your target market segment, while also identifying new markets to tap into. The types of travellers who have always loved staying at your property will appreciate the improved experience. In addition, your new technology will allow you to reach out to new markets that would not have otherwise discovered your brand.

4. Manage your hotel distribution

Your hotel will improve your reach throughout the industry. With a property management system in place that integrates with a channel manager, you will be able to advertise across many channels whilst maintaining rate parity. From the large OTAs and GDSs to individual retail travel agents, you can provide real-time booking information to your agents that will drive bookings.

5. Manage your hotel revenue

Your hotel can implement a beneficial revenue management strategy. Using innovative pricing tools that allow you to create a flexible room pricing strategy, you can maximise the revenue that you generate per room at any given moment. Pricing your rooms right is the key to succeeding in this competitive industry, and having these tools available can help you significantly.

6. Increase bookings

Your hotel will ultimately increase your bookings. At the end of the day, the point of every feature within your hotel management business solution is to boost the bookings that you get at your hotel.

Hotel property management system

All hotels need some variation of a property management system (PMS). However they come in many different forms and are not all created equal. There are still properties trying to manage their business in a traditional way with books and ledgers, others are using server-based systems, while many used web-based systems.

One of the most valuable things to a hotel manager is time, and money of course. The first two systems listed are a drain on both time and finances, while the latter has obviously become the optimal way to manage hotel operations. Cloud-based PMSs are a superior way to automate and accelerate all the important processes at your hotel such as taking and confirming bookings, managing reservations, generating bills and reports, check-in/out, room transfers, checking/editing availability, guest communication, the list goes in. Cloud-based technology can handle all these tasks with ease because of its ability to deeply integrate with channel managers, booking engines, and revenue management systems. Despite this, there are still concerns over the validity and cost effectiveness of cloud-based PMSs.

Here are five common property management system myths and why we think they're unfounded?

1. You think cloud-based technology is confusing or hard to use

Because it's intangible and seemingly floating in the air, some hotel managers believe using cloud technology will be hard to learn and too confusing to keep track of. The opposite is true. A PMS allows you to keep everything in one place and it can never be lost. You can access your data from any location so long as you have the Internet. The many tasks that you perform using multiple programs or books can be done from one central location with a fully integrated PMS. This also means you can collaborate better with other staff who need access to the same information.

2. You worry that sensitive data is insecure and vulnerable

While the information in your cloud PMS isn't kept under lock and key it is encrypted and backed-up. Nothing is stored 'onsite' so even if your computer breaks or your laptop is lost, your data will remain accessible to you. With data in the cloud you don't have to worry about viruses or bugs, and hacking is much less likely to succeed thanks to firewalls and authentication gateways.

3. Your current software works just as well as cloud-based technology

It's unlikely this is true and even if it is, it won't be for long. Cloud software is constantly being updated and evolved meaning users automatically get the benefits included in their monthly fee. If your current server isn't updated, it becomes slow and vulnerable, while updating it requires extra time and greater cost that has to be done too regularly.

4. You believe a web PMS is only suitable for large hotels

The reality is that smaller or independent hoteliers are often stretched thinner than anyone. With less staff and more responsibility, the time and hassle saved by using a cloud-based PMS is vital and could be the difference between getting the bookings needed for maximum occupancy or losing revenue on empty rooms.

5. You think hotel technology is too expensive

Cloud-based systems are actually very cost effective. You never require any additional hardware, backup solutions, licensing, updates, fixes. There's also no lengthy setup process and with the time you save using it, more resources can be directed towards increasing guest experience and revenue streams. Overall a cloud-based PMS will give you more control over your hotel business, with:

List of hotel property management systems may include as below:

There are literally hundreds of property management systems on the market. The most important aspect when choosing one is to ensure it's easy to use, has all the functions you need, and that it is able to integrate with your other important systems, such as your channel manager.

Some popular examples you might come across include:

Little Hotelier

Mews

Sirvoy

CloudBeds

Frontdesk Anywhere

eZee Frontdesk

Hotelogix

Maestro

OPERA

Avvio

Online booking engine

Essential if your hotel wants to capture direct bookings and reduce the commission you pay to online travel agents (OTAs). The majority of travellers will visit your hotel website even if they discover your property on an OTA.But if you're looking to capitalise on this traffic, your booking engine needs certain features beyond booking as a minimum including:

Seamless online experience for your guests via a customised, two-step booking process. Multi-language and currency capabilities to convert guests from around the globe. Mobile-friendly and Facebook-compatible to reach travellers on-the-go. Upselling capability so you can offer a more personalised stay for your guests. However your hotel booking engine can be a much more powerful tool that you can customise to suit any marketing strategy, allowing your business to maximise its revenue.

Ensure your hotel gets as much value as possible out of your booking engine by following these steps:

1. Prioritise booking engine and website integration

Seamless integration between booking engine and website will make a guests booking experience so much easier. It will be more responsive to mobile, put less pressure on you to design the look of your booking engine, and will maintain your branding throughout the entire booking process. All of this will enhance the trust your customers have in your hotel.

2. Create a strong foundation for search engine optimisation

While not directly related to your booking engine, SEO is vital. If your website isn't optimised for SEO it won't matter how amazing your booking engine is, you won't be attracting sufficient traffic to drive bookings.

3. Implement urgency messages

Urgency messages do exactly what they imply; invoke urgency in the shopper. By drawing attention to rates through urgency messages you can make your guests think they are in danger of missing out, or else getting something other customers aren't. They're a great way of speeding up the booking process and increasing conversions. Examples include 'Book now, pay later!' or 'Only two rooms left!'.

4. Use promo code banners

If you're running a promotion, you want guests to notice it. Display a prominent promo banner on your website using your booking engine so guests can easily view and select applicable dates and benefit from the promotion.

5. Set up an early-bird rate

By selling discounted early-bird rates you can improve your short-term cash flow by collecting full prepayment from the booker. You can control when to flag an early-bird rate via your booking engine extranet.

6. Introduce last-minute rates

Setting attractive last minute rates are good for increasing your short-term occupancy or filling any remaining rooms. Offset the rate by taking a high deposit to limit the amount of cancelled bookings or no-shows. Clearly display these and use them in conjunction with urgency messages.

7. Entice guests with a stay pay deal

Maintain your occupancy by increasing the length of your guests stay. Offer them a discount for one or more of their dates, clearly indicating the price difference and encourage them to book additional nights. Make sure you have control over what night is to be discounted; first, last, cheapest etc.

8. Interest guests in package deals

Packaging up extras like entry to events, attractions, or restaurants gives guests a one-stop shopping experience that they enjoy. Offer options guests can't find on OTAs and again entice them to stay longer. If used intelligently a booking engine can be a hotel marketing and branding tool that will incentivise guests to become loyal to your hotel, further increasing your direct bookings and revenue in the future.

Hotel room management software: Channel managers

A channel manager is a tool that will allow you to sell all your rooms on all your connected booking sites at the same time. It will automatically update your availability in real-time on all sites when a booking is made, when you close a room to sale, or when you want to make bulk changes to your inventory. There's a lot more to a channel manager than simply making life easier for when updating your rates and availability. You can use it to perform many tasks when managing your hotel and its benefits are two-fold in how it can increase bookings and revenue, and enable long term business planning.

Take a look at this comprehensive list of how a channel manager can be used to benefit a hotel.

1. Increase online bookings

With telephone and walk-in bookings on the decline and online bookings on the rise, a channel manager places you in the best position to take advantage of this new traveller booking habit. Connect to more online channels, where more travellers than ever are locking in their stays.

2. Increase hotel revenue

Given a channel manager displays live rates and availability across all your channels at the same time, and updates automatically you can accept bookings faster and almost eliminate the chance of double bookings. In addition, the data you can analyse from your channel manager can ensure your rates are always optimised and you're using the most lucrative channels.

3. Reduce the risk of overbookings

Without a channel manager, you're forced to split your inventory between channels and risk double-bookings or failing to reach full occupancy. Pooled inventory and automated updates of availability and rates in real time means guests can only ever book a room that is actually available.

4. Improve brand recognition

A powerful channel manager will provide two-way unrestricted access to hundreds of booking channels where travellers who would never hear of you can now make reservations at your property. It also makes OTAs more likely to accept your listing because they can be sure your inventory will always be accurate.

5. Boost direct bookings

It may seem illogical but it's true! Many travellers will discover your property first on an OTA, but they want to learn more about you before they book. Often they will visit your website and then make the decision to book their stay. So you get a direct sale, but it was born on the OTA site – resulting in greater profit for your hotel. This is known as the billboard effect.

6. Remove manual processes

Manual data entry is time-consuming and frustrating, we all know that. If you were to use a channel manager and remove this friction, you'd realise just how much more productive you can be. Anything that has to be put on hold can now be prioritised to improve your business.

7. Create a seamless, integrated tech stack

Instead of being required to update information in multiple extranets, a channel manager can integrate with your property management system, central reservation system, or revenue management system as well as your booking engine to create a central control system for the entirety of your hotel's operations. Some channel managers, like SiteMinder, also have a unique connection to Airbnb. Although boutique hotels have already been using Airbnb for some time, there hasn't been a solution for them to manage this channel in conjunction with other partners such as online travel agents – until SiteMinder's partnership.

8. Transform into a powerful business platform

A good channel allows complete transparency of data across all systems and channels, meaning you can use the received information to see which channels or rooms are performing the best. This means you can constantly update your business strategy. Look at reports such as channel yield and channel analysis and your reservation trends to see where things are going right – or wrong!

9. Reduce reliance on traditional booking channels

There's certainly no suggestion that you should leave behind traditional methods such as taking reservations over the phone or via walk-ins. It can be very profitable to save some of your inventory for these methods. However, using a channel manager will ensure you don't have to worry about filling your rooms in this manner. Connecting to a significant number of online booking sites will ensure your occupancy always remains steady.

10. Keep everyone on the same page

Quality channel managers are very easy to use and hotels will regularly have multiple staff members using the system. If the main user is going away or won't be available to make updates they can easily mark important dates in the system so everyone is aware if they need to change a rate or a close a room etc. For example, they may mark school holiday periods so rates can be increased during these peak times.

Hotel management apps technology

In order to enhance productivity at your hotel, you must first ensure you and your team are as organised as possible. This may be easier said than done when you have emails arriving non-stop, content to post and people to manage . Technology has evolved to solve almost any problem. There are many apps in the market to help with everyday challenges. Organised teams get more done and having everything under control also gives you a better grip on the overall success of the business.

Here are five hotel apps to help stay on top of hotel management:

1. Pocket

Have you ever come across interesting articles, videos or websites and ended up forgetting about them? Whenever you find something you want to view later, you can add it to your Pocket – an application and web service for managing reading lists. You can save content directly from your browser or from apps like Twitter, Flipboard, Pulse and Zite. Once saved to Pocket, the list of content is visible on any device (phone, tablet or computer) with access to your account – online and offline helping you share interesting articles with your hotel's team.

2. Astro

If a large part of your day-to-day duties includes sending and receiving emails, Astro will help you focus on what is most important. Astro brings along email and calendar features, powered by an Artificial Intelligence (AI) assistant, which will prioritise your emails, tell you what to follow up on, and help you clean up your inbox. Astro also adds reminders, snoozed emails, and scheduled emails to your calendar, so you can get a complete view of your day. You can also customise the emails you send with Open Tracking, Send Later, Custom Signatures, and much more.

3. Google Calendar

One of the most important parts of management is time management and having your calendar with you on the go can be crucial. Stay on track with your appointments and tasks with Google Calendar. Your events or any meeting requests received via Gmail can be automatically added to your calendar and you'll spend less time managing your schedule. Add images and maps to your appointments, and access your schedule for the day, week and month from any device at any time. You can also gain visibility of your team's work schedule and share your calendar view with them so you can make the most of your day.

4. Trello

Stay up to speed with your team projects using Trello – an easy, free, flexible, and visual way to manage and organise workflow. Trello is divided in boards, with lists representing the workflow. For example, you can have your Social Media Marketing board and inside the lists: To Do, Doing and Done. Every list has cards, representing tasks containing relevant information. For example, the New Years 7 Nights Promotion card will contain the specification of this promotion, such as due date, hotel team members that need to follow the task, checklists and more. As tasks progress along the way, the card will navigate to the next list. With Trello you have a clear and real-time view of the stage your project is at and you'll never lose track of them.

5. Evernote

If sometimes you feel the need for a second brain, meet Evernote – an app designed for note taking, organising tasks lists, and archiving. You can collect everything that matters in one place and find it when you need it, fast. Capture, organise, and share notes from any device and always keep your best ideas in sync and only a click away.

Evernote is not a simple note taking app, you can enhance your notes with links, checklists, tables, attachments, and audio recordings. Even handwritten notes are searchable. From initial brainstorm to finished project, Evernote will give you productivity bliss.

Apps the key to establishing self-service experiences

It's no secret modern-day travellers are becoming more accustomed to hyper-personalised and streamlined service from their hotels. In fact, if the hotel is going to deliver on its promise of quality, your guests expect a personalised and convenient experience.

Hotels can adapt to this growing need by prioritising data, technology, and connectivity. It's important to know what guests want, and also how to provide the appropriate services through hotel systems and applications. The tradition of limiting service and interaction to just your hotel staff and physical property is being outgrown by the ability of technology to automate and make many processes easier for guests. Where travellers once expected to be greeted by a front desk operator, they might now prefer the self-service experience that mobile check-in offers. Given the average person wastes an hour each week waiting in line, it's no surprise that self-service is catching on.

The self-service approach allows staff to be less transactional and focus on establishing genuine connections with guests. With technology in place, hotel employees will no longer be confined to stationary positions within the lobby or left to guess what guest expectations might be. For a better idea of the trends in this area and the enabling power of technology and connectivity, we spoke to four hotel applications to get their perspective.

Being able to adapt, meet challenges, and place yourself on a scale of personal growth is vital for a hotel manager. Hotel management is about overseeing every operation of the property. This requires knowledge of distribution strategy, finance, customer service, staff management, marketing, and more. Effective inventory management for hotels involves both creating and managing demand, and maximising returns. Revenue management is another huge part of managing your hotel. How do you get more money coming in and achieve business goals?

In the hospitality industry almost everything revolves around the customer, and they're the quickest party to point out any flaws. Good management eliminates as many mistakes as possible. Hotel management sometimes also requires the management of a restaurant.

Turn your hotel restaurant into a premium dining experience that focuses on the whole package including the food, lighting, music, decor, and wine lists. This way, your restaurant won't only be the bait to bring new customers in, but also an incentive for current guests to return when they revisit the area.

Similar to search engines such as Google, OTAs have their own algorithms for how your property will rank, meaning you need to pay close attention to how you build your profile on them. Fighting food waste at your hotel goes beyond feeding people and helping the environment – it also improves your property's bottom line. Reporting on performance is essential to hotel management. You need to collect and analyse accurate data regularly to see where things are working, and what you need to improve on. Hotel management software is technology that allows hotel operators and owners to streamline their administrative tasks while also increasing their bookings in both the short- and long-term.

Managing a hotel isn't all about managing the physical property, it's also about managing intangible things like reputation. There are many apps in the market to help with everyday challenges. Organised teams get more done and having everything under control also gives you a better grip on the overall success of the business.

- Keys to an effective hotel distribution strategy

How to increase your hotel's occupancy rate

Effective revenue management strategies for hotels

Essential strategies to increase your hotel room sales

Facility management, or FM, is a broad discipline that includes a variety of industries, from food to technology, manufacturing to e-commerce and beyond. But, though the core of each business may be completely different from even its closest competition, successful facility management practices are easily interchangeable from enterprise to enterprise. As a matter of fact, it is one of the only job titles that can be found in, basically, any small to large organizations, including public entities, like schools and hospitals, to private businesses, like those that manage their inventory in warehouses.But, reciprocal tendencies aside, facility management procedures and techniques must be highly-specialized for the business in which they are being used. Because the discipline covers complex specifics, including business continuity planning and even fire safety, it's key that your organization offers a holistic outlook on its facility management procedures.

- The Core Competencies of Hotel Facility Management strategy

According to the International Facilities Management Association (IFMA), facility management is an interdisciplinary practice that "considers the coordination of people, place, process, and technology." Broken down, this means that a facility manager is responsible for the success of the all facets of the facility, including organization, safety, security, and maintenance, along with the key, everyday operational practices. Facility Management Core Competencies

It may seem like an overwhelming job to put on one person or one small team – and it is an overwhelming job – but what's important to remember is the fact that facility management is just one aspect of what makes a healthy business. Simply put, all necessary departments must work with facility managers to build a business' overall success.

Safety – It's the facility management team's job to ensure the safety of all of the employees and customers occupying the property. This responsibility spans all possible environmental health and safety issues, particularly ones that concern the building and its equipment, specifically. Failure to do so can mean serious business in the form of fines, lost business, or even prosecution if it was deemed that the manager or business' negligence caused casualties or permanent environmental damage. Fire, for example, is usually right at the top of the radars of facility managers because it's a preventable tragedy that, when prepared for sufficiently, can save lives and valuable inventory. A thorough facility management team can protect its company best by guaranteeing that all parts of the facility are up-to-code, its employees are trained well, and all permits and certificates are completely valid. This function entails everything from safe and efficient lighting to flooring choices.

Security – In regards to importance, second to safety is facility security, yet another important piece of the puzzle in which the facility management team must answer to. Though larger companies or ones with particularly pricey inventory or equipment might make the wise choice to outsource its security needs in the form of a private firm, it's still the role of the facility manager to ensure that the firm performs competently. Technology advancements like biometrics and wearables are making it possible to maintain strict access control for high-security areas, but it's up to facility managers to stay on top of these developments and make smart security technology investments. In addition to general safety, it's also important that the facility management team has the technological know-how to safeguard and maintain its priciest hardware. This role is a key one as it doubly affirms that assets are protected just as closely as the safety of the community.

Maintenance and Inspections – No matter the focus of the organization, one of the most heedless things that a facility management team can do is slack off on its building maintenance duties. Every part of the building, including installed machinery such as HVAC systems, must be maintained by the facility management team. Because some facilities contain countless elements that need regular maintenance, establishing and following strict maintenance schedules helps to ensure that all moving and permanent parts of the facility stay up-to-date and working well into the future. Along with general maintenance, inspections are also something that facility management teams must always be ready for. They can prepare the business by conducting internal inspections, as needed, for the many formal regulatory inspections they might incur annually. Of course, the team must also take into account any time the facility undergoes a major change in hardware, level of inventory, or capacity – and, they must also keep their eyes on all changes in laws that could affect their current procedures.

Business Continuity Planning – Part of leading an effective facility management team means planning for "worst case scenarios." This means that each team must sit down with the powers that be to come up with a plan in case disaster strikes and the business can't afford to shut down operations. For example, let's say that a community college endures a major fire and the authorities have deemed the entire main building a total loss. The community college is currently in the middle of a semester which it can't cut short – this is a situation where prior business continuity planning is key. If this were done in the aforementioned scenario, the facility management team would have already come up with alternate locations to hold classes and operate the organization's administrative duties. In addition to the new venue, the team would have already made a solid plan for the temporary facility's security, maintenance, and hardware needs.

Daily Operational Duties – In addition to serving as the safety and security liaisons for the facility, it's also important that facility management teams are organized to handle the inherent day-to-day challenges that might arise. Depending on how the given organization is structured, this can mean anything from mending a leaky roof in the women's restroom to even fixing a jammed fax machine.

Maintenance Operations

No matter the size of the organization, it's key that the higher-ups bring on a facility manager that can hire or outsource a reliable, competent team. And, because not every company is filled with safety-minded individuals, it is the job of this manager to act as an advocate for the workers and/or customers that occupy their facility. Having this level of tenacity and attention-to-detail in the facility management spectrum is necessary – in fact, it can save a business or even a life.

Operations and Management Strategies

The current presiding global facilities management organization, the International Facility Management Association, calls for these leaders to take a more tactical and shrewd approach when it comes to protecting the future of their business' properties. In the IFMA's Strategic Facility Planning white paper, the organization makes a call for facility managers to carry out SFP (strategic facility planning) as it "helps to avoid mistakes, delays, disappointments, and customer dissatisfaction." In addition to the aforementioned safety and maintenance-heavy responsibilities, the IFMA wants managers to begin looking beyond their normal duties so that they can better aid in the efficiency of their organizations.To do this effectively, managers must compile two things: 1) a strategic facility plan and 2) a master plan for the facility. Let's take a look at how each one can better strengthen the overall productivity of the business:

Strategic Facility Plan (SFP) – In order to compile a comprehensive SFP, the IFMA urges managers to first become acquainted with three very important things: the core values or changing values of the organization and how facilities must reflect the values, the compiling of an in-depth analysis of the facility, including location, capability, and condition, and, finally, a fundamental understanding of how the organization's goals might make for the ramping up or down in regards to facilities. If the manager can confirm each and every one of these benchmarks with the appropriate departments and find a way to support their organization's ambitions while carrying out effective day-to-day practices, then they will be acting as a truly "strategic" support system. This blend of "current" and "future" allows for all parties involved to grapple with changes as they come in the most effective manner possible.

Facility Master Plan – Any facility manager should already be constantly re-working their facility's master plan, a framework that looks at the "physical environments that incorporate the buildings," but that doesn't mean that each is as comprehensive as it could be. Let's take a look at what a holistic master plan that takes both the day-to-day tasks as well as the future space use analyses into consideration.

Here's what a facility master plan in a hotel should include:

Zoning, regulation, covenant assessments

Space standards/benchmarks descriptions

Program of space use

Workflow analyses

Engineering assessment and plan

Block, fit, or stacking plans

Concept site plan or campus plan

Architectural image concepts

Long-term maintenance plan

Construction estimates

Phasing or sequencing plan (the sequence or projects)

Once a hotel facility manager does the proper footwork to make contact with all departments that influence their facility, they will be better equipped to support their organization as it makes profitable moves in the future.

Project Management for Streamlined Facilities

Because the name of the game for facility managers is safety, maintenance, and planning, it surely comes as no surprise to you that the manager must also develop and execute a laundry list of projects to ensure that everything on and in the building is running smoothly. Facility Management Equipment Log.

Here are some examples of how project management tactics can streamline a facility's overall efficiency:

The establishment of project schedules that include both scope and budgetary needs

Advising all workers, including employees and consultants, on development and work progress

Maintaining transparent databases on each and every project to ensure that higher-ups are advised of any changes to schedule, budget, or manpower in real time

The compiling of comprehensive training schedules to ensure that all employees are properly certified for any regulatory changes that may arise

Conducting budget estimates for all proposed construction projects

Coordinating any service or maintenance upgrades for the facility's systems

Conduct meetings and get approval for necessary space alterations which might be necessary for the modernization of the space

Developing internal audit processes to ensure that all applicable regulatory standards are met, including the new ISO 41001, Facility management – Management systems – Requirements with guidance for use

Hotel Facilities Demand Organization

Best Leadership Practices for Facility Managers

Facility management is a big, often complex job that requires a strong, forward-thinking, and most of all, responsible leader who thinks about their facility's needs in as holistic of a manner as possible. In addition to possessing these qualities, the most informed managers either have years of diverse industry experience under the belt or have earned a specialized degree in the discipline. Continuing education is also common in the field, and there are a number of facilities management courses that can help facility managers stay up-to-date on current trends and best practices.

Facility Management Role

So, now that we have an idea of what an adept facility manager might look like on paper, let's delve into the most effective leadership practices they can implement to guarantee the safety and efficiency of their organization:

They are on the same page as the higher-ups in regards to the future – As mentioned throughout this guide, being a powerful facility manager means looking ahead into the future. From compiling business continuity plans in the event of a disaster to keeping an open line of communication with other departments, the manager understands that they will only be a true leader if their facility and staff are ready to roll with the changes.

They know how to plan and budget – Facility managers know the current value of every part of their facility's infrastructure – and how much it will take to upgrade. They also have an acute understanding of how their budgetary needs might ebb and flow moving forward so that they can accurately propose budgetary changes to the powers that be.

They have a feel for developing a great team – Depending on the specific needs of the organization, the facility manager might be responsible for the hiring and training of the facility workers, contractors, or even consultants. This means that the manager needs to have an innate understanding of the duties and restraints of each position and how they can best work together to make the most capable team possible. Remember, these team members are ultimately in control of the safety and security of the facility, very important jobs that can break an organization in regards to liability if something were to go awry.

They are willing to listen – It's only natural for facility managers to become frustrated with higher-ups calling for big shifts who might be physically disconnected with the facility, but that doesn't mean that they are wrong. Dynamic leaders collaborate with all departments by listening to their propositions and ideas. By doing so, they create an open, safe line of communication that, no matter the outcome, will strengthen interdepartmental relations.

Hotel Facility management is a challenging job, and it's one that grows increasingly complex as technology advancements reshape old processes into newer, streamlined approaches. The best facility managers understand exactly how to balance smart technology investments that boost efficiency while minimizing risks (e.g., fiscal and safety risks) for a positive influence on the bottom line. In short, facility management is the backbone of operations across a multitude of industries today.

In business world, the perspectives of entrepreneurial Strategies are crucial for growth. Driven by this urge, the strategic management has modeled concepts and principles towards this managerial cause. In its approach, the strategy evaluates the business operational environment and focus on the inner working of a company. In this case, it develops methodological advances and ideas that follow and target at predicting the transformation of the management practice. This paper aims to examine the strategies of management employed by the Marriott Hotels executives. For example, The Marriott Hotels choose the 'generic' strategy. The differentiation Strategy is the 'generic' approach chosen by The Marriott Hotels to market it products in the highly competitive hotel industry. Marriot International is an enterprise that has successfully employed the business-level generic strategies. The business is a global franchise or and a lodging and hotel facilities entity. These products display the Marriott facility to be the one of the top players in the accommodation sector, and the phenomenon is projected to be stabilised for a number of future years. This projection is anchored on the various competitive advantages at the disposal of the company (Marriott International Brands 34). These advantages include cost, uniqueness, and their competitiveness extent. The Marriott Global Incorporation follows a variety of strategies at the entrepreneurial level. The plans are showcased by the Marriott's vast brand portfolio that enables them to command a strong market presence in the hospitality industry. This approach is part of the strategy for the entity persuinng differentiation. The Marriot Incorporation differentiation plan is factored in developing a service and product that satisfies, in a unique way, the need of its customer. The approach is affected by the provision of several options of lodging that ranges from average to premium priced packages. The secret of value-addition offered by the uniqueness of the firm warrant it to peg a higher premium charge for hotels in the upmarket.

The way through which Marriott Hotels is implementing its strategy of differentiation

For example, Marriott Hotels is implementing its strategy of differentiation by integrating its market segmentation strategies with its every operation step. The Marriott management immediately realized, from the beginning, that one brand of the whole hotel enterprise could not offer adequate catering to every need of the guests (Harmon 2). As a result, the hotel chain utilized an extensive strategy of differentiation by creating various hotel brands. Each of the product names offered services to varied clients in the hospitality market. In this strata, products range from the low-end to high-end services. The upscale offers comprise of such products as Marriott JW Resorts, Ritz Carlton and Spas that are packaged for customers who desire luxurious and high-end accommodations (Marriott International Brands 34). Others are the Marriott Courtyard with a designed in-room space offices for the business traveler. The Fairfield Inn product offers quality service for the budget travelers. This mix of a variety of brands ensures that the Marriott International meets and fulfills any desire of every consumer regardless of her or his purchasing power. In this segmentation, the JW Marriott, Ritz Carlton, Marriott Resorts, and Hotels are promoted towards the clients desiring more experience in upscale lodging. These customers also have a strong will to pay a relatively higher cost of an added luxurious amenity. The Marriott Courtyard segment offers the business travelers an office space set-up in their units where they may be productive after business trip hours. Springhill Suites segments is a hotel offering that is moderate for a family or a single traveler with living area for unwinding before embarking on a good rest at nights (Harmon 2). The Townplace Suites and Residence Inn give accommodations an extended stay for traveler's searching for a place that is more like home. These hostels encompass living areas, full-size kitchens and sleeping quarters. In addition, the hospitality chain has a budget traveler suite with accommodations of Marriott quality. In overall, the firm has as a Marriott for all form of occasions. These products and helps the chain in its noble mission of molding loyalty to its customers. As illustrated, through this segmentation Marriott Hotels has implemented its strategy of differentiation in a unique way.

Evaluation of the Marriott Hotels' current strategy in the light of the analysis

In my opinion, the market segmentation strategy used by the hotels is a proper approach to creating a wide base of consumer. There is success for the company in this strategy, especially by segmentation its market in threefold and allocating specific price to each brand. These three categories of products. For example, the company has substantially served the high-end market in the Marriott JW Resorts, Ritz Carlton, and Spas products that are packaged for customers who desire luxurious and high-end accommodations. In addition, The Marriott Courtyard segment offers the business travelers an office space set-up in their units where they may be productive after business trip hours (Harmon 2). Springhill Suites segments is a hotel offering that is moderate for a family or a single traveler with living area for unwinding before embarking on a good rest at nights. The Townplace Suites and Residence Inn give accommodations an extended stay for traveler is searching for a home-like place. As a result, every consumer need is properly and adequately catered for without compromise in the high-quality service pursued by the Marriott Hotels management.

In my opinion, the hotel has other strategies that it may exploit. These include the Franchising and the approach Cost Leadership in its marketing mix. In addition to the market segmentation, the company should try to strengthen each brand as per its category. In this case, the firm will be able to create a strong brand identity with its consumers at all its levels of the market. As a result, it will be able to capture the mass market for its products. The increased demand will enable the firm to move high volumes of products thereby increasing its turnovers. As a result, it will be able to design a proper pricing system, as high turnovers will have high-profit levels. In addition, the company may employ the franchising strategy. In this case, it will be able to forego its traditional direct control of its hotels especially in the economies overseas. As a result, it might now concentrate its crucial business (Harmon 2). Furthermore, it will win in substantially reduce the financial risk associated with enormous businesses while allowing a more non-participatory global growth. The company may use this opportunity of franchising, as many investors are willing to collaborate with it due to its strong Marriott brand. This strategy will offset the threat of stiff competition the company is facing from its rival as Hilton and other hotels.

● Hotel cost / expense control management strategy

For hotel owners looking to grow their business, a robust revenue management strategy is of the utmost importance, helping to optimise business results. However, under the broader revenue management umbrella, there are many smaller strategies that can help to facilitate growth. In this article, you find nine revenue management strategies that those in the hotel industry can employ to achieve this ultimate objective.

What is Revenue Management?

Revenue management is a popular concept within the hotel industry, and is used to optimise a hotel or resort's financial results by maximising revenue. The accepted definition is: selling the right hotel room, to the right customer, at the right time, for the right price, via the right channel, with the best cost efficiency.Typically, it requires businesses to make effective use of performance data and analytics to predict demand, establish a dynamic pricing model and maximise the amount of revenue that the company brings in. Although revenue management is applicable to other industries, it has significance in the hospitality industry because hotels deal with a perishable inventory, fixed costs and varied levels of demand. Revenue management is considered important because it takes the guesswork out of key pricing decisions. More extended information about revenue management you can read in the article "What is revenue management?".

Revenue Management Strategies

1. Understand Your Market

In order to implement a successful revenue management strategy, it is imperative that you have a clear understanding of your market, where demand comes from and the various different local factors that might affect seasonal demand. You also need to be aware of your audience and their needs, wants and expectations.

Learn From Our Expert Partners

Moreover, you need to understand the competition that exists within the market and make strategic decisions regarding price, discounts and advertising with this competition in mind. Remember, this competition may not always be obvious, and may not always be in the same location as your hotel.

2. Segmentation and Price Optimisation

The concept of selling the right room to the right person at the right price requires you to appropriately segment your customer base. To do this, you need to identify different 'types' of customer and then look at these different segments and evaluate when they book hotel rooms or hotel facilities, how they book them and other habits. When this is carried out, it allows you to optimise prices for those different segments. One of the key advantages of this is that once prices are optimised for a particular segment, price changes can be minimised. This, in turn, can help to generate customer loyalty from those who appreciate the price consistency you offer.

3. Work Closely With Other Departments

Next, it is important to achieve close collaboration between the various different hotel departments, such as sales and marketing, in order to ensure that your revenue management strategies and their individual departmental strategies are in alignment with one another, and so that you can address challenges collectively. Identify key departmental decision-makers and bring them on board. Work with them to make adjustments to your revenue management strategies, rather than imposing your will, which might be met with resistance. Close collaboration will also help to ensure that you are always presenting consistent messages to customers and clients.

4. Forecasting Strategies

One of the most important aspects of revenue management is forecasting, which allows you to anticipate future demand and revenue, enabling necessary adjustments to be made. Within the hospitality industry, high-quality forecasting relies on accurate records being kept, including occupancy, room rates and revenue. Most forecasting strategies rely heavily on using historical data to spot trends. For example, if you notice an upturn in business in the past three Julys, it is sensible to assume the same may occur next time. However, forecasting also requires an awareness of current bookings, competitors' performance, local events and wider industry trends.

5. Embrace Search Engine Optimisation

Search engines offer one of the single biggest opportunities for those operating in the hotel industry to attract customers, which makes search engine optimisation an important part of a robust revenue management strategy. Through SEO, hotel owners can improve the visibility of their website on search engine results pages. As a consequence, you can improve the chances of attracting business from customers who are not specifically searching for your hotel, but who are searching for a hotel in your location. To achieve this, it is best to operate a solid content marketing strategy, and ensure your website's design is optimised for SEO purposes.

6. Choose the Right Pricing Strategy

There are many different pricing strategies out there, and no one strategy will guarantee success. Instead, those in the hospitality sector need to consider the best strategy for their particular hotel, based on what they have to offer, who they are trying to attract and what strategy their competitors are employing. A competitive pricing strategy, where prices are set based on other hotels prices, puts your business in direct competition and is good when your hotel has more to offer than your rivals do. Yet, in slow seasons, a discount strategy might be best, because a low-paying customer is better than an empty room. Another option is the value-added approach, where rates are higher, but additional value is provided through extras and freebies.

7. Incentives For Direct Bookings

While it is certainly important to cater for all distribution channels and meet customers where they are, rather than where you want them to be, it is also sensible to try to maximise the number of direct bookings that are made. The primary reason for this is because direct bookings do not require the commission to be paid to third parties, which means they are ideal for maximising revenue. One option is to offer exclusive incentives, such as loyalty points, or freebies, for customers who book directly through your own website.

Increase Revenue by Outsourcing Revenue Management

Revenue management is a proven concept, based on the idea of using data and analytics to optimise financial results. It also requires specific skills and knowledge, which means that it can be more effective to outsource revenue management to a third party that specialises in this area.

8. Focus on Mobile Optimisation

For those in the hotel industry, mobile has become one of the single most important revenue streams. As a result, any hotel or resort that is operating without having prioritised mobile optimisation is already operating at a distinct disadvantage compared to their competitors. Make sure your website is optimised for mobile viewing, meaning it loads quickly, the pages display properly on mobile devices and all buttons are fully functional. In addition, you need to ensure your booking process is also optimised, so that customers can book rooms from their mobile device, without needing to switch to desktop.

9. Work With a Freelance Revenue Manager

Finally, in many cases it can be beneficial to enlist the help of a freelance revenue manager, who will be able to bring knowledge, expertise and experience into your organisation. Freelancers are used to coming into hotels and getting to work quickly, and can work as and when you need them. Appointing a full-time revenue manager internally means employing them full-time, but a freelancer will only need to be paid for the work they actually do, meaning less of their time will be wasted. Moreover, because of their established expertise, you will be able to save money on costs associated with training them.

The concept of selling the right hotel room, to the right customer, at the right moment, for the right price, via the right channel is important for maximising revenue and facilitating growth. By following the nine revenue management strategies above, owners in the hospitality industry can improve their chances of achieving this.–

● Hotel service management strategy

For hotels, successful marketing depends on addressing a number of key points. These include: what a company or an industry like a hotel is going to produce; how much a hotel is going to charge; how that particular hotel is going to deliver its products or services to the guests; and how it is going to tell its customers about its products and services. Traditionally, these considerations were known as the 4Ps of the hotel industry — Product, Price, Place, and Promotion. As marketing became a more sophisticated discipline in the hospitality industry, a fifth 'P' was added and implemented— People. And recently, two further 'P's were added, mainly for service industries (like the hospitality industry)— Process and Physical evidence. These considerations are now known as the 7 Ps of service marketing in the hotel industry and sometimes referred to as the marketing mix of the hospitality industry!

In the realm of hotels, marketing is a technique of guiding the customers to choose your goods and service rather than electing the products of your rivals. If a hotel is not accounting for this aspect to make their brand more relevant, they are hampering their profit level, sales, and occupancy. The key for all hotels is to search the correct channel of marketing (which may be Display Advertising, Email Marketing, Pay-Per-Click Advertising (PPC) or Online Public Relations) and disclosing the accurate message in order to influence the targeted guests.

How to manage luxury hotel

The hotel industry has welcomed an unprecedented level of luxury. The rising demand for this extravagance is the increasing guest pursuit of meaningful, personalized experiences that are at the same time unique, exclusive and memorable. At luxury hotels, we work with a number of hotels that offer such services. From this first-hand experience, we have seen that luxury hotel guests don't want to be seen as capricious and wasteful. They value their privacy, yet seek out luxury stays for the unique surprises and thrills that hotel management can offer.However, it may have different kinds of service peformance strategies for luxury and not luxury hotel service perfomance, it may differ as below:

Outstanding Luxury Hotel Services hotel positioning strategy

1. Paparazzi Police

Keeping their vacation private is the minimum that your guests can ask of your luxury hotel, right? But, if for instance you have celebrity guests whose daily life involves being followed by paparazzi, maintaining such privacy presents challenges.To solve this paparazzi problem, for example the Las Ventanas hotel in Los Cabos, Mexico came up with an innovative solution to ensure their guests' privacy and an enjoyable stay. This hotel's staff are equipped with reflective screens, which protect their guests from prying photographers. These "Paparazzi Police" use their screens to shine light at the photographers, which ruins their photos.

2. Personalized Firework Display

We focus on Las Ventanas again, as the luxury hotel offers a spectacular personalized, private fireworks show. Costing around $1,700 per minute, guests can easily personalize it to their liking. It is another service that helps create a truly unique, unforgettable experience in a part of the world that is known for its mesmerizing natural beauty.

3. Hot Air Balloon Ride

Breathtaking experiences are a favorite of luxury hotel guests prepared to pay extra for the privilege. One such experience is a ride in a hot air balloon. And one such hotel that offers this service is the Kale Konak Hotel, located atop Cappadocia in Turkey. Leveraging its position amid a location of natural splendor, this hotel helps its guests by organizing a hot air balloon ride, which promises a stunning experience of a lifetime.

How can your hotel take advantage of its surroundings to offer thrilling adventures and experiences?

4. Sunscreen-Spraying Booths

Hotel guests don't want to worry about anything when they enjoy the beach or the resort pool at remote and exclusive locations. And if there's one thing that can ruin a vacation, it's sunburn. Proactive hotels take it upon themselves to help guests prevent burning up by including sunscreen-spraying booths as a standard luxury hotel service. In particular, many Caribbean hotels offer this service, loved by solo travelers, couples and families alike. After all, even if a guest carelessly forgets to apply sunscreen and suffers the consequences, they are much more likely to associate your hotel with the negative experience. By offering sunscreen-spraying booths, you cancel out this possibility and create a value-added service for your guests, so they can enjoy their vacation in full.

5. Sunscreen-Spraying Booth

For hotels that are located with expansive countryside hills nearby, paragliding is a luxury service that ticks all the boxes. It can be relatively inexpensive to run, offers a riveting add-on experience, and will hep move you head and shoulders above your competition. A novel twist is to offer a paragliding route from atop a hill to the hotel entrance at the bottom. With the help of a professional paragliding expert, the most demanding and fearless of guests can enjoy an extreme sport and make a rock-star entrance at your hotel.

6. Secret, Invite-Only Room

It is an increasing trend to offer a secret or hidden service. But the catch is that it can't be bought by money. Certain luxury desires can only be attained with the right contact, recommendation, knowledge or invite. Think of the appeal of speakeasy bars, or exclusive, secret societies. Take advantage of this winning trend by creating a secret, invite-only room in your hotel. Make it exceptionally beautiful or intriguing, or offer services that are unobtainable to "regular" guests. Choose a secluded or forbidden area of your hotel for its location. And of course, this secret room cannot be advertised on your official channels, such as your website.

7. In-Suite Shopping

Luxury is never having to pack a suitcase, no matter where you go or for how long. Take inspiration from London's

Hotel Café Royal, which offers its guests a personalized, curated styling service for all occasions during their stay. Guests check in without luggage and find a selection of clothes handpicked by a personal stylist to choose from in their suite upon arrival. By offering your guests this luxury option, you make them feel like pop stars. And not only is it extremely convenient, everyone loves discovering a new outfit to wear and feeling like a VIP.

8. Complimentary Luxury Car Drives

Some of the very best 5-star luxury hotels offer their guests luxury cars during their stay too, for free. Hotels like The Peninsula Beverly Hills in California provide their guests with Rolls-Royce and Infiniti cars, having developed a strong relationship with the high-end car manufacturers. If you have the budget to ramp up your luxury hotel with this complimentary service, it will help serve as a magnet for guests eager for exclusive experiential stays. And if not, there are other options. For instance, you can approach high-end car leasing companies to enquire about reaching an agreement. And it doesn't have to be luxury cars. You could also tap into the growing importance of sustainability to guests by offering premium eco-friendly cars.

9. No-Internet Digital Detox Zone

C-suite executives and stressed millionaires with companies and scores of people dependent on their decisions and attention find it difficult if not impossible to disconnect. With so much responsibility on their shoulders, they are often available around the clock, seven days a week. Even if they do get an opportunity to get some much needed time off, they are often interrupted by a colleague who needs their input on the latest emergency or major decision at their company. Cue the growing prevalence of no-internet resorts. No WiFi, no mobile internet signal and no onsite computers to access the web. Completely and utterly offline.

This digital detox is increasingly sought after by hyper-connected individuals who want to get away from it all, even if only for a few days, offering them total peace and quiet, without the fear of their phone blowing up with calls, messages and emails. For typically busy company executives and such individuals in an ultra-connected world, this kind of opportunity to unwind and relax "off the grid" is an increasingly exclusive luxury.

On conclusion, more and more hotels are trying to make their guests' stay as special as possible so in the near future, many of these unconventional services will be offered by more luxurious hotels all over the world. This being said, a great hotel manager goes beyond what customers say they want, helping them to realize their wildest dreams by combining fun, joyful experiences with exclusive, unique services that make them feel important.

For hotels, successful marketing depends on addressing a number of key points. These include: what a company or an industry like a hotel is going to produce; how much a hotel is going to charge; how that particular hotel is going to deliver its products or services to the guests; and how it is going to tell its customers about its products and services. Traditionally, these considerations were known as the 4Ps of the hotel industry — Product, Price, Place, and Promotion. As marketing became a more sophisticated discipline in the hospitality industry, a fifth 'P' was added and implemented— People. And recently, two further 'P's were added, mainly for service industries (like the hospitality industry)— Process and Physical evidence. These considerations are now known as the 7 Ps of service marketing in the hotel industry and sometimes referred to as the marketing mix of the hospitality industry!

Hence, in the realm of hotels, marketing is a technique of guiding the customers to choose your goods and service rather than electing the products of your rivals. If a hotel is not accounting for this aspect to make their brand more relevant, they are hampering their profit level, sales, and occupancy. The key for all hotels is to search the correct channel of marketing (which may be Display Advertising, Email Marketing, Pay-Per-Click Advertising (PPC) or Online Public Relations) and disclosing the accurate message in order to influence the targeted guests.

Before providing an excellent service is experienced, it first has to be delivered. It, therefore, means that the process of choosing to use a service might be perceived as risky since one is buying something that is intangible. To reduce this uncertainty, physical evidence such as case studies should be used. This can be done by keeping the facilities clean, well decorated and tidy. The physical evidence that is demonstrated by an organization should be able to confirm the assertions of the customers. Although it might not be possible for the customers to experience the service before they have purchased, the customers can talk to other customers with experience!

GUEST ENGAGEMENT GUEST EXPERIENCE HOTEL INDUSTRY HOTEL MARKETING HOTEL REVENUE MANAGEMENT MARKETING

Hotel-sales-strategies-direct-bookings

Your worst nightmare as a hotelier is walking down the halls of your hotel and realising that rooms are empty. There's a sad stillness that not only marks the sign of a quiet moment, but also the sign of a failing business strategy. In order to avoid this situation at any point during the year – even during the slow travel season – you need to implement sales strategies that will improve business and continually bring in more guests. The first, and most obvious reason, to focus on increasing hotel room sales is because this will drive revenue. With additional revenue on-hand, you are able to provide guests with the service they expect, as well as move the hotel forward into the future. Before you can dabble in additional packages, add-on excursions and luxury upgrades, you must be able to sell rooms. Another reason to prioritise hotel room sales techniques is to provide guests with the atmosphere that they expect. A vacant or nearly empty hotel is not a good look to people who are staying there. You want to be able to sell as many rooms as possible so that you can provide your guests with a lively, charismatic environment.

● Essential hotel room sales strategies

Every hotelier needs to implement sales strategies that work best for their own target market as well as for their local destination. Ultimately, it is up to the hotel operator or manager to create a customised sales strategy that will drive the most room sales at their own individual property, but these are some of the top hotel room sales strategies to consider:

1. Hotel group sales strategy

This strategy may require an overhaul of your normal marketing and sales approach. The idea is to sell rooms and meeting spaces to corporate groups; it's important you can offer a deal for both. Landing these types of sales requires innovation but it can be very beneficial for repeat business if you do. The most cost effective way to secure group bookings is by connecting directly to planners. You can list your property on venue marketplaces where planners can view floorplans, photos, and unique differentiators. It's also important to segment your target audience so you can make compelling offers to the right kind of groups for your property.

2. Hotel direct sales strategy

With this sales strategy, the priority is to earn direct bookings online from as many guests as possible. Direct bookings are the most beneficial booking for hotel operators because these bookings generate the most revenue. There are no agents or other distribution partners that must be paid a commission when a guest books directly online. In order to implement a direct booking strategy, hotel managers should invest in an online booking system that syncs with their existing website and property management system. Hotel operators should also prioritise their social media strategy when focusing on increasing direct bookings.

3. Destination marketing sales strategy

This type of sales strategy requires a hotel operator to work with other tourism business professionals in their destination to promote the region as a whole. Through a destination marketing campaign, local businesses team up to target the most powerful inbound tourism markets and drive more traffic to the general area.

4. Cross-promotional sales strategy

With this sales strategy, hotel managers need to identify and evaluate various large events that will be taking place in the local region throughout the calendar year. Then, the hotel operator needs to come up with a promotion that can coincide with the event, ultimately allowing them to earn an influx of bookings that they may not otherwise have had. Opportunities that are ideal for a cross-promotional sales strategy include an upcoming industry conference, a concert or a major sporting event.

5. Guest rewards sales strategy

Many travellers today, particularly the powerful millennial generation, value the opportunity to earn rewards with the companies that they do business with. Hotels, in particular, have great success with rewards programs. In a guest rewards sales strategy, the manager or operator should develop a system that rewards guests for staying frequently, for purchasing upgrades, and for referring friends and family members. A rewards sales strategy often generates repeat bookings, which are particularly lucrative for hotel operators.

6. Revenue management sales strategy

This type of sales strategy aims to maximise the number of rooms booked at any point in the year, regardless of the typical travel traffic at that particular point in time. Typically, a revenue management plan requires hotel operators to drop room rates during the low season in order to encourage bookings, while raising rates during high traffic times. During these moments, guests are going to be willing to pay higher rates to get a room, so it's worthwhile raising rates to generate more revenue per available room.

Other room selling techniques in hotels

Large, overarching, strategies are vital to drive a consistent level of business at your hotel but there are other smaller tactics you can use to sell your rooms or generate more revenue from each guest:

Upselling – Upselling is the process of selling a more expensive version of the service or product your customer is buying. The methods you use to upsell need to be handled with a degree of delicacy. The timing, tone, and regularity with which you upsell is the key to the success of your efforts. You don't want to seem pushy so treat it as an exercise in awareness rather than a sales pitch. Make sure guests know what options are available to them but let them initiate any further interest.

Re-marketing – Re-marketing allows you to reach out to potential guests who have visited your site without finalising their booking. Many travellers will visit a variety of different websites to explore their options during the research phase of their online booking journey. With re-marketing strategies, you can access these customers again at different points during their online booking experience and remind them to visit your site again to book with you.

Incentives or cross-selling – Cross-selling is the process of selling an additional, supplementary product or service to complement the product or service your customer is buying. Offering incentives in the form of additional products or services may just be the thing that gets your guest to confirm a booking. Think added-value items like a free massage, or a local tour.

Build local partnerships – Unless your hotel is located in a remote or isolated destination, there should be plenty of other businesses and attractions you can form a mutually beneficial partnership with. Co-promoting with restaurants, specialty shops like ski hire, adventure companies, theme parks, or museums can help lead to easy and effective marketing. And these kind of partnerships can work no matter how the guest is planning their trip – be it to book accommodation first, or create their itinerary before looking for a hotel.

Make booking easy on your website – The importance of a good website experience for travellers can't be overstated. Nothing will drain their excitement quicker than a slow, confusing, or convoluted website. Make sure yours is clean, intuitive, mobile-friendly, and has clear action buttons such as 'book now' for potential guests to click. When direct bookings are so valuable, your website has to be a priority.

● Hotel promotion strategy

Promotions are great because you can be very flexible and targeted with what you offer, and often they'll grab the attention of travellers searching online. This is where it can actually be useful to steer into what guests might expect, such as promotions around seasons, themes, events, direct, bookings, or partnerships.

1. Seasonal promotions

Most destinations experience a low season, where tourism is not as active as other parts of the year. However, with the right deals your hotel doesn't have to suffer through empty rooms and hallways. Try to incorporate discounts with eye-catching promotions like 'Summer Getaways' and 'Winter Retreats' and remind travellers how beautiful your destination is and how much they can see when there are less crowds.

2. Themed promotions

These will be attention-grabbing and very relevant for travellers looking into booking a stay in the area. For example you might offer promotions around honeymoons or anniversaries if you're in a romantic locale, adventure deals if you're out of the major cities, or ultimate relaxation experiences if you're a coastal hotel. Appealing to different lifestyles or family setups is always a good idea.

3. Event-based promotions

It makes a lot of sense to capitalise on events and include them in your promotions. People will already be researching these events so if your hotel has a deal on in conjunction with them, awareness of your hotel should increase along with site traffic. These events might include music or art festivals, Easter or Christmas events, circuses, travelling markets, sporting events etc. With a booking you might offer discounted tickets, adapt the hotel experience to match the events, create special rates.

4. Direct booking promotions

Placing exclusive promotions within your booking engine on your website will give travellers an incentive to book direct instead of via an OTA. It will also help establish your hotel website as your most important distribution channel and help increase profit by eliminating OTA commission fees. The incentive might be a discount, or it might also be an added extra such as a bottle of wine, restaurant voucher, or amenity gift cards.

5. Partnership promotions

Combining with other businesses will reduce the cost of promotion and marketing, and give you wider coverage as long as your partner holds up their end of the bargain. It may also give you access to a new market and create ongoing business. Common partnerships include those with theme parks, restaurants, cinemas, museums, sporting arenas, adventure and tour guides. It's one thing to create your promotions, but remember you need people to see them. Always advertise on your social media channels and ensure your search engine optimisation is strong

6. Mobile-only promotions

Year on year, nearly every statistic points to an upsurge of mobile usage on hotel, travel, and booking websites, with projected numbers even more prominent. As quick as online booking overtook more traditional and outdated methods, mobile is starting to usurp desktop. Implementing smart and effective mobile strategies will boost customer experience and keep your hotel competitive within an industry that never stops innovating.

● Hotel packages strategy

Use other businesses to enrich your packages – Combining your services with that of another tourist attraction in the area is a surefire way to add value to your packages. It also gives you a lot of flexibility on what you can offer guests. Tickets to zoos, tours, theme parks, museums are always popular as are restaurant vouchers. Even concerts or one-off events can be leveraged as short-term packages. This way you can cater for many different guests, those interested in adventure and those more excited by shopping or fine dining.

Promote one-stop shopping – Savvy travellers will look at your packages and wonder exactly what kind of deal they're getting. Unless you and your business partner agree to offer discounted prices it's likely the combined price of a room and a tour package will be similar to the components purchased separately. This is why you need to advertise the convenience and quality of what you're offering, rather than spruiking the cost.

Be creative with your choices – Guests might become rather bored if they see yet another 'romance' package. Try incorporating more interesting content into your packages and their names. For instance a 'bucket list' package might include a selection of passes or discounts to the absolute must-sees of the local area. This will be an attractive option for guests because it's likely they already interested in visiting those landmarks. For business travellers, always focus on convenience such as a package delivering breakfast to their room, free dry cleaning, and transport services.

Use your own property to add value – While most packages include a room and some type of external activity, you can make your packages even more enticing by adding your own service to the mix such as spa-treatments or a bar tab. Guests will want to experience your amenities and they'll be more likely to pay to do so if it's included in a package.

Cater for speciality markets – Never ignore families. Often it's the children you're appealing to most because parents will be looking for activities that will occupy the kids. The same principle applies if you're a pet-friendly hotel. You must also consider guests with disabilities and people with specific occupations that you can give personalised packages to. Don't forget to promote any new packages you create, be they long-term or one-off. Use Facebook, Twitter, Instagram, and your email sends to drum up business. Send any information along to your local tourism office so they can do the same. Another thing to consider is what you want to achieve with your packages. Sometimes they can create a lot of brand awareness, even if they don't attract much business directly.

direct-sales-hotel

To the average traveller you and your competitors will often appear very similar. That's why you need to present an offer that tips the balance and convinces an undecided traveller yours is the best hotel for them. Package deals and extras are an easy, but extremely effective way of doing this, providing you take the right approach.

Your hotel distribution strategy and how it impacts sales

Implementing a successful sales strategy requires you to have an effective distribution strategy. Hotel operators must network with industry professionals as well as agents to sell their rooms to the maximum number of people in a variety of target market segments. Common agents that are included in any distribution strategy include retail travel agents, visitor information centres, local businesses, online travel agents, and destination marketing organisations. Hotel operators and managers must recognise that their distribution network is a fluid, living entity, and they should constantly be looking for new and innovative ways to reach out to new agents and distributors.

In addition to expanding and developing a diverse distribution network, hotel operators must be able to effectively distribute their rooms to all of their agents in real-time. The only way to do this is to partner with a channel manager that connects to your property management system. With a channel manager, hotel operators can provide their live availability to every distribution agent that they have, regardless of their location or time zone. This allows them to sell as many rooms as possible — including securing those valuable last-minute bookings. It also significantly reduces the risk of overbooking rooms at the property, particularly during high-volume times. A channel manager is necessary to implement any sales strategy that a manager wishes to employ at their individual property.

Hotel sales tools

Your hotel sales tools include anything that enable you to bring a guest into your hotel. This might mean your social media accounts, your email marketing campaigns, the phone on your front desk, guest feedback, or back-end hotel technology solutions.Though when you think of tools as objects or functional pieces of software you might consider these to help inform your sales strategy:

Social networks

Analytics tools such as Google

Survey tools

Online travel agents

Property management tools

Booking engines

Channel managers

Website builders

Identifying and using the right tools will depend on your property and the guests you want to attract but for the most part all properties need the same tools. The difference comes in how you use them. Data is extremely important so using tools that can give you detailed reporting functions is a great step to take. With enough data at your disposal, you can make informed decisions about how you sell, gaining an edge over any competitors who are following a 'cookie-cutter' approach. Obviously you need to be smart about you use the budget at your hotel and look at tools which will make life easier while helping deliver more revenue to the business.

Hotel sales software

When you think of sales software in a hotel context, it's better to think distribution software. Three key pieces of technology that could help you are a channel manager, online booking engine, and website builder. While they may not be strictly thought of as sales software, they are the key to driving sales and revenue in the hotel industry.

Channel manager

This is one of your greatest allies when distributing your rooms because it's a tool that manages all the different online travel agents (OTAs) you sell your rooms through, such as Booking.com, Expedia or Airbnb. The main operating principle is called "pooled inventory" which means updates to rates and availability are made automatically across all connected channels whenever and wherever a booking is made. Enabling a more effective way to promote your rooms will naturally create an increase in sales. Read our guide on channel managers to learn more.

Booking engine

Also a reservation system, this will secure online bookings from direct channels such as your own website and social media pages like Facebook. An online booking engine has become essential, especially with the rise of social media. Creating a friction-less experience for guests when they book direct will boost your conversion and improve your sales results. Read our guide on booking engines to learn more.

Website builder

This takes away the need for you to hire a web designer. Instead you can use this software to create a beautiful, search engine optimised, guest converting website in minutes. You simply have to provide your content and choose from a number of available templates. Your website is a major selling point for travellers – winning them over with an amazing first impression is imperative. With the right technology in place, you will be able to easily and effectively implement your hotel room sales strategies. To learn more about these hotel sales tools and to find out if they are the right choice for your hotel property, check out how they work in a video demo.

What to expect from these hotel room sales strategies ? When you sell hotel rooms, you do more than just get another guest in the door of your property. You are able to improve your hotel business in its entirety. Here are a few of the benefits that you will realise when you employ hotel room sales strategies that are designed to increase hotel room sales:

You will generate more revenue consistently throughout the entire year. An effective hotel sales strategy allows you to earn as much revenue as possible, regardless of the seasonal ebbs and flows of the tourism industry. You will be able to make improvements to your property. As you begin to earn more revenue from your bookings, you can make improvements that will generate buzz about your brand and continue to sell more rooms. Finally, you will be able to move beyond standard sales strategies and begin creating packages that increase the revenue you generate per guest. Once your sales steadily increase, you can begin to expand your offerings. Romance packages, adventure packages and luxury upgrades allow you to sell more rooms while also boosting the revenue you earn per booking.

- Hotel revenue management technology

What is revenue management for the hospitality industry? Revenue management refers to the strategic distribution and pricing tactics you use to sell your property's perishable inventory to the right guests at the right time, to boost revenue growth. Other products such as your amenities and food and beverage offerings will also come into the picture. Revenue management revolves around measurement of what customers from different segments are willing to pay, and this can only be done by measuring and monitoring the supply and demand of your hotel rooms.

Every traveller has a maximum value they can offer your hotel; revenue management is about capturing as much of this value as you possibly can. Preferably you'll do this by convincing the guest to book direct, purchase extensions, up-sells or extras, and become a return visitor. The best strategies are based on the understanding that hotel pricing is fluid, and can change from one day to the next. This is why you should never be afraid to increase your rates. Customers actually expect increases over time – most businesses where consumers spend money are varying their prices based on demand and shifts in costs.

Effective hotel revenue management strategies can also help hoteliers:

Better manage resources

Protect against rostering too many staff during slow periods

Ensure adequate numbers of staff are working during the busiest times

With all this in mind, revenue management can drive the entire business plan when implemented effectively. Your hotel distribution strategy is also a vital part of your revenue management plan. Make sure you are on the internet distribution channels that promote your destination online. They have strong marketing power and can put your hotel in front of many customers you can't contact directly.

How to increase hotel revenue ? Many strategies come into play when driving more revenue to your hotel, and many of them don't involve raising prices or playing with your rates much at all. Not least of these is satisfying your customer. If the product you offer is universally recognised as quality, you have the grounding to charge a higher price. If guests feel like they are getting maximum value for their money, it's very likely they'll be willing to spend more. Getting more out each individual guest who stays with you is a great way to increase the overall revenue of your hotel. For instance, guaranteed revenue from a guest you convince to stay an extra night by discounting the additional night might be worth your while, especially in low season.

A list of general tactics you can use to improve your hotel's revenue stream:

Be bookable online

These days travellers enjoy the flexibility, convenience, and value of booking online. By connecting to online travel agents/more online travel agents you'll easily see an uplift.

Build a revenue culture

Who's on your revenue team? Everyone! Anticipatory service + proactive revenue-minded employee = emotionally connected customer with engaged loyalty and higher revenue returns.

Sell other hotel products

Revenue opportunities extend far beyond simply selling your rooms. Think about the amenities you have on site and what your are charging for them, and go even further by offering hotel guests the chance to purchase items like soap, utensils, towels etc – especially if your hotel has a unique sense of style.

Leverage events and attractions

Local events and attractions are a great opportunity to put together packages for guests or offer additional services such as transport. The benefits are two-fold – guests will enjoy their stay more and your hotel will generate more income.

As you move away from tactics and towards fully fledged strategies around your revenue and room sales, you need to start understanding your key performance indicators (KPIs). Once you know what you should be looking at you can start analysing the data and developing ways to manipulate them in your favour.

As an introduction, these are the metrics you can explore:

Occupancy rate

ADR (Average daily rate)

RevPAR (Revenue per available room)

TrevPAR (RevPAR + ancillaries)

GOPPAR (Gross operating profit per available room)

RevPASH (Revenue per available seat hour) – useful if you have a hotel restaurant

The principle that you should always keep in mind is to assess market conditions in real-time and adapt accordingly.

Revenue management strategies

You need a revenue management strategy to remain sustainable – that's the short story. Ideally, you'll even be able to turn a tidy profit each year. The best hotel revenue management strategies recognise that hotel pricing is fluid, and can change from one day to the next. It's critical that any hotelier creates a revenue management strategy that is adaptable to the current conditions. Often it's more important to focus on your own business and be confident than to worry too much about competitors, at least at first.

Every hospitality business strategy has to have the customer at its heart. How do travellers behave in the current landscape? How do they book and travel? How do they experience and explore? What do they require? What are their expectations? It's vital you have an idea of these factors if you want to squeeze the most value out of each guest that enters your door. The better you know the guest the more guest loyalty you can generate, which is extremely important for recurring revenue. If you know you have a certain amount of guests returning each year, that's more rooms you don't have to worry about and you can focus more on upselling and cross-selling.

Hotel pricing strategies

There's no pricing strategy that is perfect for any hotel. Each property must consider the pricing strategy, or strategies, that work best for its particular brand. A revenue manager will spend a lot of time analysing data and other influencing factors to ensure the business is operating with the best possible chance to maximise income.

There are a number of questions that should surround your pricing strategies:

What do your guests want?

Which strategy will complement the business mix?

How will different strategies affect connected channels and distribution partners?

How does your strategy integrate with your channels?

Who are the experts that can help determine the right strategy?

With all that in mind, the first priority of pricing should be forecasting. This way you can predict demand so you can get travellers to book early. Then you can raise rates later as availability drops and demand increases. (This is an ideal pricing structure known as the "ascending model" whereby pricing increases closer to an arrival day.) We'll talk more about forecasting and analysis later.

What is dynamic pricing?

Dynamic pricing involves changing room rates daily or even within the day based on real-time market data. Taking supply and demand into account, prices should fluctuate regularly if you want to maximise revenue. This pricing option is well suited in today's market and is one many hoteliers opt to use.

Dynamic pricing examples

Put simply, there will be days where supply and demand will be very different depending on the time of day. In the morning you may have lower rates because your occupancy is low, as is demand. However by that evening supply may have reduced and demand grown. Many factors can drive this, such as competitors putting up their no vacancy signs or setting rates slightly too high, or travellers arriving late for events the next day and so on. You can raise your rates to take advantage of the shifting market and earn more revenue than if you'd kept your rates static.

What is open pricing?

Open pricing defines the flexibility hotels around the globe have to set their prices at different levels depending on the various target markets and distribution channels they deal with.

This luxury of choice allows hotels to forecast more accurately. For example, a high-end hotel may usually attract guests who no budget constraints but in the off-season bookings will drops and the hotel can drop rates to attract travellers who normally would not be able to afford the stay. While the average daily rate of the hotel will be lower, occupancy will remain steady and revenue will continue to turnover.

Other hotel pricing strategies

There are numerous pricing strategies you can use at your hotel as part of your broader revenue management strategy, many of them in conjunction. Here's a list of the most common pricing strategies your hotel might find useful:

1. Value-added pricing

You can set your room rates higher than the local competition while also offering more extras in the basic package. This gives the illusion that the hotel offers a premium experience that focuses on value rather than just low rates.

2. Discount pricing

Used in slow seasons to boost occupancy by dropping base rates. Revenue can be made up through other services in the hotel.

3. Price per segment

Offering the same product at different prices to different types of customers. E.g 'family rate'

Length of stay

When demand outweighs supply, it can help to implement a rule where guests are 'obligated' to stay a minimum number of days. In such cases, lower rates may not be necessary.

4. Positional pricing

Basing your rates off brand strength and reputation.

5. Penetration pricing

Positioning yourself as the cheapest in the market. Be mindful of how travellers will perceive your hotel – you need to retain the opportunity to sell at higher rates.

6. Skimming

Positioning your hotel among the most expensive. Price leaders often achieve among the highest profitability, however the consumers need to clearly understand the reasons that they would pay more for staying at your hotel.

What does hotel market segmentation mean?

Segmenting is a key aspect of revenue management. It allows you to differentiate between the travellers who are coming to your hotel and devise uniques strategies for all of them. For example, the approach you take with young adventurers will be very different to a business professional. However segmentation is more complex than simply business vs leisure, and you can use it to discover trends within your hotel business.

One of the best ways to identify and filter segments is by their reason for travel. Think family holiday, wedding, tourist event, adventure, relaxation, business, etc. However, more and more hotels are adopting a different strategy and defining market segment by how a reservation was made, e.g. Expedia as a market segment. This is known as "blended segmentation" – combining the reason for stay and method of booking. Hotel chains have adopted different applications of this traditional definition of a market segment and channels. Some hotel chains and groups identify a channel as an OTA, and then identify the likes of Booking.com's reward program and Expedia's Egencia (for corporate travel) as sub-channels.

Further segmentation factors that you should take into account include:

Length of stay

Days of the week of stays

Lead time (how long before arrival do they book)

Cancellations

No show ratio

Once you have a good grip on market segments you can start to decide which groups your business wants to focus on more, and which to close out at different times of the year. By drilling down further you might realise certain segments have higher cancellation rates and you could want to resist marketing to them. Each segment will have a unique opportunity for you to gain extra business or revenue.

Here's a quick snapshot of the possibilities:

Loyalty or rewards members – Offer discounts

Mobile booking – Use mobile exclusive promotions

Direct bookings – Make offers that only exist on your website

Walk-ins – Entice extra spending with your amenities

Corporate – A chance to negotiate rates with large companies

Online travel agents – Advertise special event packages

Groups – Combine with tour operators and attractions

Every piece of analysis you do helps you build the optimal business mix for your hotel, so it's important to look at all your options. If selling is a problem, there's always a new way to sell or new market to target. If spending is the problem, there's always a way to entice customers to open their wallets again.

Hotel price forecasting

Forecasting is not only important for rate setting, but also for budgeting purposes. Accurate and effective forecasting requires a strong foundation in historical data. By budgeting and forecasting in advance you'll have plenty of time and opportunity to make strategy adjustments. If you know one point in the year is particularly valuable to your hotel, write your forecast immediately for that period a year in advance. For example, try writing your December 2021 forecast on January 1st 2020.

Key components of an effective forecast include:

Occupancy

Revenue

Room rates

Turnaways/Regrets/Denials – tracking of reservations that are turned away or not booked, and is a critical measurement of demand. Ideally your turnaways are captured and measured on your online as well as direct/ telephone requests.

Spend per room

Reservations

Market trends

Hotel budgeting and demand forecasting

It's a good idea to create demand calendar prior to setting your budgeting plan so you know exactly what you're dealing with. Most hotels forecast every day for next 30 days and every week for next 90 days. A lot of hoteliers do this in a spreadsheet after extracting data from their PMS, but this is where you need really cool tech – and a really easy system – that can do it all in one place.

Take into account factors from last year and also the upcoming year. Mark the following as things to track:

RevPAR last year

Groups or events last year

Demand level indicator last year (High, Medium, Low, Distressed)

Public/bank holidays

School holidays

Indications of increased demand

This will allow you to make informed pricing strategies based on solid data sets.

Before you reach your ideal budget you have to take into account influences such as sales resources, online marketing and distribution, refurbishment needs, and developments your competitor set is making. Your budget should be developed on the basis of this question: at which rate and how many rooms can you sell for every future day? For example, how do you anticipate the business demand and the leisure demand per country? At which rate can you sell on the upcoming months? How will your main corporate accounts behave?

Two distinct demand measurements are constrained demand and unconstrained demand.

1. Constrained demand

Maximum demand for amount of rooms (the maximum number of bookings you could get based on the number of rooms) limited by the physical inventory.

2. Unconstrained demand

Maximum bookings you could get with unlimited rooms based on demand and not limited by the actual physical inventory.

You should identify when unconstrained demand is above the capacity of the hotel. This is an important part of your hotel revenue management strategy. The unconstrained demand will help you calculate your Last Room Value for certain dates, and possible length of stay restrictions that may apply.

Hotel benchmarking

Hotels will commonly benchmark against their competition to evaluate performance. It's not the definitive way to track performance, nor should it be treated as an authority, but it does enable you to see where you stand and how travellers might react.

You'll be required to benchmark on criteria such as:

Prices

Product (luxury, mid-range, economy?)

Level of service

Location

Distribution channel

Remember a competitor is only a competitor if they're targeting the same markets as you, and even then you might not be competing for the same segments at the same time. However, if you can anticipate their strategies, making your own adjustments will become much easier. In the context of the competitor set, results can often look very different. Perhaps you thought you only had an average year when in fact your competitors were much worse off and you were the stellar hotel in the area. Or vice versa.

On conclusion, hotel price control/income management strategy may bring below these benefits to any hotels as below, they may include as below:

1. Less costly errors

While larger hotels might be able to hide or easily overcome a pricing mistake, smaller hotels have less margin for error. An incorrect price at a small hotel will have a bigger impact on ADR and RevPAR.

2. Get more revenue out of every room

With fewer rooms, maximising the rate for each room becomes more critical. The data your technology provides will help you understand who you should be targeting and when. What will be the most valuable demand for you? For example, do you offer rates for group business? Do you offer discounts for long stays?

3. Know your competitors better

To get your own pricing strategy right, you need to know what your immediate competitors are doing. With a pricing intelligence tool you can get an instant all-in-one overview of your competitors rate activity, meaning you can concentrate on why they are adjusting and how/if you should respond.

4. It makes your hotel 'bigger'

Large, branded hotels will already have an RMS in place – and dedicated revenue managers to manage them – and while independent hotels may not be able to afford a robust solution, pricing intelligence tools are an affordable substitute. These use the data and its own algorithms to carry out a real-time analysis of the state of the market, and of demand, in order to calculate ideal room rates. Increasing your data visibility and analysis capabilities gives you more ammunition to compete with large hotel groups who are able to devote full-time staff to revenue management.

5. Manage your time efficiently

Automated market intelligence will allow you to instantly access and act upon pricing data. Knowing when the market will be an easy sell-out or in a quiet period will not only enable you to optimise rates, but with a dependable forecast, you can organise your staff more effectively and improve the guest experience.

6. You can be proactive

The more data you have access to, the less reactive you'll be. Rather than reacting to your competitors all the time, you'll better understand demand, make your own projections, and set intelligent rates.

7. Understand your guests better

A RMS can tell you more about customer behaviour and allow you to attract more bookings. For example, do guests prefer it when your rate applies to every night of their stay, or will they accept varying rates, or do they prefer a total stay price?

8. Your data will come from a single source

Instead of combing through your own data, and then individually doing the same for competitors, an RMS will collate everything for you in one place. Depending on your system, you can do this for up to 15 competitors. If you are a smaller hotel that is new to revenue management strategies, doing everything manually might have you tearing your hair out.

Hence, any hotels can not neglect to consider how to implement price and income management strategy in order to achieve the highest profit aim.

Hotel room living service consumer psychological factors

What are some noticeable hotel service trends in the industry ?

Travellers of today are diverse and want to stay in a place which lets them live out their individuality. They want a hotel which adapts to them, not the other way around. The quest for individualised experiences sets them apart from older generations and has created a challenge for many hoteliers. Guests expect convenience, simplicity and the same instant gratification they enjoy in other areas of their lives. However, hotel and resort staff face the daunting task of handling an endless array of guest issues with a limited team. No matter how well trained front desk staff might be, there are always occasions where long lines form and waiting guests become frustrated. Even a five-minute wait in a check-in line can result in a 50% reduction in guest satisfaction scores. Moreover, guests have become accustomed to the Airbnbs of the world where everything offered to them is extremely relevant and guest has the option to tweak the experience themselves. A similar trend is seen among major hotel chains, where they are using loyalty solutions to promote offers and services based on the guests' preferences and guests have the ability to check-in using mobile. Independent hotels are slowly but steadily starting to embrace such solutions. Personalisation of guest service is no longer a trend, but an obligation for hotels. For example, traditional check-in times were designed for a guest that no longer exists. With long haul travel now very much mainstream, 40% of guests are either arriving on flights before 7AM or leaving on flights that take off after 6PM. Tailoring check-in/check out times to your guest's travel plans is the next battleground of personalisation."

What's the power of automation for hotels and guests?

By combining powerful segmentation with a high-conversion platform, upselling can really help deliver the five R's of revenue management: Selling the right room on the right channel to the right customer at the right time at the right price. Using segmentation properly allows you to target and market to a variety of potential buyers with varying needs, behaviors and budgets. Doing this well will provide you data needed to understand the success of your current revenue strategies and adjust them to maximise your topline in the future. Software providers can take most of that work off your hands. Setting up your segments is done in a matter of minutes, and the software handles the rest, like making sure the segments you choose are offered attractive deals in automatically sent emails."

Can AI platforms or chatbots raise travellers living hotel room choice need ?

Artificial Intelligence (AI) platforms or chatbots can be used to answer simple guest questions and requests freeing up hotel staff to focus on the most complicated guest issues. With mobile keys, bluetooth technology allows mobile devices to communicate directly with the door lock on a guest room.Automation technology can also be leveraged to enhance communication between the hotel staff and guest. Platforms like ours at OpenKey also gives hotels the ability to offer mobile dining, valet requests, concierge, and other guest services – in addition to a digital key – from a mobile app.

I believe that AI technology can boost your hotel brand perception. Automating guest communication opens up a tremendous potential for the hotel. Typically pre-arrival or confirmation emails have been seen as just a system-generated message verifying that a reservation has been made. But this is the first time guest hears about you. "Wouldn't it be nice, if you could delight the guest with a warm greeting, in their own language, with offers that are specific to their profile or segment? With proper tools, this can be easily achieved. For exmaple, if a guest booked a standard room, the system may automatically offer the deluxe room. Or if the airport is far away, offer them a fully arranged taxi service. If targeted properly, upsell and cross-sell efforts can significantly improve guest satisfaction as offers are more relevant. When should you send the offer and who should you send it to? Hotels often send their upsell offers too early when the pain point the hotel is looking to solve is not front of mind for the guest. How should you change your offer depending on the nature of the guest? We'll change how we target and what we offer guests depending on nationality and travel time.

Moreover, AI technology is helping hotels to be more efficient. From the perspective of some hotels which apply AI technology, these hotels look to elevate their service, mobile technology will help us deliver a simplified and efficient guest experience. Today's traveller wants to save time and enjoy their travel, not wait in check-in lines. These hotels could help their customers can be happier about adding a tech solution that will ultimately benefit to their per booking hotel rooms service before they catch pair planes to arrive their country. So, they do not need to spend much time to find the best suitable hotel to live when the hotel can apply AI technology to help them to make hotel choice decision. For example, hoteliers are slowly beginning to understand that technology is not here to replace the human touch but to complement it. Historically guest-facing technology was seen as a toy they can live without. But more and more guests expect these types of convenience services and hotels are realising, this is the new norm. Most guests are not overly expressive about their wants and needs. This means, without tech, it will become extremely difficult to deliver superior guest experience.

How important is connectivity for hoteliers and the platforms they use? As a minimum we need the reservation data from hotel guests, which can be gleaned from the PMS, channel manager, or OTA. So it's important these systems are able to integrate easily with each other. Connectivity is the most important influential factor: Without it any lacking AI technological communication assistance hotels can't automate their services for their clients, which means adding manual work to the hotel's front desk, which simply doesn't work. The ability for technology to continue to help hotels run their businesses, hinges on the providers ability to connect into the hotel's tech stack. Moreover, hoteliers completely understand the pivotal role of tech, but their hands have been tied by the lack of connectivity offered by their incumbent technology systems.

On conclusion, hotel management is about overseeing every operation of the property. This requires knowledge of distribution strategy, finance, customer service, staff management, marketing, and more. Effective inventory management for hotels involves both creating and managing demand, and maximising returns. Revenue management is another huge part of managing your hotel. How do you get more money coming in and achieve business goals?

In the hospitality industry almost everything revolves around the customer, and they're the quickest party to point out any flaws. Good management eliminates as many mistakes as possible. Hotel management sometimes also requires the management of a restaurant. Turn your hotel restaurant into a premium dining experience that focuses on the whole package including the food, lighting, music, decor, and wine lists. This way, your restaurant won't only be the bait to bring new customers in, but also an incentive for current guests to return when they revisit the area. Similar to search engines such as Google, OTAs have their own algorithms for how your property will rank, meaning you need to pay close attention to how you build your profile on them. Fighting food waste at your hotel goes beyond feeding people and helping the environment – it also improves your property's bottom line. Reporting on performance is essential to hotel management. You need to collect and analyse accurate data regularly to see where things are working, and what you need to improve on. Hotel management software is technology that allows hotel operators and owners to streamline their administrative tasks while also increasing their bookings in both the short- and long-term. Managing a hotel isn't all about managing the physical property, it's also about managing intangible things like reputation. There are many apps in the market to help with everyday challenges. Organised teams get more done and having everything under control also gives you a better grip on the overall success of the business.

● How and why hotel managers need to attempt to predict customer booking hotel room behavior or booking hotel room need psychology?

Any hotel management ought need to learn how to predict hotel entertainment consumer individual need in order to attract consumer living choice or increase consumers number easily. I assume that if the hotel can provide the room living service can let any hotel consumers to feel such ad themselves homes feeling. It will influence them to live longer time to stay in the hotel (prolonging hotel room booking days) in the hotel because they can feel themselves homes living feeling. How can make hotel room booking consumers to feel the hotel rooms are such as their homes living feeling? it is one interesting question to discuss. I shall explain as below;

Building hotel living holiday leisure feeling, this factor is very important to influence hotel living consumers to make final extending proplonging living consumers to make final extending or prolonging living days in the hotel. Holidays, by definition , are non-working times, an extended period of anticipated recreation, especially away from home, they can be days of festivity when no work is done. The prolem and opportunity for hotel living entertainment service providers, is that when hotel living customers are on holiday, or at leisure. Hotels need to give a chance of getting away from living holidays, new changing the batteries and for some a change of holiday living of entertainment lifestyle. Hence, if the hotel can let all customers to feel home comfortable living feeling to enjoy their one part of entertainment activity in the whole journeys. The hotel may persuade any one customer (hotel room living customers to prolong any one customer (hotel room living customers to prolong living days in the hotel).

Will the broad framework of leisure defined as time, there are many variations. In general, defining leisure as the time when someone is not working primarrily for money. So, if the hotel room living customer can feel that he/she spends the booking room living fee is value to choose the hotel room to live. The hotel room is such as unoccupied time or free time in whose journey time. Due to he/she feels that this living hotel room time is whose entertainment time. It is essential, then this unoccupied time may persuade him/her to prolong booking hotel room living time in the hotel. For example, he planned to stay 5 days in the hotel, but because he/she feels that the hotel can provide entertainment activities time to attract him/her to stay longer time in the hotel, e.g. gym sport facilities are very attractive sport playing entertainment or hotel restaurant can provide good taste food eating time in special dinner, breakfast, lunch time or swimming pool is beautiful design and large size and it can let him/her to feel actual natural beach environment feeling. Then, any one these extra entertainment facilities or services factors may influence any one customer to spend extending living time in the hotel. Such as this cause, this hotel living customer may feel need to live more two to three days, even more days in this hotel. Hence, hotel leisure as time psychological factor is also important to influence any one hotel room living customer to influence any one hotel oom living consumer to make extending living time decision easily, when they feel this hotel has themselves homes feeling.

Kraus & Bates (1975) add experiencing to the activity. Recreation consists of activities or experiences with are carried on volutarily in leisure time. They are chosen by participants, either for pleasure or to satisfy certain personal needs when provided as part of organized community programs, creation must be designed to achieve constructive goals.

Hence, if the hotel can consist any recreation actvities or experiences to let any one hotel living customer to enjoy to live when are carried on voluntarily in their leisure time. They can choose any kinds of leisure activities to play and live in the hotel, if the hotel any one kind of leisure activity can satisfy their leisure needs. Then, the hotel's any kind of leisure activity can achieve constructive goals to persuade any one hotel room living consumer likes to spend extra money to enjoy any kinds of hotel leisure facilties, instead of spending extra hotel room living expenditure to proplong hotel time in the hotel. Hence, it seems that whether the hotel can provide attractive leisure facilities to let consumers to relationship to influence they their long living or staying time in the hotel.

When asked what were the three most important factors in the development of hotel. Thus equality applied to most leisure facilities ideally, a public transport location may influence any one hotel room customer to choose which hotel location is the nearest to public transport in order to pay cheap transport fee to catch the public transport. This is one low transport fee cost factor to influence the potential hotel room customer choice.

Hence, any hotel's location will be chosen to build to near many public transport tools, e.g. buses, underground trains, taxis, trains station locations. It aims to attract the hotel room booking potential customers can pay cheap public transport fee to arrive their hotel conveniently. They do not need to spend long walking time to arrive their hotels after they catch any one kind of public transport tool to arrive their hotel destinations. Moreover, they do not need to spend long time to find where the hotel locates when they leave the bus stop. So, geographical location factor will be another main factor to influence hotel consumer choices.

The model is based on comparing demand and supply economc theory:

1. identifying where hotel demand is located, whether and to what extent, hotel rooms number demand exceeds hotel rooms number supply in the geographical area and whether , and where, the city has much land to provide space capacity to permit to build hotels number exists in the geographical area in the city.

2. Moreover, local demand is measured on the basis of the number of hotel visits per week in peack period for any hotel room needs determined by:

The total number of travelling visitors in the month rate , the demand rate, the proportion of residents who want to book room to live in the hotel, instead of overseas travelling visitors, the desired frequency of visits, how often overseas travellers want to visit the country and the proportation of visits which arise in the normal peiods per month, such as christmas, New Year etc. public holidays.

So, all of these hotel visitors public transport fee cheap demand number and hotel geographical locations, hotel entertainment facilities , hotel comfortable living feeling, hotel safety, hotel food taste, public holiday and visitor individual travelling need, air ticket price main factors which will influence any one hotel's room demand and supply number absolutely in behavioral economic theory view, instead of hotel environment and service performance basic element factor.

On conclusion, all of these any one element may influence any one hotel customers numner increases or decreases absolutely. Hence, any one hotel management can not neglect to learn how to implement their hotel management strategies effectively.

ref.

Kraus , R. & Batees , B. (1975). Creation leadership and supervision, W.B. Saunders, philadelphia, P.A.

How to supervise teams in hospitality industry

Any hotels need effective supervisors to supervise their teams in different department in order to raise service efficiency. How to supervise teams which is one important question to any hotels? I shall attempt to explain as below: In hospitaloty industry, alomst everything depends on the psycical labour of many hours (non-managerial workers), waiters, mix drinks, wash dishes, checkquests, clean room, carry bags, mop floors, even security etc. All of these teams must need a supervisor to manage their make products and/or perform services. The human resources for personnel, and training departments are example of staffs who advise line departments, such as the food and beverage department on matters including hiring, disciplining and training.

In general, supervisor responsibility may include: achieving or exceeding the expected results, on time and on budget, planning or determining priorities. Organizing (scheduling), motivating (creative a positive work environment), controlling (monitoring and taking corrective action if mistakes are outside acceptable limits), communicating effectively.

In the reality, in a hotel you may have 5,000 minimum customers are day. You deal with your supervisors. You deal with your subordinates, and you deal with your guests, all coming at you from different directons. Salepeople , deliveries, inspectors, customer complaints and applicants . You jobs interrupt you. So , you are likely to have only a few seconds available when you make many important decisons.

You will feel bus to deal any of either above, these matters every day. Hence, in effective hotel organization, it needs have effective scientific management, it incudes these elements: Standardization, of work procedures, tool and conditions of work through design of work methods by specialists, careful selection of competent people, after training, and elimination of these (traineers) who could not or would not perform, complete and constant overseeing of the work, with total obedience from the worker' incenive pay for meeting the fair day for meeting the fair day's work standard, the worker's share of the increased productivity.

How to innovate hotel tasks to be work simplification or searching for the best way of performance tasks ? Supervisors can use time-and-motion study techniques, developing ways of simplifying tasks than often doubled or triples what a worker would do. This methods and principles had a great impact in food service kitchen, where work simplification techniques have been explored widely adopted. This methods ewere adopted although the idea that have hotel worker should share in the benefits of increased productivity seldom went along with the rest of the system. For example, in hotel kitcehen department , every cooking steep is systematized, and the cooker, dish cleaner is simply taught to run the kitchen dish cleaning machines, cooking machines follow the rules, and speak given phrases. When the kitchen bell rings, the cooker turns the hamburgers on dispenser one time, where is no room for deviation.

How a supervisor can build a positive work climate in his/her hotel department ? He/She needs to know his/her employee expectation and need. You may wonder whethet their performance will meet your expectation, and you may have some plans for improving productivity. But you may not realize that what there people expect from you and how you meet their expectations may have as much to do with their performance as your expectation of them. However, your staffs also expect you to be qualified to supervise. First, they want you to have worked in the area in which you are supervising: a hotel, room, a hotel kitchen, a hotel restaurant, lowing into a big motel from a job in a budget motel, you may also improve yourself. Your staffs want to feel that you understand the operation well and appreciate the work , they are doing. They want to feel that they and their jobs are in good hands, that you are truly capable of directing their work.

● Behavior modification supervising strategy

Behavior modification explains a newer method for improving performance. It explains all behavior is a function of its consequences; people behave as they do because of positive or negative consequences to them. If the consequences are positive, they will trend to repeat the behaviors, if they are negative, they will trend not to . Hence, if you are hotel kitchen cookers their supervisor, you need to give praise , or appreciation to the cookers , whose cooking skills can be improved when they can cook good taste foods ro satisfy hotel restaurant customer individual eatting feeling. Every time, you need to give praise to the excellent cooker's cooking performance. Then, his/her cooking skills will be improved , due to your praise.

It is possible that he/she feels salary will be increased by your praise. Otherwise, when you feel the cooker's cooking skill is worse and your cookers their cooking foods taste are also worse and they can not satisy your cookers their customers' eatting taste needs often. Then , you ought not punish or blam to let him/her by your oral blaming or pubishment threat (without salary increasing threat). Consequently, his /her cooking skill can not be improved, even worse. You ought attempt to help him/her to find whether which aspects of cooking skills , he/she is felt to need to learn how to improve hir/her cooking skill to be better, and you ought teach him/her how to cool the kinds of food to be better taste. Consequently, his/her cooking skill will be improved by your teaching and patience excuse attitude.

● How to design clear job analysis?

Any one hotel team ought need have clear job analysis to let their departments supervisors and staffs to know whether what aspects of tasks , they need to do in order to achieve actual work performance improvement. For example, sever job units example, it may include: Stock service station, set tables, great quests, explain menu to customers, take food and beverage orders and complete guest check, pick up order and complete plate preparation, serve food, recommand wines and serve them, total and present check, perform side work, operate equipment , meet dress and grooming stantards, observe sanitation procedures and requirements, maintain good customer relations, and desired check arrange.

Hence, any one hotel restaurant server can know whether how they require the setting standards, training and evaluation jst as the actual work sequences do. Such units appears in ither jobs as well , and the same standards will apply in each case in the hotel any departments performance standards from the heart of the job description and they describe the what, how to and how wells of a job.

1. What the employee is to do?

2. How it is to be done?

3. To what extent it is to be done?

It means that any hotel department staffs and supervisors they need to know concern their job requirement such as : How much, how well, how soon. For example, " one waitor or waitress job at acertain restaurant. The server will take food and beverage orders for up to five tables with 100 % accuracy, using standard house procedures." It is the hotel restaurant waitor/waitress general job standard acceptance level.

Hence, waitor/waitress supervisor can folle this guideline to know how to supervise his/her staffs and evaluate whose job performance in the hotel restaurant.

On conclusion, due to hotel is one service industry, any hotel's different department effective supervising management, they need have good job standard, training and fair evaluation performance system, fair compensation and pubishment system, instead of the department supervisor whose supervising effort or ability whether is proficient or worse in order to influence whose team serving performance effectively and efficiently . However, any organization itself management team and supervising team will need have good communicating technique in order to let any department supervisor knows how to supervise his/her team effectively in order to achieve improvement service performance aim.

CHAPTER VII

How Business Strategy Influences Consumer Behavioral Change

Human Behavioral network job brings social economic benefits

What does human network job mean ? Why may human network job be popular? Why human network job behavior may influence economy ?

Nowadays internet is popular to use. We can apply internet to find data , search any new things, even earn money. Why does internet

may become huma network job source. For example, e-publish may be one kind of new human network job. Any authors may apply internet

channel to help them to sell electronic or paper books from e-publisher web store. They may apply facebook, you tub etc. any online

channel to promote themselves new books to let new readers to know whether when they may buy themselves favourable new topic books to read

from electronic publisher web store.

Thus, future electronic publisher industry may help any authors to build internet network platform to help them to sell and promote

ot advertise their any one new electronic or paper book topic to let global any one reader to choose to buy their any new topic books from electronic publisher web store easily and conveniently. However, it implies that electronic network platform author may be one kind of future new human network job in our societies.

How electronic network platform author job may bring economy benefit in macro economy view? A person can have few friends, contacts and still be very influential if these few

friends and contacts are themselves highly influential, e.g. one author must not need to know any one reader in global society. When they like to choose any electronic books from electronic internet network platform. They may become the author's any one topic book buyer, when they feel the author's any one topic book is fun and attract they make decision to buth the strange author whose the topic book from electronic book publisher's platform web store conventiently in short time. Although, they are strangers, they do not know themselves , but the reader can understand what it way that made Google from writing platofrm to create new creative mind and typing network job method to replace traditional hand writing book method for global authors. It will be one kind of new human network writing job.

Hence, global any one reader can apply an innovative search engine , such as google.com to find whether whom author personal new topic books are value to read from internet.

Then, the electroniuc publisher's web store may be new book store platform sale network to help the author to sell many electronic or paper books from electronic network platform

in short time. So, internet may be future new network plaform to help global any one author to create network writing job absolutely. Furthermore, internet may be popular social media

to help any one author to build goold relationship between his/her readers. It is one kind of new network, human network job. New authors do not need to buy many paper books to prepare to put in any one book shop warehouse. Their every book can print on demand to reduce out of book stock in any one book shop. They may choose to sell either electronic books or paper books both from any one book publisher web store. So, electronic network platform may be one kind of good writing channel to help human authors to create income and it can also help authors to bring new creative mind and new topic fun content books to let readers to know and buy to read from electronic publisher network platform.

Why does human behavior may be one kind of new human network job to bring global economic advantages. ALthough, it may be free income or without inocme, but the person does the network behavior, his/her behavior may be bring advantages to influence many other people's health. For this case, when a worker in a coffee shop in an airport gets a vaccination aganinst the flu, it does not only helps him or her stay healthy, but also helps the many travellers who might otherwise have been inflected if that workers caught the flu. So, the externality , the result implies the vaccination of even a part of a community conveys benefits to the whole community. For example, governments pay special attention to the vaccinations of school children, teachers, health mothers, and the elderly, categories of people particularly susceptible not only to catching, but also to transmitting a disease.

It is not accidential that governments are heavily involved with vaccination . When there are externalities, free market, fail to persuade individual incentives with society's
their the worker's decision of whether to get a vaccine ends up attracting whether other people get sick. The workers might not fully take all these other people's potential suffering into account when making her or his vaccination decision.

As Stanford University does many suggestions, understand this and tries to help them make the right decisions and so providers free flu vaccines for its staff and students.
Small pockets of unvaccinated individuals can allow a disease to gain a spread more widely well-being. For example, parent weighing the costs and benefits of a vaccine for their child is not always thinking of the consequences of that vaccination to other people. THese are markets in which subsidizing or regulating behavior can make everyone better off. Because the reason for requiring that a child be vaccinated before enrolling in school is not just to protect that child, because each child's vaccination affects others via potential contagions.

Robots take our jobs behavioral and economy influences
Robot job behavior brings economy influences

If one day robots can replace human to do simple, even complex jobs. They will bring what influences to our global societial economy.The popular economic refrain declares that the
global middle class is dying and robots will soon take our jobs, e.g. shopping center customer service jobs, library service jobs, cinema ticket sale jobs, restaurant kitchen cooker jobs,
even, bus drivers, taxi drivers etc. public transport driving jobs, accountant, doctors etc. professional jobs. Whether it is beautiful or petty matter if our future societies have many human jobs can be replaced to do from robots. Businessman must may reduce to employ employees and reduce to pay salary or wage, when robots can be replaced to do their employees tasks. But, societies must bring unemployement rate rises , due to societies will have many people loss jobs when their employers choose to buy robots to serve their clients or do any office tasks or customer service or cleaning etc. tasks.

In micro economy view, employers may save money in long term, but in macro economy view, it will cause unemployment ratio rises , even crime rate rises when there are many people lose
jobs in societies. These models of doom, though, fail to account for the hundreds of businesses riding the waves of change in their industries when robots may be invented to replace human to do many simple , even complex tasks in our future societies.

WE may image that one small factory needs to manufacture fishes canes to sell to supermarket, the small , cheaper stuff and higher margin parts of the fishes manufacture industry. Before, this factory needs to employe many human factory workers need to help every fresh customer makeing the perfect fishing gear, designed for performance, durability, and cost in order to achieve to manufacture every fish cane in whole fished processing manufacturing stages. Every worker needs to spend about 15 to twenty minutes to finish every fish cane , till to delivery to any supermarket to sell. If this fish canes manufacturing factory can apply manufacturing robots to help them to finish any one working tasks , every robot can only spend five minutes to finish whole fresh fish cane manufacturing process. Thus, every robot can
help this factory save 10 to 15 minutes time to finsh every fish cane manufacturing process. IN fact, time is money, because when every robot can help this factory to reduce 10 to 15 minutes time to compare human worker. Then, this

factory can finish about 20 fish canes in one hour if it can use robot to help it to manufacture fish canes. Otherwise, if this factory still use human workers to help it to manufacture fish canes, then it can finsh about 3 to 4 fish canes in one hour. SO, the manufacturing efficiency ensures that robots must help this fish manufacturing factory to raise fish canes number more than human workers. So, in robotic behavioral economy view, manufacturing robots must help this fish canes manufacturing factory to raise fish canes manufacturing number and deliver increasing number to supermarkets to prepare to sell every day. Robots can help this fish canes manufacturing factory bring manufacturing time saving, rising manufacturing efficiency, improving performance and reducing wages expenditure long time advantages in micro economy view. However, manufacturing robots can also bring disadvanages to society, e.g. increasing unemployment ratio, increasing crime rate,

this factory workers will lose jobs and income, they need earn social welfare from government and increasing government finance pressure in short time, even long time in macro economic view.

Stanford University graduate program in economics, Scott lecturer explained that "in demand and supply economic theory for robots supply and demand case, robots supply number increasing may influence human workers demand number decrease. It sometimes calls " the efficient frontier".

No specific human beings were mentioned in any of economics classes. As robots supply and demand in market case, They (robots) may be purely theoretical " agents" who reached to the most reasonable sale prices in order to persuadc any one businessman buyer to make manufacturing robot buying decision whether robots can help him / her to bring how much saving time , saving money, saving cost, improving performance, efficiency economic benefit before he/she plans to reduce workers number when he/she decides to apply robots to replace human workers in his/her factory or office or any service department, e.g. cinema ticket sale service, shopping center customer service, shopping center cleaning , supermarket customer service etc. service or sale tasks. When robots can replace human to do any one of these tasks in any organizations. So, robots may be human worker agents who reached to prices the way robots would react to a software

command. There was nothing that explained why some people thrived and others did n't or why truly brilliant, hardworking people could fail when much lazier folks succeeded." Having been admitted to the Stanford University graduate program in economics, Scott lecturer hoped to get his answers there.

How robots influence our future social changing? Using the right technology can be a boon to your business in this economy. For internet example, it is easier than ever to find well-matched customers all around the world, to stay in contact with them, and to more quickly design the products they want. If you focus solely on being cutting -edge, though you risk letting the technology

take over what should be very robust relationships with your customers , employees, and colleagues. IN nowaddays society, technoligical advances and cutomation, personal

relationships in business are more crucial than ever. I mean that robots can not replace human to serve clients to let them to feel more comfortable and passion more easily. For shoe shop case example, if the shoe shop apply one robot to serve its clients to replace human shoe salesperson to serve its shoe customers. Robots ensure that they can not persuade every shoe potential buyer to make shoe buying decision more easily when robots need to contact every shoe potential buyer. The reason is simple, because robots can not touch any one shoe buyer individual emotion very easier.

If the shoe buyer needs the robots to help him/her to choose any right shoe styles when he/she can not feel himself / herself can make the most right shoe style choice decision. The robots can not replace human shoe salesperson to make shoe style choice judgement more easily. They must need longer time to analyze whether which shoe style may be the most suitable to the shoe buyer. Otherwise, human shoe salesperson may attempt to make the most right shoe style choice decision to help any one shoe buyer to chooce the most right style shoe because he/she owns shoe style sale experience, shoe style knowledge, the most important reason is that they can feel every shoe customer individual emotion to touch whether he/she will feel comfortable or happy when they attempt to help every shoe customer to seek the most right shoe style in every shoe customer whole shoe searching processing. Othwerwise, serving robots are only one machine, they can not touch or feel every shoe customer individual emotion whether he/she feel comfortable or unhappy or happy when they need to contact them in whole shoe searching processing.

Hence, I believe that some tasks robots can

not repalce human staff to do very easily. Otherwise, robots may bring disadvanatges to let any one businessman to loss his/her customers, due to robots can not touch every customer

emotion to compare human staff in service tasks more easily. Robots serving customer behaviors may cause money lose and customers number lose to the shop in micro economic view.

Intellectual human economic behaviors

What does intellectual human economic behaviors mean ? I believe that when we choose or decide to do intellectual behaviors, then our societies will be influenced to bring economic growth in consequence.I shall attempt to indicate pollution case to explain how and why eithet our intellectual or foolish behaviors may bring economic growth or recession in consequence as below:

On one hand, for air pollution social case aspect example, if we only consider to buy cars to drive for working aimr or holiday leisure aim. Then, our societies air will be polluted. Our health will be influenced to bad. Our car driving behaviors may cause global environment air pollution serously. In long tiem, global air pollution will bring our bodies health to be bad. Although, ourselves car driving behaviors may bring our driving travelling leisure enjoyment and comfortable feeling in short time, also we so not need to pay public transport fare often, but we need to compensate ourselves health economic intangible loss due to air pollution , when cars number increases, dirty air will cause ouselves health to become bad.

In the result, we will need to pay more medical expenditure when we are old age, due to ourselves bodies will become bad, due to we breathe global dirty air every day, due to ourselves cars pollute air in long time, e.g. 10 to 20 years, even 30 more without limited air pollution environment. So, driving cars behavior may be one kind of human foolish behavior and our foolish behavior may bring ourselves future long time medical expenditure absolutely.

One the other hand, water pollution social aspect, if we often keep much rubblish to pollute sea, oil exploration porcessing pollute ocean , ships gas pollute ocaen, then fishes will eat polluted food and drive dirty water, due to global ocean is polluted.

In fact, because human only to conside how to buy boats to carry on leisure enjoyment activities, or catch cruises to travel on the sea. Also, oil manufacturers only consider researching anywhere to find new oil exploration places to manufacture oil product, when their oil exploration processes pollute ocarn . Consequently, global fishes drink polluted warer or eat polluted food. They will have poison. SO, human will have high chance to eat poison polluted fishes, due to fishes are poison or are polluted.

So, human is doing foolish activities, we only hope to find oil exploration places to pollute ocean or we only spend money to buy ticket to catch ships to travel anywhere in global ocean. All of these human foolish behaviors will bring pollution to global ocean. On consequently, we will need to compensate to eat polluted or dirty or poision fishes, ourselves bodies health will be bad. In long time, we need have high chance to pay medical expenditure when we are old. So, pollution case may be one good example to explain how and why human foolish behavior may influence ourselves future need to compensate serious medical loss.

All of these human foolish behavior will bring pollution to global ocean. On consequently, we will need to compensate to eat polluted or dirty or poison fished , ourselves bodies health will be bad. In long time, we will have high chance to pay medical expenditure, when we are old. So, pollution case may be one good example to explain how and why human ourselves intellectual or foolish behaviors may influence future long time economic loss or economic growth or recession in micro and micro economic view.

On another water pollution aspect hand, if we often keep rubbish to sea, oil exploration processing pollutes ocean and ships' gas pollute ocean, then fishes will eat polluted food and drink dirty water, due to fishes will eat polluted food and drink dirty sea water because the global ocean is polluted seriously.

In fact, because human only consider how to buy boats to carry on any leisure water activities, or catches cruises to travel on the sea. Also, oil manufacturers only consider any where to find oil exploratin places to manufacture oil products from ocean, when their pol exploration processes can plooute ocean. Consequently, global fishes drink polluted water or eat direty food. They will have poison. So, human will have high chance to eat poison fishes.

Otherwise, such as pollutin case, it can infuence inflation or deflation. Consequently, the reason indicates supply and demand theory. If air pollution is serious, then we will consider health issue, global cars demand number may be influenced to reduce, when global cars number demand will reduce, global car prices and supply number will need to change to fall down in order to attract or persuade global car consumers choose to make car purchase decision.

Hence, global car manufacture number and car price will be influenced to reduce, due to global air pollution issue. Consequently, deflation will occur because when the country citizen usually does not spend much extra saving money to buy car expensive goods. Money value will be low. Otherwise, if global cair pollution is not serious, human considers to buy cars to enjoy driving leisure lives. So, global car demand is influenced to increase , also global car price will also influenced to increase.

Consequently, gobal human will choose to buy cars to drive. Due to we accept to spend extra saving to buy expensive car goods. Car sale price and supply may be influenced to rise up. Money value is influenced to reduce. Inflation may be influenced, due to global car consumers number increases, we would not have extra money to spend easily. Car expensive goods expenditure influences our spending habit to avoid to make car purchase decision more easily. So, human intellectual or foolish activities may bring inflation or deflation consequency in possible indirectly in macro economic view.

On conclusion, above pollution case explain that how and why human intellectual or foolish economic behaviors may bring inflation or deflation consequency as wll as economic growth or recession consequency as well as any goods demand and supply increasing or decreasing consequency. It implies that human behavior may have indirect relationship to influence any goods dcmand and supply number to either increase or decrease result as well as any goods price will be influenced to increase or decrease in micro and macro economic view.

The relationship between social change and human behavior

Why does economic changes may influence human individual behavioral change? I shall attempt to indicate shopping behavior and staying at home behavior to explain their case and effect relationsip as below:

Human behavior can be influenced by economic change or economic change can be influenced by human behavior? Why does recession may influence consumers reduce shopping desire? In social recession suitation, it is possible that many people lose jobs suddenly, due to businessmen lose many customers. They need to make decision to reduce employees number in order to continue to keep businesses. Consequently, many firms (organizations) their employees may lose jobs. When they have much time, due to lose jobs, they will feel to avoid to spend too much time and money to go to shopping often. Many losing jobs people, they will often stay at homes.

So, they will reduce time to go to shopping, then non essential products won't their preferable choice purchase products. Hence, recession will change many losing jobs people their shopping or consumption desires to avoid to buy non essential products often . Usually when economic boom, many people have jobs to do because consumers number must increase when many people have jobs to do. Then, many people can accept to spend money to buy non essential products often. Many people feel spend time to go to shopping can satisfy their purchase of any kinds of new products useful psychology or desire. So, recession is one good example to explain it can influence many people do not like often to leave homes to go to shopping easily. Many people like to stay at homes, becaue they feel worry about spending too much shopping time when they leave homes. Their staying home time is one good negative shopping behavior example. So, economic change may influence human individual behavior changes , they have direct cause and efect relationship in behavioral economic view.

May human behavior influence economic change? Is it possible that human behavior may bring the country social economic change in macro economic or micro behavioral economic view ? I shall indicate publishing industry example. Do you feel that if there are many students feel learning is very important when they read many books or many of students feel interesting to read or they have reading new books in habit, then it is possible that the country will have many students like to spend time to go to any book shops to choose the books, they feel that they can help they learn new knowledge. Then the country will increase students number, they often spend time to visit any one book shop every week. Their visiting book shops behavior which may become their habits. So, the country will increase students number, they often spend time to visit book shops. Also, it implies that visiting book shops behaviors may be their behavioral habits.

So, when the country has many students often spend time to visit book shops , their visiting book shops behaviors may help any one book shop to raise books sale chance. So, the country's student individual often visiting book shop behaviors, their habitual visiting book shops behaviors must may assist help any one book shop to increase books sale number absolutely.

Consequently, any one book shop , its books sale bumber must be influenced to increase to increase because the country will have many students like or feel need visit book shops habit in order to choose any suitable books to buy to read at home in order to raise themselves learning effort. When the country has many bok shops often have many students visit their book shops, then their books sale number may be influenced to increase. It explain why student individual visiting book shop behavior may help any one book shop sale number increases also.

How human productive behavior may influence economic development

May any country which citizen behavior assist themselves country development? It is one cause and effect economic question. I mean that if the country itself citicen can not concentrate mind or energy to choose to do one kind of industry in order to let themselves country can bring the most benefit, then whether the counry itself economy can bring the most serious economic benefit. I shall attempt to indicate these countries themselves indistry choice to explain whether these countries themselves citizen productive behavior may help themselves countries to achieve the largest economic benefits. I shall indicate as below:

New Zealand farmer individual wine productive behavior

For New Zealand country example, this country concerns itself effort is foucs on farming agricultural aspect. So, this country has many farmers concentrate on farming agricultural aspect. May New Zealanders choose to spend time to produce different kinds of wines, e.g. wine or red grape wine is for the people are eating meat, or they are eating dinner.

When these New Zealanders their behaviors choose to do farming or agriculture to grow and produce different kinds of taste of white or red grape wine drinking products job. Themselves grape agriculture behavior will influence these New Zealanders themselves, they can learn how to improve different kinds of grape wine drinking products in order to achieve every kinds of white or read grape wines taste improving aim during their white or red grape producing process.

Why can New Zealander every individual white or read grape wine producers improve their white or read grape wine taste more easily? In behavioral economic view, it can explain that why any one New Zealander white or read grape wine producer can be encouraged or excited or persuaded to concentrate nervous and energy and effort to learn how to improve their white or red grape wine products easily.

In fact, New Zealand is one agricultural food export country. It has good natural environment resource , e.g. land, seed to provide any one farmer to produce themselves any kinds of agricultrual food products, e.g. fruit, or wine food products. Because New Zealanders know themselves country has enough natural resource . So, in common, many New Zealanders choose to attempt to do farming agricultural jobs in order to export themselves any kinds of fruit or meat or wine products to overseas or sell to domestic in order to earn profit.

So, when these New Zealand farmers number has been increasing every year. This country farmers will feel themsleves competition between this New Zealand farmers themselves are serious due to they may feel New Zealanders choose to do agriculture businesses in order to export themselves different kinds of farming food to overseas or sell to local to earn profit.

Hence, when many New Zealand farmers feel that farmers number has been increasing every year. They will feel themselves competition is serious. They must need to spend much time and nervous and effort to research what method is the best how to produce the best taste of white or red grape wine products in order to let local or overseas wine buyers to choose to buy his/her producing white or read grpae products to drink.

Hence, in competition psychological view, may influence many New Zealand white or reaad wine producers had been beginning to change their learning behavior on researching what method is the best in order to produce the best quality of taste red or white wine products to sell in order to attract overseas or local white or read grape wine drinkers to choose to buy his/her wine products. Their behavior will focus on learning how to raising or improving white or read grape wine taste method more than only focus on producing a large number white or red grape wine products. They believe wine quality is more important to compare wine producing number. So, New Zealand wine producers themselves wine producers behaviors have been changing on concentrating on researching wine quality method aspect more then wine producing number aspect in behavioral economic view.

America high technological productive behavior

For America example, US is one high technological country, it owns many high technological knowledge talent inventors, e.g. computer science inventors. Hence, US must attract many diferent countries owning high technological computer inventors choose to go to US to develop their computer science profession career. Also, it seems that when many computer science inventors or professions choose to go to US to develop themselves computer science new career. In behavioral economic view, due to their leaving themselves countries choice, which may bring influence themselve country job behaviors need to be changed. They must need to adapt US new live. Because they will forgive their past computer science job. These computer science professionals need to spend time to adapt US new lives. They " past computer science job behaviors" will need to be changed to their new US any computer employer's new computer science job model.

Because their traditional computer science jobs needed to be forgot in their themselves countries. They will feel their old computer science job knowledge and behavior needed to change in order to let their US any one new of computer company employer feels satisfactory to accept their new working behavior in any one US computer organization.

So, on the other hand, many US computer company employer will feel that they must need time to accept any one new overseas computer science professions their working behaviors, their working attitude daily, because these foreign comouter science professional, their past computer working behaviors and working attitude must be different to US domestic computer science professions.

In behavioral economic view, these overseas computer science professions, their working behaviors and attitude must be needed to change in order to adapt any one US new computer company itself domestic or local computer science professional stafs themselves daily working behaviors and attitude because these overseas and local computer science professionals must need to team work together.

In behavioral economic view, it is only one way that foreign computer science professionals must need to change themselves past country traditiona daily working behaviors and attitude in order to cooperate with these US local computer science professionals in teams more easily.

Consequently, if these foreign compute science professionals can change their past working behaviors and attitude to let any one US local computer science professional feels to cooperate with them easily in short time. Then, the US computer company itself whole computer professional teams themselves efficiencies will be influenced to raised or improved by the changing past working attitude and working behaviors of these foreign computer science professionals. So, in behavioral economic view, only if US any one computer company hopes itself computer teams themselves efficiency can be raised or improved when it decides to employ foreign computer science professionals and US domestic computer science professionals. They need to work in teams together. They must need to let these foreign computer science professionals to know how to change their working behaviors and attitude to let their domestic computer science professionals feel easy to work together. Then, the US computer company itself whole team efficiency must be rasied or improved easily in short time.

● China share market investing behavior

For China share market example, economic development depends on financial market. Because if many Chinese have interest to invest to carry on shares buying and selling activities in orde to learn how to earn shares interest and share profit when the China shareholder can make decision to sell himself/herself shares in the the high price, then he/she can earn money when he/she can sell the China company's shares in the high sale share price position.

If China has many Chinese like to spend time to carry on investing shares activities. Themselves shares buying and selling behaviors will influence China has many companies can increase fund from many Chinese shareholders in order to have enough money to expand or develop themselves businesses in China in long term.

Consequently, when China can have many Chinese like to attempt to carry on buying and selling shares investing behaviors in China share market. Themselves buying and selling shares behaviors can help many Chinese companies have effort to increase enough money or capital in order to continue to do their businesses in long term absolutely.

So, it explains why when many Chinese become shareholders , they can assist China will have many companies continue to develop their businesses if many Chinese like to carry on shares buying and selling investing behaviors in long time in China financial investment market nowadays in behavioral economic view.

Why has any individual country have many people invest share behavior which can influence the country's macro consumption desire?

I shall apply shares market buying and selling investment behavior to explaiin why shares investment behavior which may impact the country's overal consumption desire as below:

In behavioral economic view, I assume that when the coutry has many people have interest to attempt to carry on shares buying and selling investment behavior, then their frequent shares buying and selling behaviors which may bring negactive consumption desire or shopping desire of these shares investors their consumer behavior.

The reason is simple, when the country has many share buyers number suddenly been increasing rapidly. Consequently, these large group share investors must need to spend much time to research any kinds of company shares variations, whether when their share prices will rise up of fall down in order to achieve buying the company's shares in the lowest price and selling the company's shares in the highest price level in order to earn profit.

Basic on this reason, they must need to spend much extra time to research share prices changing behavior every day, e.g. one working person will wait to leave his/her job, after he/she can spend time to gather data to research the day's share price changing behavior after dinner. So, the working person's right time may be his/her share price market research behavior. Before he/she may spend his/her night time to go to shopping after dinner, but nowadays, he/she will fogive to do his/her shopping behavior before dinner or after dinner at hight sometime. He/she will make decision to spend much night time to turn on computer to click on share market website to research his/her share purchase choice to investigate whether his/her share price whether it rises up or falls down at the moment in order to make his/her share buying or selling decision at ever night time.

I mean the when the country has many people are share investors, their shares investment behavioral spenging time which will influence many shops lose customers at might often because the country will have many people feel need to spend night time to turn on computer or watch television to investigate share price variation. So, the country will have many people / share investors choose to stay at home in order to carry on share price variation investigation behavior, they need to listen share market update news from radios or watch the share market update news from computer or TV at home every night. Consequenly, they must reduce times to leave themselves homes at night. So, their shopping behavior also will be reduced. Because these share investors feel need to spend time to investigate share price variation news at homes which can bring economic benefits (high opportunity benefits) when they choose to forgive to leave homes to go to shopping times (opportunity cost) every night.

On conclusion, it seems that when the country has many people are share investors, then their share price investigating behavior may bring negative shopping emotion at night. Consequently, the country's any one shop may lose many customers from this share investor consumer group in behavioral economic view. Hence, when the country's share investors number had been increasing rapidly, it will influence any shops lose many customers from this share investing customer group at night frequenly in short time, even long time in behavioral economic view, because their shopping desires or shopping emotion will be brought negative feeling when they make decisions to spend much time to listen radios or watch TV or computers share price update nes at night. Hence, share market will bring negative impact to influence consumer shopping desire or negative shopping emotion in behavioral economic view.

Can technology influence human shopping behavioral change?

Nowadays, technological development has reached mature stage, whether technological mature stage may bring positive or negative shopping emotion influence to global consumers. I shall aplly internet inventin or ecommerce shopping channel tool to explain whether internet technology can bring postive or negative influence to global consumer behavior in behavioral economic view.

Internet is a good technological tool, it brings e-commerce business chance. In fact, commonly, global has have many businessmen choose to use internet channel to carry on their products transactions between global online-buyers and their electronic websites. So, global many shoppers had begun to feel online shopping is more convenient to compare visiting shops shopping. Their shopping behaviors have been changed from internet technological tool. Global has many shoppers choose to buy any products from any overseas or local businessmen their web stores. They only need to spend time to find any businessmen their webstores to choose the most suitable products to pay visa to buy from their webstores. at homes. So, in general, global had have may shoppers had changed their shopping behaviors from visiting shops to visiting webstores at homes often.

So, it seems that internet technological tool had influenced global many shops disappear, but internet webstores will be replaced their actual shops on streets. Some of businessmen either they choose webstores to replace shops or choose websotes and shops both or still keep shops only. Hence, internet tool influences global businessmen have three kinds of products sale channels to let globa local and overseas consumers to choose how to buy their products. However, in fact, many of global shoppers, youngers and olders had begun to accept to buy any products from webstores. They feel to spend time to leave homes to visit shops , their shopping behaviors will be wasted time to not essential part to their daily lives. Hence, since internet technological invention, it had changed many consumers their traditional visiting shops shopping habit to change to buying products from webstores channel.

However, on the one hand, internet creates webstores ecommerce shopping channel to let global many consumers do not need to leave homes to go to shopping. It brings negative visiting shops shopping emotion to global general consumers nowadays. But on the other hand, it also brings positive visiting internet webstores shopping emotion to global general consumer nowadays. So, it seems that global many consumers feel that they often do not need to spend much time to go out shopping. Many global consumers feel convenient and enjoy to choose any products to buy from different internet webstores, when the online buyer chooses the most suitable product, he she only needs to pay visa card to buy the product from the online seller's webstore conveniently at home.

Hence, online shopping can bring economic benefit to online buyers, e.g. avoiding walking time or spending transport fare to visit the shop to go to shopping, shortening or reducing shopping time to do another important matter.

On conclusion, global many consumers began feel online shopping can bring more economic benefits on shortening shopping time, avoiding transport fare spending aspect. So, online shopping will be popular shopping behavior for future long time. It may encourage global many shoppers can make rapid shopping decision in short time in order to carry on any products buying transaction to global any one online shopper in short time easily in behavioral economic view. So, global many businessmen had begun to build themselves one attraction webstore in order to persuade different countries consumers to choose to click themselves webstores from internet channel to buy any kinds of products in short time easily.

So, internet technology had changed consumers traditional shopping behaviors to build positive online shopping emotion as well as raise online sellers' any products sale chance easily in behavioral economic view.

Why and how human behavior may influence the country's economic growth or recession?

When one country has many people choose to do the same matter for one period, whether their behavior may influence the country's pvera; economic growth or recession . I shall attempt to indicate cases toexplain their relationship as below:

For flowing rubblish behavioral case example, do you feel that when the country has many people often flow rubblish on the streets, instead of their flowing rubblish behavior may bring streets dirty? But, their flowing rubblish behavior may explain that this country has people may have enough money to buy food to ear, or enough cloths to wear, enough bottles of water to drink, even they may have enough money to buy new television, radio, refrigeraters , washing machines, desktops or laptops electronic home products from old to new to use in order to satisfy their living needs. So, when they flow old electronic home products, their flowing old home electronic products behaviors may seem that they have enough money to buy other new home electronic products to replace old home electronic products to use at homes.

However, it seems thaat this country ought have many people have jobs to do. So, many of them, they can easy to make purchase decison to flow any old home electronic products and buy any new home electronic products to use . Because this country has many people have jobs to do. So, they can often not use old home electonic products to become rubblishs to flow on streets after they had bought any kinds of new home electronic homes.

In fact, it also implies that this country's economy grows rapidly. So, many businesses can glow up rapdly. When they expanded their businesses, they must need to increase employees number in order to let they help themselves to raise productivity or serve their clients absolutely. So, when the country has many businesses can grow up, it seems that its economy must be better or it is improved to compare past. Due to many different kinds of home electronic products had been often bought to use by this country people in this period. So, this country's any streets can be observed that expensive electronic home products were flowed on streets anywhere. then, this country will have many electronic home products sellers can sell their home electronic products very easily. When this country has many people can find any kinds of jobs to do easily. So, due to unemploymen rate had been decreasing.

In behavioral economic view, as this many electronic home products rubblish country case, we can observe this country may have many people have jobs to do. So, consumption number has been increased long time. So, cheap food, or expensive home electronic products may be rubblish on any streets. This country's people , their flowing rubblish behaviors may be explained that many of people have enough jobs to do, so they have ability to buy any good taste food to eat or buy any kinds of expensive electronic home products to use. So, this country's economy may be improved for this long period. So, in behavioral economic view, when this country can have many electronic home products rubblishs are flowed on anywherer in streets frequently. It seems that this country will have many people have jobs to do, so it causes they often change old home electronic products or replaced them easily, when they have enough income to spend to buy any kinds of new home electronic products to use at homes easily. Moreover, their flowing old electronic home products behaviors also indicate that this country has many people their salaries may be increased in possible from their emplyers. When this country can have many different kinds of home electornic products are sold. It means that this country's electronic home products needs or demand had been increasing, due to many people have jobs to do and income increases to excite their living of needs also improve. Consequently, this country may seem have better economic improvement. We can observe from this country's electronic home products rubblish increasing income in theis period.

On conclusion, this country ought experience economic growth at this period. So, " flowing expensive electronic home rubblish increasing number " may seem that this country's economic growth is rapidly in this period, due to many people have jobs to do as well as salaries increase in this period.

Technology how impacts human behavior changing?

Technology how influences human behavior to bring changing? For example, online share purchase and sale transaction from smart phone brings share investor can do share buying or selling transation in any where and any time conveniently, non manual driving auto vehicle, bring car owner feels comfortable and spends free time to do other matter, e.g. reading, listening mucis in himself or herself car freely. electrical energy vehicle can help car owner to reduce air polluton and it can brings the drivers do not feel drive long time in any journeys in order to avoid air pollution for environmental protection responsible car drivers in our societies. Thus, they will drive long time in any journeys when they can drive electronic energy cars to replace oil energy cars.

However, online technology can also bring consumers can choose to stay at homes to buy any things from seller individual online webstore conveniently. Such as online technology can bring shoppers do not need to spend much time to visit shops to buy any things. They can choose any kinds of products from any online sellers individual online webstores conveniently at homes. Online technology excite busy consumers can make purchase decision easily as well as it can help online sellers sell any kinds of products from internet easily.

In behavioral economic view, technology can change human behavior to be improved, it can let human feels comfortable, more free time ro use, rapid making any decisions, such as apply smart phones to make share purchase or sale transaction decision, online shopping decision, even travelling any where decision in short time, when the traveller finds the most cheap hotel accommodation room price and air ticket price frm any travel agent online tourism webstore, then the potential travel customer can follow the online hotel accommodation price and air ticket price data to make decision when to buy the air ticket from the airline travel agent or make decision when to prebook which hotel accommodation room to go to the country to travel from online travel agent tourism webstores. So, technology can encourage global any country travelers to make anywhere to trvel rapidly. If the traveler can find the country's general hotel rooms and airline tickets prices had been decreasing more sightly. The traveler may make travel decision to choose the country to travel in short time, then he/she can prebook the country;s any hotel room and airline ticket to pay by visa fraom the country's any hotel and airline travel agent webstores., before one week, even one month or more easily. Hence, online technology can also encourage traveler individual frequent travel times to be increased, due to global travelers can find any hotel rooms and airline tickets prices from internet conveniently at homes. They do not need to spend time to visit any airline travel agent to enquire travel choice country's hotel rooms prices and airline ticket prices. They can compare global travel of countries choices ' all hotels rooms and airline agents air tickets prices to make prebook airline seat and hotel room decision before one week, one month even six months early.

On conclusion, online technology can encourage global travelers can make travelling any where and when traveling time desicions easily. It can excite tourism industry develops in long time. Also, such as electricity cars invention can encourage environment protection car owners do car purchase decision easily, because they can choose to drive electronic energy cars to replace oil energy cars in order to avoid air pollution occurs easily. So, electronic cars can increase electronic car purchasrs number, due to many of environmental protection attitude of car owners can choose to drive electricity cars to bring air cleans, even non -manual driving cars can encourage lazy driving and free time driving car owners to choose to buy non-manual (artificial intelligent) cars to drive , because they can spend much free time to read, listen music or do any matters in themselves cars, they do not need to drive cars, robotic (AI) auto driving machine is such one non-manual driver to help them to drive themselves cars confidently. So, non-manual driving cars can attract lazy and enjoying free time driving car owners to choose to buy to replace traditional manual cars to drive easily. Moreover, online share transaction can help any share investors to make share buying and selling decision in short time easily. When they can apply smart phones technological tool to carry on share buying and selling activities easily. They can observe any share rising or falling price suitation from smart phones in any where any any time easily. So, smart phone technology can help global any shareholders to make share purchase and sale transaction easily. So, technology can encourage human makes decision in short time rapidly.

How and why employees behaviors may influence economy development?

In behavioral economy view,I believe the country's any organizational employees behavior may bring indirect relationship to influence the country's long term economic development. I shall indicate past manufacture industry social development period to explain their relationship. For many countries' past business activities had belonged to manufacturing industry, such as US, UK past before 1980 year, it focused on steel manufacturing and steel manufacturing related machine products. So, US, Uk developed countries manufacturing industries may be past main country's economic income sources. I assume US , UK past had one million number different kinds of industries. They ought had about seven houndred thousand number organizational businesses were belonged to manufactured industry. They may include:

Steel manufacturing and steel related machine manufacturing, e.g. vehicle manufacturing, home appliances, e.g. washing machine, television, radio, refrigerate cooler, heater, air condition etc. different kinds of different kinds of steel -related manufacturing machine, they were manufactured from US, UK steel machine manufacturers. So, US, Uk the other three hundred thousand number industry may be general service industry, e.g. hotel service, restaurent, cinema, public transport service, tourism lesiure , wine bar, supermarket etc. different kinds of non-manufacturing industries business organizations were operated in UK, US past before 1980 year.

So, in UK, US developed countries industry development history, they ought have high percentage of businesses belonged to steel related manufacturing machine and steel products. Also, in the past before 1980 year, US, Uk business employers , they employed many workers are manufacturing workers. They needed to spend long time to work in factories. They were skillful workers, and they are trained to manufacturing cars, washing machine, television, heater, etc. even steel itself different kinds of steel related products to prepare to deliver to their shops to sell to US, Uk local or overseas clients.

So, I believe that past UK, US ought employ many employees, they belonged to skillful manufacturing workers, manufacture increasing steel machine or steel related machine number of products rapidly daily. So, if UK, US had had many of these manufacturing factories owned high skillful workers, then their manufacturing steel-related machine or steel both kinds of products number must be influenced to raise rapidly. Consequently, their steel machine manufacturing products would been exported to overseas or would been sold to local both markets , they may be influenced to raise sale number. They (these manufacturing workers) needed to be trained to know how to manufactur these different kinds of machine products in the efficient teams and they ought to be trained to raise their efficiencies in order to shorten time to manufacturing many kinds of steel related manufacturing machine or steel itself products rapidly. So , if their efficiencies and manufacturing performance was improved, these US, UK any one manufacturing worker and their teams ought achieve raising productivities significantly.

Hence, when past UK, US manufacturing industry development period, if these two countries' any manufacturing factories could have many manufacturing workers could be trained to be skillful and proficient manufacturing workers. Then, in past every day to these factories workers, they ought help their steel or steel related manufacturing employers to raise any kinds of machine or steel products number in every team. So, when past in the manufacturing industry development, US, UK could have many factories' manufacturing workers themselves steel or steel related machine products manufacturing skill could be trained to to improve to any kinds of these machine or steel manufacuring products quality as well as their products number could be influenced to raise by themselves skillful improvement significantly every day.

Then, what would be influenced to occur to past UK, US manufacturing industry period? In behavioral economic view, when these two manufacturing industry developed countries, such as UK, US , if they had many factories workers can be trained to improve their skill in order to achieve any kinds of steel or steel-related machine products quality could be improved as well as products manufacturing number could be also increased absolutely.

In consequence, past UK and US both countries ought increase themselves any kinds of steel and steel related machine products number to be supplied to themselves local shops to let local clients to choose any one kind of machine manufacturing products to buy easily as well as they could also export to supply overseas any countries to buy their different kinds of steel or steel related machine products to let overseas steel or steel related manufacturing machine product buyers, they can have many of these different kinds of these steel or steel-related different kinds of manufacturing machine from UK and UK these both countries easily to compare other countries.

On conclusion, I believe that past US, and UK macro manufacturing industry income GDP would increase significantly. So, they would have good economic growth performance because when many of these manufacturing workers themselves manufacturing effort could be improved. So, it explained when employees manufacturing abilities can influence economic growth indirectly.

Robots invention whether they can help organizations to raise efficiencies or inefficiencies?

In behavioral economic view, in any organizations, when the organization hopes its worker teams can raise efficiencies , the organization may choose to increase more workers number and/or it can provide training to improve these workets themselves skills in order to raise their efficiencies. For one warehouse example, when the warehouse increases many goods , they are needed to delivered these goods from the shelves to the delivering destination locations. If this warehouse supervisors feel these workers themselves goods delivery speeds are slow, which is possible due to this warehouse's workers number is not enough. So, this warehouse supervisor ought increase workers number in order to increase their goods delivery speed in order to deliver goods from the shelves to every indicated goods delivery destination in order to let any one lorry driver can transport the right kinds of goods and ensure the accurate goods number to transport to any one client home rapidly.

However, if this warehouse supervisor planed to buy several warehouse goods delivery robots to assist these warehouse workers to find the right kinds of goods from shelves and then deliver to the right destination location in the warehouse. So, these warehouse orkers can concentrate on counting the accurate goods number and ensuring the right kinds of goods in order to prepare to let lorry drivers to transport these goods to these goods of buyers themselvers homes rapidly. Consequently, in the first step, robots can concentrate on finding th right goods from shelves and delivers them to the right goods transportation of location destination. Then, in the second step, these warehouse workers can concentrate on counting the accurate goods number and ensuring the right kinds of goods in order to prepare to put them to the lorry. Consequently, when warehouse robots and warehouse workers can cooperate to work together, the most important, robots, can deal on finding the right kinds of goods and deal on delivering the accurate number of goods of job duty as well as these warehouse workers can only concentrte on counting the right kinds of goods number in order to avoid it has none any mistake of wrong kinds of goods and inaccurate goods of delivery number to be transported to the lorry and to deliver to any one buyer's home.

So, it seems that warehouse robots ought help any one warehouse worker to raise himself efficiency and avoid goods delivery of mistake occurrence easily as well as their help to warehouse workers that can let any one goods buyer feels their goods can be delivered to their homes rapidly. Moreover, warehouse robots can also help these warehouse workers to raise efficiencies because warehouse robots can help them to shorten goods delivery time between any one shelf and any one goods delivery destination of location in the warehuse because robots may help them to find the right kinds of goods from the right shelf in the short time. So, any one worker does not need to spend long time to seek anywhere is the right shelf location for the kind of goods when the kind of goods are needed to deliver to the buyer's home from lorry. Warehouse robots can help them to do this aspect of " finding the goods from the right shelf in short time job duty". So, any one warehouse worker only needed tospend less time to do the counting of any right kind of goods number and ensuring the right kind of goods job duty. Consequently, this warehouse 's any one worker, his any one kind of goods delivery time may be reduced, because robots' assistance and they may have more confidence to avoid mistake to deliver the wrong number of goods and/or the wrong kind of goods to any one goods buyer's home.

On conclusion, it seems that warehouse robots ought may help any one warehouse worker to raise efficiency for any one team in the warehouse as well as the warehouse any one supervisor does not need to spend much time to observe any one worker individual performance for " goods delivery job duty aspect" because their goods delivery job duty that had been replaced to do by these several warehouse robots. Robots can achieve the more accurate of right kinds of goods and the right number of goods delviery job performance to compare any one of human warehouse worker themselves right kinds of goods of delivery and right number of goods of delivery job performance. So, when robots can participate to cooperate with this warehouse's any one worker to do their goods of delivery job duty in this warehouse every day. Then, robots can raies any one of supervisor individual confidence in order to let they do not need to spend time to observe any one of worker individual whose goods of delivery job performane. They can concentrate on supervising any one worker whose goods transport to lorry in the final step in order to avoid to deliver wrong goods number and / or wrong kind of goods to any one goods buyer's home every day. Consequently, this warehouse's overall teams of their delviery of goods performance many be improved by robotss' participatin to goods of delivery task as well as this warehouse's oveall teams themselves efficiencies may be influenced to raise by robots' goods of delivery task participation.

Why social behavior may influence organizational strategy needs to be changed ?

Why any organizations need to know whether nowadays social behaivor how has been changing in order to implement the kind of the most right strategy to achieve the profit aim pursue in possible. I shall indicate nowadays ecommerce or online, customer shopping behavior to explain above question concerns they ought have close relationship between social behavior and organizational strategic choice or organizational behavioral changing need.

On nowadays ecommerce business, or online shopping model, this kind of shopping model in global many young and old age consumers like to apply internet tool to choose any country sellers website stores in order to stay at home to buy any kinds of products from themselves webstores in global societies.

In fact, online shopping model had been popular for long time above to twenty years. Most of global sellers will make decision to design themselves webstores in order to attract global many online buyers to choose to buy their products from themselves webstores. So, it seems that social consumers purchase behaviors had been changed to online shopping from internet invention.

Hence, social consumers purchase behavioral changes may influence any organizations' strategies need to be changed from visiting shops purchase strategy model to online purchase strategy model, if the seller still concentrate on concentrate on considerate how to design itelf , but neglects to considerate how to design itself webstore, e.g. how to design attract product photos to put on itself webstore, how to arrange sale price information location to be putted on webstore and visa card payment location on itself webstore in order to let any one online buyer can feel very easier to buy itself any kinds of products from itself webstore. Then, its potential online buyers will be influenced to increase number when they can find this online seller itself any kinds of products photes and every kinds of product sale price information and visa card payment channel locations easily from itself webstore.

So, it implies that nowadays any one seller ought need to design one webstore to let any one online overseas and domestic consumers can have chance to click itself webstore to choose any one kind of product to buy conveniently when he/she does not hope to leave him/her home to go to shop, because nowadays social shopping behaviors had been influenced to change when internet invention, them it gives another online purchase method to replace visiting shops purchase method to global any one buyer in nowadays societies.

So, if nowadays any one seller still concentrate on how to design itself shop display in order to put any kinds of product on shelf in order to let any one visiting shop customer to find the kind of product to buy, but it neglects to change to choose to pursue another new technological shopping method, such as webstore purchase method in order to implement effective strategy to design the most right webstore as well as in order to attract global overseas and local consumers to find itself webstore easily from website and find its any one kind of product phots and sale price and visa card payment button in order to choose to buy itself any kinds of products in the short time. Consequently I believe that the seller will lose many customers from overseas and local when its other same or similar product sellers choose to design themselves webstores in order to let global any one product buyer can buy themselves any one kind of product when they can pay visa card to buy their products from them webstores conveniently when they stay at home habitly. Then, the seller will lose many global potential customers in long time.

On conclusion, in behavioral economic view, any consumer behavioral social changing, which will influence any in order to avoid customers number loses significantly . In future time, organizations need to make rapid decision in order to implement the most reasonable and the most useful strategy in order to avoid global potential customers number reduces or lose them in long time. So, social behavioral changing environment ought influence any global organizations need to decide how to change themselves strategies in order to avoid customers loses significantly in future time.

How and why human behavior may influence economic growth or recession?

May ourselves daily behaviors influence our global societial continue economic growth or recession? Do they have cause and effect close relationship between human behaviors and global economic growth or recession? I shall apply behavioral economic theory to analyze and explain whether ourselves daily behaviors and our global societial economic growth or recession which have close cause and effect relationship as below:

Every country itself economic development must depend on any business activities, otherwise, any kinds of business activities must need ourselves business activities or behaviors in order to achieve any business activities as well as achieve the country's overall economic development in macro view.

However, any country's overall business activites or behaviors which must depend on any kinds of individual businessmen, themselves employees daily working behavior or activity or performance in order to help them to attract or increase many clients number to acieve " earning profit" aim. So, it seems that any individual business, itself overall every department individual working behavior is one main factor to influence the company's overall business performance.

For agricultural fruit and meat food farming industry example, such as New Zealand is a farming main target industry country. It had had many New Zealanders were daily themselves own farming businesses for many years. Their farming businesses include growing fruit, sheep, cow, pig pork, meat etc. food sale business. If the New Zealand farmer owned a large size farming land, then he will choose either growing fruit or feeding sheeps, pigs, cows to be meat to to transport to New Zealand supermarkets to help them to sell to their farmers meet to New Zealanders in order to earn profit. Thus, if the New Zealand farmer owned large size of farming lands, then he needs to employ many farming employees (farming workers) to help him to carry on farming business daily tasks, e.g. picking up friuts, feeding pigs, cows, sheeps to eat food daily. These daily farming jobs are very important to influence this New Zealand farmer's meats or fruits sale number whether they can be easy or diffcult to sell in New Zealand supermarkets , if these farming workers can own encough farming knowledge or skill to know how to pick up fruits method and make judgement to know whether it is right time to pick up the kind of fruits from the trees , as well as know how feed this pigs, sheeps, cows to eat food in order to let they are better health. Consequently, their farming behaviors which can let these animals can provide the best taste and enough meat from these animals to let New Zealander to buy to eat from New Zealand any one supermarket. Even these New Zealand farming workers can know whether the kinds of fruits, e.g. oranges, apples, gapes etc. fruits whether they ought be picked up from the trees at the right time. Consequently, they can make judgement to decide to pick up any kinds of the best taste fruits to let any one New Zealander to buy to eat from any one supermarket in New Zealand. Otherwise, if they do not make judegement to know whether the kind of fruit ought not be picked up because they still need longer time to continue grow up to increase fruit size and better taste from the trees in order to let any one fruit buyer can feel better taste when they eat this kind of fruit later. If they can buy this kind of fruit to eat later, then this New Zealand farmer's his fruit buyers can buy the best taste of this kind of fruit to eat from an yone supermarket in New Zealand. Consequently, many New Zealand supermarkets will choose to buy any kinds of fruits from this farmer fruit supplier when they feel this farmer's fruits can provide more better taste fruits to compare other farmers' fruits.

Thus, due to New Zealand is one farming main income source country. It's any kinds of fruits and meats need to be export to overseas to sell , instead of local sale. It's GDP percent is very high to whole country 's overall income source. So, any one New Zealand farmer individual and any one farming worker individual working behavior will influence its economy whether it is influenced to grow or recession possible. Moreover, it also seems that farming workers' farming knowledge and skill will influence themselves farming daily activities to achieve the aim of the number of increase or decrease to any kinds of fruits whether they are better taste or the number of increase of decrease to any kinds of meats whether they are better taste to supply to any one New Zealand fruit or meat buyers to eat from any one New Zealand supermarket. So, it implies that any one New Zealand farming worker individual farming behavior may influence any kinds of fruits or any kinds of meat taste because they are transported to any one supermarket to sell in New Zealand.

Consequently, if New Zealans had many farmers can teach god farming knowledge and skill to let their any one farming workers know how to decide judgement to decide when it is right time to pick up any kinds of fruits from trees , or how to grow them on soil in order to let they can grow rapidly. Then, many different kinds of fruits can be provided to let any one New Zealanders can eat the best taste of fruits when their fruits are supplied to any one New Zealand supermarkets. Even, if they knew how to feed foods to pigs, cows, sheeps to eat daily. Then they can be more health and they can provide the best taste of meats to let any one New Zealanders can buy their meats from any one New Zealand supermarkets. Moreover, their fruits and meats can be transported to overseas to let any one country fruits or meats buyers can choose any kinds of New Zealand meats and fruits to buy to eat from themselves countries supermarkets. Then, many overseas fruit and meat buyers will perfer to choose New Zealand any kinds of fruits or meats to buy to compare other countries fruits or meats to buy when they go to any one local supermarkets. On conclusion, it seems that New Zealand farming workers themselves farming behavior may influence their farming employers any kinds of fruits or meats sale number and income because their farming task behaviors must influence whether their fruits or meats taste are the better taste or worse taste to compare their other local farmers (the farmer competitors) whose fruits or meats taste. If tthe farmer's any one farming worker can be trained to learn how to know to feed animals skill and when is the most right time to pick up any kinds of fruits from trees or how to grow them on the soil methods. Due to these farming worker individual farming behavior may influence his different finds of fruits and meats sale number to be increase or decrease, so these any one New Zealand farmer must need to depend on any one farming worker whose farming working methods, if their farming working behaviors can be the best to influence any kinds of fruits to grow rapid or any kinds of pigs, cows, sheeps animals grow up rapidly , then their sale number may be increase significantly and their taste can be improved to let any New Zealand or overseas meat or fruit buyer to buy to eat to feel from any one New Zealand or overseas supermarkets, then New Zealand's agriculture industry must be influenced to increase. In the world, any one fruit or meat buyer must choose to buy New Zealand's fruit and meat to eat in prefer to compare other countries' fruits and meats. So, New Zealand's GDP may be influenced to raise from any one New Zealand farming worker individual farming working behaviors.